W9-BJA-874

The Intentional Stance

The Intentional Stance

Daniel C. Dennett

A Bradford Book
The MIT Press
Cambridge, Massachusetts
London, England

First MIT Press paperback edition, 1989

© 1987 by The Massachusetts Institute of Technology

All rights reserved. No part of this book may be reproduced in any form by any electronic or mechanical means (including photocopying, recording, or information storage and retrieval) without permission in writing from the publisher.

This book was set in Palatino by Achorn Graphic Services and printed and bound by Halliday Lithograph in the United States of America.

Library of Congress Cataloging-in-Publication Data

Dennett, Daniel Clement.
  The intentional stance.

  "A Bradford book."
  Bibliography: p.
  Includes index.
  1. Intentionality (Philosophy)   I. Title.
B105.I56D46   1987   128'.3   87-3018
ISBN 0-262-04093-X (hardcover)
      0-262-54053-3 (paperback)

Dedicated to the memory
of Basil Turner,
neighbor, friend, and teacher.

Contents

Preface

The theory of intentionality presented in this book has been gradually evolving over about twenty years. While the central ideas found rudimentary expression in *Content and Consciousness* in 1969, it was the publication in 1971 of "Intentional Systems" that initiated the series of articles about what I call the intentional stance and the objects one discovers from that stance: intentional systems. The first three of these articles (Dennett 1971, 1973, 1976b) were reprinted in *Brainstorms* in 1978, and critics and students often treat that book as the canonical, target expression of my view. I soon found, however, that the defense of my position was evolving further in response to criticism, and so I was driven to compose a series of post-*Brainstorms* essays in which I attempted to revise, re-express, and extend my view.

Most of these essays were scattered, however, in relatively inaccessible volumes, thanks to the inexorable effect of Limelight Gravity: as one's ideas become a Center of Attention, one is invited to contribute to more and more conferences, which proceed to suck one's entire corpus into delayed publication in conference proceedings and special-interest anthologies. Nothing is left over to submit to refereed journals, for ready reading. The point of this book is to overcome the bad side effects of that otherwise gratifying diffusion.

Six of those scattered essays are reprinted in this volume (chapters 2–7), introduced by an essay on their aspirations and methodological presuppositions, tied together with reflections, and followed by two new essays (chapters 8 and 9), in which the themes and arguments of the preceding chapters converge on some rather surprising claims about the relationship between evolution, brain design, and intentionality. Chapter 10 is my attempt to adopt the stance of an impartial observer toward my own work and describe its place in the development of current thinking about "the intentionality of mental states."

This book does not present my whole view of the mind, but only, one might say, the first half: content. The other half—consciousness—is also in need of a second retelling (part three of *Brainstorms* was the first), but that will require another volume, to which I am currently devoting my attention. Consciousness is regularly regarded, especially by people outside the field of philosophy, as the outstanding (and utterly baffling) challenge to materialist theories of the mind. And yet, curiously enough, most of the major participants in the debates *about mental content* to which this volume is primarily addressed have been conspicuously silent on the topic of consciousness. No theory, or even theory-sketch, of consciousness is to be found in the writings of Fodor, Putnam, Davidson, Stich, Harman, Dretske, or Burge, for instance. I, on the other hand, do have a theory of consciousness (and have always had difficulty understanding how the others can suppose they may ignore or postpone the issue), but its latest version is too unwieldy for inclusion in this volume. Anyone impatient to see how the new version of this second half of my theory of the mind comes out can extrapolate (at my own risk) from the ideas expressed in such published and forthcoming essays as "How to Study Human Consciousness Empirically: or, Nothing Comes to Mind" (1982b), "Why Do We Think What We Do About Why We Think What We Do?" (1982d), "Reflection, Language and Consciousness" (*Elbow Room*, 1984d, pp. 34–43), "Julian Jaynes' Software Archeology" (1986d), "Quining Qualia" (forthcoming d), and "The Self as the Center of Narrative Gravity" (forthcoming g).

Another challenge, also popularly deemed insurmountable by materialistic theories of the mind, is the problem of free will. I have devoted a separate book to that challenge, *Elbow Room*, so the topic will scarcely be mentioned again in these pages. If there are other major challenges to my view, they have not yet been drawn to my attention.

Since the previously published essays in this volume appeared over a five-year span, punctuated by their share of controversy, misconstrual, and amendment, it is no wonder that few have been able to discern the resulting equilibrium position. I have sometimes been described, in fact, as presenting a moving target to my critics. There is some truth to this. I have been ready to learn from my mistakes and willing to retract ill-considered claims. Motion is relative, however, and when something appears to an observer to be protean and wandering, it may be because the observer is only gradually coming to discern the shape it has had all along. Recently I was congratulated by a neuroscientist for "coming around" to a view I have unswervingly maintained since *Content and Consciousness* in 1969, a sobering experience that has led me to reassess my expository strategy over the years. Rereading that book, now in paperback after being out of print for some years, I am struck more by my doctrinal constancy than by my developments. Most of the changes seem to me to be extensions, extrapolations, and further arguments, not shifts. Be that as it may, I have probably seriously underestimated the potential for misdirection in my playful and unsystematic style. In this book I do my best, therefore, to come to a halt, draw my wagons into a circle, and present and defend my considered view in a more orderly fashion.

Some of the previously unpublished parts of this book are drawn from my Gavin David Young Lectures at the University of Adelaide in 1984, from my lectures at the Ecole Normale Supérieure in Paris in 1985, and from lectures given at various workshops, conferences, and colloquia in the last two or three years, from which I gained a bounty of insights that have found their way into this volume.

I am also grateful to many people for advice and criticism on earlier drafts of the unpublished material in this volume: especially to Kathleen Akins, who not only helped organize and edit the entire book, but also convinced me to make major revisions in the presentation and defense of my views; and to Peter Bieri, Bo Dahlbom, Debra Edelstein, Doug Hofstadter, Pierre Jacob, Jean Khalfa, Dan Lloyd, Ruth Millikan, and Andrew Woodfield. I am also very pleased to add my voice to the now traditional chorus of authorial praise for my good friends Harry and Betty Stanton, who have made me so proud, over the years, to be a Bradford Books author. And thanks, as always, to my wife Susan for her support and forbearance, and to my colleagues at Tufts.

Tufts University
January 1987

1   Setting Off on the Right Foot

Talking about the mind, for many people, is rather like talking about sex: slightly embarrassing, undignified, maybe even disreputable. "Of course it exists," some might say, "but do we have to talk about it?" Yes, we do. Many people would rather talk about the brain (which, after all, *is* the mind) and would like to think that all the wonderful things we need to say about people could be said without lapsing into vulgar, undisciplined *mentalistic* talk, but it is now quite clear that many things need saying that cannot be said in the restricted languages of neuroanatomy, neurophysiology, or behavioristic psychology. It is not just the arts and humanities that need to talk about the mind; the various puritanical attempts to complete the biological and social sciences without ever talking about it have by now amply revealed their futility.

In fact there is something approaching a new consensus among cognitive scientists and the more liberated neuroscientists, to the effect that there can be—must be, somehow—a responsible, materialistic science not only of the brain, but also of the mind. There is no consensus yet, however, about just how this responsible science of the mind will be conducted.

This book is about how to talk about the mind. It is a philosophical book, written by a philosopher and dealing primarily with the issues as they have appeared in the philosophical literature; but it is not for philosophers only. Those in other disciplines who are newly eager, or at any rate reluctantly willing, to indulge in various mentalistic sorts of talk find that philosophers, who have never been shy about talking about the mind, have a lot to tell them about how to do it. In fact we philosophers have rather too much to tell. Only a small portion of what we have said could possibly be true, or useful, and much of even the best is apt to be misinterpreted. Philosophy does not often produce stable, reliable "results" the way science does at its best. It can, however, produce new ways of looking at things, ways of thinking about things, ways of framing the questions, ways of seeing what is important and why.

This can be a valuable contribution, since everyone who is trying to think about the mind is beset by tactical problems about which questions to try to answer. We are all faced with the baffling phenomena; how could anything be more familiar, and at the same time more weird, than a mind? We also have an overwhelming array of data about the most complex object we have encountered in the universe—the human brain—and about the enormous variety of behavior that brain can modulate. Finally, we are bemused by an intrusive gaggle of persistent intuitions deriving from heaven knows where. Theorists in every field, then, run the risk of following their distinguished predecessors and setting off on the wrong foot because of one "philosophical" misconception or another about the nature of the phenomena, the range of available theoretical options, the shape of the theoretical tasks, or the conditions that must be met by a successful account of the mind.

There is no way to avoid having philosophical preconceptions; the only option is whether to examine them explicitly and carefully at some point in one's endeavors. It is of course possible that some of today's philosophically untutored theorists are lucky enough to harbor only the soundest philosophical preconceptions—perhaps the ambience of the age will ensure this without any direct communication with philosophers. And it must certainly be borne in mind that some of the most debilitating philosophical misconceptions of the past have been all too potent gifts from academic philosophy that scientists have misconstrued, typically by enthusiastic exaggeration and oversimplification: logical positivism and, more recently, incommensurability of Kuhnian paradigms come to mind. Still, we philosophers think we can help and are gratified to find a growing number of others who have turned to us for help—with an entirely appropriate attitude of cautious skepticism.

This book presents the foundations for my theory of the mind: my account of the intentional stance. Those familiar with that account will find few major innovations of theory but several innovations of exposition and defense, especially in the reflections following each reprinted essay, where I attempt to clarify and amplify my previous arguments. The last chapter is devoted to a systematic comparison of my view with others that have been defended recently, using the criticisms and objections of others to focus the problematic points. In these new essays I have tried to present and answer all the objections to my account that have appeared in the literature and to correct the misapprehensions and misconstruals. I also make explicit along the way some of the main points of agreement and disagreement with others who have written on these topics, and draw attention to some generally unrecognized implications of my position regarding current controversies.

The basic introduction to my theory of the intentional stance is to be found in the next chapter, "True Believers," which I now consider to replace "Intentional Systems" (1971) as the flagship expression of my position. In the rest of this chapter, I step back a few paces and comment on some unargued assumptions of the other essays.

Common Sense and the Third-Person Point of View

Here on planet Earth are many complicated life forms. Common sense tells us that many of them have mental lives—minds—of one dimly envisaged sort or another. What common sense tells us is not enough. Not only does it leave too many pressing questions unresolved, but it often yields persuasive intuitions that contradict each other. From some vantage points it is "obvious" that warm-blooded animals have minds like ours, while insects appear to be "mere automata"; from other vantage points the gulf between us and even the chimpanzee appears larger than the gulf between a pigeon and a robot. The idea that no automaton could possibly be conscious the way we are is perennially popular but can be made to look suspiciously unimaginative and parochial, a case of misguided wishful thinking. Some of the apparently well-attested pathologies of human mind and brain are so counterintuitive that recounting them often provokes derisive dismissal. A student of mine recently relayed to her literature professor the account I had presented in class of the strange but well-studied pathologies of blindness denial and hemi-neglect. He firmly assured her that I had been making it all up, that I must have been performing some experiment on the credulity of my students. To him it was obvious that Professor Dennett was just inventing another of his wild science-fiction fantasies, yet another intuition pump to bamboozle the gullible. When so many "obvious facts" compete with each other, common sense is not enough.

No rules govern the way we as theorists must appeal to common sense. We must all in one way or another start from the base of common sense if we hope to be understood, or to understand ourselves. But reliance on any particular item of common sense is treacherous; one person's bedrock certainty is another's spuriously convincing relic of an outmoded world view. Even if some portions of what passes as common sense are shining, immutable Truth, other portions are probably just the cognitive illusions of our species—overwhelmingly persuasive to us because of design shortcuts in our cognitive systems. (To a phototropic moth, it may seem to be an *a priori* truth that it is always Right to head toward the Light; no alternative is conceivable to it.) Other deliverances of common sense are just diluted, popularized versions of the science of yesteryear.

Sorting out these portions of common sense into the true, the false, the misleading, and the unreliable is a good task for a philosopher. Indeed philosophers specialize in this sort of task. One thing we have learned from the distinguished failures of the past is that this is not a systematic task, amenable to a purely foundational or axiomatic approach. Rather, we must wade in opportunistically and attempt to achieve a stable vision by playing off against each other a variety of intuitions, empirical findings and theories, rigorous arguments, and imaginative thought experiments.

Some useful skirmishes in this campaign do consist of rigorous, formal explorations of particular sets of hunches. That is in fact the best light in which to view the various formalist failures of philosophy—as if they had been prefaced with "What if we made *these* assumptions and proceeded under *these* constraints?" As Fodor says, "The form of a philosophical theory, often enough, is: *Let's try looking over here.*" (1981a, p. 31) Every formal system in philosophy must be "motivated," and the informal task of providing that motivation typically contributes more philosophical illumination (or at least doctrine) than the system for which it paves the way. There is always more than one candidate system or perspective crying out for philosophical exploration and development, and in such an unruly arena of thought, tactical considerations play an unusually important role. These tactical considerations often masquerade, however, as first principles.

I begin, then, with a tactical choice. I declare my starting point to be the objective, materialistic, third-person world of the physical sciences. This is the orthodox choice today in the English-speaking philosophical world, but it has its detractors, most notably Nagel, who has devoted a book, *The View From Nowhere* (1986), to deploring the effects of this tactical choice. Since Nagel's is the major alternative starting point to mine, let us compare them briefly to see what we might be missing.

I am not certain that Nagel is one of those who thinks he can *prove* that my starting point is a mistake, but he certainly *asserts* that it is:

There are things about the world and life and ourselves that cannot be adequately understood from a maximally objective standpoint, however much it may extend our understanding beyond the point from which we started. A great deal is essentially connected to a particular point of view, or type of point of view, and the attempt to give a complete account of the world in objective terms detached from these perspectives inevitably leads to false reductions or to outright denial that certain patently real phenomena exist at all. (p. 7)

My intuitions about what "cannot be adequately understood" and what is "patently real" do not match Nagel's. Our tastes are very different. Nagel, for instance, is oppressed by the desire to develop an evolutionary explanation of the human intellect (pp. 78–82); I am exhilarated by the prospect. My sense that philosophy is allied with, and indeed continuous with, the physical sciences grounds both my modesty about philosophical method and my optimism about philosophical progress. To Nagel, this is mere scientism.

To the extent that such no-nonsense theories have an effect, they merely threaten to impoverish the intellectual landscape for a while by inhibiting the serious expression of certain questions. In the name of liberation, these movements have offered us intellectual repression. (p. 11)

Nagel is both courageous and clever. It takes courage to stand up for mystery, and cleverness to be taken seriously. Nagel repeatedly announces that he has no answers to the problems he raises, but prefers his mystification to the demystifying efforts of others. Oddly enough, then, Nagel would agree with me that his tactical starting point leads not just to perplexity, but to a perplexity from which he himself offers no escape. For me, that impasse is tantamount to a *reductio ad absurdum* of his method, but Nagel bravely recommends embracing the result:

Certain forms of perplexity—for example, about freedom, knowledge, and the meaning of life—seem to me to embody more insight than any of the supposed solutions to those problems. (p. 4)

Nagel is the most eloquent contemporary defender of the mysteries, and anyone who suspects I have underestimated the problems I pose for my theory will be braced by Nagel's contrary assertions. Assertions, not arguments. Since Nagel and I start from different perspectives, his arguments beg the question against a position like mine: what counts for him as flat obvious, and in need of no further support, often fails to impress me. I assume that whatever the true theory of the mind turns out to be, it will overturn some of our prior convictions, so I am not cowed by having the counterintuitive implications of my view pointed out. Any theory that makes progress is bound to be *initially* counterintuitive. No doubt Nagel, who calls his book "deliberately reactionary," is equally unshaken when it is pointed out that his allegiance to certain intuitions is all that prevents him from escaping his perplexity down various promising avenues of scientific research.

The feeling then is mutual; we beg the question against each other. I do not presuppose that an alternative starting point such as Nagel's must be wrong or that everything in the universe worth taking seriously must be accessible from my starting point. I am impressed, however, with its proven yield of (apparent) comprehension, and even more so by its promise of future harvests.

Nagel claims to show that the attempt to reconcile objective and subjective is "essentially incompletable" (p. 4), and he might be right—though I remain utterly unpersuaded. Some join him in suspecting, however, that there is something subtly incoherent in the more or less standard scientists' vision of the world and our place in it—some irresolvable conflict between the subjective and objective, between the concrete and abstract, between the macro and the micro (cf. Dennett 1984d, pp. 128–29). Doesn't the self-styled objectivist covertly depend on some prior commitment to irreducible points of view? Or doesn't the goal of "reducing" these points of view to biology to chemistry to physics defeat itself in the end in any case? It is rumored that down in the subcellars of contemporary physics the modern-day alchemists are turning materialism into idealism all over again. Quantum particles do sometimes seem to be, as David Moser has said, "the dreams stuff is made of."

Perhaps those who distrust the frankly materialistic assumptions and aspirations of the current scientific image are right to do so, but I doubt it, and choose not to confront their suspicions further at the outset. The orthodoxy today of my scientific starting point *might* even be due as much to social and political factors as to any philosophical justification. Although I don't believe it, I can see the plausibility in Nagel's diagnosis: "It is like the hatred of childhood and results in a vain effort to grow up too early, before one has gone through the essential formative confusions and exaggerated hopes that have to be experienced on the way to understanding anything." (p. 12)

My tactical hunch, however, is that even if this is so, the best way to come to understand the situation is by starting here and letting whatever revolutions are in the offing foment from within. I propose to see, then, just what the mind looks like from the third-person, materialistic perspective of contemporary science. I bet we can see more and better if we start here, now, than if we try some other tack. This is not just a prejudice of mine—I have shopped around—but the only way I know to convince you I am right is to get on with the project and let the results speak for themselves.

Folk Science and the Manifest Image

What then do we see when we look at this bustling public world? Among the most complicated and interesting of the phenomena are the doings of our fellow human beings. If we try to predict and describe them using the same methods and concepts we have developed to describe landslides, germination, and magnetism, we can make a few important inroads, but the bulk of their observable macroactivity—their "behavior"—is hopelessly unpredictable from these perspectives. People are even less predictable than the weather, if we rely on the scientific techniques of meteorologists and even biologists. But there is another perspective, familiar to us since childhood and used effortlessly by us all every day, that seems wonderfully able to make sense of this complexity. It is often called *folk psychology*. It is the perspective that invokes the family of "mentalistic" concepts, such as belief, desire, knowledge, fear, pain, expectation, intention, understanding, dreaming, imagination, self-consciousness, and so on.

The important features of folk psychology can best be highlighted by drawing out its similarity to another portion of our common endowment: folk physics. Folk physics is the system of savvy expectations we all have about how middle-sized physical objects in our world react to middle-sized events. If I tip over a glass of water on the dinner table, you leap out of your chair, expecting the water to spill over the side and soak through your clothes. You know better than to try to sop up the water with your fork, just as you know you can't tip over a house or push a chain. You expect a garden swing, when pushed, to swing back.

Some folk physics might be innate, but at least some of it must be learned. Virtually from birth, infants cringe when shapes loom, and once they develop crawling and stereovision (after about six months), they exhibit reluctance to venture out over the edge of the "visual cliff"—a clear glass surface extending out over a tabletop—even though they have never learned from bitter experience about the consequences of falling off a high place (Gibson 1969). But children have to learn from particular experiences that they cannot walk on water and that unstable towers of blocks will topple. Some folk physics seems to be supported by innate perceptual bias: when shown an animation of something apparently falling (e.g., circles of color "falling" like rain on a video screen), if the acceleration rate is tampered with, one instantly and irrepressibly sees that some invisible force is "pushing" up or down on the circles to disturb their "proper" motion.

The fact that a judgment of folk physics is innate, or just irresistible, would be no guarantee of its truth. The truth in academic physics is often strongly counterintuitive, or in other words contrary to the dictates of folk physics, and we need not descend to the perplexities of modern particle physics for examples. The naive physics of liquids would not predict such surprising and apparently magical phenomena as siphons or pipettes (Hayes 1978), and an uninitiated but clever person could easily deduce from the obvious first principles of folk physics that gyroscopes, the virtual images produced by parabolic mirrors, and even sailing upwind were flat impossible.

So it is with folk psychology. So natural and effortless are its interpretations that it is almost impossible to suppress them. Imagine watching someone picking blueberries and not having any idea what he was doing. Imagine perceiving two children tugging at the same teddy bear and not having it occur to you that they both *want* it. When a blind person fails to react to something right before her eyes, this can startle us, so compelling is our normal expectation that people come to *believe the truth* about what is happening right in front of their eyes.

Some of the categories of folk psychology, like some of those of folk physics, are apparently given an innate perceptual boost; for instance, (inconclusive) evidence from studies with infants suggests that the perception of faces as a preferred category is served by innate and somewhat specialized visual mechanisms (Maurer and Barrera 1981; but see also Goren et al. 1975 and Cohen, DeLoache, and Strauss 1979). An adult who could not interpret a threatening (or seductive) gesture as such would be suspected of brain damage, not just of having led a sheltered life. And yet there is much that we must learn, at mother's knee and even in school, before we become adept at "reading" the behavior of others in mentalistic terms (see, e.g., Shaftz, Wellman, and Silver 1983; Wimmer and Perner 1983).

The intuitions generated by folk psychology are probably no more irresistible initially than those of folk physics, but perhaps because of the relatively undeveloped and unauthoritative state of academic psychology (including its close relatives, the neurosciences), there are few well-known uncontroversial cases of science directly discrediting a folk-psychological intuition.

What are the siphons and gyroscopes of psychology? As Churchland (1986) notes, "So long as the brain functions normally, the inadequacies of the commonsense framework can be hidden from view, but with a damaged brain the inadequacies of theory are unmasked." (p. 223) So we should look first at the puzzling abnormal cases. Blindsight (Weiskrantz 1983) and the split-brain phenomena (Gazzaniga 1985) have already attracted the attention of philosophers (e.g., Marks 1980 and Nagel 1979), and then there are the blindness denial and hemi-neglect that the literature professor thought I was making up. (Churchland 1986, pp. 222–35, offers an introductory survey. Sacks 1984, 1986 provides vivid descriptions of some particularly bizarre cases, including his own experience with the temporary "loss" of his left leg.) Academic psychology does not yet have an established theory of these phenomena to hold up against our folk incredulity, so they remain controversial, to say the least.

No one doubts that there are perceptual illusions, and some of these—for example, the Ames distorting room (Ittleson 1952; Gregory 1977)—outrage our naive expectations. Then there are the masochists, who are reputed to like pain (?!), and the legion of legendary (and indeed sometimes mythical) idiot savants (Smith 1983). Finally there are the people who supposedly have photographic memories, or multiple personalities, to say nothing (and I mean it) of those with alleged psychic powers.

This motley assortment of challenges to our everyday psychological hunches should have been enough to make us all cautious when advancing *a priori* claims based on an analysis of the everyday concepts about what can and cannot happen, but philosophers have typically invested a surprising authority in those concepts. Consider the philosophical debates about self-deception and weakness of the will. No one doubts that the phenomena so-called by folk psychology are ubiquitous. The controversy reigns over how, if at all, these phenomena can be described coherently in terms of belief, knowledge, intention, judgment, and the other standard terms of folk psychology. Articles with titles like "How is Weakness of Will Possible?" (Davidson 1969) attempt to say just exactly what one must believe, think, know, intend, and want in order to suffer a genuine case of weakness of will. The paradoxes and contradictions that bedevil the attempts have discouraged few of the participants. It is apparently obvious to them that the folk-psychological categories they learned in infancy are the right categories to use, whatever Nagelian perplexity their use may bring in its train.

We have all learned to take a more skeptical attitude toward the dictates of folk physics, including those robust deliverances that persist in the face of academic science. Even the "undeniable introspective fact" that you can *feel* "centrifugal force" cannot save it, except for the pragmatic purposes of rough-and-ready understanding it has always served. The delicate question of just how we ought to express our diminished allegiance to the categories of folk physics has been a central topic in philosophy since the seventeenth century, when Descartes, Boyle, and others began to ponder the metaphysical status of color, felt warmth, and the other "secondary qualities." These discussions, while cautiously agnostic about the status of folk physics, have traditionally assumed as unchallenged bedrock the folk-psychological counterpart categories: *conscious perceptions* of color, *sensations* of warmth, or *beliefs* about the "external world," for instance. (This assumption is particularly evident in Kripke's (1972) discussion of materialism, for example.)

A few of us (Quine 1960; Dennett 1969, 1978a; Churchland 1981; Stich 1983) have wondered if the problems encountered in traditional philosophy of mind may be problems with the whole framework or system of folk-psychological concepts, and have recommended putting those concepts in the same jeopardy as the concepts of folk physics. We have disagreed on the verdict, a topic for exploration in the chapters ahead, but not on the vulnerability in principle of the mentalistic concepts.

The faith we are all tempted to place in the categories of folk psychology, like our faith in the categories of folk physics, is not due just to stubborn loyalty to the world view we grew up with. In his classic essay "Philosophy and the Scientific Image of Man," Sellars (1963, chapter 1) calls this world view the manifest image and distinguishes it from the scientific image. It is no accident that we have the manifest image that we do; our nervous systems were designed to make the distinctions we need swiftly and reliably, to bring under single sensory rubrics the relevant common features in our environment, and to ignore what we can usually get away with ignoring (Dennett 1984d, forthcoming a; Akins, unpublished). The undeniable fact is that usually, especially in the dealings that are most important in our daily lives, folk science works. Thanks to folk physics we stay warm and well fed and avoid collisions, and thanks to folk psychology we cooperate on multiperson projects, learn from each other, and enjoy periods of local peace. These benefits would be unattainable without extraordinarily efficient and reliable systems of expectation-generation.

How are we enabled to do all this? What organizes our capacity to have all these effortless, confident, and largely reliable expectations? Are there general "laws" or "principles" of folk physics that we somehow internalize and then unconsciously exploit to generate the indefinitely various and sensitive expectations we have about inanimate objects? How do we manage to acquire such a *general* capacity to interpret our fellow human beings? I have no account to offer of our talents as folk physicists, or about the relation of folk physics to its academic offspring (though this is a fascinating topic deserving further study), but I do have an explanation of the power and success of folk psychology: we make sense of each other by adopting the intentional stance.

2   True Believers:
The Intentional Strategy
and Why It Works

Death Speaks

There was a merchant in Baghdad who sent his servant to market to buy provisions and in a little while the servant came back, white and trembling, and said, Master, just now when I was in the market-place I was jostled by a woman in the crowd and when I turned I saw it was Death that jostled me. She looked at me and made a threatening gesture; now, lend me your horse, and I will ride away from this city and avoid my fate. I will go to Samarra and there Death will not find me. The merchant lent him his horse, and the servant mounted it, and he dug his spurs in its flanks and as fast as the horse could gallop he went. Then the merchant went down to the market-place and he saw me standing in the crowd, and he came to me and said, why did you make a threatening gesture to my servant when you saw him this morning? That was not a threatening gesture, I said, it was only a start of surprise. I was astonished to see him in Baghdad, for I had an appointment with him tonight in Samarra.

W. Somerset Maugham

In the social sciences, talk about *belief* is ubiquitous. Since social scientists are typically self-conscious about their methods, there is also a lot of talk about *talk about belief*. And since belief is a genuinely curious and perplexing phenomenon, showing many different faces to the world, there is abundant controversy. Sometimes belief attribution appears to be a dark, risky, and imponderable business—especially when exotic, and more particularly religious or superstitious, beliefs are in the limelight. These are not the only troublesome cases; we also

Originally presented as a Herbert Spencer Lecture at Oxford in November 1979, and reprinted, with permission, from A. F. Heath, ed., *Scientific Explanation* (Oxford: Oxford University Press, 1981).

court argument and skepticism when we attribute beliefs to nonhuman animals, or to infants, or to computers or robots. Or when the beliefs we feel constrained to attribute to an apparently healthy, adult member of our own society are contradictory, or even just wildly false. A biologist colleague of mine was once called on the telephone by a man in a bar who wanted him to settle a bet. The man asked: "Are rabbits birds?" "No" said the biologist. "Damn!" said the man as he hung up. Now could he *really* have believed that rabbits were birds? Could anyone really and truly be attributed that belief? Perhaps, but it would take a bit of a story to bring us to accept it.

In all of these cases belief attribution appears beset with subjectivity, infected with cultural relativism, prone to "indeterminacy of radical translation"—clearly an enterprise demanding special talents: the art of phenomenological analysis, hermeneutics, empathy, *Verstehen,* and all that. On other occasions, normal occasions, when familiar beliefs are the topic, belief attribution looks as easy as speaking prose and as objective and reliable as counting beans in a dish. Particularly when these straightforward cases are before us, it is quite plausible to suppose that in principle (if not yet in practice) it would be possible to confirm these simple, objective belief attributions by *finding something inside the believer's head*—by finding the beliefs themselves, in effect. "Look," someone might say, "You either believe there's milk in the fridge or you don't believe there's milk in the fridge" (you might have no opinion, in the latter case). But if you do believe this, that's a perfectly objective fact about you, and it must come down in the end to your brain's being in some particular physical state. If we knew more about physiological psychology, we could in principle determine the facts about your brain state and thereby determine whether or not you believe there is milk in the fridge, even if you were determined to be silent or disingenuous on the topic. In principle, on this view physiological psychology could trump the results—or nonresults—of any "black box" method in the social sciences that divines beliefs (and other mental features) by behavioral, cultural, social, historical, *external* criteria.

These differing reflections congeal into two opposing views on the nature of belief attribution, and hence on the nature of belief. The latter, a variety of *realism,* likens the question of whether a person has a particular belief to the question of whether a person is infected with a particular virus—a perfectly objective internal matter of fact about which an observer can often make educated guesses of great reliability. The former, which we could call *interpretationism* if we absolutely had to give it a name, likens the question of whether a person has a particular belief to the question of whether a person is immoral, or has style, or talent, or would make a good wife. Faced with such questions, we preface our answers with "well, it all depends on what you're interested in," or make some similar acknowledgment of the relativity of the issue. "It's a matter of interpretation," we say. These two opposing views, so baldly stated, do not fairly represent any serious theorists' positions, but they do express views that are typically seen as mutually exclusive and exhaustive; the theorist must be friendly with one and only one of these themes.

I think this is a mistake. My thesis will be that while belief is a perfectly objective phenomenon (that apparently makes me a realist), it can be discerned only from the point of view of one who adopts a certain *predictive strategy*, and its existence can be confirmed only by an assessment of the success of that strategy (that apparently makes me an interpretationist).

First I will describe the strategy, which I call the intentional strategy or adopting the intentional stance. To a first approximation, the intentional strategy consists of treating the object whose behavior you want to predict as a rational agent with beliefs and desires and other mental stages exhibiting what Brentano and others call *intentionality*. The strategy has often been described before, but I shall try to put this very familiar material in a new light by showing *how* it works and by showing *how well* it works.

Then I will argue that any object—or as I shall say, any *system*—whose behavior is well predicted by this strategy is in the fullest sense of the word a believer. *What it is* to be a true believer is to be an *intentional system*, a system whose behavior is reliably and voluminously predictable via the intentional strategy. I have argued for this position before (Dennett 1971, 1976b, 1978a), and my arguments have so far garnered few converts and many presumed counterexamples. I shall try again here, harder, and shall also deal with several compelling objections.

The Intentional Strategy and How It Works

There are many strategies, some good, some bad. Here is a strategy, for instance, for predicting the future behavior of a person: determine the date and hour of the person's birth and then feed this modest datum into one or another astrological algorithm for generating predictions of the person's prospects. This strategy is deplorably popular. Its popularity is deplorable only because we have such good reasons for believing that it does not work (*pace* Feyerabend 1978). When astrological predictions come true this is sheer luck, or the result of such vagueness or ambiguity in the prophecy that almost any eventuality can be construed to confirm it. But suppose the astrological strategy did in fact work well on some people. We could call those people *astrological systems*—systems whose behavior was, as a matter of fact, predictable by the astrological strategy. If there were such people, such astrological systems, we would be more interested than most of us in fact are in *how the astrological strategy works*—that is, we would be interested in the rules, principles, or methods of astrology. We could find out how the strategy works by asking astrologers, reading their books, and observing them in action. But we would also be curious about *why* it worked. We might find that astrologers had no useful opinions about this latter question—they either had no theory of why it worked or their theories were pure hokum. Having a good strategy is one thing; knowing why it works is another.

So far as we know, however, the class of astrological systems is empty, so the astrological strategy is of interest only as a social curiosity. Other strategies have better credentials. Consider the physical strategy, or physical stance; if you want to predict the behavior of a system, determine its physical constitution (perhaps all the way down to the microphysical level) and the physical nature of the impingements upon it, and use your knowledge of the laws of physics to predict the outcome for any input. This is the grand and impractical strategy of Laplace for predicting the entire future of everything in the universe, but it has more modest, local, actually usable versions. The chemist or physicist in the laboratory can use this strategy to predict the behavior of exotic materials, but equally the cook in the kitchen can predict the effect of leaving the pot on the burner too long. The strategy is not always practically available, but that it will always work *in principle* is a dogma of the physical sciences (I ignore the minor complications raised by the subatomic indeterminacies of quantum physics.)

Sometimes, in any event, it is more effective to switch from the physical stance to what I call the design stance, where one ignores the actual (possibly messy) details of the physical constitution of an object, and, on the assumption that it has a certain design, predicts that it will behave *as it is designed to behave* under various circumstances. For instance, most users of computers have not the foggiest idea what physical principles are responsible for the computer's highly reliable, and hence predictable, behavior. But if they have a good idea of what the computer is designed to do (a description of its operation at any one of the many possible levels of abstraction), they can predict its behavior with great accuracy and reliability, subject to discon-firmation only in cases of physical malfunction. Less dramatically, almost anyone can predict when an alarm clock will sound on the basis of the most casual inspection of its exterior. One does not know or care to know whether it is spring wound, battery driven, sunlight powered, made of brass wheels and jewel bearings or silicon chips— one just assumes that it is designed so that the alarm will sound when it is set to sound, and it is set to sound where it appears to be set to sound, and the clock will keep on running until that time and be-yond, and is designed to run more or less accurately, and so forth. For more accurate and detailed design stance predictions of the alarm clock, one must descend to a less abstract level of description of its design; for instance, to the level at which gears are described, but their material is not specified.

Only the designed behavior of a system is predictable from the design stance, of course. If you want to predict the behavior of an alarm clock when it is pumped full of liquid helium, revert to the physical stance. Not just artifacts but also many biological objects (plants and animals, kidneys and hearts, stamens and pistils) behave in ways that can be predicted from the design stance. They are not just physical systems but designed systems.

Sometimes even the design stance is practically inaccessible, and then there is yet another stance or strategy one can adopt: the inten-tional stance. Here is how it works: first you decide to treat the object whose behavior is to be predicted as a rational agent; then you figure out what beliefs that agent ought to have, given its place in the world and its purpose. Then you figure out what desires it ought to have, on the same considerations, and finally you predict that this rational agent will act to further its goals in the light of its beliefs. A little practical reasoning from the chosen set of beliefs and desires will in many—but not all—instances yield a decision about what the agent ought to do; that is what you predict the agent *will* do.

The strategy becomes clearer with a little elaboration. Consider first how we go about populating each other's heads with beliefs. A few truisms: sheltered people tend to be ignorant; if you expose someone to something he comes to know all about it. In general, it seems, we come to believe all the truths about the parts of the world around us we are put in a position to learn about. Exposure to *x*, that is, sensory confrontation with *x* over some suitable period of time, is the *normally sufficient* condition for knowing (or having true beliefs) about *x*. As we say, we come to *know all about* the things around us. Such exposure is only *normally* sufficient for knowledge, but this is not the large escape hatch it might appear; our threshold for accepting abnormal ignorance in the face of exposure is quite high. "I didn't know the gun was loaded," said by one who was observed to be present, sighted, and awake during the loading, meets with a variety of utter skepticism that only the most outlandish supporting tale could overwhelm.

Of course we do not come to learn or remember all the truths our sensory histories avail us. In spite of the phrase "know all about," what we come to know, normally, are only all the *relevant* truths our sensory histories avail us. I do not typically come to know the ratio of spectacle-wearing people to trousered people in a room I inhabit, though if this interested me, it would be readily learnable. It is not just that some facts about my environment are below my thresholds of discrimination or beyond the integration and holding power of my memory (such as the height in inches of all the people present), but that many perfectly detectable, graspable, memorable facts are of no interest to me and hence do not come to be believed by me. So one rule for attributing beliefs in the intentional strategy is this: attribute as beliefs all the truths relevant to the system's interests (or desires) that the system's experience to date has made available. This rule leads to attributing somewhat too much—since we all are somewhat forgetful, even of important things. It also fails to capture the false beliefs we are all known to have. But the attribution of false belief, *any* false belief, requires a special genealogy, which will be seen to consist in the main in true beliefs. Two paradigm cases: S believes (falsely) that *p*, because S believes (truly) that Jones told him that *p*, that Jones is pretty clever, that Jones did not intend to deceive him, . . . etc. Second case: S believes (falsely) that there is a snake on the barstool, because S believes (truly) that he seems to see a snake on the barstool, is himself sitting in a bar not a yard from the barstool he sees, and so forth. The falsehood has to start somewhere; the seed may be sown in hallucination, illusion, a normal variety of simple misperception, memory deterioration, or deliberate fraud, for instance, but the false beliefs that are reaped grow in a culture medium of true beliefs.

Then there are the arcane and sophisticated beliefs, true and false, that are so often at the focus of attention in discussions of belief attribution. They do not arise directly, goodness knows, from exposure to mundane things and events, but their attribution requires tracing out a lineage of mainly good argument or reasoning from the bulk of beliefs already attributed. An implication of the intentional strategy, then, is that true believers mainly believe truths. If anyone could devise an agreed-upon method of individuating and counting beliefs (which I doubt very much), we would see that all but the smallest portion (say, less than ten percent) of a person's beliefs were attributable under our first rule.[1]

Note that this rule is a derived rule, an elaboration and further

---

1. The idea that most of anyone's beliefs *must* be true seems obvious to some people. Support for the idea can be found in works by Quine, Putnam, Shoemaker, Davidson, and myself. Other people find the idea equally incredible—so probably each side is calling a different phenomenon belief. Once one makes the distinction between belief and opinion (in my technical sense—see "How to Change Your Mind" in *Brainstorms*, chapter 16), according to which opinions are linguistically infected, relatively sophisticated cognitive states—*roughly* states of betting on the truth of a particular, formulated sentence—one can see the near triviality of the claim that most beliefs are true. A few reflections on peripheral matters should bring it out. Consider Democritus, who had a systematic, all-embracing, but (let us say, for the sake of argument) entirely false physics. He had things *all wrong*, though his views held together and had a sort of systematic utility. But even if every *claim* that scholarship permits us to attribute to Democritus (either explicit or implicit in his writings) is false, these represent a vanishingly small fraction of his *beliefs*, which include both the vast numbers of humdrum standing beliefs he must have had (about which house he lived in, what to look for in a good pair of sandals, and so forth) and also those occasional beliefs that came and went by the millions as his perceptual experience changed.

But, it may be urged, this isolation of his humdrum beliefs from his science relies on an insupportable distinction between truths of observation and truths of theory; all Democritus's beliefs are theory-laden, and since his theory is false, they are false. The reply is as follows: Granted that all observation beliefs are theory laden, why should we choose Democritus's *explicit*, sophisticated theory (couched in his *opinions*) as the theory with which to burden his quotidian observations? Note that the least theoretical compatriot of Democritus also had myriads of theory-laden observation beliefs—and was, in one sense, none the wiser for it. Why should we not suppose Democritus's observations are laden with the same (presumably innocuous) theory? If Democritus forgot his theory, or changed his mind, his observational beliefs would be *largely* untouched. To the extent that his sophisticated theory played a discernible role in his routine behavior and expectations and so forth, it would be quite appropriate to couch his humdrum beliefs in terms of the sophisticated theory, but this will not yield a *mainly false* catalogue of beliefs, since so few of his beliefs will be affected. (The effect of theory on observation is nevertheless often underrated. See Churchland 1979 for dramatic and convincing examples of the tight relationship that can sometimes exist between theory and experience. [The discussion in this note was distilled from a useful conversation with Paul and Patricia Churchland and Michael Stack.])

specification of the fundamental rule: attribute those beliefs the system *ought to have*. Note also that the rule interacts with the attribution of desires. How do we attribute the desires (preferences, goals, interests) on whose basis we will shape the list of beliefs? We attribute the desires the system *ought to have*. That is the fundamental rule. It dictates, on a first pass, that we attribute the familiar list of highest, or most basic, desires to people: survival, absence of pain, food, comfort, procreation, entertainment. Citing any one of these desires typically terminates the "Why?" game of reason giving. One is not supposed to need an ulterior motive for desiring comfort or pleasure or the prolongation of one's existence. Derived rules of desire attribution interact with belief attributions. Trivially, we have the rule: attribute desires for those things a system believes to be good for it. Somewhat more informatively, attribute desires for those things a system believes to be best means to other ends it desires. The attribution of bizarre and detrimental desires thus requires, like the attribution of false beliefs, special stories.

The interaction between belief and desire becomes trickier when we consider what desires we attribute on the basis of verbal behavior. The capacity to *express* desires in language opens the floodgates of desire attribution. "I want a two-egg mushroom omelette, some French bread and butter, and a half bottle of lightly chilled white Burgundy." How could one begin to attribute a desire for anything so specific in the absence of such verbal declaration? How, indeed, could a creature come to *contract* such a specific desire without the aid of language? Language *enables* us to formulate highly specific desires, but it also *forces* us on occasion to commit ourselves to desires altogether more stringent in their conditions of satisfaction than anything we would otherwise have any reason to endeavor to satisfy. Since in order to get what you want you often have to say what you want, and since you often cannot say what you want without saying something more specific than you antecedently mean, you often end up giving others evidence—the very best of evidence, your unextorted word—that you desire things or states of affairs far more particular than would satisfy you—or better, than would have satisfied you, for once you have declared, being a man of your word, you acquire an interest in satisfying exactly the desire you declared and no other.

"I'd like some baked beans, please."

"Yes sir. How many?"

You might well object to having such a specification of desire demanded of you, but in fact we are all socialized to accede to similar requirements in daily life—to the point of not noticing it, and certainly not feeling oppressed by it. I dwell on this because it has a parallel in the realm of belief, where our linguistic environment is forever forcing us to give—or concede—precise verbal expression to convictions that lack the hard edges verbalization endows them with (see Dennett 1969, pp. 184–85, and *Brainstorms,* chapter 16). By concentrating on the *results* of this social force, while ignoring its distorting effect, one can easily be misled into thinking that it is *obvious* that beliefs and desires are rather like sentences stored in the head. Being language-using creatures, it is inevitable that we should often come to believe that some particular, actually formulated, spelled and punctuated sentence *is true,* and that on other occasions we should come to want such a sentence to *come true,* but these are special cases of belief and desire and as such may not be reliable models for the whole domain.

That is enough, on this occasion, about the principles of belief and desire attribution to be found in the intentional strategy. What about the rationality one attributes to an intentional system? One starts with the ideal of perfect rationality and revises downward as circumstances dictate. That is, one starts with the assumption that people believe all the implications of their beliefs and believe no contradictory pairs of beliefs. This does not create a practical problem of clutter (infinitely many implications, for instance), for one is interested only in ensuring that the system one is predicting is rational enough to get to the particular implications that are relevant to its behavioral predicament of the moment. Instances of irrationality, or of finitely powerful capacities of inferences, raise particularly knotty problems of interpretation, which I will set aside on this occasion (see chapter 4, "Making Sense of Ourselves," and Cherniak 1986).

For I want to turn from the description of the strategy to the question of its use. Do people actually use this strategy? Yes, all the time. There may someday be other strategies for attributing belief and desire and for predicting behavior, but this is the only one we all know now. And when does it work? It works with people almost all the time. Why would it *not* be a good idea to allow individual Oxford colleges to create and grant academic degrees whenever they saw fit? The answer is a long story, but very easy to generate. And there would be widespread agreement about the major points. We have no difficulty thinking of the reasons people would then have for acting in such ways as to give others reasons for acting in such ways as to give others reasons for . . . creating a circumstance we would not want. Our use of the intentional strategy is so habitual and effortless that the role it plays in shaping our expectations about people is easily overlooked. The strategy also works on most other mammals most of the time. For instance, you can use it to design better traps to catch those mammals, by reasoning about what the creature knows or believes about various things, what it prefers, what it wants to avoid. The strategy works on birds, and on fish, and on reptiles, and on insects and spiders, and even on such lowly and unenterprising creatures as clams (once a clam believes there is danger about, it will not relax its grip on its closed shell until it is convinced that the danger has passed). It also works on some artifacts: the chess-playing computer will not take your knight because it knows that there is a line of ensuing play that would lead to losing its rook, and it does not want that to happen. More modestly, the thermostat will turn off the boiler as soon as it comes to believe the room has reached the desired temperature.

The strategy even works for plants. In a locale with late spring storms, you should plant apple varieties that are particularly *cautious* about *concluding* that it is spring—which is when they *want* to blossom, of course. It even works for such inanimate and apparently undesigned phenomena as lightning. An electrician once explained to me how he worked out how to protect my underground water pump from lightning damage: lightning, he said, always wants to find the best way to ground, but sometimes it gets tricked into taking second-best paths. You can protect the pump by making another, better path more *obvious* to the lightning.

True Believers as Intentional Systems

Now clearly this is a motley assortment of "serious" belief attributions, dubious belief attributions, pedagogically useful metaphors, *falçcons de parler*, and, perhaps worse, outright frauds. The next task would seem to be distinguishing those intentional systems that *really* have beliefs and desires from those we may find it handy to treat *as if* they had beliefs and desires. But that would be a Sisyphean labor, or else would be terminated by fiat. A better understanding of the phenomenon of belief begins with the observation that even in the worst of these cases, even when we are surest that the strategy works *for the wrong reasons*, it is nevertheless true that it does work, at least a little bit. This is an interesting fact, which distinguishes this class of objects, the class of *intentional systems*, from the class of objects for which the strategy never works. But is this so? Does our definition of an intentional system exclude any objects at all? For instance, it seems the lectern in this lecture room can be construed as an intentional system, fully rational, believing that it is currently located at the center of the civilized world (as some of you may also think), and desiring above all else to remain at that center. What should such a rational agent so equipped with belief and desire do? Stay put, clearly, which is just what the lectern does. I predict the lectern's behavior, accurately, from the intentional stance, so is it an intentional system? If it is, anything at all is.

What should disqualify the lectern? For one thing, the strategy does not recommend itself in this case, for we get no predictive power from it that we did not antecedently have. We already knew what the lectern was going to do—namely nothing—and tailored the beliefs and desires to fit in a quite unprincipled way. In the case of people or animals or computers, however, the situation is different. In these cases often the only strategy that is at all practical is the intentional strategy; it gives us predictive power we can get by no other method. But, it will be urged, this is no difference in nature, but merely a difference that reflects upon our limited capacities as scientists. The Laplacean omniscient physicist could predict the behavior of a computer—or of a live human body, assuming it to be ultimately governed by the laws of physics—without any need for the risky, short-cut methods of either the design or intentional strategies. For people of limited mechanical aptitude, the intentional interpretation of a simple thermostat is a handy and largely innocuous crutch, but the engineers among us can quite fully grasp its internal operation without the aid of this anthropomorphizing. It may be true that the cleverest engineers find it practically impossible to maintain a clear conception of more complex systems, such as a time-sharing computer system or remote-controlled space probe, without lapsing into an intentional stance (and viewing these devices as asking and telling, trying and avoiding, wanting and believing), but this is just a more advanced case of human epistemic frailty. We would not want to classify these artifacts with the true believers—ourselves—on such variable and parochial grounds, would we? Would it not be intolerable to hold that some artifact or creature or person was a believer from the point of view of one observer, but not a believer at all from the point of view of another, cleverer observer? That would be a particularly radical version of interpretationiʋm, and some have thought I espoused it in urging that belief be viewed in terms of the success of the intentional strategy. I must confess that my presentation of the view has sometimes invited that reading, but I now want to discourage it. The decision to adopt the intentional stance is free, but the facts about the success or failure of the stance, were one to adopt it, are perfectly objective.

Once the intentional strategy is in place, it is an extraordinarily powerful tool in prediction—a fact that is largely concealed by our typical concentration on the cases in which it yields dubious or unreliable results. Consider, for instance, predicting moves in a chess game. What makes chess an interesting game, one can see, is the *un*predictability of one's opponent's moves, except in those cases where moves are "forced"—where there is *clearly* one best move—typically the least of the available evils. But this unpredictability is put in context when one recognizes that in the typical chess situation there are very many perfectly legal and hence available moves, but only a few—perhaps half a dozen—with anything to be said for them, and hence only a few high-probability moves according to the intentional strategy. Even when the intentional strategy fails to distinguish a single move with a highest probability, it can dramatically reduce the number of live options.

The same feature is apparent when the intentional strategy is applied to "real world" cases. It is notoriously unable to predict the exact purchase and sell decisions of stock traders, for instance, or the exact sequence of words a politician will utter when making a scheduled speech, but one's confidence can be very high indeed about slightly less specific predictions: that the particular trader *will not buy utilities today*, or that the politician *will side with the unions against his party*, for example. This inability to predict fine-grained descriptions of actions, looked at another way, is a source of strength for the intentional strategy, for it is this neutrality with regard to details of implementation that permits one to exploit the intentional strategy in complex cases, for instance, in *chaining predictions* (see *Brainstorms*). Suppose the US Secretary of State were to announce he was a paid agent of the KGB. What an unparalleled event! How unpredictable its consequences! Yet in fact we can predict dozens of not terribly interesting but perfectly salient consequences, and consequences of consequences. The President would confer with the rest of the Cabinet, which would support his decision to relieve the Secretary of State of his duties pending the results of various investigations, psychiatric and political, and all this would be reported at a news conference to people who would write stories that would be commented upon in editorials that would be read by people who would write letters to the editors, and so forth. None of that is daring prognostication, but note that it describes an arc of causation in space-time that could not be predicted under *any* description by any imaginable practical extension of physics or biology.

The power of the intentional strategy can be seen even more sharply with the aid of an objection first raised by Robert Nozick some years ago. Suppose, he suggested, some beings of vastly superior intelligence—from Mars, let us say—were to descend upon us, and suppose that we were to them as simple thermostats are to clever engineers. Suppose, that is, that they did not *need* the intentional stance—or even the design stance—to predict our behavior in all its detail. They can be supposed to be Laplacean super-physicists, capable of comprehending the activity on Wall Street, for instance, at the microphysical level. Where we see brokers and buildings and sell orders and bids, they see vast congeries of subatomic particles milling about—and they are such good physicists that they can predict days in advance what ink marks will appear each day on the paper tape labeled "Closing Dow Jones Industrial Average." They can predict the individual behaviors of all the various moving bodies they observe without ever treating any of them as intentional systems. Would we be right then to say that from *their* point of view we really were not believers at all (any more than a simple thermostat is)? If so, then our status as believers is nothing objective, but rather something in the eye of the beholder—provided the beholder shares our intellectual limitations.

Our imagined Martians might be able to predict the future of the human race by Laplacean methods, but if they did not also see us as intentional systems, they would be missing something perfectly objective: the *patterns* in human behavior that are describable from the intentional stance, and only from that stance, and that support generalizations and predictions. Take a particular instance in which the Martians observe a stockbroker deciding to place an order for 500 shares of General Motors. They predict the exact motions of his fingers as he dials the phone and the exact vibrations of his vocal cords as he intones his order. But if the Martians do not see that indefinitely many *different* patterns of finger motions and vocal cord vibrations—even the motions of indefinitely many different individuals—could have been substituted for the actual particulars without perturbing the subsequent operation of the market, then they have failed to see a real pattern in the world they are observing. Just as there are indefinitely many ways of *being a spark plug*—and one has not understood what an internal combustion engine is unless one realizes that a variety of different devices can be screwed into these sockets without affecting the performance of the engine—so there are indefinitely many ways of *ordering 500 shares of General Motors*, and there are societal sockets in which one of these ways will produce just about the same effect as any other. There are also societal pivot points, as it were, where which way people go depends on whether they *believe that p*, or *desire A*, and does not depend on any of the other infinitely many ways they may be alike or different.

Suppose, pursuing our Martian fantasy a little further, that one of the Martians were to engage in a predicting contest with an Earthling. The Earthling and the Martian observe (and observe each other observing) a particular bit of local physical transaction. From the Earthling's point of view, this is what is observed. The telephone rings in Mrs. Gardner's kitchen. She answers, and this is what she says: "Oh, hello dear. You're coming home early? Within the hour? And bringing the boss to dinner? Pick up a bottle of wine on the way home, then, and drive carefully." On the basis of this observation, our Earthling predicts that a large metallic vehicle with rubber tires will come to a stop in the drive within one hour, disgorging two human beings, one of whom will be holding a paper bag containing a bottle containing an alcoholic fluid. The prediction is a bit risky, perhaps, but a good bet on all counts. The Martian makes the same prediction, but has to avail himself of much more information about an extraordinary number of interactions of which, so far as he can tell, the Earthling is entirely ignorant. For instance, the deceleration of the vehicle at intersection *A*, five miles from the house, without which there would have been a collision with another vehicle—whose collision course had been laboriously calculated over some hundreds of meters by the Martian. The Earthling's performance would look like magic! How did the Earthling know that the human being who got out of the car and got the bottle in the shop would get back in? The coming true of the Earthling's prediction, after all the vagaries, intersections, and branches in the paths charted by the Martian, would seem to anyone bereft of the intentional strategy as marvelous and inexplicable as the fatalistic inevitability of the appointment in Samarra. Fatalists—for instance, astrologers—believe that there is a pattern in human affairs that is inexorable, that will impose itself *come what may*, that is, no matter how the victims scheme and second-guess, no matter how they twist and turn in their chains. These fatalists are wrong, but they are *almost* right. There *are* patterns in human affairs that impose themselves, not quite inexorably but with great vigor, absorbing physical perturbations and variations that might as well be considered random; these are the patterns that we characterize in terms of the beliefs, desires, and intentions of rational agents.

No doubt you will have noticed, and been distracted by, a serious flaw in our thought experiment: the Martian is presumed to treat his Earthling opponent as an intelligent being like himself, with whom communication is possible, a being with whom one can make a wager, against whom one can compete. In short, a being with beliefs (such as the belief he expressed in his prediction) and desires (such as the desire to win the prediction contest). So if the Martian sees the pattern in one Earthling, how can he fail to see it in the others? As a bit of narrative, our example could be strengthened by supposing that our Earthling cleverly learned Martian (which is transmitted by X-ray modulation) and disguised himself as a Martian, counting on the species-chauvinism of these otherwise brilliant aliens to permit him to pass as an intentional system while not giving away the secret of his fellow human beings. This addition might get us over a bad twist in the tale, but might obscure the moral to be drawn: namely, *the unavoidability of the intentional stance with regard to oneself and one's fellow intelligent beings.* This unavoidability is itself interest relative; it is perfectly possible to adopt a physical stance, for instance, with regard to an intelligent being, oneself included, but not to the exclusion of maintaining at the same time an intentional stance with regard to oneself at a minimum, and one's fellows *if* one intends, for instance, to learn what they know (a point that has been powerfully made by Stuart Hampshire in a number of writings). We can perhaps suppose our super-intelligent Martians fail to recognize *us* as intentional systems, but we cannot suppose them to lack the requisite concepts.[2] If they observe, theorize, predict, communicate, they view *themselves* as intentional systems.[3] Where there are intelligent beings, the patterns must be there to be described, whether or not we care to see them.

It is important to recognize the objective reality of the intentional patterns discernible in the activities of intelligent creatures, but also important to recognize the incompleteness and imperfections in the patterns. The objective fact is that the intentional strategy *works as well as it does*, which is not perfectly. No one is perfectly rational, perfectly unforgetful, all-observant, or invulnerable to fatigue, malfunction, or design imperfection. This leads inevitably to circumstances beyond the power of the intentional strategy to describe, in much the same way that physical damage to an artifact, such as a telephone or an automobile, may render it indescribable by the normal design terminology for that artifact. How do you draw the schematic wiring diagram of an audio amplifier that has been partially melted, or how do you characterize the program state of a malfunctioning computer? In cases of even the mildest and most familiar cognitive pathology— where people seem to hold contradictory beliefs or to be deceiving themselves, for instance—the canons of interpretation of the intentional strategy fail to yield clear, stable verdicts about which beliefs and desires to attribute to a person.

Now a *strong* realist position on beliefs and desires would claim that in these cases the person in question really does have some particular beliefs and desires which the intentional strategy, as I have described it, is simply unable to divine. On the milder sort of realism I am advocating, there is no fact of the matter of exactly which beliefs and desires a person has in these degenerate cases, but this is not a sur-

---

2. A member of the audience in Oxford pointed out that if the Martian included the Earthling in his physical stance purview (a possibility I had not explicitly excluded), he would not be surprised by the Earthling's prediction. He would indeed have predicted exactly the pattern of X-ray modulations produced by the Earthling speaking Martian. True, but as the Martian wrote down the results of his calculations, his prediction of the Earthling's prediction would appear, word by Martian word, as on a Ouija board, and what would be baffling to the Martian was how this chunk of mechanism, the Earthling predictor dressed up like a Martian, was able to yield this *true* sentence of Martian when it was so informationally isolated from the events the Martian needed to know of in order to make his own prediction about the arriving automobile.

3. Might there not be intelligent beings who had no use for communicating, predicting, observing . . . ? There might be marvelous, nifty, invulnerable entities lacking these modes of action, but I cannot see what would lead us to call them *intelligent*.

render to relativism or subjectivism, for *when* and *why* there is no fact of the matter is itself a matter of objective fact. On this view one can even acknowledge the *interest relativity* of belief attributions and grant that given the different interests of different cultures, for instance, the beliefs and desires one culture would attribute to a member might be quite different from the beliefs and desires another culture would attribute to that very same person. But supposing that were so in a particular case, there would be the further facts about *how well* each of the rival intentional strategies worked for predicting the behavior of that person. We can be sure in advance that no intentional interpretation of an individual will work to perfection, and it may be that two rival schemes are about equally good, and better than any others we can devise. That this is the case is itself something about which there can be a fact of the matter. The objective presence of one pattern (with whatever imperfections) does not rule out the objective presence of another pattern (with whatever imperfections).

The bogey of radically different interpretations with equal warrant from the intentional strategy is theoretically important—one might better say metaphysically important—but practically negligible once one restricts one's attention to the largest and most complex intentional systems we know: human beings.[4]

Until now I have been stressing our kinship to clams and thermostats, in order to emphasize a view of the logical status of belief attribution, but the time has come to acknowledge the obvious differences and say what can be made of them. The perverse claim remains: *all there is* to being a true believer is being a system whose behavior is reliably predictable via the intentional strategy, and hence *all there is* to really and truly believing that *p* (for any proposition *p*) is being an intentional system for which *p* occurs as a belief in the best (most predictive) interpretation. But once we turn our attention to the truly interesting and versatile intentional systems, we see that this apparently shallow and instrumentalistic criterion of belief puts a severe constraint on the internal constitution of a genuine believer, and thus yields a robust version of belief after all.

Consider the lowly thermostat, as degenerate a case of an inten-

---

4. John McCarthy's analogy to cryptography nicely makes this point. The larger the corpus of cipher text, the less chance there is of dual, systematically unrelated decipherings. For a very useful discussion of the principles and presuppositions of the intentional stance applied to machines—explicitly including thermostats—see McCarthy 1979.

tional system as could conceivably hold our attention for more than a moment. Going along with the gag, we might agree to grant it the capacity for about half a dozen different beliefs and fewer desires—it can believe the room is too cold or too hot, that the boiler is on or off, and that if it wants the room warmer it should turn on the boiler, and so forth. But surely this is imputing too much to the thermostat; it has no concept of heat or of a boiler, for instance. So suppose we *de-interpret* its beliefs and desires: it can believe the A is too F or G, and if it wants the A to be more F it should do K, and so forth. After all, by attaching the thermostatic control mechanism to different input and output devices, it could be made to regulate the amount of water in a tank, or the speed of a train, for instance. Its attachment to a heat-sensitive transducer and a boiler is too impoverished a link to the world to grant any rich semantics to its belief-like states.

But suppose we then enrich these modes of attachment. Suppose we give it more than one way of learning about the temperature, for instance. We give it an eye of sorts that can distinguish huddled, shivering occupants of the room and an ear so that it can be told how cold it is. We give it some facts about geography so that it can conclude that it is probably in a cold place if it learns that its spatio-temporal location is Winnipeg in December. Of course giving it a visual system that is multipurpose and general—not a mere shivering-object detector—will require vast complications of its inner structure. Suppose we also give our system more behavioral versatility: it chooses the boiler fuel, purchases it from the cheapest and most reliable dealer, checks the weather stripping, and so forth. This adds another dimension of internal complexity; it gives individual belief-like states *more to do*, in effect, by providing more and different occasions for their derivation or deduction from other states, and by providing more and different occasions for them to serve as premises for further reasoning. The cumulative effect of enriching these connections between the device and the world in which it resides is to enrich the semantics of its dummy predicates, F and G and the rest. The more of this we add, the less amenable our device becomes to serving as the control structure of anything other than a room-temperature maintenance system. A more formal way of saying this is that the class of indistinguishably satisfactory models of the formal system embodied in its internal states gets smaller and smaller as we add such complexities; the more we add, the richer or more demanding or specific the semantics of the system, until eventually we reach systems for which a unique semantic interpretation is practically (but never in principle) dictated (cf. Hayes 1979). At that point we say this device (or animal or person) has beliefs *about heat* and *about this very room*, and so forth, not only because of the system's actual location in, and operations on, the world, but because we cannot imagine another niche in which it could be placed *where it would work* (see also chapters 5 and 8).

Our original simple thermostat had a state we called a belief about a particular boiler, to the effect that it was on or off. Why about *that* boiler? Well, what other boiler would you want to say it was about? The belief is about the boiler because it is *fastened* to the boiler.[5] Given the actual, if mimimal, causal link to the world that happened to be in effect, we could endow a state of the device with *meaning* (of a sort) and *truth conditions*, but it was altogether too easy to substitute a different minimal link and completely change the meaning (in this impoverished sense) of that internal state. But as systems become perceptually richer and behaviorally more versatile, it becomes harder and harder to make substitutions in the actual links of the system to the world without changing the organization of the system itself. If you change its environment, it will *notice*, in effect, and make a change in its internal state in response. There comes to be a two-way constraint of growing specificity between the device and the environment. Fix the device in any one state and it demands a very specific environment in which to operate properly (you can no longer switch it easily from regulating temperature to regulating speed or anything else); but at the same time, if you do not *fix* the state it is in, but just plonk it down in a changed environment, its sensory attachments will be sensitive and discriminative enough to respond appropriately to the change, driving the system into a new state, in which it will operate effectively in the new environment. There is a familiar way of alluding to this tight relationship that can exist between the organization of a system and its environment: you say that the organism continuously *mirrors* the environment, or that there is a *representation* of the environment in—or implicit in—the organization of the system.

---

5. This idea is the ancestor in effect of the species of different ideas lumped together under the rubric of *de re* belief. If one builds from this idea toward its scions, one can see better the difficulties with them, and how to repair them. (For more on this topic, see chapter 5, "Beyond Belief.")

It is not that we attribute (or should attribute) beliefs and desires only to things in which we find internal representations, but rather that when we discover some object for which the intentional strategy works, we endeavor to interpret some of its internal states or processes as internal representations. What makes some internal feature of a thing a representation could only be its role in regulating the behavior of an intentional system.

Now the reason for stressing our kinship with the thermostat should be clear. There is no magic moment in the transition from a simple thermostat to a system that *really* has an internal representation of the world around it. The thermostat has a minimally demanding representation of the world, fancier thermostats have more demanding representations of the world, fancier robots for helping around the house would have still more demanding representations of the world. Finally you reach us. We are so multifariously and intricately connected to the world that almost no substitution is possible— though it is clearly imaginable in a thought experiment. Hilary Putnam imagines the planet Twin Earth, which is just like Earth right down to the scuff marks on the shoes of the Twin Earth replica of your neighbor, but which differs from Earth in some property that is entirely beneath the thresholds of your capacities to discriminate. (What they call water on Twin Earth has a different chemical analysis.) Were *you* to be whisked instantaneously to Twin Earth and exchanged for your Twin Earth replica, you would never be the wiser— just like the simple control system that cannot tell whether it is regulating temperature, speed, or volume of water in a tank. It is easy to devise radically different Twin Earths for something as simple and sensorily deprived as a thermostat, but your internal organization puts a much more stringent demand on substitution. Your Twin Earth and Earth must be virtual replicas or you will change state dramatically on arrival.

So which boiler are *your* beliefs about when you believe the boiler is on? Why, the boiler in your cellar (rather than its twin on Twin Earth, for instance). What other boiler would your beliefs be about? The completion of the semantic interpretation of your beliefs, fixing the referents of your beliefs, requires, as in the case of the thermostat, facts about your actual embedding in the world. The principles, and problems, of interpretation that we discover when we attribute beliefs to people are the *same* principles and problems we discover when we look at the ludicrous, but blessedly simple, problem of attributing beliefs to a thermostat. The differences are of degree, but never-

theless of such great degree that understanding the internal organization of a simple intentional system gives one very little basis for
understanding the internal organization of a complex intentional system, such as a human being.

Why Does the Intentional Strategy Work?

When we turn to the question of *why* the intentional strategy works as
well as it does, we find that the question is ambiguous, admitting of
two very different sorts of answers. If the intentional system is a
simple thermostat, one answer is simply this: the intentional strategy
works because the thermostat is well designed; it was designed to be
a system that could be easily and reliably comprehended and manipulated from this stance. That is true, but not very informative, if what
we are after are the actual features of its design that explain its performance. Fortunately, however, in the case of a simple thermostat
those features are easily discovered and understood, so the other
answer to our *why* question, which is really an answer about *how the
machinery works*, is readily available.

  If the intentional system in question is a person, there is also an
ambiguity in our question. The first answer to the question of why
the intentional strategy works is that evolution has designed human
beings to be rational, to believe what they ought to believe and want
what they ought to want. The fact that we are products of a long and
demanding evolutionary process guarantees that using the intentional strategy on us is a safe bet. This answer has the virtues of truth
and brevity, and on this occasion the additional virtue of being an
answer Herbert Spencer would applaud, but it is also strikingly uninformative. The more difficult version of the question asks, in effect,
how the machinery which Nature has provided us works. And we
cannot yet give a good answer to that question. We just do not know.
We do know how the *strategy* works, and we know the easy answer to
the question of why it works, but knowing these does not help us
much with the hard answer.

  It is not that there is any dearth of doctrine, however. A Skinnerian
behaviorist, for instance, would say that the strategy works because
its imputations of beliefs and desires are shorthand, in effect, for as
yet unimaginably complex descriptions of the effects of prior histories
of response and reinforcement. To say that someone wants some ice
cream is to say that in the past the ingestion of ice cream has been

reinforced in him by the results, creating a propensity under certain background conditions (also too complex to describe) to engage in ice-cream-acquiring behavior. In the absence of detailed knowledge of those historical facts we can nevertheless make shrewd guesses on inductive grounds; these guesses are embodied in our intentional stance claims. Even if all this were true, it would tell us very little about the way such propensities were regulated by the internal machinery.

A currently more popular explanation is that the account of how the strategy works and the account of how the mechanism works will (roughly) *coincide:* for each predictively attributable belief, there will be a functionally salient internal state of the machinery, decomposable into functional parts in just about the same way the sentence expressing the belief is decomposable into parts—that is, words or terms. The inferences we attribute to rational creatures will be mirrored by physical, causal processes in the hardware; the *logical* form of the propositions believed will be copied in the *structural* form of the states in correspondence with them. This is the hypothesis that there is a *language of thought* coded in our brains, and our brains will eventually be understood as symbol manipulating systems in at least rough analogy with computers. Many different versions of this view are currently being explored, in the new research program called cognitive science, and provided one allows great latitude for attenuation of the basic, bold claim, I think some version of it will prove correct.

But I do not believe that this is *obvious.* Those who think that it is obvious, or inevitable, that such a theory will prove true (and there are many who do), are confusing two different empirical claims. The first is that intentional stance description yields an objective, real pattern in the world—the pattern our imaginary Martians missed. This is an empirical claim, but one that is confirmed beyond skepticism. The second is that this real pattern is *produced by* another real pattern roughly isomorphic to it within the brains of intelligent creatures. Doubting the existence of the second real pattern is not doubting the existence of the first. There *are* reasons for believing in the second pattern, but they are not overwhelming. The best simple account I can give of the reasons is as follows.

As we ascend the scale of complexity from simple thermostat, through sophisticated robot, to human being, we discover that our efforts to design systems with the requisite behavior increasingly run foul of the problem of *combinatorial explosion*. Increasing some parameter by, say, ten percent—ten percent more inputs or more degrees of freedom in the behavior to be controlled or more words to be recognized or whatever—tends to increase the internal complexity of the system being designed by orders of magnitude. Things get out of hand very fast and, for instance, can lead to computer programs that will swamp the largest, fastest machines. Now somehow the brain has solved the problem of combinatorial explosion. It is a gigantic network of billions of cells, but still finite, compact, reliable, and swift, and capable of learning new behaviors, vocabularies, theories, almost without limit. Some elegant, *generative*, indefinitely extendable principles of representation must be responsible. We have only one model of such a representation system: a human language. So the argument for a language of thought comes down to this: what else could it be? We have so far been unable to imagine any plausible alternative in any detail. That is a good enough reason, I think, for recommending as a matter of scientific tactics that we pursue the hypothesis in its various forms as far as we can.[6] But we will engage in that exploration more circumspectly, and fruitfully, if we bear in mind that its inevitable rightness is far from assured. One does not well understand even a true empirical hypothesis so long as one is under the misapprehension that it is necessarily true.

---

6. The fact that all *language of thought* models of mental representation so far proposed fall victim to combinatorial explosion in one way or another should temper one's enthusiasm for engaging in what Fodor aptly calls "the only game in town."

Reflections:
Real Patterns,
Deeper Facts, and
Empty Questions

Several of the themes that receive a brisk treatment in "True Believers" expand into central topics in subsequent chapters. Perhaps the major source of disquiet about my position over the years has been its delicate balancing act on the matter of the observer-relativity of attributions of belief and other intentional states. On my view, is belief attribution (or meaning) in the eye of the beholder? Do I think there are *objective truths* about what people believe, or do I claim that all attributions are just *useful fictions*? My discussion of Nozick's objection attempts to place my view firmly on the knife-edge between the intolerable extremes of simple realism and simple relativism, but this has not been recognized as a stable and attractive option by many others in the field, and my critics have persistently tried to show that my position tumbles into one abyss or the other.

My view is, I insist, a *sort* of realism, since I maintain that the patterns the Martians miss are really, objectively there to be noticed or overlooked. How could the Martians, who "know everything" about the physical events in our world, miss these patterns? What could it mean to say that some patterns, while objectively there, are visible only from one point of view? An elegant two-dimensional microworld provides a clear instance: John Horton Conway's Game of Life (Gardner 1970), a simple yet extraordinarily rich source of insights that should become a part of everyone's imaginative resources as a versatile testbed for thought experiments about the relation of levels in science.

Imagine a huge piece of graph paper. The intersections (not the squares) of this grid are the only places—called cells—in the Life microworld, and at any instant each cell is either ON or OFF. Each cell has eight neighbors: the four adjacent cells north, south, east, and west of it, and the four nearest diagonal cells (northeast, southeast, southwest, northwest). Time in the Life world is also discrete, not continuous; it advances in ticks, and the state of the world changes between each tick according to the following rule:

Each cell, in order to determine what to do in the next instant, counts how many of its eight neighbors is ON at the present instant. If the answer is exactly two, the cell stays in its present state (ON or OFF) in the next instant. If the answer is exactly three, the cell is ON in the next instant whatever its current state. Under all other conditions, the cell is OFF.

The entire, deterministic physics of the Life world is captured in that single unexceptioned law. (While this is the fundamental law of the "physics" of the Life world, it helps at first to conceive this curious physics in biological terms: think of cells going ON as births, cells going OFF as deaths, and succeeding instants as generations. Either overcrowding or isolation causes death; birth occurs only under propitious circumstances.) By the scrupulous application of the law, one can predict with perfect accuracy the next instant of any configuration of ON and OFF cells, and the instant after that, and so forth. So the Life world is a fine Laplacean playpen: a simplified deterministic world in which we finite creatures can adopt the physical stance and predict the future with supreme confidence. Many computer simulations of the Life world exist, in which one can set up configurations on the screen and then watch them evolve according to the rule. In the best simulations, one can change the scale of both time and space, alternating between close-up and bird's-eye view.

One soon discovers that some simple configurations are more interesting than others. There are things that blink back and forth between two configurations, things that grow and then disintegrate, "glider guns" that emit "gliders"—configurations that reproduce themselves translated a few cells over, gradually gliding across the two-dimensional landscape—puffer trains, strafing machines, eaters, antibodies, space rakes. Once one understands the behavior of these configurations, one can adopt the design stance and ask oneself how to design larger assemblages of these objects that will perform more complicated tasks. One of the triumphs of the design stance in the Life world is a universal Turing machine—a configuration whose behavior can be interpreted as the state-switching, symbol-reading, and symbol-writing of a simple computer, which can be "programmed" to compute any computable function. (For more on Turing machines, see "The Abilities of Men and Machines" in *Brainstorms*, and Dennett 1985a.)

Anyone who hypothesizes that some configuration in the Life world is such a Turing machine can predict its future state with precision, efficiency, and a modicum of risk. Adopt the "Turing machine stance" and, ignoring both the physics of the Life world and the design details of the machine, just calculate the function being computed by the Turing machine; then translate the function's output back into the symbol system of the Life world machine. That configuration of ONs and OFFs will soon appear, you can predict, provided that no stray gliders or other noisy debris collide with the Turing machine and destroy it or cause it to malfunction.

Is the pattern that enables you to make this prediction "real"? So long as it lasts it is, and if the pattern includes "armor" to insulate the machine from noise, the pattern may survive for quite some time. The pattern *may* owe its existence to the intentions (clear-sighted or confused) of the machine's designer, but its reality in any interesting sense—its longevity or robustness—is strictly independent of historical facts about its origin.

Whether one can see the pattern is another matter. In one sense it would be visible to anyone who watched the unfolding of the particular configurations on the Life plane. One of the delights of the Life world is that nothing is hidden in it; there is no backstage. But it takes a big leap of insight to see this unfolding *as* the computation of a Turing machine. Ascending to the point of view from which this level of explanation and prediction is readily visible is optional, and might be difficult for many.

I claim that the intentional stance provides a vantage point for discerning similarly useful patterns. These patterns are objective—they are *there* to be detected—but from our point of view they are not *out there* entirely independent of us, since they are patterns composed partly of our own "subjective" reactions to what is out there; they are the patterns made to order for our narcissistic concerns (Akins 1986). It is easy for us, constituted as we are, to perceive the patterns that are visible from the intentional stance—and only from that stance.[1]

---

1. Anscombe spoke darkly of "an order which is there whenever actions are done with intentions" (1957, p. 80) but did not say *where* in the world this order was to be discerned. In the brain? In behavior? For years I could not make sense of this, but now I see what she may have intended and why she was so coy in her description (and location) of the order. It is as hard to say where the intentional order is as it is to say where the intentional patterns are in the Life world. If you "look at" the world in the right way, the patterns are obvious. If you look at (or describe) the world in any other way, they are, in general, invisible.

Martians might find it extremely difficult, but they can aspire to know the regularities that are second nature to us just as we can aspire to know the world of the spider or the fish.

So I am a sort of realist. I decline the invitation to join Rorty's (1979, 1982) radical perspectivalism (Dennett 1982a). But I also maintain that when these objective patterns fall short of perfection, as they always must, there will be uninterpretable gaps; it is always possible in principle for rival intentional stance interpretations of those patterns to tie for first place, so that no further fact could settle what the intentional system in question *really* believed.

This idea is not new. It is a quite direct extension of Quine's (1960) thesis of the indeterminacy of radical translation, applied to the "translation" of not only the patterns in subjects' dispositions to engage in external behavior (Quine's "stimulus meanings"), but also the further patterns in dispositions to "behave" internally. As Quine says, "radical translation begins at home" (1969, p. 46), and the implications of his thesis extend beyond his peripheralism or behaviorism.

The metaphor of the black box, often so useful, can be misleading here. The problem is not one of hidden facts, such as might be uncovered by learning more about the brain physiology of thought processes. To expect a distinctive physical mechanism behind every genuinely distinct mental state is one thing; to expect a distinctive mechanism for every purported distinction that can be phrased in traditional mentalistic language is another. The question whether . . . the foreigner *really* believes *A* or believes rather *B*, is a question whose very significance I would put in doubt. This is what I am getting at in arguing the indeterminacy of translation. (Quine 1970, pp. 180–81)

My argument in "Brain Writing and Mind Reading" (1975) enlarged on this theme, exposing the error of those who had hoped to *find something in the head* to settle the cases Quine's peripheralism left indeterminate: exactly the same considerations applied to the translation of any "language of thought" one might discover once one abandoned behaviorism for cognitive science. Another Quinian[2] who has defended this position with regard to belief is Davidson (1974a):

---

2. Some non-Quinians have maintained versions of this idea. Wheeler (1986) insightfully shows that Derrida can be seen to "provide important, if dangerous, supplementary arguments and considerations" to those that have been advanced by Davidson and other Quinians. As Wheeler notes:

For Quineans, of course, it is obvious already that speech and thought are brainwriting, some kind of tokenings which are as much subject to interpretation as any other. . . . Still, there seems in non-Quinean circles to be a covert belief that somehow inner speech is directly expressive of thought. (p. 492)

This covert belief is exposed to attack in chapter 8.

Indeterminacy of meaning or translation does not represent a failure to capture significant distinctions; it marks the fact that certain apparent distinctions are not significant. If there is indeterminacy, it is because when all the evidence is in, alternative ways of stating the facts remain open. (p. 322)

More recently another application of the idea of indeterminacy has been ably defended by Parfit (1984), who has argued that the principles we (should) rely on to determine questions of *personal identity* will also inevitably leave open the possibility in principle of puzzling indeterminate cases. This is extraordinarily hard for many people to accept.

Most of us are inclined to believe that, in any conceivable case, the question "Am I about to die?" must have an answer. And we are inclined to believe that this answer must be either, and quite simply, Yes or No. Any future person must either be me, or someone else. These beliefs I call the view that *our identity must be determinate.* (p. 214)

We are just as strongly attracted to the view that *the contents of our thoughts or beliefs must be determinate* and resist the suggestion that the question "Do I believe there is milk in the fridge?" could fail to have a determinate answer, yes or no. Parfit shows that there are other cases in which we rest content without an answer to such questions.

Suppose that a certain club exists for several years, holding regular meetings. The meetings then cease. Some years later, some of the members of this club form a club with the same name, and the same rules. We ask: "Have these people reconvened the *very same* club? Or have they merely started up *another* club, which is exactly similar?" There might be an answer to this question. The original club might have had a rule explaining how, after such a period of non-existence, it could be reconvened. Or it might have had a rule preventing this. But suppose that there is no such rule, and no legal facts, supporting either answer to our question. And suppose that the people involved, if they asked our question, would not give it an answer. There would then be no answer to our question. The claim "This is the same club" would be *neither true nor false.*

Though there is no answer to our question, there may be nothing that we do not know. . . . When this is true of some question, I call this question *empty.* (p. 213)

We recognize that in the case of the club's existence, and in similar cases, there is no "deeper fact" that would settle the matter, but in the case of personal identity, the supposition that there is—must be—just such a deeper fact dies hard. Not surprisingly, this is one of the brute convictions that Nagel (1986) cannot abandon:

Why isn't it enough to identify myself as a person in the weaker sense in which this is the subject of mental predicates but not a separately existing thing—more like a nation than a Cartesian ego?

I don't really have an answer to this, except the question-begging answer . . . (p. 45)

I make the analogous case for what we might call belief identity or belief determinacy. In chapter 8, "Evolution, Error, and Intentionality," I show how Searle, Fodor, Dretske, Kripke, and Burge (among others) all are tempted to search for this deeper fact, and how their search is forlorn. I claim, in other words, that some of the most vigorously disputed questions about belief attribution are, in Parfit's sense, empty questions.

How is this persistent illusion created? In the reflections on "Making Sense of Ourselves," I describe a false contrast (between our beliefs and those of lower animals) that creates the mistaken conviction that our own beliefs and other mental states must have determinate content.

Another *leitmotif* that gets its first play in "True Believers" is the comparison between Putnam's Twin Earth thought experiment and various simpler environmental dislocations or exchanges—of thermostats, in this instance. The theme is developed more fully in chapter 5, "Beyond Belief," and in the example of the "two-bitser" in chapter 8.

Finally, the attenuated and conditional endorsement of the idea of a language of thought at the end of "True Believers" is further elaborated in chapter 5 and in chapter 6, "Styles of Mental Representation," and the reflections following it.

3

Three Kinds of Intentional Psychology

Folk Psychology as a Source of Theory

Suppose you and I both believe that cats eat fish. Exactly what feature must we share for this to be true of us? More generally, recalling Socrates's favorite style of question, what must be in common between things truly ascribed an *intentional* predicate—such as "wants to visit China" or "expects noodles for supper"? As Socrates points out, in the *Meno* and elsewhere, such questions are ambiguous or vague in their intent. One can be asking on the one hand for something rather like a definition, or on the other hand for something rather like a theory. (Socrates of course preferred the former sort of answer.) What do all magnets have in common? First answer: they all attract iron. Second answer: they all have such-and-such a microphysical property (a property that explains their capacity to attract iron). In one sense people knew what magnets were—they were things that attracted iron—long before science told them what magnets were. A child learns what the word "magnet" means not, typically, by learning an explicit definition, but by learning the "folk physics" of magnets, in which the ordinary term "magnet" is embedded or implicitly defined as a theoretical term.

Sometimes terms are embedded in more powerful theories, and sometimes they are embedded by explicit definition. What do all chemical elements with the same valence have in common? First answer: they are disposed to combine with other elements in the same integral ratios. Second answer: they all have such-and-such a mi-

Originally presented to the Thyssen Philosophy Group and the Bristol Fulbright Workshop, September 1978, and reprinted, with permission, from R. Healy, ed., *Reduction, Time and Reality* (Cambridge: Cambridge University Press, 1981).

crophysical property (a property which explains their capacity so to combine). The theory of valences in chemistry was well in hand before its microphysical explanation was known. In one sense chemists knew what valences were before physicists told them.

So what appears in Plato to be a contrast between giving a definition and giving a theory can be viewed as just a special case of the contrast between giving one theoretical answer and giving another, more "reductive" theoretical answer. Fodor (1975) draws the same contrast between "conceptual" and "causal" answers to such questions and argues that Ryle (1949) champions conceptual answers at the expense of causal answers, wrongly supposing them to be in conflict. There is justice in Fodor's charge against Ryle, for there are certainly many passages in which Ryle seems to propose his conceptual answers as a bulwark against the possibility of *any* causal, scientific, psychological answers, but there is a better view of Ryle's (or perhaps at best a view he ought to have held) that deserves rehabilitation. Ryle's "logical behaviorism" is composed of his steadfastly conceptual answers to the Socratic questions about matters mental. If Ryle thought these answers ruled out psychology, ruled out causal (or reductive) answers to the Socratic questions, he was wrong, but if he thought only that the conceptual answers to the questions were not to be given by a microreductive psychology, he was on firmer ground. It is one thing to give a causal explanation of some phenomenon and quite another to cite the cause of a phenomenon in the analysis of the concept of it.

Some concepts have what might be called an essential causal element (see Fodor 1975, p. 7, n6). For instance, the concept of a genuine Winston Churchill *autograph* has it that how the trail of ink was in fact caused is essential to its status as an autograph. Photocopies, forgeries, inadvertently indistinguishable signatures—but perhaps not carbon copies—are ruled out. These considerations are part of the *conceptual* answer to the Socratic question about autographs.

Now some, including Fodor, have held that such concepts as the concept of intelligent action also have an essential causal element; behavior that appeared to be intelligent might be shown not to be by being shown to have the wrong sort of cause. Against such positions Ryle can argue that even if it is true that every instance of intelligent behavior is caused (and hence has a causal explanation), exactly *how* it is caused is inessential to its being intelligent—something that could be true even if all intelligent behavior exhibited in fact some common pattern of causation. That is, Ryle can plausibly claim that no account in causal terms could capture the class of intelligent actions except *per accidens*. In aid of such a position—for which there is much to be said in spite of the current infatuation with causal theories—Ryle can make claims of the sort Fodor disparages ("it's not the mental activity that makes the clowning clever because what makes the clowning clever is such facts as that it took place out where the children can see it") without committing the error of supposing causal and conceptual answers are incompatible.[1]

Ryle's logical behaviorism was in fact tainted by a groundless anti-scientific bias, but it need not have been. Note that the introduction of the concept of valence in chemistry was a bit of *logical chemical behaviorism*: to have valence *n* was "by definition" to be disposed to behave in such-and-such ways under such-and-such conditions, *however* that disposition to behave might someday be explained by physics. In this particular instance the relation between the chemical theory and the physical theory is now well charted and understood—even if in the throes of ideology people sometimes misdescribe it—and the explanation of those dispositional combinatorial properties by physics is a prime example of the sort of success in science that inspires reductionist doctrines. Chemistry has been shown to reduce, in some sense, to physics, and this is clearly a Good Thing, the sort of thing we should try for more of.

Such progress invites the prospect of a parallel development in psychology. First we will answer the question "What do all believers-that-*p* have in common?" the first way, the "conceptual" way, and then see if we can go on to "reduce" the theory that emerges in our first answer to something else—neurophysiology most likely. Many theorists seem to take it for granted that *some* such reduction is both possible and desirable, and perhaps even inevitable, even while recent critics of reductionism, such as Putnam and Fodor, have warned us of the excesses of "classical" reductionist creeds. No one today hopes to conduct the psychology of the future in the vocabulary of the neurophysiologist, let alone that of the physicist, and principled ways of relaxing the classical "rules" of reduction have been proposed. The issue, then, is *what kind* of theoretical bonds can we expect—or ought we to hope—to find uniting psychological claims

---

1. This paragraph corrects a misrepresentation of both Fodor's and Ryle's positions in my critical notice of Fodor's book in *Mind* (1977) reprinted in *Brainstorms*, pp. 90–108.

about beliefs, desires, and so forth with the claims of neurophysiologists, biologists, and other physical scientists?

Since the terms "belief" and "desire" and their kin are parts of ordinary language, like "magnet," rather than technical terms like "valence," we must first look to "folk psychology" to see what kind of things we are being asked to explain. What do we learn beliefs are when we learn how to use the words "believe" and "belief"? The first point to make is that we do not really learn what beliefs are when we learn how to use these words.[2] Certainly no one *tells us* what beliefs are, or if someone does, or if we happen to speculate on the topic on our own, the answer we come to, wise or foolish, will figure only weakly in our habits of thought about what people believe. We learn to *use* folk psychology as a vernacular social technology, a craft; but we don't learn it self-consciously as a theory—we learn no metatheory with the theory—and in this regard our knowledge of folk psychology is like our knowledge of the grammar of our native tongue. This fact does not make our knowledge of folk psychology entirely unlike human knowledge of explicit academic theories, however; one could probably be a good practicing chemist and yet find it embarrassingly difficult to produce a satisfactory textbook definition of a metal or an ion.

There are no introductory textbooks of folk psychology (although Ryle's *The Concept of Mind* might be pressed into service), but many explorations of the field have been undertaken by ordinary language philosophers (under slightly different intentions) and more recently by more theoretically minded philosophers of mind, and from all this work an account of folk psychology—part truism and the rest controversy—can be gleaned. What are beliefs? Very roughly, folk psychology has it that *beliefs* are information-bearing states of people that arise from perceptions and that, together with appropriately related *desires*, lead to intelligent *action*. That much is relatively uncontroversial, but does folk psychology also have it that nonhuman animals have beliefs? If so, what is the role of language in belief? Are beliefs constructed of parts? If so, what are the parts? Ideas? Concepts? Words? Pictures? Are beliefs like speech acts or maps or instruction manuals or sentences? Is it implicit in folk psychology that beliefs

---

2. I think it is just worth noting that philosophers' use of "believe" as the standard and general ordinary language term is a considerable distortion. We seldom talk about what people *believe*; we talk about what they *think* and what they *know*.

enter into causal relations, or that they don't? How do decisions and intentions intervene between belief–desire complexes and actions? Are beliefs introspectible, and if so, what authority do the believer's pronouncements have?

All these questions deserve answers, but one must bear in mind that there are different reasons for being interested in the details of folk psychology. One reason is that it exists as a phenomenon, like a religion or a language or a dress code, to be studied with the techniques and attitudes of anthropology. It may be a myth, but it is a myth we live in, so it is an "important" phenomenon in nature. A different reason is that it seems to be a *true* theory, by and large, and hence is a candidate—like the folk physics of magnets and unlike the folk science of astrology—for incorporation into science. These different reasons generate different but overlapping investigations. The anthropological question should include in its account of folk psychology whatever folk actually include in their theory, however misguided, incoherent, gratuitous some of it may be. (When the anthropologist marks part of the catalogue of folk theory as false, he may speak of *false consciousness* or *ideology,* but the role of such false theory *qua* anthropological phenomenon is not thereby diminished.) The proto-scientific quest, on the other hand, as an attempt to prepare folk theory for subsequent incorporation into, or reduction to, the rest of science, should be critical and should eliminate all that is false or ill founded, however well entrenched in popular doctrine. (Thales thought that lodestones had souls, we are told. Even if most people agreed, this would be something to eliminate from the folk physics of magnets prior to "reduction.") One way of distinguishing the good from the bad, the essential from the gratuitous, in folk theory is to see what must be included in the theory to account for whatever predictive or explanatory success it seems to have in ordinary use. In this way we can criticize as we analyze, and it is even open to us in the end to discard folk psychology if it turns out to be a bad theory, and with it the presumed theoretical entities named therein. If we discard folk psychology as a theory, we would have to replace it with another theory, which, while it did violence to many ordinary intuitions, would explain the predictive power of the residual folk craft.

We use folk psychology all the time, to explain and predict each other's behavior; we attribute beliefs and desires to each other with confidence—and quite unselfconsciously—and spend a substantial portion of our waking lives formulating the world—not excluding ourselves—in these terms. Folk psychology is about as pervasive a part of our second nature as is our folk physics of middle-sized objects. How good is folk psychology? If we concentrate on its weaknesses we will notice that we often are unable to make sense of particular bits of human behavior (our own included) in terms of belief and desire, even in retrospect; we often cannot predict accurately or reliably what a person will do or when; we often can find no resources within the theory for settling disagreements about particular attributions of belief or desire. If we concentrate on its strengths we find first that there are large areas in which it is extraordinarily reliable in its predictive power. Every time we venture out on a highway, for example, we stake our lives on the reliability of our general expectations about the perceptual beliefs, normal desires, and decision proclivities of the other motorists. Second, we find that it is a theory of great generative power and efficiency. For instance, watching a film with a highly original and unstereotypical plot, we see the hero smile at the villain and we all swiftly and effortlessly arrive at the same complex theoretical diagnosis: "Aha!" we conclude (but perhaps not consciously), "he wants her to think he doesn't know she intends to defraud his brother!" Third, we find that even small children pick up facility with the theory at a time when they have a very limited experience of human activity from which to induce a theory. Fourth, we find that we all use folk psychology knowing next to nothing about what actually happens inside people's skulls. "Use your head," we are told, and we know some people are brainier than others, but our capacity to use folk psychology is quite unaffected by ignorance about brain processes—or even by large-scale misinformation about brain processes.

As many philosophers have observed, a feature of folk psychology that sets it apart from both folk physics and the academic physical sciences is that explanations of actions citing beliefs and desires normally not only describe the provenance of the actions, but at the same time defend them as reasonable under the circumstances. They are reason-giving explanations, which make an ineliminable allusion to the rationality of the agent. Primarily for this reason, but also because of the pattern of strengths and weaknesses just described, I suggest that folk psychology might best be viewed as a rationalistic calculus of interpretation and prediction—an idealizing, abstract, instrumentalistic interpretation method that has evolved because it works and works because we have evolved. We approach each other as *intentional systems* (Dennett 1971), that is, as entities whose behavior can be predicted by the method of attributing beliefs, desires, and rational acumen according to the following rough and ready principles:

(1) A system's beliefs are those it *ought to have,* given its perceptual capacities, its epistemic needs, and its biography. Thus, in general, its beliefs are both true and relevant to its life, and when false beliefs are attributed, special stories must be told to explain how the error resulted from the presence of features in the environment that are deceptive relative to the perceptual capacities of the system.

(2) A system's desires are those it *ought to have,* given its biological needs and the most practicable means of satisfying them. Thus intentional systems desire survival and procreation, and hence desire food, security, health, sex, wealth, power, influence, and so forth, and also whatever local arrangements tend (in their eyes—given their beliefs) to further these ends in appropriate measure. Again, "abnormal" desires are attributable if special stories can be told.

(3) A system's behavior will consist of those acts that *it would be rational* for an agent with those beliefs and desires to perform.

In (1) and (2) "ought to have" means "would have if it were *ideally* ensconced in its environmental niche." Thus all dangers and vicissitudes in its environment it will *recognize as such* (i.e., *believe* to be dangers) and all the benefits—relative to its needs, of course—it will *desire.* When a fact about its surroundings is particularly relevant to its current projects (which themselves will be the projects such a being ought to have in order to get ahead in its world), it will *know* that fact and act accordingly. And so forth and so on. This gives us the notion of an ideal epistemic and conative operator or agent, relativized to a set of needs for survival and procreation and to the environment(s) in which its ancestors have evolved and to which it is adapted. But this notion is still too crude and overstated. For instance, a being may come to have an epistemic need that its perceptual apparatus cannot provide for (suddenly all the green food is poisonous, but alas it is colorblind), hence the relativity to perceptual capacities. Moreover, it may or may not have had the occasion to learn from experience about something, so its beliefs are also relative to its biography in this way: it will have learned what it ought to have learned, viz., what it had been given evidence for in a form compatible with its cognitive apparatus—providing the evidence was "relevant" to its project then.

But this is still too crude, for evolution does not give us a best of all possible worlds, but only a passable jury-rig, so we should look for design shortcuts that in specifiably abnormal circumstances yield false perceptual beliefs, etc. (We are not immune to illusions—which we would be if our perceptual systems were *perfect*.) To offset the design shortcuts we should also expect design bonuses: circumstances in which the "cheap" way for nature to design a cognitive system has the side benefit of giving good, reliable results even outside the environment in which the system evolved. Our eyes are well adapted for giving us true beliefs on Mars as well as on Earth, because the cheap solution for our Earth-evolving eyes happens to be a more general solution (cf. Sober 1981).

I propose that we can continue the mode of thinking just illustrated *all the way in*—not just for eye design, but for deliberation design and belief design and strategy-concocter design. In using this optimistic set of assumptions (nature has built us to do things right; look for systems to believe the truth and love the good), we impute no occult powers to epistemic needs, perceptual capacities, and biography but only the powers common sense already imputes to evolution and learning.

In short, we treat each other as if we were rational agents, and this myth—for surely we are not all that rational—works very well because we are *pretty* rational. This single assumption, in combination with home truths about our needs, capacities and typical circumstances, generates both an intentional interpretation of us as believers and desirers and actual predictions of behavior in great profusion. I am claiming, then, that folk psychology can best be viewed as a sort of logical behaviorism: *what it means* to say that someone believes that *p*, is that that person is disposed to behave in certain ways under certain conditions. What ways under what conditions? The ways it would be rational to behave, given the person's other beliefs and desires. The answer looks in danger of being circular, but consider: an account of what it is for an element to have a particular valence will similarly make ineliminable reference to the valences of other elements. What one is given with valence talk is a whole system of interlocking attributions, which is saved from vacuity by yielding independently testable predictions.

I have just described in outline a method of predicting and explaining the behavior of people and other intelligent creatures. Let me distinguish two questions about it: is it something we could do, and is it something we in fact do? I think the answer to the first is obviously yes, which is not to say the method will always yield good results. That much one can ascertain by reflection and thought experiment. Moreover, one can recognize that the method is familiar. Although we don't usually use the method self-consciously, we do use it self-consciously on those occasions when we are perplexed by a person's behavior, and then it often yields satisfactory results. Moreover, the ease and naturalness with which we resort to this self-conscious and deliberate form of problem-solving provide some support for the claim that what we are doing on those occasions is not switching methods but simply becoming self-conscious and explicit about what we ordinarily accomplish tacitly or unconsciously.

No other view of folk psychology, I think, can explain the fact that we do so well predicting each other's behavior on such slender and peripheral evidence; treating each other as intentional systems works (to the extent that it does) because we really are well designed by evolution and hence we *approximate* to the ideal version of ourselves exploited to yield the predictions. But not only does evolution not guarantee that we will always do what is rational; it guarantees that we won't. If we are designed by evolution, then we are almost certainly nothing more than a bag of tricks, patched together by a *satisficing* Nature—Herbert Simon's term (1957)—and no better than our ancestors had to be to get by. Moreover, the demands of nature and the demands of a logic course are not the same. Sometimes— even *normally* in certain circumstances—it pays to jump to conclusions swiftly (and even to forget that you've done so), so by most philosophical measures of rationality (logical consistency, refraining from invalid inference) there has probably been some positive evolutionary pressure in favor of "irrational" methods.[3]

---

3. While in general true beliefs have to be more useful than false beliefs (and hence a system ought to have true beliefs), in special circumstances it may be better to have a few false beliefs. For instance it might be better for beast B to have some false beliefs about whom B can beat up and whom B can't. Ranking B's likely antagonists from ferocious to pushover, we certainly want B to believe it can't beat up all the ferocious ones and can beat up all the obvious pushovers, but it is better (because it "costs less" in discrimination tasks and protects against random perturbations such as bad days and lucky blows) for B to extend "I can't beat up x" to cover even some beasts it can in fact beat up. *Erring on the side of prudence* is a well-recognized good strategy, and so Nature can be expected to have valued it on occasions when it came up. An alternative strategy in this instance would be to abide by the rule: avoid conflict with penumbral cases. But one might have to "pay more" to implement that strategy than to implement the strategy designed to produce, and rely on, some false beliefs. (On false beliefs, see also chapter 2.)

How rational are we? Recent research in social and cognitive psychology (e.g., Tversky and Kahneman 1974; Nisbett and Ross 1978) suggests we are only minimally rational, appallingly ready to leap to conclusions or be swayed by logically irrelevant features of situations, but this jaundiced view is an illusion engendered by the fact that these psychologists are deliberately trying to produce situations that provoke irrational responses—inducing pathology in a system by putting strain on it—and succeeding, being good psychologists. No one would hire a psychologist to prove that people will choose a paid vacation to a week in jail if offered an informed choice. At least not in the better psychology departments. A more optimistic impression of our rationality is engendered by a review of the difficulties encountered in artificial intelligence research. Even the most sophisticated AI programs stumble blindly into misinterpretations and misunderstandings that even small children reliably evade without a second thought (see, e.g., Schank 1976; Schank and Abelson 1977). From this vantage point we seem marvelously rational.

However rational we are, it is the myth of our rational agenthood that structures and organizes our attributions of belief and desire to others and that regulates our own deliberations and investigations. We aspire to rationality, and without the myth of our rationality the concepts of belief and desire would be uprooted. Folk psychology, then, is *idealized* in that it produces its predictions and explanations by calculating in a normative system; it predicts what we will believe, desire, and do, by determining what we ought to believe, desire, and do.[4]

Folk psychology is *abstract* in that the beliefs and desires it attributes are not—or need not be—presumed to be intervening distinguishable states of an internal behavior-causing system. (The point will be enlarged upon later.) The role of the concept of belief is like the role of the concept of a center of gravity, and the calculations that yield the predictions are more like the calculations one performs with a parallelogram of forces than like the calculations one performs with a blueprint of internal levers and cogs.

Folk psychology is thus *instrumentalistic* in a way the most ardent

4. It tests its predictions in two ways: action predictions it tests directly by looking to see what the agent does; belief and desire predictions are tested indirectly by employing the predicted attributions in further predictions of eventual action. As usual, the Duhemian thesis holds: belief and desire attributions are under-determined by the available data.

realist should permit: people really do have beliefs and desires, on my version of folk psychology, just the way they really have centers of gravity and the earth has an Equator.[5] Reichenbach distinguished between two sorts of referents for theoretical terms: *illata*—posited theoretical entities—and *abstracta*—calculation-bound entities or logical constructs.[6] Beliefs and desires of folk psychology (but not all mental events and states) are *abstracta*.

This view of folk psychology emerges more clearly when contrasted to a diametrically opposed view, each of whose tenets has been held by some philosopher, and at least most of which have been espoused by Fodor:

Beliefs and desires, just like pains, thoughts, sensations and other episodes, are taken by folk psychology to be real, intervening, internal states or events, in causal interaction, subsumed under covering laws of causal stripe. Folk psychology is not an idealized, rationalistic calculus but a naturalistic, empirical, descriptive theory, imputing causal regularities discovered by extensive induction over experience. To suppose two people share a belief is to suppose them to be ultimately in some structurally similar internal condition, e.g. for them to have the same words of Mentalese written in the functionally relevant places in their brains.

I want to deflect this head-on collision of analyses by taking two steps. First, I am prepared to grant a measure of the claims made by the opposition. Of course we don't all sit in the dark in our studies like mad Leibnizians rationalistically excogitating behavioral predictions from pure, idealized concepts of our neighbors, nor do we derive all our readiness to attribute desires from a careful generation of them from the ultimate goal of survival. We may observe that some folks seem to desire cigarettes, or pain, or notoriety (we observe this by hearing them tell us, seeing what they choose, etc.) and without any conviction that these people, given their circumstances, ought to have these desires, we attribute them anyway. So rationalistic generation of attributions is augmented and even corrected on occasion by

---

5. Michael Friedman's "Theoretical Explanation" (1981) provides an excellent analysis of the role of instrumentalistic thinking within realistic science. Scheffler (1963) provides a useful distinction between *instrumentalism* and *fictionalism*. In his terms I am characterizing folk psychology as instrumentalistic, not fictionalistic.

6. "Our observations of concrete things confer a certain probability on the existence of *illata*-nothing more. . . . Second, there are inferences to *abstracta*. These inferences are . . . equivalences, not probability inferences. Consequently, the existence of abstracta is reducible to the existence of concreta. There is, therefore, no problem of their objective existence; their status depends on a convention." (Reichenbach 1938, pp. 211–12)

empirical generalizations about belief and desire that guide our attributions and are learned more or less inductively. For instance, small children believe in Santa Claus, people are inclined to believe the more self-serving of two interpretations of an event in which they are involved (unless they are depressed), and people can be made to want things they don't need by making them believe that glamorous people like those things. And so forth in familiar profusion. This folklore does not consist in *laws*—even probabilistic laws—but some of it is being turned into science of a sort, for example theories of "hot cognition" and cognitive dissonance. I grant the existence of all this naturalistic generalization, and its role in the normal calculations of folk psychologists—that is, all of us. People do rely on their own parochial group of neighbors when framing intentional interpretations. That is why people have so much difficulty understanding foreigners— their behavior, to say nothing of their languages. They impute more of their own beliefs and desires, and those of their neighbors, than they would if they followed my principles of attribution slavishly. Of course this is a perfectly reasonable shortcut for people to take, even when it often leads to bad results. We are in this matter, as in most, satisficers, not optimizers, when it comes to information gathering and theory construction. I would insist, however, that all this empirically obtained lore is laid over a fundamental generative and normative framework that has the features I have described.

My second step away from the conflict I have set up is to recall that the issue is not what folk psychology as found in the field truly is, but what it is at its best, what deserves to be taken seriously and incorporated into science. It is not particularly to the point to argue against me that folk psychology is *in fact* committed to beliefs and desires as distinguishable, causally interacting *illata;* what must be shown is that it ought to be. The latter claim I will deal with in due course. The former claim I *could* concede without embarrassment to my overall project, but I do not concede it, for it seems to me that the evidence is quite strong that our ordinary notion of belief has next to nothing of the concrete in it. Jacques shoots his uncle dead in Trafalgar Square and is apprehended on the spot by Sherlock; Tom reads about it in the *Guardian* and Boris learns of it in *Pravda.* Now Jacques, Sherlock, Tom, and Boris have had remarkably different experiences—to say nothing of their earlier biographies and future prospects—but there is one thing they share: they all believe that a Frenchman has committed murder in Trafalgar Square. They did not all *say* this, not even "to themselves"; *that proposition* did not, we can suppose, "occur to" any of them, and even if it had, it would have had entirely different import for Jacques, Sherlock, Tom, and Boris. Yet they all believe that a Frenchman committed murder in Trafalgar Square. This is a shared property that is visible, as it were, only from one very limited point of view—the point of view of folk psychology. Ordinary folk psychologists have no difficulty imputing such useful but elusive commonalities to people. If they then insist that in doing so they are postulating a similarly structured object in each head, this is a gratuitous bit of misplaced concreteness, a regrettable lapse in ideology.

But in any case there is no doubt that folk psychology is a mixed bag, like folk productions generally, and there is no reason in the end not to grant that it is much more complex, variegated (and in danger of incoherence) than my sketch has made it out to be. The *ordinary* notion of belief no doubt does place beliefs somewhere midway between being *illata* and being *abstracta*. What this suggests to me is that the concept of belief found in ordinary understanding, that is, in folk psychology, is unappealing as a scientific concept. I am reminded of Anaxagoras's strange precursor to atomism: the theory of seeds. There is a portion of everything in everything, he is reputed to have claimed. Every object consists of an infinity of seeds, of all possible varieties. How do you make bread out of flour, yeast, and water? Flour contains bread seeds in abundance (but flour seeds predominate—that's what makes it flour), and so do yeast and water, and when these ingredients are mixed together, the bread seeds form a new majority, so bread is what you get. Bread nourishes by containing flesh and blood and bone seeds in addition to its majority of bread seeds. Not good theoretical entities, these seeds, for as a sort of bastardized cross between properties and proper parts they have a penchant for generating vicious regresses, and their identity conditions are problematic to say the least.

Beliefs are rather like that. There seems no comfortable way of avoiding the claim that we have an infinity of beliefs, and common intuition does not give us a stable answer to such puzzles as whether the belief that 3 is greater than 2 is none other than the belief that 2 is less than 3. The obvious response to the challenge of an infinity of beliefs with slippery identity conditions is to suppose these beliefs are not all "stored separately"; many—in fact *most* if we are really talking about infinity—will be stored *implicitly* in virtue of the *explicit* storage of a few (or a few million)—the *core beliefs* (see Dennett 1975; also Fodor 1975 and Field 1978). The core beliefs will be "stored separately," and they look like promising *illata* in contrast to the virtual or implicit beliefs which look like paradigmatic *abstracta*. But although this might turn out to be the way our brains are organized, I suspect things will be more complicated than this: there is no reason to suppose the core *elements,* the concrete, salient, separately stored representation tokens (and there must be some such elements in any complex information processing system), will explicitly represent (or *be*) a subset of our *beliefs* at all. That is, if you were to sit down and write out a list of a thousand or so of your paradigmatic beliefs, *all* of them could turn out to be virtual, only implicitly stored or represented, and what was explicitly stored would be information (e.g. about memory addresses, procedures for problem-solving, or recognition, etc.) that was entirely unfamiliar. It would be folly to prejudge this empirical issue by insisting that our core representations of information (whichever they turn out to be) are beliefs *par excellence,* for when the facts are in, our intuitions may instead support the contrary view: the least controversial self-attributions of belief may pick out beliefs that from the vantage point of developed cognitive theory are invariably virtual.[7]

In such an eventuality what could we say about the causal roles we assign ordinarily to beliefs (e.g. "Her belief that John knew her secret caused her to blush")? We could say that whatever the core elements were in virtue of which she virtually believed that John knew her secret, they, the core elements, played a direct causal role (somehow) in triggering the blushing response. We would be wise, as this example shows, not to tamper with our *ordinary* catalogue of beliefs (virtual though they might all turn out to be), for these are predictable, readily understandable, manipulable regularities in psychological phenomena in spite of their apparent neutrality with regard to the explicit/implicit (or core/virtual) distinction. What Jacques, Sherlock, Boris, and Tom have in common is probably only a virtual belief "derived" from largely different explicit stores of information in each of them, but virtual or not, it is their sharing of *this* belief that would explain (or permit us to predict) in some imagined circumstances their all taking the same action when given the same new information.

---

7. See Field 1978, p. 55, n. 12 on "minor concessions" to such instrumentalistic treatments of belief.

("And now for one million dollars, Tom [Jacques, Sherlock, Boris], answer our jackpot question correctly: has a French citizen ever committed a major crime in London?")

At the same time we want to cling to the equally ordinary notion that beliefs can cause not only actions, but blushes, verbal slips, heart attacks, and the like. Much of the debate over whether or not intentional explanations are causal explanations can be bypassed by noting how the core elements, *whatever they may be,* can be cited as playing the causal role, while belief remains virtual. "Had Tom not believed that p and wanted that q, he would not have done A." Is this a causal explanation? It is tantamount to this: Tom was in some one of an indefinitely large number of structurally different states of type B that have in common just that each one of them licenses attribution of belief that p and desire that q in virtue of its normal relations with many other states of Tom, and this state, whichever one it was, was causally sufficient, given the "background conditions" of course, to initiate the intention to perform A, and thereupon A was performed, and had he not been in one of those indefinitely many type B states, he would not have done A. One can call this a causal explanation because it talks about causes, but it is surely as unspecific and unhelpful as a causal explanation can get. It commits itself to there being some causal explanation or other falling within a very broad area (i.e., the intentional interpretation is held to be supervenient on Tom's bodily condition), but its true informativeness and utility in actual prediction lie, not surprisingly, in its assertion that Tom, however his body is currently structured, has a particular set of these elusive intentional properties, beliefs, and desires.

The ordinary notion of belief is pulled in two directions. If we want to have good theoretical entities, good *illata,* or good logical constructs, good *abstracta,* we will have to jettison some of the ordinary freight of the concepts of belief and desire. So I propose a divorce. Since we seem to have both notions wedded in folk psychology, let's split them apart and create two new theories: one strictly abstract, idealizing, holistic, instrumentalistic—pure intentional system theory—and the other a concrete, microtheoretical science of the actual realization of those intentional systems—what I will call sub-personal cognitive psychology. By exploring their differences and interrelations, we should be able to tell whether any plausible "reductions" are in the offing.

Intentional System Theory as a Competence Theory

The first new theory, intentional system theory, is envisaged as a close kin of, and overlapping with, such already existing disciplines as decision theory and game theory, which are similarly abstract, normative, and couched in intentional language. It borrows the ordinary terms "belief" and "desire" but gives them a technical meaning within the theory. It is a sort of holistic logical behaviorism because it deals with the prediction and explanation from belief–desire profiles of the actions of whole systems (either alone in environments or in interaction with other intentional systems), but it treats the individual realizations of the systems as black boxes. The *subject* of all the intentional attributions is the whole system (the person, the animal, or even the corporation or nation [see Dennett 1976]) rather than any of its parts, and individual beliefs and desires are not attributable in isolation, independently of other belief and desire attributions. The latter point distinguishes intentional system theory most clearly from Ryle's logical behaviorism, which took on the impossible burden of characterizing individual beliefs (and other mental states) as particular individual dispositions to outward behavior.

The theory deals with the "production" of new beliefs and desires from old, via an interaction among old beliefs and desires, features in the environment, and the system's actions; and this creates the illusion that the theory contains naturalistic descriptions of internal processing in the systems the theory is about, when in fact the processing is all in the manipulation of the theory and consists in updating the intentional characterization of the whole system according to the rules of attribution. An analogous illusion of process would befall a naive student who, when confronted with a parallelogram of forces, supposed that it pictured a mechanical linkage of rods and pivots of some kind instead of being simply a graphic way of representing and plotting the effect of several simultaneously acting forces.

Richard Jeffrey (1970), in developing his concept of probability kinematics, has usefully drawn attention to an analogy with the distinction in physics between kinematics and dynamics. In kinematics,

you talk about the propagation of motions through a system in terms of such constraints as rigidity and manner of linkage. It is the physics of position and time, in terms of which you can talk about velocity and acceleration, but not about force and mass. When you talk about forces—*causes* of accelerations— you are in the realm of dynamics. (p. 172)

Kinematics provides a simplified and idealized level of abstraction appropriate for many purposes—for example, for the *initial* design development of a gearbox—but when one must deal with more concrete details of systems—when the gearbox designer must worry about friction, bending, energetic efficiency, and the like—one must switch to dynamics for more detailed and reliable predictions, at the cost of increased complexity and diminished generality. Similarly, one can approach the study of belief (and desire and so forth) at a highly abstract level, ignoring problems of realization and simply setting out what the normative demands on the design of a believer are. For instance, one can ask such questions as "What must a system's epistemic capabilities and propensities be for it to survive in environment *A*?" (cf. Campbell 1973, 1977) or "What must this system already know in order for it to be able to learn *B*?" or "What intentions must this system have in order to mean something by saying something?"

Intentional system theory deals just with the performance specifications of believers while remaining silent on how the systems are to be implemented. In fact this neutrality with regard to implementation is the most useful feature of intentional characterizations. Consider, for instance, the role of intentional characterizations in evolutionary biology. If we are to explain the evolution of complex behavioral capabilities or cognitive talents by natural selection, we must note that it is the intentionally characterized capacity (e.g., the capacity to acquire a belief, a desire, to perform an intentional action) that has survival value, however it happens to be realized as a result of mutation. If a particularly noxious insect makes its appearance in an environment, the birds and bats with a survival advantage will be those that come to believe this insect is not good to eat. In view of the vast differences in neural structure, genetic background, and perceptual capacity between birds and bats, it is highly unlikely that this useful trait they may come to share has a common description at any level more concrete or less abstract than intentional system theory. It is not only that the intentional predicate is a projectible predicate in evolutionary theory; since it is more general than its species-specific counterpart predicates (which characterize the successful mutation just in birds, or just in bats), it is preferable. So from the point of view of evolutionary biology, we would not want to "reduce" all intentional characterizations even if we knew in particular instances what the physiological implementation was.

This level of generality is essential if we want a theory to have anything meaningful and defensible to say about such topics as intelligence in general (as opposed, say, to just human or even terrestrial or natural intelligence) or such grand topics as meaning or reference or representation. Suppose, to pursue a familiar philosophical theme, we are invaded by Martians, and the question arises: do they have beliefs and desires? Are they that much *like us*? According to intentional system theory, if these Martians are smart enough to get here, then they most certainly have beliefs and desires—in the technical sense proprietary to the theory—no matter what their internal structure, and no matter how our folk-psychological intuitions rebel at the thought.

This principled blindness of intentional system theory to internal structure seems to invite the retort: but there has to be *some* explanation of the *success* of intentional prediction of the behavior of systems (e.g., Fodor 1985, p. 79). It isn't just magic. It isn't a mere coincidence that one can generate all these *abstracta*, manipulate them via some version of practical reasoning, and come up with an action prediction that has a good chance of being true. There must be some way in which the internal processes of the system mirror the complexities of the intentional interpretation, or its success would be a miracle.

Of course. This is all quite true and important. Nothing without a great deal of structural and processing complexity could conceivably realize an intentional system of any interest, and the complexity of the realization will surely bear a striking resemblance to the complexity of the instrumentalistic interpretation. Similarly, the success of valence theory in chemistry is no coincidence, and people were entirely right to expect that deep microphysical similarities would be discovered between elements with the same valence and that the structural similarities found would explain the dispositional similarities. But since people and animals are unlike atoms and molecules not only in being the products of a complex evolutionary history, but also in being the products of their individual learning histories, there is no reason to suppose that individual (human) believers that p—like individual (carbon) atoms with valence 4—regulate their dispositions with *exactly* the same machinery. Discovering the constraints on design and implementation variation, and demonstrating how particular species and individuals in fact succeed in realizing intentional systems, is the job for the third theory: subpersonal cognitive psychology.

Sub-personal Cognitive Psychology as a Performance Theory

The task of sub-personal cognitive psychology is to explain something that at first glance seems utterly mysterious and inexplicable. The brain, as intentional system theory and evolutionary biology show us, is a *semantic engine;* its task is to discover what its multifarious inputs *mean*, to discriminate them by their significance and "act accordingly."[8] That's what brains *are for.* But the brain, as physiology or plain common sense shows us, is just a *syntactic engine;* all it can do is discriminate its inputs by their structural, temporal, and physical features and let its entirely mechanical activities be governed by these "syntactic" features of its inputs. That's all brains *can do.* Now how does the brain manage to get semantics from syntax? How could *any* entity (how could a genius or an angel or God) get the semantics of a system from nothing but its syntax? It couldn't. The syntax of a system doesn't determine its semantics. By what alchemy, then, does the brain extract semantically reliable results from syntactically driven operations? It cannot be designed to do an impossible task, but it could be designed to *approximate* the impossible task, to *mimic* the behavior of the impossible object (the semantic engine) by capitalizing on close (close enough) fortuitous correspondences between structural regularities—of the environment and of its own internal states and operations—and semantic types.

The basic idea is familiar. An animal needs to know when it has satisfied the goal of finding and ingesting food, but it settles for a friction-in-the-throat-followed-by-stretched-stomach detector, a mechanical switch turned on by a relatively simple mechanical condition that normally co-occurs with the satisfaction of the animals "real" goal. It's not fancy and can easily be exploited to trick the animal into either eating when it shouldn't or leaving off eating when it shouldn't, but it does well enough by the animal in its normal environment. Or suppose I am monitoring telegraph transmissions and

---

8. More accurately if less picturesquely, the brain's task is to come to produce internal mediating responses that reliably vary in concert with variation in the actual environmental significance (the natural and nonnatural meanings, in Grice's (1957) sense) of their distal causes and independently of meaning-irrelevant variations in their proximal causes, and moreover to respond to its own mediating responses in ways that systematically tend to improve the creature's prospects in its environment if the mediating responses are varying as they ought to vary.

have been asked to intercept all *death threats* (but only death threats in English—to make it "easy"). I'd like to build a machine to save me the trouble of interpreting semantically every message sent, but how could this be done? No machine could be designed to do the job perfectly, for that would require defining the semantic category *death threat in English* as some tremendously complex feature of strings of alphabetic symbols, and there is utterly no reason to suppose this could be done in a principled way. (If somehow by brute-force inspection and subsequent enumeration we could list all and only the English death threats of, say, less than a thousand characters, we could easily enough build a filter to detect them, but we are looking for a principled, projectible, extendable method.) A really crude device could be made to discriminate all messages containing the symbol strings

. . . I will kill you . . .

or

. . . you . . . die . . . unless . . .

or

. . . (for some finite disjunction of likely patterns to be found in English death threats).

This device would have some utility, and further refinements could screen the material that passed this first filter, and so on. An unpromising beginning for constructing a sentence understander, but if you want to get semantics out of syntax (whether the syntax of messages in a natural language or the syntax of afferent neuron impulses), variations on this basic strategy are your only hope.[9] You must put

---

9. One might think that while in principle one cannot derive the semantics of a system from nothing but its syntax, in practice one might be able to cheat a little and exploit syntactic features that don't imply a semantical interpretation but strongly suggest one. For instance, faced with the task of deciphering isolated documents in an entirely unknown and alien language, one might note that while the symbol that looks like a duck doesn't have to mean "duck," there is a good chance that it does, especially if the symbol that looks like a wolf seems to be eating the symbol that looks like a duck, and not vice versa. Call this *hoping for hieroglyphics* and note the form it has taken in psychological theories from Locke to the present: we will be able to tell which mental representations are which (which idea is the idea of *dog* and which of *cat*) because the former will look like a dog and the latter like a cat. This is all very well as a crutch for us observers on the outside, trying to assign content to the events in some brain, but it is

together a bag of tricks and hope nature will be kind enough to let your device get by. Of course some tricks are elegant and appeal to deep principles of organization, but in the end all one can hope to produce (all natural selection can have produced) are systems that *seem* to discriminate meanings by actually discriminating things (tokens of no doubt wildly disjunctive types) that co-vary reliably with meanings.[10] Evolution has designed our brains not only to do this but to evolve and follow strategies of self-improvement in this activity during their individual lifetimes (see Dennett 1974b).

It is the task of sub-personal cognitive psychology to propose and test models of such activity—of pattern recognition or stimulus generalization, concept learning, expectation, learning, goal-directed behavior, problem-solving—that not only produce a simulacrum of genuine content-sensitivity, but that do this in ways demonstrably like the way people's brains do it, exhibiting the same powers and the same vulnerabilities to deception, overload, and confusion. It is here that we will find our good theoretical entities, our useful *illata,* and while some of them may well resemble the familiar entities of folk psychology—beliefs, desires, judgments, decisions—many will certainly not (see, e.g., the sub-doxastic states proposed by Stich 1978b). The only similarity we can be sure of discovering in the *illata* of subpersonal cognitive psychology is the intentionality of their labels (see *Brainstorms,* pp. 23–38). They will be characterized as events with content, bearing information, signaling this and ordering that.

In order to give the *illata* these labels, in order to maintain any intentional interpretation of their operation at all, the theorist must always keep glancing outside the system, to see what normally produces the configuration he is describing, what effects the system's responses normally have on the environment, and what benefit nor-

---

of no use to the brain . . . because brains don't know what dogs look like! Or better, this cannot be the brain's fundamental method of eking semantic classes out of raw syntax, for any brain (or brain part) that could be said—in an extended sense—to know what dogs look like would be a brain (or brain part) that had already solved its problem, that was already (a simulacrum of) a semantic engine. But this is still misleading, for brains in any event do not *assign* content to their own events in the way observers might: brains *fix* the content of their internal events in the act of reacting as they do. There are good reasons for positing *mental images* of one sort or another in cognitive theories (see "Two Approaches to Mental Images" in *Brainstorms,* pp. 174–89) but hoping for hieroglyphics isn't one of them, though I suspect it is covertly influential.

10. I take this point to be closely related to Davidson's reasons for claiming there can be no psycho-physical laws, but I am unsure that Davidson wants to draw the same conclusions from it that I do. See Davidson 1970.

mally accrues to the whole system from this activity. In other words the cognitive psychologist cannot ignore the fact that it is the realization of an intentional system he is studying on pain of abandoning semantic interpretation and hence psychology. On the other hand, progress in sub-personal cognitive psychology will blur the boundaries between it and intentional system theory, knitting them together much as chemistry and physics have been knit together.

The alternative of ignoring the external world and its relations to the internal machinery (what Putnam has called psychology in the narrow sense, or methodological solipsism, and Gunderson has lampooned as black world glass box perspectivalism) is not really psychology at all, but just at best abstract neurophysiology—pure

Black Box Behaviorism   Black World Glass Box Perspectivalism

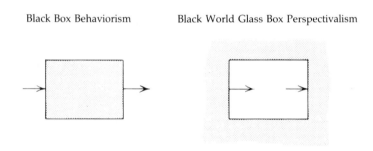

internal syntax with no hope of a semantic interpretation. Psychology "reduced" to neurophysiology in this fashion would not be psychology, for it would not be able to provide an explanation of the regularities it is psychology's particular job to explain: the reliability with which "intelligent" organisms can cope with their environments and thus prolong their lives. Psychology can, and should, work toward an account of the physiological foundations of psychological processes, not by eliminating psychological or intentional characterizations of those processes, but by exhibiting how the brain implements the intentionally characterized performance specifications of sub-personal theories.

Friedman, discussing the current perplexity in cognitive psychology, suggests that the problem is the direction of reduction. Contemporary psychology tries to explain *individual* cognitive activity independently from *social* cognitive activity, and then tries to give a *micro* reduction of social cognitive activity—that is, the use of a public language—in terms of a prior theory of individual cognitive activity. The opposing suggestion is that we first look for a theory of social activity, and then try to give a *macro* reduction of individual cognitive activity—the activity of applying concepts, making judgments, and so forth—in terms of our prior social theory. (1981, pp. 15–16)

With the idea of macro-reduction in psychology I largely agree, except that Friedman's identification of the macro level as explicitly social is only part of the story. The cognitive capacities of non language-using animals (and Robinson Crusoes, if there are any) must also be accounted for, and not just in terms of an analogy with the practices of us language users. The macro level *up* to which we should relate microprocesses in the brain in order to understand them as psychological is more broadly the level of organism–environment interaction, development, and evolution. That level includes social interaction as a particularly important part (see Burge 1979), but still a proper part.

There is no way to capture the semantic properties of things (word tokens, diagrams, nerve impulses, brain states) by a micro-reduction. Semantic properties are not just relational but, you might say, super-relational, for the relation a particular vehicle of content, or token, must bear in order to have content is not just a relation it bears to other similar things (e.g., other tokens, or parts of tokens, or sets of tokens, or causes of tokens) but a relation between the token and the whole life—and counterfactual life[11]—of the organism it "serves" *and* that organism's requirements for survival *and* its evolutionary ancestry.

The Prospects of Reduction

Of our three psychologies—folk psychology, intentional system theory, and sub-personal cognitive psychology—what then might reduce to what? Certainly the one-step micro-reduction of folk psychology to physiology alluded to in the slogans of the early identity theorists will never be found—and should never be missed, even

---

11. What I mean is this: counterfactuals enter because content is in part a matter of the *normal* or *designed* role of a vehicle whether or not it ever gets to play that role. Cf. Sober 1981 and Millikan 1984.

by staunch friends of materialism and scientific unity. A prospect worth exploring, though, is that folk psychology (more precisely, the part of folk psychology worth caring about) reduces—conceptually— to intentional system theory. What this would amount to can best be brought out by contrasting this proposed conceptual reduction with more familiar alternatives: "type-type identity theory" and "Turing machine functionalism." According to type-type identity theory, for every mentalistic term or predicate "M", there is some predicate "P" *expressible in the vocabulary of the physical sciences* such that a creature is M if and only if it is P. In symbols:

(1) $(x)\ (Mx \equiv Px)$

This is reductionism with a vengeance, taking on the burden of re-placing, in principle, all mentalistic predicates with co-extensive predicates composed truth-functionally from the predicates of phys-ics. It is now widely agreed to be hopelessly too strong a demand. Believing that cats eat fish is, intuitively, a *functional* state that might be variously implemented physically, so there is no reason to sup-pose the commonality referred to on the left-hand side of (1) can be reliably picked out by any predicate, however complex, of physics. What is needed to express the predicate on the right-hand side is, it seems, a physically neutral language for speaking of functions and functional states, and the obvious candidates are the languages used to describe automata—for instance, Turing machine language.

The Turing machine functionalist then proposes

(2) $(x)\ (Mx \equiv x$ realizes some Turing machine k in logical state $A)$

In other words, for two things both to believe that cats eat fish they need not be physically similar in any specifiable way, but they must both be in a "functional" condition specifiable in principle in the most general functional language; they must share a Turing machine de-scription according to which they are both in some particular logical state. This is still a reductionist doctrine, for it proposes to identify each mental type with a functional type picked out in the language of automata theory. But this is still too strong, for there is no more reason to suppose Jacques, Sherlock, Boris, and Tom "have the same program" in *any* relaxed and abstract sense, considering the differ-ences in their nature and nurture, than that their brains have some crucially identical physico-chemical feature. We must weaken the re-quirements for the right-hand side of our formula still further.

Consider

(3) (x) (x believes that $p \equiv x$ can be predictively attributed the belief that p)

This appears to be blatantly circular and uninformative, with the language on the right simply mirroring the language on the left. But all we need to make an informative answer of this formula is a systematic way of making the attributions alluded to on the right-hand side. Consider the parallel case of Turing machines. What do two different realizations or embodiments of a Turing machine have in common when they are in the same logical state? Just this: there is a system of description such that according to it both are described as being realizations of some particular Turing machine, and according to this description, which is predictive of the operation of both entities, both are in the same state of that Turing machine's machine table. One doesn't *reduce* Turing machine talk to some more fundamental idiom; one *legitimizes* Turing machine talk by providing it with rules of attribution and exhibiting its predictive powers. If we can similarly legitimize "mentalistic" talk, we will have no need of a reduction, and that is the point of the concept of an intentional system. Intentional systems are supposed to play a role in the legitimization of mentalistic predicates parallel to the role played by the abstract notion of a Turing machine in setting down rules for the interpretation of artifacts as computational automata. I fear my concept is woefully informal and unsystematic compared with Turing's, but then the domain it attempts to systematize—our everyday attributions in mentalistic or intentional language—is itself something of a mess, at least compared with the clearly defined field of recursive function theory, the domain of Turing machines.

The analogy between the theoretical roles of Turing machines and intentional systems is more than superficial. Consider that warhorse in the philosophy of mind, Brentano's Thesis that intentionality is the mark of the mental: all mental phenomena exhibit intentionality and no physical phenomena exhibit intentionality. This has been traditionally taken to be an *irreducibility* thesis: the mental, in virtue of its intentionality, cannot be reduced to the physical. But given the concept of an intentional system, we can construe the first half of Brentano's Thesis—all mental phenomena are intentional—as a *reductionist* thesis of sorts, parallel to Church's Thesis in the foundations of mathematics.

According to Church's Thesis, every "effective" procedure in mathematics is recursive, that is, Turing-computable. Church's Thesis is not provable, since it hinges on the intuitive and informal notion of an effective procedure, but it is generally accepted, and it provides a very useful reduction of a fuzzy-but-useful mathematical notion to a crisply defined notion of apparently equal scope and greater power. Analogously, the claim that every mental phenomenon alluded to in folk psychology is *intentional-system-characterizable* would, if true, provide a reduction of the mental as ordinarily understood—a domain whose boundaries are at best fixed by mutual acknowledgment and shared intuition—to a clearly defined domain of entities whose principles of organization are familiar, relatively formal and systematic, and entirely general.[12]

This reduction claim, like Church's Thesis, cannot be proven but could be made compelling by piecemeal progress on particular (and particularly difficult) cases—a project I set myself elsewhere (in *Brainstorms*). The final reductive task would be to show not how the terms of intentional system theory are eliminable in favor of physiological terms via sub-personal cognitive psychology, but almost the reverse: to show how a system described in physiological terms could warrant an interpretation as a realized intentional system.

---

12. Ned Block (1978) presents arguments supposed to show how the various possible functionalist theories of mind all slide into the sins of "chauvinism" (improperly excluding Martians from the class of possible mind-havers) or "liberalism" (improperly including various contraptions, human puppets, and so forth among the mind-havers). My view embraces the broadest liberalism, gladly paying the price of a few recalcitrant intuitions for the generality gained.

Reflections:
Instrumentalism
Reconsidered

"Three Kinds of Intentional Psychology," though written before "True Believers," follows it in expository order, since it presupposes somewhat more familiarity with my basic position and deals in more detail with some of the problems. In these Reflections I will concentrate on the problem of my so-called *instrumentalism*, which has occasioned much debate; but before presenting and defending my variety of instrumentalism and distinguishing it from its neighboring alternatives, I will comment briefly on four other themes in "Three Kinds" which cast their shadows ahead into other chapters and other controversies.

(1) What is the rationality presupposed by adoption of the intentional stance? The brief and allusive remarks here are supplemented in detail in the next chapter, "Making Sense of Ourselves."

(2) "The syntax of a system doesn't determine its semantics. By what alchemy, then, does the brain extract semantically reliable results from syntactically driven operations?" This way of putting the issue was echoed by Searle (1980b)—"The computer, to repeat, has a syntax but no semantics,"—and again in (1982):

Actually Dennett couldn't have shown how to get from the syntax to the semantics, from form to mental content, because his brand of behaviorism makes it impossible for him to accept the existence of semantics or mental contents literally construed. (p. 57)

This passage makes clear one of Searle's fundamental disagreements with me: while we agree that a computer is a syntactic engine, and hence can only approximate the performance of a semantic engine, he thinks an organic brain is a mechanism that somehow eludes this limitation on computers. He concludes his 1980b paper thus: "Whatever it is that the brain does to produce intentionality, it cannot consist in instantiating a program since no program, by itself, is sufficient for intentionality." Searle and I agree that brains are machines, but he thinks they are very special machines:

"Could a machine think?" My own view is that *only* a machine could think, and indeed only very special kinds of machines, namely brains and machines that had the same causal powers as brains. (1980b, p. 424)

To me, these conjured causal powers of brains are just the sort of alchemy I was warning against in my rhetorical question. A machine is a machine, and there is nothing about the construction or materials of any subvariety that could permit it to transcend the limits of mechanism and eke out "real semantics" over and above its merely syntactical churning. I pursue this disagreement with Searle in more detail in chapters 8 and 9.

(3) The suggestion that we can "reduce" the intuitive notion of mentality to the concept of an intentional system, modeled on Turing's reduction of effectiveness to Turing-computability, was first made explicit by me in the Introduction to *Brainstorms.* Searle (1980b) has called this style of thinking about the mind operationalism—a supposedly dirty word in these post-positivist times. But not to me. I make explicit my fundamental sympathy with Turing's vision, and even its reputedly shocking operationalism, in "Can Machines Think?" (1985a).

(4) The distinction between "core" beliefs and virtual or implicit beliefs is treated with more care and detail in "Styles of Mental Representation," but my main point about the distinction was already made in this essay, and in some quarters it has still not sunk in: even if considerations of compositionality or generativity drive us to the conclusion that the brain *has* to be organized into a modest, explicit set of core elements from which "the rest" is generated somehow as needed (Dennett 1975), no reason at all has thereby been given to suppose that any of the core elements will be beliefs rather than some as yet unnamed and unimagined neural data structures of vastly different properties. Those who want to be "realists about beliefs"— in opposition to my instrumentalism, for instance—often respond to my arguments about the inexhaustible supply of beliefs by saying they are realists about the core beliefs only. Some intuit that only the core beliefs are properly speaking beliefs at all (e.g., Goldman 1986, pp. 201–2). What makes them so sure there are any core *beliefs*? I am as staunch a realist as anyone about those core information-storing

elements in the brain, whatever they turn out to be, to which our intentional interpretations are anchored. I just doubt (along with the Churchlands, P. M. 1981, 1984; P. S. 1980, 1986) that those elements, once individuated, will be recognizable as the beliefs we purport to distinguish in folk psychology. In the reflections following chapter 6, I explain why I do not draw the Churchlands' moral from this shared doubt.

Instrumentalism

I propose to say that someone is a *Realist* about propositional attitudes iff (a) he holds that there are mental states whose occurrences and interactions cause behaviour and do so, moreover, in ways that respect (at least to an approximation) the generalizations of common-sense belief/desire psychology; and (b) he holds that these same causally efficacious mental states are also semantically evaluable. (Fodor 1985, p. 78)

As I said on page 37, I am a sort of realist, but I am not Fodor's Realist with a capital *R* since I expect that the actual internal states that cause behavior will not be functionally individuated, even to an approximation, the way belief/desire psychology carves things up. I have let myself be called an instrumentalist for a half-dozen years (so it is my own fault), but I am not at all happy with the guilt-by-association I have thereby acquired. For instance:

First Anti-Realist option: You could take an *instrumentalist* view of intentional explanation. . . . The great virtue of instrumentalism—here as elsewhere—is that you get all the goodness and suffer none of the pain: you get to use propositional-attitude psychology to make behavioural predictions; you get to "accept" all the intentional explanations that it is convenient to accept; but you don't have to answer hard questions about what the attitudes *are.* (Fodor 1985, p. 79)

Classical instrumentalism was an all-embracing view, a complete rejection of realism; one was instrumentalistic not only about centers of gravity and parallelograms of forces and the Equator, but also about electrons, cells, planets—everything but what could be observed with the naked senses. This embracing instrumentalism did excuse its adherents, as Fodor says, from having to answer certain hard ontological questions, but I have not ducked these interesting questions about beliefs and the other propositional attitudes. From the outset I have maintained a contrast between my realism about brains and their various neurophysiological parts, states, and processes and my "instrumentalism" about the belief-states that appear as *abstracta* when one attempts to interpret all those real phenomena by adopting the intentional stance. The distinction I meant to draw is familiar enough and (I think) uncontroversial in other contexts. As Friedman (1981) notes:

> The reduction/representation distinction is not a mere philosopher's invention; it plays a genuine role in scientific practice. Scientists themselves distinguish between aspects of theoretical structure that are intended to be taken literally and aspects that serve a purely representational function. No one believes, for example, that the so-called "state spaces" of mechanics—phase space in classical mechanics and Hilbert space in quantum mechanics—are part of the furniture of the physical world. (p. 4)

My attempt to endorse and exploit this distinction as a variety of *selective* instrumentalism was evidently a tactical error, given the confusion it has caused. I should have forsworn the term and just said something like this: My *ism* is whatever *ism* serious realists adopt with regard to centers of gravity and the like, since I think beliefs (and some other mental items drawn from folk psychology) are *like that*—in being *abstracta* rather than part of the "furniture of the physical world" and in being attributed in statements that are *true* only if we exempt them from a certain familiar standard of literality.

Some instrumentalists have endorsed *fictionalism*, the view that certain theoretical statements are *useful falsehoods,* and others have maintained that the theoretical claims in question *were neither true nor false* but mere instruments of calculation. I defend neither of these varieties of instrumentalism; as I said when first I used the term above: "people really do have beliefs and desires, on my version of folk psychology, just as they really have centers of gravity." Do I then grant that attributions of belief and desire under the adoption of the intentional stance can be *true*? Yes, but you will misunderstand me unless you grant that the following are also true:

(1) The gravitational attraction between the earth and the moon is a force that acts between two points: the two bodies' centers of gravity.

(2) Hand calculators add, subtract, multiply, and divide.

(3) A Vax 11/780 is a universal Turing machine.

(4) SHAKEY (the "seeing" robot described in Dennett 1982b) makes line drawings even when its CRT is turned off.

It is arguable that each of these is a useful, oversimplifying falsehood; I would rather say that each is a truth one must understand *with a grain of salt.* I have no official, canonical translation of that familiar phrase, but I also do not see the need for one. I would rather make my view as clear and convincing as I can by explaining why I think all belief talk has the same status (*veritas cum grano salis,* to put it technically) as (1–4). The status derives from the uses we find for the intentional stance.

One can view the intentional stance as a limiting case of the design stance: one predicts by taking on just one assumption about the design of the system in question: whatever the design is, it is optimal. This assumption can be seen at work whenever, in the midst of the design stance proper, a designer or design investigator inserts a frank homunculus (an intentional system as subsystem) in order to bridge a gap of ignorance. The theorist says, in effect, "I don't know how to design this subsystem yet, but I know what it's supposed to do, so let's just pretend there is a demon there who wants nothing more than to do that task and knows just how to do it." One can then go on to design the surrounding system with the simplifying assumption that this component is "perfect." One asks oneself how the rest of the system must work, given that this component will do its duty.

Occasionally such a design effort in AI proceeds by literally installing a human module *pro tempore* in order to explore design alternatives in the rest of the system. When the HWIM speech-recognition system was being developed at Bolt Beranek and Newman (Woods and Makhoul 1974), the role of the phonological analysis module, which was supposed to generate hypotheses about the likely phonemic analysis of segments of the acoustic input, was temporarily played by human phonologists looking at segments of spectrograms of utterances. Another human being, playing the role of the control module, could communicate with the phonology demon and the rest of the system, asking questions and posing hypotheses for evaluation.

Once it was determined what the rest of the system had to "know" in order to give the phonologist module the help it needed, that part of the system was designed (discharging, *inter alia,* the control demon) and then the phonologists themselves could be replaced by a machine: a subsystem that used the same input (spectrograms—but not visually encoded, of course) to generate the same sorts of queries and hypotheses. During the design testing phase the phonologists tried hard not to use all the extra knowledge they had—about likely words, grammatical constraints, etc.—since they were mimicking *stupid* homunculi, specialists who only knew and cared about acoustics and phonemes.

Until such time as an effort is made to replace the phonologist subsystem with a machine, one is committed to virtually none of the sorts of design assumptions *about the working of that subsystem* that are genuinely explanatory. But in the meantime one may make great progress on the design of the other subsystems it must interact with and the design of the supersystem composed of all the subsystems.

The first purported chess-playing automaton was a late-eighteenth-century hoax: Baron Wolfgang von Kempelen's wooden mannequin, which did indeed pick up and move the chess pieces, thereby playing a decent game. It was years before the secret of its operation was revealed: a human midget chess master was hidden in the clockwork under the chess table and could see the moves through the translucent squares—a literal homunculus (Raphael 1976). Notice that the success or failure of the intentional stance as a predictor is so neutral with regard to design that it does not distinguish von Kempelen's midget-in-the-works design from, say, Berliner's Hitech, a current chess program of considerable power (Berliner and Ebeling 1986). Both work; both work well; both must have a design that is a fair approximation of optimality, so long as what we mean by optimality at this point focuses narrowly on the task of playing chess and ignores all other design considerations (e.g., the care and feeding of the midget versus the cost of electricity—but try to find a usable electrical outlet in the eighteenth century!). Whatever their internal differences, both systems are intentional systems in good standing, though one of them has a subsystem, a homunculus, that is itself as unproblematic an intentional system as one could find.

Intentional system theory is almost literally a black box theory, which makes it *behavioristic* to philosophers like Searle and Nagel, but hardly behavioristic in Skinner's sense. On the contrary, intentional system theory is an attempt to provide what Chomsky, no behaviorist, calls a competence model, in contrast to a performance model. Before we ask ourselves how mechanisms are designed, we must get clear about what the mechanisms are supposed to (be able to) do. This strategic vision has been developed further by Marr (1982) in his methodological reflections on his work on vision. He distinguishes three levels of analysis. The highest level, which he misleadingly calls *computational*, is in fact not at all concerned with computational processes but strictly (and more abstractly) with the question of what function the system in question is serving—or, more formally, with what function in the mathematical sense it must (somehow or other) "compute" (cf. Newell 1982; Dennett 1986c, forthcoming e). At this computational level one attempts to specify formally and rigorously the system's proper competence (Millikan 1984 would call it the system's proper function). For instance, one fills in the details in the formula

"given an element in the set of x's as input, it yields an element in the set of y's as output according to the following formal rules . . ."

while remaining silent or neutral about the implementation or performance details of whatever resides in the competent black box. Marr's second level is the *algorithmic* level, which does specify the computational processes but remains as neutral as possible about the physical mechanisms implementing them, which are described at the *hardware* level.

Marr claims that until we get a clear and precise understanding of the activity of a system at its highest, "computational" level, we cannot properly address detailed questions at the lower levels or interpret such data as we may already have about processes implementing those lower levels. This echoes Chomsky's long insistence that the diachronic process of language learning cannot be insightfully investigated until one is clear about the end-state mature competence toward which it is moving. Like Chomsky's point, it is better viewed as a strategic maxim than as an epistemological principle. After all, it is not impossible to stumble upon an insight into a larger picture while attempting to ask yourself what turn out to be subsidiary and somewhat myopically posed questions.

Marr's more telling strategic point is that if you have a seriously mistaken view about what the computational-level description of your system is (as all earlier theories of vision did, in his view), your attempts to theorize at lower levels will be confounded by spurious artifactual puzzles. What Marr underestimates, however, is the extent to which computational level (or intentional stance) descriptions can also mislead the theorist who forgets just how idealized they are (Ramachandran 1985a, b).

The fact about competence models that provokes my "instrumentalism" is that the decomposition of one's competence model into parts, phases, states, steps, or whatever *need* shed no light at all on the decomposition of actual mechanical parts, phases, states, or steps of the system being modeled—even when the competence model is, as a competence model, excellent.[1]

Consider what we can say about the competences of two very different sorts of entities, a hand calculator and a Newfie-joke-getter. A Newfie-joke-getter is a person who laughs when told the following Newfie joke. (In Canada, the ethnic slur jokes are about "Newfies"— Newfoundlanders—and my favorite was told to me some years ago by Zenon Pylyshyn. Anyone familiar with Pylyshyn's position on mental imagery will wonder if it was foolhardy of him to divulge this particular phenomenon to me.)

A man went to visit his friend the Newfie and found him with both ears bandaged. "What happened?" asked the man, and the Newfie replied, "I was ironing my shirt when the telephone rang."—"That explains one ear, but what about the other?"—"Well, I had to call a doctor!"

If you "got" the joke, you are in the class of Newfie-joke-getters. How can we characterize the competence required to get the joke? Notice that the text is radically enthymematic—gappy. It never mentions answering the telephone or putting the iron to the ear or the similarity in shape, or heft, of an iron and a telephone receiver. Those details you fill in for yourself, and you have to have the requisite knowledge, the know-how, to do it. We could try to list all the "things you needed to know" to get the joke (Charniak 1974). These "things" are propositions, presumably, and we would create quite a long list if we worked at it. Had you not known any particular one of these "things," you would not have got the point of the joke. Your behavior on this occasion (supposing you laughed, smiled, snorted, or groaned) is almost proof positive that your intentional characterization includes, in the list of beliefs, all these items.

At the same time, no one has much of an idea what a good processing theory of your comprehension of the story would look like. Most readers, probably, would say that what happened as they were reading the joke was that they formed a visual image of some sort in their mind's eye—first of the Newfie reaching for the phone and then of him raising both hands at once—as soon as they read the bit about

---

1. Bechtel (1985) observes, "Dennett seems to reduce the question of instrumentalism *versus* realism to an empirical issue about how the human cognitive system is structured—if there turns out to be a reasonable mapping of intentional idioms onto processing states, then realism will be vindicated, while instrumentalism will be justified if there is no such mapping." (p. 479)

the phone ringing. It is easy enough to tell a sincere and plausible introspective story of this sort, but if we asked a number of readers to share their recalled phenomenology with us, it would not surprise us if there were considerable variation around the central, essential themes. And even if someone denied experiencing any imagery at all but still laughed heartily (and there are definitely such people in my sampling experience), we would suppose that a story of *unconscious* processing—having otherwise much the same content—must be true of the individual. It isn't magic, after all, and there must be an information-sensitive process in each individual that takes them from the seen words to the chuckle.

The story to be told about the actual process in different individuals will not be told by intentional system theory. Among the propositions one has to believe to get the joke is the proposition that people usually answer the telephone when it rings. Another is that answering the telephone typically involves lifting a telephone receiver with one hand and bringing it into contact with one's ear. I will not bore you with a recitation of other required beliefs. Not only do these beliefs not "come to mind" in the form of verbal judgments (which might seriously distract one from paying attention to the words of the story), but it is also highly implausible to suppose that each and every one of them is consulted, independently, by a computational mechanism designed to knit up the lacunae in the story by a deductive generation process. And yet the information expressed in those sentences has to be somehow in the heads of those who get the joke. We can predict and explain some phenomena at this level. For instance, I predict that in this day of wash-and-wear clothes, there is a generation of children growing up that includes many who really do not know what the action of ironing a shirt looks like; these sheltered individuals will be baffled by the joke because they lack some essential beliefs.

The list of beliefs gives us a good general idea of the information that must be in the head, but if we view it as a list of axioms from which a derivational procedure deduces the "point of the joke," we may have the sketch of a performance model, but it is a particularly ill-favored performance model. So even though it is far from idle to catalogue the minimal set of beliefs of the canonical Newfie-jokegetter, that intentional stance characterization, for all its predictive and even explanatory power, sheds virtually no light on the underlying mechanisms.

Now consider a familiar competence model of a hand calculator. Suppose I use my ability to do pencil-and-paper arithmetic to predict the behavior of my pocket calculator (philosophers often like to make life difficult for themselves). The formalism of arithmetic makes for an exemplary "computational level" model: rigorous and precise to a fault, it provides rules for predicting exactly which output the black box will yield for any input. These rules transform the input ("26 × 329") through a series of phases ("six times nine is fifty-four, put down the four, carry the five . . .") until eventually an output is yielded, which (if we've done the computation right) is borne out by the behavior of the calculator. But do the component stages of the process by which I calculated my prediction mirror any component stages in the process by which the calculator produced its predicted result? Some do and some don't. Those that do on one occasion need not on another; the "fit," when it exists, can be accidental. There are indefinitely many ways of engineering a calculator to fit our competence model, and only some of them "bear a strong resemblance" to the details of the competence model calculations.

There isn't just one arithmetical competence model for my hand calculator, of course. Arithmetic ignores finitude, but my calculator doesn't. In its finite way, it uses a process that involves approximation and either truncation (two-thirds comes out .6666) or round-off (two-thirds comes out .6667). A prediction and experiment will determine which. Arithmetic says that 10, divided by 3, times 3 is 10, and that 20, divided by 3, times 3, is 20, but my calculator says that the first answer is 9.9999999, and the second is 19.999999. Discovering this mismatch between perfection and reality gives us a powerful clue about the actual machinery of the calculator.

Here I can use the initial competence model to generate hypotheses the falsification of which sheds light on the actual organization of the machinery. This permits a refinement of the competence model itself—in the direction of turning it into a performance model. To ask which of the many possible algorithms for approximate arithmetic is used by the calculator is to descend to the algorithmic level. If, when we descend to the algorithmic level, we lose a few of the familiar categories of the computational level (perhaps nothing counts as the step where you "put down the four and carry the five"), this will not diminish the practical utility of using the pure competence model as a predictor or as an ideal, a specifier of what the system ought to do, but it will certainly prevent us from discovering the (material) identity of what appear, from that perspective, to be the components and phases of the process.[2]

Moving away from an oversimple ideal toward greater realism is not always a wise tactic. It depends on what you want; sometimes quick-and-dirty prediction is more valuable than an extension of one's fine-grained scientific understanding even in science. The fact that an object can be reliably expected to approximate optimality (or rationality) may be a deeper and more valuable fact than any obtainable from a standpoint of greater realism and detail.

I have always stressed the actual predictive power of the pure intentional stance. I have claimed, for instance, that one can use the intentional stance to predict the behavior of an unknown chess opponent (human or artifact), and this sometimes provokes the objection (e.g., Fodor 1981, chapter 4) that what makes chess an interesting game is precisely that one's opponent's moves are *not* predictable from the intentional stance. If they were, the game would be boring.

This objection sets the standards for prediction too high. First of all, there are those situations during the endgame when we speak of "forced moves" and these are predictable from the intentional stance (and only from the intentional stance) with virtual 100 percent reliability. (One's only serious source of doubt is whether or when one's opponent is going to resign rather than take the next forced move.) Forced moves are forced only in the sense of being "dictated by reason." An irrational opponent (human or artifact) might self-defeatingly fail to make a forced move, and for that matter a rational opponent (again, human or artifact) might have a higher ulterior motive than avoiding defeat at chess.

What about the opponent's moves in the middle game? These are seldom reliably predictable down to uniqueness (and as the critics claim, that is what makes chess interesting), but it is a rare situation when the thirty or forty *legal* moves available to the opponent can't be cut down by the intentional stance to an unordered short list of half a dozen most likely moves on which one could bet very successfully if given even money on all legal moves. This is a tremendous predictive advantage plucked from thin air in the face of almost total ignorance

---

2. Please note that *our* capacity to "do arithmetic" without succumbing directly to round-off or truncation error does not at all show that we are not mechanisms or not finite! Perhaps we are just bigger and fancier finite mechanisms. There are computer systems (such as MACSYMA) that are adept at algebraic manipulations and have alternative ways of representing irrational numbers, for instance.

of the intervening mechanisms, thanks to the power of the intentional stance.

This is how chess programs themselves are designed to economize. Instead of devoting equal attention to all possible continuations of the game, a chess program at some point will concentrate on those branches of the decision tree on which its opponent makes (what the program calculates to be) *its* best response. It makes no difference to the chess program whether its opponent is human or artifact; it simply calculates on the assumption that any opponent worth playing will try to make the best moves it can. Bold "blunders" can thus be ways of surprising—upsetting the expectations of—a program that economizes too optimistically about its opponents. Ought the program be redesigned to keep on the lookout for patterns of such "suboptimal" choice in its opponents—as a step in the direction of greater realism, a more fine-grained understanding of its individual opponents? Perhaps. It all depends on the costs of maintaining, and accessing, such detail while under the pressure of the time clock. Probably the risks of being tricked by deliberate "blunders" are so low that they are a tolerable cost of the speed and efficiency of using the less realistic optimality assumption.

Fodor (1981b) misses this when he suggests that the rationality assumption would actually prevent a chess player from planning a threat.

> So, if I am assuming Black's rationality, I am assuming, inter alia, that Black notices the threat. Whereas, what I hope and predict is precisely that the threat will go unmarked. Nor, in so predicting, have I abandoned the intentional stance. On the contrary, I may rationally predict Black's lapse precisely *because* of what I know or believe about Black's intentional states: in particular, about what he is and is not likely to notice. (p. 108)

What is Black not likely to notice? I can tell you without even knowing who Black is. Being approximately rational, Black is not likely to notice threats that would take a great deal of time and effort to discover and is extremely likely to notice obvious threats. If Black is, as Fodor supposes, rather unlikely to notice the threat, it must be because the threat is somewhat distant in the search tree and hence may well fall outside Black's more or less optimal focus of attention.

So even when we are planning to exploit another rational agent's foibles, we make use of the rationality assumption to guide our efforts (see Dennett 1976, reprinted in *Brainstorms*). Since the general power of the intentional stance is thus not explained by any knowledge we might happen to have about mechanisms in the objects we thereby comprehend, I continue to resist the brand of realism that concludes from the stance's everyday success that there must be belief-like and desire-like states in all such objects. Bechtel (1985) has suggested, constructively, that this still does not bar me from a variety of realism. I could reconstrue my instrumentalism as realism about certain abstract relational properties: properties that relate an organism (or artifact) to its environment in certain indirect ways. Millikan (1984) has a positive account in the same vein. So far as I can see, this is indeed a viable ontological option for me, but as chapter 5 will show, the properties one would end up being a realist about are hardly worth the effort.[3]

---

3. I considered a similar tactical move in Chapter 1 of *Content and Consciousness*, where the option was a similarly convoluted identity theory, and I decided against it: "Hasn't one lost the point of *identity* theory once one begins treating whole sentences as names in effect of situations or states of affairs which are then proclaimed identical with other situations or states of affairs?" (p. 18n)

4 Making Sense of Ourselves

In "Dennett on Intentional Systems" (1981), Stephen Stich gives a lively, sympathetic, and generally accurate account of my view with detailed objections and counterproposals (see also Stich 1980 and Dennett 1980c). My proposed refinement of the folk notion of belief (via the concept of an *intentional system*) would, he claims, "leave us unable to say a great deal that we now wish to say about ourselves." For this to be an objection, he must mean it would leave us unable to say a great deal we *rightly* want to say—because it is true, presumably. We must see what truths, then, he supposes are placed out of reach by my account. Many of them lie, he says, in the realm of facts about our cognitive shortcomings, which can be given no coherent description according to my account: "if we trade up to the intentional-system notions of belief and desire . . . then we simply would not be able to say all those things we need to say about ourselves and our fellows when we deal with each other's idiosyncracies, shortcomings, and cognitive growth" (p. 48). He gives several examples. Among them are the forgetful astronaut, the boy at the lemonade stand who gives the wrong change, and the man who has miscalculated the balance in his checking account. These three are cases of simple, unmysterious cognitive failure—cases of people *making mistakes*—and Stich claims that my view cannot accommodate them. One thing that is striking about all three cases is that in spite of Stich's summary expression of his objection, these are *not* cases of "familiar irrationality" or cases of "inferential failings" at all. They are not cases

Originally published, along with Stich's "Dennett on Intentional Systems," in *Philosophical Topics* 12, no. 1 (1981), a special issue with a variety of excellent papers, subsequently published as *Mind, Brain, and Functionalism*, edited by J. Biro and J. Shahan (Norman: University of Oklahoma Press, 1982).

of what we would ordinarily call irrationality, and since there are quite compelling cases of what we *would* ordinarily call irrationality (and since Stich knows them and indeed cites some of the best documented cases [Wason and Johnson-Laird 1972; Nisbett and Ross 1980]), it is worth asking why he cites instead these cases of miscalculation as proof against my view. I shall address this question shortly, but first I should grant that these are in any case examples of suboptimal behavior of the sort my view is not supposed to be able to handle.

I hold that such errors, as either *malfunctions* or the outcomes of *misdesign,* are unpredictable from the intentional stance, a claim with which Stich might agree, but I go on to claim that there will inevitably be an instability or problematic point in the mere *description* of such lapses at the intentional system level—at the level at which it is the agent's beliefs and desires that are attributed. And here it seems at first that Stich must be right. For although we seldom if ever suppose we can *predict* people's particular mistakes from our ordinary folk-psychological perspective, there seems to be nothing more straightforward than the folk-psychological *description* of such familiar cases. This presumably is part of the reason why Stich chose these cases: they are so uncontroversial.

Let's look more closely, though, at one of the cases, adding more detail. The boy's sign says "LEMONADE—12 cents a glass." I hand him a quarter, he gives me a glass of lemonade and then a dime and a penny change. He's made a mistake. Now what can we *expect* from him when we point out his error to him? That he will exhibit surprise, blush, smite his forehead, apologize, and give me two cents. Why do we expect him to exhibit surprise? Because we attribute to him the belief that he's given me the right change—he'll be surprised to learn that he hasn't (see Weizenfeld 1977). Why do we expect him to blush? Because we attribute to him the desire not to cheat (or be seen to cheat) his customers. Why do we expect him to smite his forehead or give some other acknowledgment of his lapse? Because we attribute to him not only the belief that $25 - 12 = 13$, but also the belief that that's obvious, and the belief that no one his age should make any mistakes about it. While we can't predict his particular error—though we might have made an actuarial prediction that he'd probably make some such error before the day was out—we can pick up the skein of our intentional interpretation once he has made his mistake and predict his further reactions and activities with no more than the usual attendant risk. At first glance then it seems that belief attribution in this instance is as easy, predictive, and stable as it ever is.

But now look yet more closely. The boy has made a mistake all right, but *exactly which mistake?* This all depends, of course, on how we tell the tale—there are many different possibilities. But no matter which story we tell, we will uncover a problem. For instance, we might plausibly suppose that so far as all our evidence to date goes, the boy believes:

(1) that he has given me the right change
(2) that I gave him a quarter
(3) that his lemonade costs 12 cents
(4) that a quarter is 25 cents
(5) that a dime is 10 cents
(6) that a penny is 1 cent
(7) that he gave me a dime and a penny change
(8) that $25 - 12 = 13$
(9) that $10 + 1 = 11$
(10) that $11 \neq 13$

Only (1) is a false belief, but how can he be said to believe *that* if he believes all the others? It surely is not plausible to claim that he has *mis-inferred* (1) from any of the others, directly or indirectly. That is, we would not be inclined to attribute to him the inference of (1) directly from (7) and—what? Perhaps he would infer

(11) that he gave me 11 cents change

from (9) and (7)—he ought to, after all—but *it would not make sense* to suppose he *inferred* (1) from (11) unless he were under the misapprehension

(12) that 11 cents is the right change from a quarter.

We would expect him to believe *that* if he believed

(13) that $25 - 12 = 11$

and while we might have told that tale so that the boy simply had this false belief—and didn't believe (8)—(we can imagine, for instance, that he thought that's what his father told him when he asked), this would yield us a case that was not at all a plausible case of either irrationality or even miscalculation, but just a case of a perfectly rational thinker with a single false belief (which then generates other false beliefs such as (1)). Stich rightly does not want to consider such a case, for of course I do acknowledge the possibility of mere false belief, when special stories can be told about its acquisition. If we then attribute (13) *while retaining* (8), we get a blatant and bizarre case of irrationality: someone believing simultaneously that $25 - 12 = 13$, $25 - 12 = 11$ and $13 \neq 11$. This is not what we had supposed at all, but so strange that we are bound to find the conjoined attributions frankly incredible. Something has to give. If we say, as Stich proposes, that the boy "is not yet very good at doing sums in his head," what is the implication? That he doesn't *really* believe the inconsistent triad, that he *sort of* understands arithmetical notions well enough to have the cited beliefs? That is, if we say what Stich says and *also* attribute the inconsistent beliefs, we still have the problem of brute irrationality too stark to countenance; if we take Stich's observation to temper or withdraw the attribution, then Stich is agreeing with me: even the simplest and most familiar errors require us to resort to scare-quotes or other *caveats* about the literal truth of the total set of attributions.

There is something obtuse, of course, about the quest exhibited above for a total belief-set surrounding the error. The demand that we find an inference—even a *mis*-inference—to the false belief (1) is the demand that we find a practice or tendency with something like a rationale, an exercise of which has led in this instance to (1). No mere succession in time or even regular causation is enough in itself to count as an inference. For instance, were we to learn that the boy was led directly from his belief (6) that a penny is 1 cent to his belief (2) that I gave him a quarter, then no matter how habitual and ineluctable the passage in him from (6) and (2), we wouldn't call it *inference*. Inferences are passages of thought for which there is a reason, but people don't make mistakes for reasons. Demanding reasons (as opposed to "mere" causes) for mistakes generates spurious edifices of belief, as we have just seen in (11–13), but simply acquiescing in the attribution of reasonless belief is no better. It is not as if *nothing* led the boy to believe (1); it is not as if that belief was utterly baseless. We do not suppose, for instance, that he would have believed (1) had his hand been empty, or filled with quarters, or had I given him a dollar or a credit card. He does somehow base his mistaken belief on a distorted or confused or mistaken perception of what he is handing me, what I have handed him, and the appropriate relationships between them.

The boy is basically on top of the situation, and is no mere change-giving robot; nevertheless, we must descend from the level of beliefs and desires to some other level of theory to describe his mistake, since no account in terms of his beliefs and desires will make sense completely. At some point our account will have to cope with the sheer senselessness of the transition in any error.

My perhaps tendentious examination of a single example hardly constitutes an argument for my general claim that this will always be the outcome. It is presented as a challenge: try for yourself to tell the total belief story that surrounds such a simple error and see if you do not discover just the quandary I have illustrated.

Mistakes of the sort exhibited in this example are slips in good procedures, not manifestations of an allegiance to a bad procedure or principle. The partial confirmation of our inescapable working hypothesis that the boy is fundamentally rational is his blushing acknowledgment of his error. He doesn't defend his action once it is brought to his attention, but willingly corrects his error. This is in striking contrast to the behavior of agents in the putative cases of genuine irrationality cited by Stich. In these instances, people not only persist in their "errors," but also stubbornly defend their practice—and find defenders among philosophers as well (see Cohen 1981). It is at least *not obvious* that there are any cases of systematically irrational behavior or thinking. The cases that have been proposed are all controversial, which is just what my view predicts: no such thing as a cut-and-dried or obvious case of "familiar irrationality." This is not to say that we are always rational, but that when we are not, the cases defy description in ordinary terms of belief and desire. There is no mystery about why this should be so. An intentional interpretation of an agent is an exercise that attempts to *make sense* of the agent's acts, and when acts occur that make no sense, they cannot be straightforwardly interpreted in sense-making terms. Something must give: we allow that the agent either only "sort of" believes this or that, or believes this or that "for all practical purposes," or believes some falsehood which creates a context in which what had appeared to be irrational turns out to be rational after all (see, e.g., Cohen's suggestions, 1981). These particular fall-back positions are themselves subject to the usual tests on belief attribution, so merely finding a fall-back position is not confirming it. If it is disconfirmed, the search goes on for another saving interpretation. If there is no saving interpretation—if the person in question is irrational—no interpretation at all will be settled on.

The same retreat from the abyss is found in the simple cases of miscalculation and error of which Stich reminds us, but with a few added wrinkles worth noting. In the case of the lemonade seller, we might excuse ourselves from further attempts to sort out his beliefs by just granting that while he knew (and thus believed) all the right facts, he "just forgot" or "overlooked" a few of them temporarily—until we reminded him of them. This has the appearance of being a modest little psychological hypothesis: something roughly to the effect that although something or other was stored safe and sound inside the agent's head where it belonged, its address was temporarily misplaced. Some such story may well in the end be supported within a confirmed and detailed psychological theory (cf. Cherniak 1983, 1986; Thomason 1986), but it is important to note that at the present time we make these hypotheses simply on the basis of our abhorrence of the vacuum of contradiction.

For instance, consider absentmindedness—a well-named affliction, it seems. At breakfast I am reminded that I am playing tennis with Paul instead of having lunch today. At 12:45 I find myself polishing off dessert when Paul, in tennis gear, appears at my side and jolts me into recollection. "It completely slipped my mind!" I aver, blushing at my own absentmindedness. But why do I say *that*? Is it because, as I recall, not a single conscious thought about my tennis date passed through my head after breakfast? That might be true, but perhaps no conscious thought that I was going to lunch today occurred to me in the interim either, and yet here I am, finishing my lunch. Perhaps if I *had* thought consciously about going to lunch as usual, that very thought would have reminded me that I wasn't, in fact. And in any case, even if I remember now that it *did* occur to me in mid-morning that I was to play tennis today—to no avail, evidently—I will still say it subsequently slipped my mind.

Why, indeed, am I eager to insist that it completely slipped my mind? To assure Paul that I haven't stood him up on purpose? Perhaps, but that should be obvious enough not to need saying, and if my eagerness is a matter of not wanting to insult him, I am not entirely succeeding, since it is not at all flattering to be so utterly forgotten. I think a primary motive for my assertion is just to banish the possibility that otherwise would arise: I am starkly irrational; I believe that I am playing tennis at lunch and that I am free to go to lunch as usual. I cannot act on both beliefs at once; whichever I act on, I declare the other to have slipped my mind. Not on any introspective evidence (for I may, after all, have repeatedly thought of the matter in the relevant interim period), but on *general principles*. It does not matter how close to noon I have reflected on my tennis date; if I end up having lunch as usual, the tennis date *must have* slipped my mind at the last minute.

There is no direct relationship between our conscious thought and the occasions when we will say something has slipped our mind. Suppose someone asks me to have lunch today and I reply that I can't: I have another appointment then, but for the life of me I can't recall what it is—it will come to me later. Here although in one regard my tennis date has slipped my mind, in another it has not, since my belief that I am playing tennis, while not (momentarily) consciously retrievable, is yet doing some work for me: it is keeping me from making the conflicting appointment. I hop in my car and I get to the intersection: left takes me home for lunch; right takes me to the tennis court; I turn right this time without benefit of an accompanying conscious thought to the effect that I am playing tennis today at lunchtime. It has not slipped my mind, though; had it slipped my mind, I would no doubt have turned left (cf. Ryle 1958). It is even possible to have something slip one's mind while one is thinking of it consciously! "Be careful of this pan," I say, "it is very hot"—reaching out and burning myself on the very pan I am warning about. The height of absentmindedness, no doubt, but possible. We would no doubt say something like "You didn't think what you were saying!"—which doesn't mean that the words issued from my mouth as from a zombie, but that if I had believed—*really* believed—what I was saying, I *couldn't* have done what I did. If I can in this manner not think what I am saying, I could also in about as rare a case not think what I was thinking. I could think "careful of that hot pan" *to myself*, while ignoring the advice.

There is some temptation to say that in such a case, while I knew full well that the pan was hot, I just forgot for a moment. Perhaps we want to acknowledge this sort of forgetting, but note that it is not at all the forgetting we suppose to occur when we say I have forgotten the telephone number of the taxicab company I called two weeks ago or forgotten the date of Hume's birth. In those cases we presume the information is gone for good. Reminders and hints won't help me recall. When I say "I completely forgot our tennis date," I don't at all mean I completely forgot it—as would be evidenced if on Paul's arrival in tennis gear I was blankly baffled by his presence, denying any recollection of having made the date.

Some other familiar locutions of folk psychology are in the same family: "notice," "overlook," "ignore," and even "conclude." One's initial impression is that these terms are applied by us to our own cases on the basis of direct introspection. That is, we classify various conscious acts of our own as concludings, noticings, and the like—but what about ignorings and overlookings? Do we find ourselves doing these things? Only retrospectively, and in a self-justificatory or self-critical mood: "I ignored the development of the pawns on the queen side," says the chess player, "because it was so clear that the important development involved the knights on the king side." Had he lost the game, he would have said, "I simply overlooked the development of the pawns on the queen side, since I was under the misapprehension that the king side attack was my only problem."

Suppose someone asks, "Did you notice the way Joe was evading your questions yesterday?" I might answer "yes," even though I certainly did not *think any conscious thoughts* at the time (that I can recall) about the way Joe was evading my questions; if I can nevertheless see that my reactions to him (as I recall them) took appropriate account of his evasiveness, I will (justly) aver that I did notice. Since I did the appropriate thing in the circumstances, I must have noticed, mustn't I?

In order just now for you to get the gist of my tale of absent-mindedness, you had to conclude from my remark about "polishing off dessert" that I had just finished a lunch and missed my tennis date. And surely you did so conclude, but did you consciously conclude? Did anything remotely like "Mmm, he must have had lunch . . ." run though your head? Probably not. It is no more likely that the boy selling lemonade consciously thought that the eleven cents in his hand was the right change. "Well, if he didn't consciously think it, he unconsciously thought it; we must posit an unconscious controlling thought to that effect to explain, or ground, or *be* (!) his belief that he is giving the right change."

It is tempting to suppose that when we retreat from the abyss of irrationality and find a different level of explanation on which to flesh out our description of errors (or, for that matter, of entirely felicitous passages of thought), the arena we properly arrive at is the folk-psychological arena of thinkings, concludings, forgettings, and the like—not mere abstract mental *states* like belief, but concrete and clockable episodes or activities or processes that can be modeled by psychological model builders and measured and tested quite directly in experiments. But as the examples just discussed suggest (though they do not by any means prove), we would be unwise to model our serious, academic psychology too closely on these putative *illata* of folk theory. We postulate all these apparent activities and mental processes in order to make sense of the behavior we observe—in order, in fact, to make as much sense as possible of the behavior, especially when the behavior we observe is our own. Philosophers of mind used to go out of their way to insist that one's access to one's own case in such matters is quite unlike one's access to others', but as we learn more about various forms of psychopathology and even the foibles of apparently normal people (see Nisbett and Wilson 1977), it becomes more plausible to suppose that although there are still some small corners of unchallenged privilege, some matters about which our authority is invincible, each of us is in most regards a sort of inveterate auto-psychologist, effortlessly *inventing* intentional inter-pretations of our own actions in an inseparable mix of confabulation, retrospective self-justification, and (on occasion, no doubt) good theorizing. The striking cases of confabulation by subjects under hyp-nosis or suffering from various well-documented brain disorders (Korsakoff's syndrome, split brains, various "agnosias") raise the prospect that such virtuoso displays of utterly unsupported self-interpretation are not manifestations of a skill suddenly learned in response to trauma, but of a normal way unmasked (see Gaz-zoniga and Ledoux 1978; also Gardner 1975, for graphic accounts of such cases).

As creatures of our own attempts to make sense of ourselves, the putative mental activities of folk theory are hardly a neutral field of events and processes to which we can resort for explanations when the normative demands of intentional system theory run afoul of a bit of irrationality. Nor can we suppose their counterparts in a developed cognitive psychology, or even their "realizations" in the wetware of the brain, will fare better.

Stich holds out the vision of an entirely norm-free, naturalized psychology that can *settle* the indeterminacies of intentional system theory by appeal, ultimately, to the presence or absence of real, functionally salient, causally potent states and events that can be identified and ascribed content independently of the problematic canons of ideal rationality my view requries. What did the lemonade seller really believe? Or what, in any event, was the *exact content* of the sequence of states and events that figure in the cognitivistic description of his error? Stich supposes we will be able in principle to say, even in cases where my method comes up empty-handed. I claim on the contrary that just as the interpretation of a bit of *outer*, public communication—a spoken or written utterance in natural language, for instance—depends on the interpretation of the utterer's beliefs and desires, so the interpretation of a bit of inner, subpersonal cognitivistic machinery must inevitably depend on exactly the same thing: the whole person's beliefs and desires. Stich's method of content ascription depends on mine and is not an alternative, independent method.

Suppose we find a mechanism in Jones that reliably produces an utterance of "It is raining" whenever Jones is queried on the topic and it is raining in Jones's epistemically accessible vicinity. It also produces "yes" in response to "Is it raining?" on those occasions. Have we discovered Jones's belief that it is raining? That is, more circumspectly, have we found the mechanism that "subserves" this belief in Jones's cognitive apparatus? Maybe—it all depends on whether or not Jones believes that it is raining when (and only when) this mechanism is "on." That is, perhaps we have discovered a weird and senseless mechanism (like the "assent-inducing tumor" I imagined in "Brain Writing and Mind Reading," *Brainstorms*, p. 44) that deserves no intentional interpretation at all—or at any rate not this one: that it is the belief that it is raining. We need a standard against which to judge our intentionalistic labels for the *illata* of sub-personal cognitive theory; what we must use for this standard is the system of *abstracta* that fixes belief and desire by a sort of hermeneutical process that tells the best, most rational story that can be told. If we find that Jones passes the right tests—he demonstrates that he really understands what the supposition that it is raining means, for instance—we may find confirmation of our hypothesis that we have uncovered the mechanistic realization of his beliefs. But where we find such fallingsshort, such imperfect and inappropriate proclivities and inactivities, we will *thereby* diminish our grounds for ascribing belief content to whatever mechanisms we find.

It is unlikely, I have said, that the *illata* we eventually favor in academic psychology will resemble the putative *illata* of folk theory enough to tempt us to identify them. But whatever *illata* we find, we will interpret them and assign content to them by the light of our holistic attribution to the agent of beliefs and desires. We may not find structures in the agent that can be made to line up belief-by-belief with our intentional system catalogue of beliefs for the agent. On Stich's view, and on Fodor's, we would be constrained to interpret this outcome—which all grant is possible—as the discovery that *there were no such things as beliefs after all*. Folk psychology was just false. On my view we would instead interpret this discovery—and a very likely one it is—as the discovery that the concrete systems of representation whereby brains realize intentional systems are simply not sentential in character (see "Beyond Belief," chapter 5).

Of course sometimes there are sentences in our heads, which is hardly surprising, considering that we are language-using creatures. These sentences, though, are as much in need of interpretation via a determination of our beliefs and desires as are the public sentences we utter. Suppose the words occur to me (just "in my head"): "Now is the time for violent revolution!"—did I thereby *think* the thought with the content that now is the time for violent revolution? It all depends, doesn't it? On what? On what I happened to believe and desire and intend when I internally uttered those words "to myself." Similarly, even if "cerebroscopes" show that while the boy was handing me my change he was internally accompanying his transaction with the conscious or subconscious expression in his natural language or in Mentalese: "this is the right change," that would not settle the correct interpretation of that bit of internal language and hence would not settle the intentional interpretation of his act. And since he has made a mistake, there is no unqualified catalogue of his intentional states and acts of the moment.

So I stick to my guns: even for the everyday cases of error Stich presents, the problems of belief interpretation encountered by my view *really are there* in the folk-psychological practice, although they often lurk behind our confabulations and excuses. Nor will they go away for Stich's proposed alternative theory of content ascription. This is not to say that such phenomena cannot be given any coherent description. Of course they can be coherently described from either the design stance or the physical stance—a point on which Stich and I agree. So I do not discover any truths of folk theory I must regretfully forswear.

In thus resisting Stich's objections, and keeping rationality at the foundation of belief and desire attribution, am I taking what Stich calls the "hard line," or the "soft line"? The hard line, according to Stich, insists that intentional system theory's idealizing assumption of rationality is actually to be found in the folk practice from which intentional system theory is derived. The soft line "proposes some fiddling with the idealized notion of an intentional system" to bring it more in line with folk practice, which does not really (Stich insists) invoke considerations of rationality at all. These distinct lines are Stich's inventions, born of his frustration in the attempt to make sense of my expression of my view, which is both hard and soft—that is to say, flexible. The *flexible line* insists both that the assumption of rationality is to be found in the folk practice and that rationality is not what it appears to be to some theorists—so the idealization will require some "fiddling." What, then, do I say of the ideal of rationality exploited self-consciously by the intentional system strategist and as second nature by the rest of the folk?

Here Stich finds me faced with a dilemma. If I identify rationality with *logical consistency and deductive closure* (and the other dictates of the formal normative systems such as game theory and the calculus of probability), I am embarrassed by absurdities. Deductive closure, for instance, is just too strong a condition, as Stich's case of Oscar the engineer witnesses (cf. also Fodor 1981a). If, flying to the other extreme, I identify rationality with *whatever it is that evolution has provided us,* I either lapse into uninformative tautology or fly in the face of obvious counterexamples: cases of evolved manifest irrationality. What then do I say rationality is? I don't say.

Stich is right; for ten years I have hedged and hinted and entertained claims that I have later qualified or retracted. I didn't know what to say, and could see problems everywhere I turned. With that *mea culpa* behind me, I will now take the offensive, however, and give what I think are good reasons for cautiously resisting the demand for a declaration on the nature of rationality while still insisting that an assumption of rationality plays the crucial role I have seen for it.

First, a few words on what rationality is *not*. It is not deductive closure. In a passage Stich quotes from "Intentional Systems" I present the suggestion that "If S were ideally rational . . . S would believe every logical consequence of every belief (and ideally, S would have no false beliefs)" and I make a similar remark in "True Believers." That is, after all, the logically guaranteed resting point of the universally applicable, indefinitely extendable demand that one believe the "obvious" consequences of one's genuine, fully understood beliefs. But Stich's example of Oscar nicely reveals what is wrong with letting sheer entailment expand a rational agent's beliefs, and, as Lawrence Powers shows in his important article "Knowledge by Deduction" (1978), there is work to be done by a theory of knowledge *acquisition* by deduction: one comes to know (and believe) what one didn't already know (or believe) by deducing propositions from premises already believed—a familiar and "obvious" idea, but one that requires the very careful exposition and defense Powers gives it. And it is important to note that in the course of making his case for what we might call implication-insulated cognitive states, Powers must advert to neologism and caveat: we must talk about what our agent "pseudo-believes" and "pseudo-knows" (p. 360ff). It puts one in mind, in fact, of Stich's own useful neologism for belief-like states lacking the logical fecundity of beliefs: "sub-doxastic states" (Stich 1978b).

Nor is rationality perfect logical consistency, although the *discovery* of contradiction between propositions one is inclined to assent to is always, of course, an occasion for sounding the epistemic alarm (de Sousa 1971). Inconsistency, when discovered, is of course to be eliminated one way or another, but making the rooting out of inconsistency the pre-eminent goal of a cognizer would lead to swamping the cognitive system in bookkeeping and search operations to the exclusion of all other modes of activity (Cherniak 1986 and Darmstadter 1971). Now how can I talk this way about inconsistency, given my account of the conditions of correct belief attribution? Who said anything about inconsistency of *beliefs*? When one enters the domain of considerations about the wise design of cognitive structures and operations, one has left belief proper behind and is discussing, in effect, structurally identified features with more-or-less apt intentionalistic labels (see "Three Kinds of Intentional Psychology" and *Brainstorms*, pp. 26–27).

If I thus do not identify rationality with consistency and deductive closure, what then could be my standard? If I turn to evolutionary considerations, Stich suggests, "such established theories as deductive and inductive logic, decision theory and game theory" will be "of no help in assessing what an organism 'ought to believe'." This is just not true. The theorist who relinquishes the claim that these formalisms are the final benchmark of rationality can still turn to them for help, can still exploit them in the course of criticizing (on grounds of irrationality) and reformulating strategies, designs, interpretations. The analogy is imperfect, but just as one may seek help from a good dictionary or a good grammar book in supporting one's criticism of someone's spelling, word choice, or grammar, so may one appeal to the defeasible authority of, say, decision theory in objecting to someone's strategic formulation. One can also reject as wrong—or irrational—the advice one gets from a dictionary, a grammar, a logic, or any other normative theory, however well established (Cohen 1981; Stich and Nisbett 1980).

What of the evolutionary considerations? I am careful *not* to define rationality in terms of what evolution has given us—so I avoid outright tautology. Nevertheless, the relation I claim holds between rationality and evolution is more powerful than Stich will grant. I claim, as he notes, that if an organism is the product of natural selection we can assume that most of its beliefs will be true and most of its belief-forming strategies will be rational. Stich disagrees: "it is simply not the case that natural selection favors true beliefs over false ones," because all natural selection favors is beliefs "that yield selective advantage" and "there are many environmental circumstances in which false beliefs will be more useful than true ones." I do not think it is *obvious* that it is *ever* advantageous to be designed to arrive at false beliefs about the world, but I have claimed that there are describable circumstances—rare circumstances—where it can happen, so I agree with Stich on this point: *"better safe than sorry* is a policy that recommends itself to natural selection," Stich says, echoing my claim in "Three Kinds of Intentional Psychology,"—"Erring on the side of prudence is a well-recognized good strategy, and so Nature can be expected to have valued it on occasions when it came up."

But does this go any way at all toward rebutting my claim that natural selection guarantees that most of an organism's beliefs will be true, most of its strategies rational? I think not. Moreover, even if a strategy is, as I grant it very well may be, a "patently invalid" strategy that works most of the time in the contexts it is invoked—does this show it is an *irrational* strategy? Only if one is still clinging to the ideals of Intro Logic for one's model of rationality. It is not even that there are no "established" academic canons of rationality in opposition to the logicians' to which one might appeal. Herbert Simon is duly famous for maintaining that *it is rational* in many instances to *satisfice*—for example, to leap to possibly "invalid" conclusions when the costs of further calculations probably outweigh the costs of getting the wrong answer. I think he is right, so I for one would not tie rationality to any canons that prohibited such practices. Stich declares:

So long as we recognize a distinction between a normative theory of inference or decision-making and a set of inferential practices which (in the right environment) generally get the right (or selectively useful) answer, it will be clear that the two need not, and generally do not, coincide. (pp. 53–54)

This is a puzzling claim, for there are normative theories for different purposes, including the purposes of "generally getting the right answer." If one views these as at odds with one another, one makes a mistake. Deductive logic might be held to advise that in the face of uncertainty or lack of information one should simply *sit tight and infer nothing*—bad advice for a creature in a busy world, but fine advice if avoiding falsehood at all costs is the goal. It is better to recognize the various uses to which such strategies can be put and let rationality consist in part of a good sense of when to rely on what. (It is also useful to remind ourselves that only a tiny fraction of all the "rational animals" that have ever lived have ever availed themselves self-consciously of *any* formal techniques of the normative theories that have been proposed.)

The concept of rationality is indeed slippery. We agree, it seems, that a system would be improperly called irrational if although its *normal, designed* operation were impeccable (by the standards of the relevant norms), it suffered occasional *malfunctions*. But of course a system that was particularly delicate, particularly prone to uncorrected malfunctions, would hardly be a well-designed system; a system that was foolproof or failsafe would in this regard be better. But which would be better—which would be more rational—all things considered: a very slow but virtually failsafe system, or a very fast but only 90 percent malfunction-free system? It depends on the application, and there are even normative canons for evaluating such choices in some circumstances.

I want to use "rational" as a general-purpose term of cognitive approval—which requires maintaining only conditional and revisable allegiances between rationality, so considered, and the proposed (or even universally acclaimed) methods of getting ahead, cognitively, in the world. I take this usage of the terms to be quite standard, and I take appeals to rationality by proponents of cognitive disciplines or practices to require this understanding of the notion. What, for instance, could Anderson and Belnap (1974) be appealing to, what could they be assuming about their audience, when they recommend their account of entailment over its rivals, if not to an assumably shared rationality which is such that it is an *open question* which formal system best captures it? Or consider this commentary on the discovery that a compartmentalized memory is a necessary condition for effective cognition in a complex, time-pressured world:

> We can now appreciate both the costs and the benefits of this strategy; *prima facie*, the resulting behavior can be characterized as departures from rationality, but on the assumption that exhaustive memory search is not feasible, such memory organization is advisable overall, despite its costs. Correspondingly, a person's action may seem irrational when considered in isolation, but it may be rational when it is more broadly considered as part of the worthwhile price of good memory management. (Cherniak 1983, p. 23)

The claim is that it is rational to be inconsistent sometimes, not the pseudo-paradoxical claim that it is rational sometimes to be irrational. As the example shows, the concept of rationality is systematically pre-theoretical. One may, then, decline to *identify* rationality with the features of any formal system or the outcome of any process and still make appeals to the concept, and assertions about appeals to it (such as mine), without thereby shirking a duty of explicitness.

When one leans on our pre-theoretical concept of rationality, one relies on our shared intutitions—when they *are* shared, of course—about what makes sense. What else, in the end, could one rely on? When considering what we *ought to do,* our reflections lead us eventually to a consideration of what we *in fact do;* this is inescapable, for a catalogue of our considered intuitive judgments on what we ought to do is both a compendium of what we do think, and a shining example (by our lights—what else?) of how we ought to think:

> Thus, what and how we do think is evidence for the principles of rationality, what and how we ought to think. This itself is a methodological principle of rationality; call it the *Factunorm Principle.* We are (implicitly) accepting the Factunorm Principle whenever we try to determine what or how we ought to think. For we must, in that very attempt, think. And unless we can think that what and how we do think there is correct—and thus is evidence for what and how we ought to think—we cannot determine what or how we ought to think. (Wertheimer 1974, pp. 110–11)

Now it will appear that I am backing into Stich's own view, the view that when we attribute beliefs and other intentional states to others, we do this by comparing them to ourselves, by projecting ourselves into their states of mind. One doesn't ask: "what ought this creature believe?" but "what would I believe if I were in its place?" (I have suggested to Stich that he call his view *ideological solipsism*, but he apparently feels this would court confusion with some other doctrine.) Stich contrasts his view with mine and claims that "the notion of idealized rationality plays *no role at all*" (Stich's emphasis) in his account. "In ascribing content to belief states we measure others not against an idealized standard but against ourselves." But for the reasons just given, measuring "against ourselves" *is* measuring against an idealized standard.

Stich at one point observes that "since we take ourselves to approximate rationality, this explains the fact, noted by Dennett, that intentional description falters in the face of egregious irrationality." He must grant, then, that since we take ourselves to approximate rationality, it is also true that the results of his method and my method will coincide very closely. He, asking "what would I do if . . . ?" and I, asking "what ought he to do . . . ?" will typically arrive at the same account, since Stich will typically suppose that what he ought to do is what I would do if I were in his shoes. If the methods were actually extensionally equivalent, one might well wonder about the point of the quarrel, but is there not room for two methods to diverge in special cases? Let us see.

Can it be like this? Stich, cognizant of his lamentable and embarrassing tendency to affirm the consequent, imputes this same tendency to those whose beliefs and desires he is trying to fathom. He does this instead of supposing they might be free from his own particular foible, but guilty of others. Unlikely story. Here is a better one. Having learned about "cognitive dissonance," Stich is now prepared to find both in himself and in others the resolution of cognitive dissonance in the favoring of a self-justifying belief over a less comfortable belief better supported by the evidence. This is a fine example of the sort of empirical discovery that can be used to tune the intentional stance, by suggesting hypotheses to be tested by the attributer, but how would Stich say it had anything to do with *ourselves*, and how would this discovery be put into effective use independently of the idealizing assumption? First, is it not going to be an empirical question whether all people respond to cognitive dissonance as we do? If Stich builds this (apparently) suboptimal proclivity into his very method of attribution, he forgoes the possibility of discovering varieties of believers happily immune to this pathology.

Moreover, consider how such an assumption of suboptimality would get used in an actual case. Jones has just spent three months of hard work building an addition to his house; it looks terrible. Something must be done to resolve the uncomfortable cognitive dissonance. Count on Jones to slide into some belief that will save the situation. But which one? He might come to believe that the point of the project, really, was to learn all about carpentry by the relatively inexpensive expedient of building a cheap addition. Or he might come to believe that the bold thrust of the addition is just the touch that distinguishes his otherwise hackneyed if "tasteful" house from the run of the neighborhood houses. Or, . . . for many possible variations. But which of these is actually believed will be determined by seeing what he says and does, and then asking: what beliefs and desires would make those acts rational? And whatever delusion is embraced, it must be—and will be—carefully surrounded by plausible supporting material, generatable on the counterfactual assumption that the delusion is an entirely rationally held belief. Given what we already know about Jones, we might be able to predict which comforting delusion would be most attractive and efficient for him—that is, which would most easily cohere with the rest of the fabric of his beliefs. So even in a case of cognitive dissonance, where the beliefs we attribute are not optimal by anyone's lights, the test of rational coherence is the preponderant measure of our attributions.

I do not see how my method and Stich's can be shown to yield different results, but I also do not see that they could not. I am not clear enough about just what Stich is asserting. An interesting idea lurking in Stich's view is that when we interpret others we do so not so much by *theorizing* about them as by *using ourselves as analog computers* that produce a result. Wanting to know more about your frame of mind, I somehow put myself in it, or as close to being in it as I can muster, and see what I thereupon think (want, do. . .). There is much that is puzzling about such an idea. How can it work without being a kind of theorizing in the end? For the state I put myself in is not belief but make-believe belief. If I make believe I am a suspension bridge and wonder what I will do when the wind blows, what "comes to me" in my make-believe state depends on how sophisticated my knowledge is of the physics and engineering of suspension bridges. Why should my making believe I have your beliefs be any different?

In both cases, knowledge of the imitated object is needed to drive the make-believe "simulation," and the knowledge must be organized into something rather like a theory. Moreover, establishing that we do somehow arrive at our interpretations of others by something like simulation and self-observation would not by itself show that the guiding question of our efforts is "what would I believe?" *as opposed to* "what ought he to believe?" A wary attributer might exhibit the difference by using the trick of empathy or make-believe to *generate* a candidate set of attributions to *test* against his "theory" of the other before settling on them. Note that the issue is far from clear even in the case of imagined *self*-attribution. What would your state of mind be if you were told you had three weeks to live? How do you think about this? In a variety of ways, probably; you do a bit of simulation and see what you'd say, think, and so on, and you also reflect on what kind of person you think you are—so you can conclude that a person *like that* would believe—ought to believe—or want such-and-such.

I close with one final rejoinder. Stich seeks to embarrass me in closing with a series of rhetorical questions about what a frog *ought to believe*—for I have made my determination of what a frog *does* believe hinge on such questions. I grant that such questions are only problematically answerable under even the best conditions but view that as no embarrassment. I respond with a rhetorical question of my own: does Stich suppose that the exact content of what a frog does in fact believe is any more likely of determination?

Reflections:
When Frogs (and Others)
Make Mistakes

Stich has a fine knack for asking just the right questions—not the unsympathetic killer questions, but the telling provokers of better second thoughts. Now, with more time to think about his challenges and more space in which to respond, I want to address two of them in more detail: the lemonade seller and the frog. What do they *really* believe? My answers to these two questions lead to some further reflections on why Realism about beliefs is so unrealistic.

The Lemonade Seller's Mistake

The lemonade seller has made a simple mistake, and Stich correctly draws out the striking implication of my view about such mistakes: I must claim that unless the mistake has one of the normal etiologies that we might call peripheral—he has misperceived the coins in his hand or has been misinformed about the value of the coins or the truths of arithmetic—there is sure to be a surd spot, an uninterpretable gap, in the tale we tell of him from the intentional stance. Put bluntly, on my view there is no saying what someone actually believes whenever he makes a cognitive mistake! Stich suggests that this is obviously false. Presumably every such mistake is some particular mistake, from which it would seem to follow that there will always be (even if we can't find it) a best complete belief story to tell about it.

A complete belief story would assign truth or falsity to every relevant belief attribution. Think of it on the model of a cross-examination in a trial. Did the defendant believe he gave the right change? Did he believe the two coins he handed over were a dime and a penny? Did he know the value of a penny, or didn't he? Yes or no? I grant that it does seem obvious that these are all fair questions which have to have correct answers, even if no one can determine them, but I claim that this is an illusion. It is close kin to the illusion, first pointed out by Quine, that there has to be a best translation manual between any two languages even if we can't find it. Quine has often been challenged to give a convincing example of a genuine (even if imaginery) case of indeterminacy of radical translation (most memorably at the conference on Intentionality, Language, and Translation anthologized in *Synthese*, 1974). He has been unable to give a detailed and realistic example, not because his thesis is false but because it postulates the possibility of a case poised on a knife-edge—two radically disagreeing translation manuals such that *all* the available relevant information fails to favor one over the other. The actual world abhors knife-edges even more than vacuums. Almost inevitably, grubby details begin to mount faster on one side than the other, ruining any realistic case for the role as Quine's Example.

One might anticipate a similar fate for my indeterminacy claim, and yet it seems to me to be easier to sustain the claim that the gap is real and unclosable in the case of cognitive errors (cf. Wheeler 1986). For although in every case I can imagine, the not-so-grubby details do mount up to favor one story or another about the nature of the mistake, these shed no uncontroversial light on *what the person believed*. Consider how we might complete the story of the lemonade seller.

Suppose it is determined by conclusive tests in the laboratories of cognitive scientists that once he is "warmed up," he makes change in a semi-automatic way, while thinking of other things. A temporary change-making "module" is located in his brain, and Nuclear Magnetic Resonance Imaging shows it to have been operating at the time. Moreover, it is established that 350 milliseconds before the change-making module completed its task, the smile of a girl in a passing car caught his eye, indirectly causing the penny-fetching submodule to Exit after gathering only one penny instead of three. Visual and tactile feedback, which would normally have detected the error, were received but ignored, thanks to an attention shift caused by my noisy slurping of the lemonade and the fact that the module reported back successful completion of its task before shutting down.

Now what did he believe? Did he believe he gave me a dime and a penny change? He did see what he was doing and suffered no visual hallucination (*ex hypothesi* on this telling). Had he been asked immediately after I took the change to say what he had given me, he would have said a dime and a penny. Of all the powers such a belief might be expected to have, the only one lacking in this case, we may suppose, is the power to *initiate* a correction (remember: as soon as the fact that he gave me a dime and a penny is drawn to his attention, he recognizes and corrects his error).

"He had the belief, but just didn't attend to it."

Fine; did he also believe he gave me thirteen cents change?

"Yes, but he didn't attend to that belief either. If he had attended to both of them, he would have noticed the contradiction."

Couldn't he have attended to both and *not* noticed the contradiction?

"No; if he *really understands* those two propositions he *must* recognize their incompatibility."

But then isn't it just as constitutive of belief in such a proposition that one recognize when one is being contradicted? He must not *really believe* those propositions, since among their definitive powers as beliefs must be that they raise alarms, draw attention to themselves, when contradictory propositions are accepted or entertained.

This debate could go on, but notice how it has left the imagined sub-personal cognitive psychology behind. That is because the imagined mechanisms are just as much in need of interpretation as the outward behavior, and the same rules apply—and hence conflict. The grounds for saying that "I gave him a dime and a penny" is tacitly represented by the state of the module plus visual memory (etc.) are strong, but so are the grounds for saying they are not strong enough for full belief. So it will be for any telling, I claim. One can always legislate, sweeping the indeterminate cases one way or another for the sake of tidiness. But then one is not using the facts about the inner processes as clues leading to discoveries about a person's beliefs, but just using them as more behavioral grounds for attribution of the sort already gathered—and then running out of patience. Just as "But Bill *told* him that *p*" is powerful but defeasible grounds for attributing the belief that *p* to him (he may not have understood, and he may have forgotten), so is "But the module *told* the rest of the system that it had successfully given change."

This suggests that we are looking in the wrong place when we look at the "peripheral" modules, the sense organs and effectors. Shouldn't we look more "centrally" to the arena wherein "fixation of belief" occurs? (Fodor 1983; Dennett 1984a) The myth that one might find the truth written down in little cubbyholes in the Belief Box dies hard. (See the next two chapters.) It is less compelling, however, in the case of nonhuman objects of the intentional stance, such as frogs.

Frog Psychology

Stich closes his paper with a series of questions:

Ought the frog to believe that there is an insect flying off to the right? Or merely that there is some food there? Or perhaps should it only have a conditional belief: if it flicks its tongue in a certain way, something yummy will end up in its mouth? Suppose the fly is of a species that causes frogs acute indigestion. Ought the frog to believe this? Does it make a difference how many fellow frogs he has seen come to grief after munching on similar bugs? (pp. 60–61)

Let us look more closely at the suggested contrast between us and the frogs. The frog is situated in its environment in a very complicated way, bathed in potentially useful information thanks to the myriad interactions between its sensory receptors and items in the world around it. It is capable at any waking moment of exploiting that bath of information in ways that can be *roughly summarized* by saying things like this:

Now the frog sees your shadow looming. He wants to get away from you. He believes you are right behind him, and since he can't see your net guarding the opening on the left, he thinks that's the way to escape, so he'll jump left.

Let us consider one at a time the mentalistic idioms that are exploited in this adoption of the intentional stance toward a frog. Frogs have eyes so of course in some sense they *see*. Do they really see? (Does a flea really see? Does a blue-eyed scallop really see? It has dozens of eyes that permit it to react to moving patterns of light and shade.) Frog vision, we now know, is quite unlike ours. If our ancestors had guessed how impoverished frog vision was compared with our own, they might not have said that frogs can actually see. Does *any* action-guiding benefit derived from photosensitivity count as seeing? Where do we draw the line? The problem is minor, and largely just lexical, but it can be turned into a philosophical puzzle if one seeks out just the right sort of borderline case.

What about the blind people who have been fitted with prosthetic vision devices? They wear a simple television camera on their heads, and its signal is typically spread over an array of a few hundred tinglers on their back or belly. These people can train themselves to respond perceptually to the crude patterns of light and dark that are detectable by their television cameras, even to the point of being able to identify letters of the alphabet and hence "read" large signs. Does such a prosthesis enable them to *see*? The phenomenon is fascinating, but the philosophical puzzle is not. Once one knows just which perceptual powers enjoyed by normally sighted people can (and cannot) be acquired with such a device, all that remains is to make a tactical lexical decision about whether it would be misleading to call that phenomenon seeing.

From the first-person perspective this seems to leave out the all-important matter: *what it is like* to be informed about the distal world in such a manner. But this has not in fact been left out. In canvassing the perceptual powers of adept users of the device, one learns that the tingles on their skin soon drop out of their awareness; their "point of view" shifts to a point above their heads, and swings as they rotate their heads (Livingston 1978). Doesn't that settle it that this is a sort of seeing? Not for some philosophers. They worry about whether such a system would provide its user with what they take to be the essential intrinsic properties of real seeing. But whatever further essential intrinsic property of seeing they take themselves to distill for our endorsement, they must admit that their supposition that frogs have it (or don't have it) is sheer guesswork. Either we have no way at all of knowing whether frogs really see, or we can go by the capacities of their information-gathering systems, in which case prosthetic human vision is, obviously, one sort of seeing on the same footing as the others. (As usual, the third-person point of view makes progress, while the first-person point of view peters out into a systematically mysterious question about imagined intrinsic properties (see *Brainstorms*, chapter 11, and "Quining Qualia," forthcoming d).

So a frog can see. Frogs also exhibit the sorts of tricky evasive behavior that lead us to interpret them as *wanting to escape,* an interpretation that makes all the more sense because we can easily think of good, justificatory reasons for frogs to "want" to keep their distance from us. And what should we call the contribution of those eyes to the control of those limbs if not *beliefs* about the location of this and that? But do frogs really have beliefs and desires? The gulf between us and frogs seems even greater here than in vision. No frog could believe that whales are mammals or that Friday comes after Thursday, or could want a pizza or hope to visit Rio. It is not just a matter of the remoteness of those topics from frogs' interests either. I believe that frogs have webbed feet and catch flying insects with their tongues, but (it seems) no frog could be properly said to believe those propositions. Does any frog so much as *want to find lots of insects today?*

Even when, in the best possible sort of case, we feel comfortable attributing a belief to the frog—perhaps the belief that a large predator behind it is about to strike—there are apparently no principles available for rendering the content of the attributed belief precise. That is what impresses Stich. What concept of a predator does the frog have? Can we distinguish between its believing that a predator is behind it and believing (more vaguely) that a thing-to-avoid is behind it? When it looks around for flies, can it be said to be looking for flies *qua* flies, or merely *qua* dark, darting, edible things or *qua* something still less specific (see Dennett 1969, chapters 4 and 10)? The occasions that lend themselves to characterizing frogs in terms of their "beliefs" and "desires" are preposterously narrow and imprecise compared to ours. Davidson (1975, p. 16) and Dretske (1985, p. 30) have made similar points.

And yet this anthropomorphizing way of organizing and simplifying our expectations about the frog's next moves is compelling and useful. Treating frogs, birds, monkeys, dolphins, lobsters, honeybees—and not just men, women, and children—from the intentional stance not only comes naturally, but also works extremely well within its narrow range. Try catching frogs without it.

The vast difference in range between an adult human believer and a frog suggests that the application of belief talk and desire talk to frogs is only a metaphorical extension of its proper use in application to human beings, the true believers. This suggestion is immensely persuasive. It is probably the single most powerful source of skepticism toward my position, which maintains that there is nothing more to *our* having beliefs and desires than our being voluminously predictable (like the frog, but more so) from the intentional stance.

I am hit by critics from two sides: those who think that really only we humans have beliefs and those who think that really there are no such things as beliefs. I can rebut both opponents at once by showing just where in tracing out our shared ground they part company from me and then diagnosing the subtle error I take them to be making.

Consider the frog again. As it lies poised motionless on the lily pad, its nervous system is humming with intricate activity. The products of millions of interactions among photons, acoustic pressure waves, receptor cells, internal secretions, and the like interact with each other to produce yet more activities, which eventually yield among their sums the efferent pulses that contract the frog's leg muscles and send it hurtling leftward into the net. One could have predicted that leap if one had known enough biology and had calculated the interactions from a functional blueprint of the frog's nervous system. That would be prediction from the design stance. In principle, one could have been ignorant of the biological principles but known enough physics to predict the frog's leap from a voluminous calculation of the energetic interactions of all the parts, from the physical stance. Laplace's celebrated demon need not have the concept of an efferent neuron whose *function* is to carry a signal that causes a muscle contraction in the frog's leg; it can predict the leap by just tracing the expected physical effects of all those ion-membrane excursions along the path that the biologist would identify, from the design stance, as the axon.

In principle, then, the frog's behavior can be calculated and explained without any invocation of "psychology" at all, from either the ground-floor stance of physics or the slightly elevated design stance of biology. *Frog psychology* can be viewed as a practically useful but theoretically gratuitous shortcut: some pragmatic rules-of-thumb for oversimplifying the complexity. Frog psychology is gratuitous in just this sense: predictions from the physical stance or biological design stance have hegemony over predictions from the intentional stance; no intervening unpredictable "emergent property" or "critical mass effect" stands in the way of, or threatens to falsify, laborious prediction from the lower stances; only complexity stands (practically) in the way of prediction.

Laplace's demon would say exactly the same thing about frog biology, of course; all you really need is frog physics, he would say. But even if we grant that the demon is right in principle, it no doubt seems that the categories of frog biology have a more robust reality than the categories of frog psychology. You can see the frog's nervous system, after all. You can individuate the neurons under a high-powered microscope and measure the state a neuron is in with an implanted microelectrode.

Here is what many, perhaps most, writers on this topic would say: It is obvious that talking of the frog's *desire to escape* or *belief that you are behind him* is not talking precisely about a particular salient state of his nervous system, but just alluding, in an indirect and imprecise way,

to a certain dispositional trend or cast to his current neurophysiological state amenable in principle to an accurate and exhaustive fine-
grained description. It is a vivid and efficient *façon de parler*, but there
are other more scientific ways of speaking. Eventually we will find
the right one for describing the operation of the frog's nervous system. This mature theory of frog neurophysiology may well describe
things in terms of information being carried here and there, processed this way and that, by various neuronal subcomponents, but it
will be silent about the frog's beliefs and desires, because, strictly
speaking, the frog has none.

This is all eminently plausible, and indeed I endorse it all, except
for the tone and the last line: "strictly speaking" implies a mistaken
contrast. It suggests to one school of my critics (Fodor, Dretske, and
other "Realists" about belief) that we are different: we human beings
really have beliefs and desires, and when we attribute a belief to a
human being, this is a nonmetaphorical statement capable of considerable precision. I'm not altogether clear where the individual Realists
draw the line. Fodor (1986) is sure that paramecia don't have beliefs,
but perhaps frogs make it into the charmed circle.

The other school of critics (Stich, the Churchlands, and other
"Eliminativists" about belief) accept the implied contrast and with it
the first group's vision of what *really having a belief* would be. Strictly
speaking, they agree, frogs have no beliefs; but, strictly speaking,
neither do we! There are no such things as beliefs.

I agree that if beliefs had to be what the Realists think they are,
there wouldn't be any beliefs, for frogs or any of us. I am not
tempted, as both groups of critics are, by the contrast between the
frog (as described) and us. No one supposes we are entirely unlike
the frog, of course. We too are bathed in information and have as-
tronomically complicated nervous systems, and many of the transactions that occur within them exhibit froggy under-specificity when
characterized from the intentional stance. For instance, what exactly
is the content of your perceptual "belief" when a looming shadow in
your visual field makes you flinch?

The Illusions of Realism

It seems to the Realists, however, that in addition to those features of
our own behavior that admit of merely metaphorical intentional char-

acterization in the manner of the frog's behavior, we have our genuine beliefs and desires and the actions that we choose to perform on the basis of those beliefs and desires. When we go to explain Mary's suddenly running upstairs by citing her belief that she's left her purse on the bed and her desire to take her purse with her when she goes out, we are not speaking metaphorically, and if we happen to speak imprecisely (didn't she really actually believe just that she'd left her purse *on some flat surface in the bedroom?*), this is always correctable in principle, because there is a definite fact of the matter—say the Realists—about just which content her beliefs and desires have.

Consider Quine's agenda-setting example:

> There is a certain man in a brown hat whom Ralph has glimpsed several times under questionable circumstances on which we need not enter here; suffice it to say that Ralph suspects he is a spy. Also there is a gray-haired man, vaguely known to Ralph as rather a pillar of the community, whom Ralph is not aware of having seen except once at the beach. Now Ralph does not know it, but the men are one and the same. (1956, p. 179)

There is a world of difference between Ralph's believing the proposition that the man in the brown hat is a spy and his believing the proposition that the man he knows as Ortcutt is a spy, even when the man he knows as Ortcutt is the man in the brown hat. Every nuance of meaning capable of expression in our language is capable in principle of distinguishing different human beliefs or desires. As Davidson puts it, "Without speech we cannot make the fine distinctions between thoughts that are essential to the explanations we can sometimes confidently supply. Our manner of attributing attitudes ensures that all the expressive power of language can be used to make such distinctions." (1975, pp. 15–16) It remains true on this view, however, that in the ordinary run of affairs, large families of beliefs travel together in our mental lives. (At one instant Mary believes her purse is on the bed *and* believes her handbag is on some horizontal surface *and* believes the item containing her comb is supported by the article of furniture she sleeps in, etc.—a very long, perhaps indefinitely long, list of further contemporaneous beliefs follows.)

According to this vision, beliefs and desires are *propositional attitudes* and hence are as numerous and distinct as the propositions that are available as completers or objects of the attitudes. Frogs—or at least paramecia—don't strictly speaking have propositional attitudes. That is what is revealed by the problematic looseness and awkwardness of fit when we attempt to get precise about their beliefs and desires. But we human beings do, and "propositional attitude psychology" is psychology properly so called.

The next chapter explores in detail the quandaries that beset anyone who takes this Realist path. Here I am just pointing to the moment where I think the wrong turning occurs: it occurs when the implied contrast is accepted. My view is that belief and desire are like froggy belief and desire *all the way up*. We human beings are only the most prodigious intentional systems on the planet, and the huge psychological differences between us and the frogs are ill described by the proposed contrast between literal and metaphorical belief attribution.

This mispolarization is an illusion born of the fact that we are not just bathed in information the way the frog is; we are also bathed in words. We don't just leap and duck and walk and eat. We assert, deny, request, command, and promise. And in addition to our outer activities of public communication, we have our highly verbal contemplative lives, in which we consider and hypothesize and distinguish and rehearse. When we aren't talking to others, we are talking to ourselves. These words we are bathed in are the words of our natural languages, such as English and Chinese.

Whether or not there is also a language of thought, a more basic symbolic medium realized in our nervous systems and enough like a language to deserve the name, is a distinct question. One of the powerful sources of inspiration for the language of thought hypothesis is an illusion that can arise from the failure to distinguish between the two baths: the bath of information both we and the frogs are immersed in, and the bath of words to which all creatures but humans are oblivious. Given the ubiquity of words, and our incessant working, playing, and fiddling with words, there is an inexhaustible and ever-growing supply of human artifacts composed of words: not just public utterances and inscriptions, but sentences running through our heads to be contemplated, endorsed, discarded, denied, memorized, avowed. These products of human activities are easily confused with beliefs (and desires and other mental states). (See "How to Change Your Mind" in *Brainstorms*.) That is, there is a strong and seldom-resisted temptation to suppose that in identifying one of these verbally infested acts, products, or states one has identified an underlying "internal state exhibiting intentionality," being in which would explain what we take having beliefs to explain when we indulge in folk psychology.

What does Ralph believe about Ortcutt? If we were to suppose that Ralph was a fox terrier or a small child, it would be clear that whatever Ralph believes about Ortcutt, it won't be about Ortcutt *qua* a man named Ortcutt, and it won't be to the effect that he is a spy. The concept of a spy is as dependent on its role in a verbal society as the concept of Thursday or surname. But suppose (as Quine does) that Ralph is an adult language-user, glimpsing the furtive Ortcutt being somehow galvanized by this perceptual event into action. Is this like the frog leaping left? Certainly the "total" content of his perceptual "belief" state is as resistant to precise specification in terms of propositional attitudes as its counterpart in the frog, but it may seem that we can extract or distill a few critical propositions as the completers of the belief attributions we are interested in. This is just because Ralph's action is not to leap to the left (if that is all he was provoked to do, we would consider the whole incident to be nothing more than frog psychology) but to reach for the telephone, or jot down a note, or perhaps just say to himself something that links the man perceived to the word-borne concept of spyhood.

What if Ralph is not galvanized on the occasion into relating himself somehow to any such explicit verbal production, but nevertheless is put by his experience into a dispositional state of some relatively specific wariness *vis-à-vis* Ortcutt? Can *that* state be catalogued via precise propositional attitude attributions? It is a state, let us suppose, determinate enough to control a voluminous verbal response from Ralph were he cross-examined. "What do you make of that man in the brown hat?" would elicit explicit English expressions of propositions in abundance, among them the assertion, "the man is a spy." One thing that happens when we are asked what we ourselves believe is that sentences of our natural languages arise in us as candidates for our endorsement and possible public expression.

This phenomenon is often considered to be (tantamount to) the direct introspective examination of one's beliefs. "How can I tell what I think until I see what I say?" asked E. M. Forster. There is much to be said about this wonderful remark (see *Brainstorms*, chapter 16), but here one point is paramount: while it is certainly true that there is in general no better way to tell what someone (oneself included) thinks than seeing what he says, if one views the clues one gets thereby on the model of, say, the publication of a poem or the release (by the Vatican Library) of a heretofore sequestered volume, one may well be making a mistake along the lines of supposing that a head cold is composed of a large set of internal sneezes, some of which escape. The self-questioning process that individuates belief expressions so crisply need not be revealing any psychologically important underlying individuation (or beliefs, presumably) but be just an artifact of the environmental demand for a particular sort of act. (Churchland 1981, p. 85, offers a speculative account of declarative utterance as a "one-dimensional *projection*—through the compound lens of Wernicke's and Broca's areas onto the idiosyncratic surface of the speaker's language—a one-dimensional projection of a four- or five-dimensional 'solid' that is an element in his true kinematical state." See also Rosenberg 1987.)

No one mistakes reciting a creed with believing what the creed expresses, and no one mistakes saying a sentence to oneself with believing it. Why then do churches and states put so much importance on getting people to perform these acts? Because although such saying is only indirectly connected with believing, it is powerfully connected with it. What church and state hope to achieve is the inculcation of the belief "behind" the saying. They want to turn mere saying into wholehearted judging. Is there then also judging that is not wholehearted? Suppose one "makes a judgment" in one's head. This is commonly supposed to be an act that quite directly manifests a belief—perhaps inaugurates a belief state, perhaps *is* an "occurrent belief." Can one make a judgment without believing it? Is there such a phenomenon as insincere judgment? (A puzzle within folk psychology.)

We can agree in any case that what explains one's actions is not the peripheral state of having related oneself to a public language product, but the more central state of belief. We don't explain Lulu's buying the lasagna by just citing the fact that she earlier wrote "lasagna" on her list; she has to have the relevant beliefs and desires to back up her interpretation of the inscription as a shopping list. And suppose she has the list memorized; she still has to interpret the words running through her head as a shopping list, and for this she needs those same beliefs and desires. What are they? Still more linguistic objects, but this time in Mentalese, not English—so sayeth the believers in the language of thought.

The language of thought hypothesis does not deny the obvious fact that we often do have *natural-language* sentences and phrases parading in our heads; it claims that behind the production of natural-language sentences (in the head or in public) are yet more sentences, in a more fundamental, unlearned language. As we shall see (in the next two chapters) there are good reasons for wanting to talk of a systematic medium of representation in the brain, but the idea that the elements of such a medium, the vehicles of meaning, must gather content in the sorts of bunches typical of sentences of natural language needs independent support. Without that support, what reason is there to suppose that human belief is all that different from frog belief? In both cases behavior is controlled by a complex internal state that can be *alluded to* more or less effectively by the everyday folk practices of belief attribution and desire attribution. If in one case it seems that the beliefs are much more finely and precisely individuated by their contents, this may be because we are attending not to the "individual beliefs" themselves (there may not be any such scheme of individuation), but to the products of linguistic behaviors controlled by those complex internal states, which products are *ipso facto* as distinct as the discriminations in that language allow.

Consider one of Fodor's examples of the doctrine of "Standard Realism": "To know that John thinks that Mary wept is to know that it's highly probable that he thinks that somebody wept. To know that Sam thinks that it is raining is to know that it's highly probable that he thinks that either it is raining or that John left and Mary wept." (1985, p. 87) The use of the verb "thinks" throughout this example is symptomatic of the Realist confusion, on my view. It is not implausible to claim that if John can be provoked to think (in the sense of occurrent "saying-to-oneself") "Mary wept," he can, without further instruction, be provoked to think (to assent to the sentence) "Somebody wept." As a doctrine about what it is probable that people *would do* in the thinking department under various provocations, this has some plausibility. As a doctrine about what different, individuated, internal states a suitably equipped theorist probably *would find* on peering into the subject's belief center, it has no plausibility at all.

If we pumped Ralph long enough, we would get some declarations that would best be ignored as unreliable or misleading indicators of Ralph's state. Perhaps Ralph, not really having a good grasp of the terms "insidious" and "double agent," makes some assertions that ill inform us about families of his expectations, his dispositions to infer, and so forth. Even if Ralph is master of his vocabulary, his attempts to express himself, as we say, may be halfhearted or injudicious.

On the Realist view, there has to be a fact—however hard to determine—about exactly what content (which means: exactly which *proposition*) is to be found in Ralph's belief. The artifactual puzzles that arise when one tries to articulate a coherent and psychologically plausible set of principles for characterizing this content have spawned such a cottage industry of philosophical theory tinkering that one group of neighboring universities has for years had a "propositional attitude task force" hard pressed to keep up with the literature. Recently, however, there have been some notable changes of heart, as the quandaries have mounted. As Loar (forthcoming) notes, "It seems to me now somewhat extraordinary that we should have thought that psychological states are captured by a neat set of content-specifications."

I agree wholeheartedly, then, with Stich and the Churchlands that the ingenuity of this recent outpouring puts one in mind of the late blooming of Ptolemaic epicycles. But the guiding Realist vision of "propositional attitude psychology" of human beings is still for many people in stark contrast to what it seems comfortable to acknowledge in the case of the frog as an intentional system: an intentional stance characterization of a frog is always an idealization, and any idealization will fit the brute facts at the physical or design level only so well. Beyond the facts about just where and how the best approximation at the intentional level proves to be misleading, there simply are no facts about what the frog "really believes." The strategy, applied to a frog, neither needs nor permits that sort of precision.[1]

Some may still not be convinced that the same moral applies to us. Some may still hold out hope of salvaging a Realist theory of *human* propositional attitudes. The next two chapters, and the reflections that follow them, should dash that hope and replace it with a more realistic (if less Realistic) sense of what academic psychology might make of folk psychology.

---

1. The limits of precision in attribution of intentional states to a frog have recently been examined in considerable, and compelling, detail by Israel (unpublished). In the years since the classic paper "What the Frog's Eye Tells the Frog's Brain" by Lettvin, Maturana, McCulloch, and Pitts (1959), philosophers have often featured frogs (and toads) in their analyses of mental content. It is instructive to compare the discussions in Dennett (1969, pp. 48, 76–83), Stich (1981), Millikan (1986), and chapter 8 of this volume to Israel's much more elaborate account, a brand of "naturalized realism" presented as an alternative to Fodor's Realism, and to Ewert (forthcoming), a detailed presentation of what can currently be said from the design stance about prey-catching in toads.

5   Beyond Belief

Suppose we want to talk about beliefs. Why might we want to talk about beliefs? Not just "because they are there," for it is far from obvious that they *are* there. Beliefs have a less secure position in a critical scientific ontology than, say, electrons or genes, and a less robust presence in the everyday world than, say, toothaches or haircuts. Giving grounds for believing in beliefs is not a gratuitous exercise, but not hopeless either. A plausible and familiar reason for wanting to talk about beliefs would be: because we want to explain and predict human (and animal) behavior. That is as good a reason as any for wanting to talk about beliefs, but it may not be good enough. It may not be good enough because when one talks about beliefs one implicates oneself in a tangle of philosophical problems from which there may be no escape—save giving up talking about beliefs. In this essay I shall try to untangle, or at least expose, some of these problems and suggest ways in which we might salvage some theoretically interesting and useful versions of, or substitutes for, the concept of belief.

Here is a synopsis of the exploratory journey lying ahead. First, I focus the principal problem: while it is widely accepted that beliefs are *propositional attitudes*, there is no stable and received interpretation of that technical term. In the next section, "Propositional Attitudes," I describe several incompatible doctrines about propositions, and hence about propositional attitudes, that have been developed as responses to Frege's demands on propositions or "Thoughts." Recently, Putnam and others have presented attacks, with a common theme, on all versions of the standard doctrine. In "Sentential At-

Originally published in A. Woodfield, ed., *Thought and Object* (Oxford: Clarendon Press, 1982), and reprinted with permission.

titudes" I discuss the retreat from these attacks that leads (as do other theoretical considerations) to postulating a "language of thought," but I show there are serious unsolved problems with this position. In"Notional Attitudes" I sketch an alternative midway, in effect, between propositional attitudes and sentential attitudes—neither purely syntactic nor fully semantic. It involves positing a theorists's fiction: the subject's *notional world*. In the final section, "*De re* and *de dicto* Dismantled," the foregoing reflections yield alternative diagnoses of the panoply of intuitions conjured up by the *de re/de dicto* literature. These observations grant us the prospect of getting along just fine without anything that could properly be called the distinction between *de re* and *de dicto* beliefs.

I shall be going over very familiar territory, and virtually everything I shall say has been said before, often by many people, but I think that my particular collection of familiar points, and perhaps the order and importance I give them, will shed some new light on the remarkably resilient puzzles that have grown up in the philosophical literature on belief: puzzles about the content of belief, the nature of belief-states, reference or *aboutness* in belief, and the presumed distinction between *de re* and *de dicto* (or *relational* and *notional*) beliefs. No "theory" of belief will be explicitly propounded and defended. I have not yet seen what such a philosophical theory would be for, which is just as well, since I would be utterly incapable of producing one in any case. Rather, this essay is exploratory and diagnostic, a prelude, with luck, to empirical theories of the phenomena that we now commonly discuss in terms of belief.

If we understand the project to be *getting clear about the concept of belief*, there are still several different ways of conceiving of the project. One way is to consider it a small but important part of the semantics of natural language. Sentences with ". . . believes that . . ." and similar formulae in them are frequently occurring items of the natural language English, and so one might wish to regiment the presuppositions and implications of their use, much as one would for other natural-language expressions, such as "yesterday" or "very" or "some." Many of the philosophers contributing to the literature on belief contexts take themselves to be doing just that—just that and nothing more—but typically in the course of explicating their proposed solutions to the familiar puzzles of the semantic theory of "believes" in English, they advert to doctrines that put them willynilly in a different project: defending (that is, defending *as true*) a *psychological* theory (or at least a theory-sketch) of beliefs considered as psychological states. This drift from natural-language semantics (or for that matter, conceptual analysis or ordinary-language philosophy) to metatheory for psychology is natural if not quite inevitable, traditional if not quite ubiquitous, and even defensible—so long as one recognizes the drift and takes on the additional burdens of argument as one tackles the metatheoretical problems of psychology. Thus Quine, Putnam, Sellars, Dummett, Fodor, and many others have observations to make about how a psychological theory of belief *must go*. There is nothing wrong with drawing such conclusions from one's analysis of the concept of belief, just so long as one remembers that if one's conclusions are sound, and no psychological theory *will* go as one concludes it *must*, the correct further conclusion to draw is: so much the worse for the concept of belief.

If we still want to talk about beliefs (pending such a discovery), we must have some way of picking them out or referring to them or distinguishing them from each other. If beliefs are real—that is, real psychological states of people—there must be indefinitely many ways of referring to them, but for some purposes some ways will be more useful than others. Suppose for instance it was books rather than beliefs that we wished to talk about. One can pick out a book by its title or its text, or by its author, or by its topic, or by the physical location of one of its copies ("the red book on the desk"). What counts as *the same book* depends somewhat on our concerns of the moment: sometimes we mean *the same edition* ("I refer, of course to the First Folio *Hamlet*"); sometimes we mean merely *the same text* (modulo a few errors or corrections); sometimes merely the same text or a good translation of it (otherwise how many of us could claim to have read any books by Tolstoy?). This last conception of a book is in some regards privileged: it is *what we usually mean* when we talk—without special provisos or contextual cues—about the books we have read or written or want to buy. We use "a copy of . . ." to prefix the notion of a book in more concrete transactions. You might refute your opponent with *Word and Object* or, failing that, hit him over the head with *a copy of . . . Being and Time*.

There is similar room for variation in talking about beliefs, but the privileged way of referring to beliefs, what we usually mean and are taken to mean in the absence of special provisos or contextual cues, is *the proposition believed*: e.g., the belief that snow is white, which is *the same belief* when believed by Tom, Dick, and Harry, and also when believed by monolingual Frenchmen—though the particular belief *tokens* in Tom, Dick, Harry, Alphonse, and the rest, like the individual, dog-eared and ink-stained personal copies of a book, might differ in all sorts of ways that were not of interest to us given our normal purposes in talking about beliefs (Burge 1979).

Beliefs, standardly, are viewed as *propositional attitudes*. The term is Russell's (1940). There are three degrees of freedom in the formulae of propositional attitude: person, attitude type, proposition; x believes that p, or y believes that p; x *believes* that p or *fears* that p or *hopes* that p; x believes that p or that q, and so forth. So we can speak of a person believing many different propositions, or of a proposition being believed by many different people, or even of a proposition being variously "taken" by different people, or by the same person at different times—I used to doubt that p, but now I am certain that p. There are other ways of referring to beliefs, such as "the belief that made Mary blush" or "McCarthy's most controversial belief," but these are parasitic; one can go on to ask after such a reference: "and which belief is that?" in hopes of getting an *identifying* reference—e.g., "Mary's belief that Tom knew her secret." Some day (some people think) we will be able to identify beliefs neurophysiologically ("the belief in Tom's cortex with physical feature F"), but for the present, at least, we have no way of singling out a belief the way we can single out a book by a physical description of one of its copies or tokens.

The orthodoxy of the view that beliefs are propositional attitudes persists in spite of a host of problems. There have always been relatively "pure" *philosophers'* problems, about the metaphysical status and identity conditions for propositions, for instance, but with the new-found interest in cognitive science, there must now be added the *psychologists'* problems, about the conditions for individual instantiation of belief-states, for instance. The attempt to harness propositional attitude talk as a descriptive medium for empirical theory in psychology puts a salutary strain on the orthodox assumptions and is prompting a rethinking by philosophers. In the nick of time, one might add, since it is distinctly unsettling to observe the enthusiasm with which nonphilosophers in cognitive science are now adopting propositional attitude formulations for their own purposes, in the innocent belief that any concept so popular among philosophers must be sound, agreed upon, and well tested. If only it were so.

Propositional Attitudes

If we think that a good way of characterizing a person's psychological state is characterizing that person's propositional attitudes, then we must suppose that a critical requirement for getting the *right* psychological description of a person will be specifying the *right* propositions for those attitudes. This in turn requires us to make up our minds about what a proposition is and, more important, to have some stable view about what counts as two different propositions and what counts as one. But there is no consensus on these utterly fundamental matters. In fact, there are three quite different general characterizations of propositions in the literature.

(1) Propositions are *sentence-like entities,* constructed from parts according to a syntax. Like sentences, propositions admit of a type-token distinction; proposition tokens of the same proposition type are to be found in the minds (or brains) of believers of the same belief. It must be this view of propositions that is being appealed to in the debate among cognitive scientists about *forms of mental representation*: is all mental representation propositional, or is some imagistic or analogue? Among philosophers, Harman (1973, 1977) is most explicit in the expression of this view of propositions.

(2) Propositions are *sets of possible worlds.* Two sentences express the same proposition just in case they are true in exactly the same set of possible worlds. On this view propositions themselves have no syntactic properties, and one cannot speak of their having instances or tokens in a brain or mind, or on a page. Stalnaker (1976, 1984) defends this view of propositions. See also Field (1978) and Lewis (1979) for other good discussions of this oft-discussed view.

(3) Propositions are something like *collections or arrangements of objects and properties in the world.* The proposition that Tom is tall consists of Tom (himself) and the attribute or property tallness. Russell held such a view, and Donnellan (1974), Kaplan (1973, 1978, 1980), and Perry (1977, 1979) have recently defended special versions of it. Echoes of the theme can be heard in many different places—for instance in correspondence theories of truth that claim that what makes a sentence true is correspondence with a fact "in the world"—where a fact turns out to be a true proposition.

What seems to me to unite this disparate group of views about what propositions *are* is a set of three classical demands about what propositions must *do* in a theory. The three demands are due to Frege, whose notion of a *Thought* is the backbone of the currently orthodox understanding of propositions (see Perry 1977). And the diversity of doctrine about propositions is due to the fact that these three demands cannot be simultaneously satisfied, as we shall see. According to the Fregean view, a proposition (a Fregean Thought) must have three defining characteristics:

(a) It is a (final, constant, underived) *truth-value-bearer*. If *p* is true and *q* is false, *p* and *q* are not the same proposition. (See Stich 1978a: "If a pair of states can be type identical . . . while differing in truth value, then the states are not beliefs as we ordinarily conceive of them.") (See also Fodor 1980.)

This condition is required by the common view of propositions as the ultimate medium of information transfer. If I know *something* and communicate *it* to you (in English, or French, or by a gesture or by drawing a picture) what you acquire is *the proposition* I know. One can befriend condition (a) without subscribing to this view of communication or information transfer, however. Evans (1980) is an example.

(b) It is composed of *intensions*, where intensions are understood *à la* Carnap as extension-determiners. Different intensions can determine the same extension: the intension of "three squared" is not the intension of "the number of planets" but both determine the same extension. Different extensions cannot be determined by one intension, however.

To say that intensions determine extensions is not to say that intensions are *means* or *methods* of figuring out extensions. Evans, in lectures in Oxford in 1979, has drawn attention to the tendency to slide into this understanding of intensions and has suggested that it contributes plausibility to views such as Dummett's (1973, 1975) to the effect that what one knows when one knows meanings (or intensions) is something like a route or method of verification or procedure. Whether this plausibility is entirely spurious is an open, and important, question.

Condition (b) cuts two ways. First, since the intensions of which a proposition is composed fix their extensions in the world, *what a proposition is about* is one of its defining characteristics. If *p* is about *a* and q is not about a, p and q are not the same proposition. Second, since extension does not determine intension, the fact that p and q are both about a, and both attribute F to a, does not suffice to show that p and q are the same proposition; p and q may be about a "in different ways"—they may refer to a via different intensions.

(For Frege, conditions (a) and (b) were unified by his doctrine that a declarative sentence in its entirety had an extension: either the True or the False. In other words, the intensional whole, the Thought, determines an extension just as its parts do, but whereas its parts determine objects or sets as extensions, the Thought itself has as its extension either the True or the False.)

(c) It is "graspable" by the mind.

Frege does not tell us anything about what grasping a Thought consists in, and has often been criticized for this. What mysterious sort of transaction between the mind (or brain) and an abstract, Platonic object—the Thought—is this supposed to be? (See, e.g., Fodor 1975, 1980; Field 1978; Harman 1977.) This question invites an excursion into heavy-duty metaphysics and speculative psychology, but that excursion can be postponed by noting, as Churchland (1979) urges, that the catalogue of propositional attitude predicates bears a tempting analogy with the catalogue of physical measure predicates. A small sample:

. . . believes that p	. . . has a length of meters of n
. . . desires that p	. . . has a volume in meters^3 of n
. . . suspects that p	. . . has a velocity in m/sec of n
. . . is thinking that p	. . . has a temperature in degrees K of n

Churchland's suggestion is that the metaphysical implications, if any, of the propositional attitude predicates are the same as those of the physical measure predicates:

The idea that believing that p is a matter of standing in some appropriate relation to an abstract entity (the proposition that p) seems to me to have nothing more to recommend it than would the parallel suggestion that weighing 5 kg is at bottom a matter of standing in some suitable relation to an abstract entity (the number 5). For contexts of this latter kind, at least, the relational construal is highly procrustean. Contexts like

x weighs 5 kg
x moves at 5 m/sec
x radiates at 5 joules/sec

are more plausibly catalogued with contexts like

x weighs very little
x moves quickly
x radiates copiously.

In the latter three cases, what follows the main verb has a transparently *adverbial* function. The same adverbial function, I suggest, is being performed in the former cases as well. The only difference is that using singular terms for number in adverbial position provides a more precise, systematic, and useful way of modifying the main verb, especially when said position is open to quantification. (1979, p. 105).

This construal of propositional attitudes does not by itself dissolve the metaphysical problems about propositions, as we shall see, but by binding their fate to the fate of numbers in physics, it disarms the suspicion that there is a *special* problem about abstract objects in psychology. Moreover, it permits us to distinguish two views that are often run together. It is often thought that *taking propositions seriously* in psychology must involve taking propositions to *play a causal role* of some sort in psychological events. Thus one is led to ask, as Harman (1977) does, about the *function* of propositions *in thought.* For propositions to have such a function, they must be concrete—or have concrete tokens—and this leads one inevitably to a version of view (1): propositions are sentence-like entities. One could not suppose that sets of possible worlds or arrangements of things and properties were themselves "in the head," and only something in the head could play a causal role in psychology. One might take propositions seriously, however, without committing oneself to this line; one might take them just as seriously as physicists take numbers. On Churchland's construal, the *function* of a proposition is just to be the denotation of a singular term completing the "adverbial" modifier in a predicate of propositional attitude, a predicate we want to use to characterize someone's thought or belief or other psychological state. This is *not* the view that takes propositional attitude predicates to have no logical structure; indeed it holds out the promise that the formal relations among propositions, like the formal relations among numbers, can be usefully exploited in forming the predicates of a science. It is the view that propositions are abstract objects useful in "measuring" the psychological states of creatures. This leaves it open for us to prove or discover later that whenever a creature has a particular propositional attitude, something in the creature mirrors the "form" of the proposition—e.g., is somehow isomorphic or homomorphic with the (canon-ically expressed) clause that *expresses* the proposition in the sentence of propositional attitude. One need not, and should not, presuppose any version of this strong claim, however, as part of one's initial understanding of the meaning of propositional attitude predicates.[1]

Failure to make this distinction, and stick to it, has created a frustrating communication problem in the literature. In a typical instance, a debate arises about the *form* of the propositions in some special context of propositional attitude: e.g., are the propositions in question universally quantified conditionals, or indefinitely long disjunctions, or is there self-reference within the propositions? What is not made clear is whether the debate is taken to be about the actual form of internal cerebral structures (in which case, for instance, the unwieldiness of indefinitely long disjunctions poses a real problem), or is rather a debate just about the correct logical form of the abstract objects, the propositions that are required to complete the predicates under discussion (in which case infinite disjunctions need pose no more problems than π in physics). Perhaps some debaters are beguiled by a tacit assumption that the issue cannot be real or substantial unless it is an issue *directly* about the physical form of structures ("syntactic" structures) in the brain, but other debaters understand that this is not so, and hence persist on their side of the debate

---

1. Field (in a postscript to Field 1978, in Block 1980, vol. 2) sees this view leading inevitably to the strong claim:

The theory of measurement . . . explains why real numbers can be used to "measure" mass (better: to serve as a scale for mass). It does this in the following way. First, certain properties and relations among massive objects are cited—properties and relations that are specifiable without reference to numbers. Then a representation theorem is proved: such a theorem says that if any system of objects has the properties and relations cited, then there is a mapping of that system into the real numbers which "preserves structure." Consequently, assigning real numbers to the objects is a convenient way of discussing the intrinsic mass-relations that those objects have, but those intrinsic relations don't themselves require the existence of real numbers. . . .

Can we solve Brentano's problem of the intentionality of propositional attitudes in an analogous way? To do so we would have to postulate a *system of entities* [my italics] inside the believer which was related via a structure-preserving mapping to the system of propositions. The "structure" that such a mapping would have to preserve would be the kind of structure important to propositions; viz., logical structure, and this I think means that the system of entities inside the believer can be viewed as a system of sentences—an internal system of representation. (p. 114)

For massive objects we postulate or isolate "properties and relations"; why not properties and relations, rather than "a system of entities," in the case of psychological subjects? Whatever might be "measured" by propositional attitude predicates is measured indirectly, and Field's opting for a language of thought to "explain" the success (the extent of which is still uncharted) of propositional measurement is a premature guess, not an implication of this view of the predicates.

without acknowledging the live possibility that the two sides are talking past each other. To avoid this familiar problem I shall cleave explicitly to the minimal, Churchland interpretation as a neutral base of operations from which to explore the prospects of the stronger interpretations.

With this metaphysically restrained conception of propositional attitudes in mind, we can then define Frege's elusive notion of graspability quite straightforwardly: propositions are graspable if and only if predicates of propositional attitude are projectible, predictive, well-behaved predicates of psychological theory. (One might in the same spirit say that the success of physics, with its reliance on numbers as predicate-forming functors, shows that numbers are graspable by physical objects and processes!) The rationale for this version of graspability is that Frege's demand that propositions be something the mind can grasp is tantamount to the demand that propositions *make a difference* to a mind; that is to say, to a creature's psychological state. What a person does is supposed to be a function of his psychological state; variations in psychological state should predict variations in behavior. (That's what a psychological state is supposed to be: a state, variation in which is critical to behavior.)[2] Now if people's psychological states vary directly with their propositional attitude characterizations so that, for instance, changing one's propositional attitudes is changing one's psychological state and sharing a propositional attitude with another is being psychologically similar in some way to the other, then propositions figure systematically in a perspicuous interpretation of the psychology of people—and a vivid way of putting this would be to say that people (or dogs or cats, if that is how the facts turn out) grasp the propositions that figure in the psychological predicates that apply to them. No more marvelous sort of "entertaining" of either abstract objects or their concrete stand-ins is—*as of yet*—implied by asserting condition (c). Frege no doubt had something more ambitious in mind, but this weaker version of graspability is sufficiently demanding to create the conflict between condition (c) and conditions (a) and (b).

---

2. *Having a big red nose* is a state that can figure prominently in one's psychology, but it is not itself a psychological state. *Believing that one has a big red nose* is one of the many psychological states that would typically go with having a big red nose, and without which the state of having a big red nose would tend to be psychologically inert (like having a big red liver). (This just ostends, and does not pretend to explicate, the intuitive distinctions between psychological states and the other states of a creature.)

A number of writers have recently offered arguments to show that conditions (a–c) are not jointly satisfiable; what is graspable cannot at the same time be an extension-determiner or ultimate truth-value-bearer: Putnam (1975a), Fodor (1980), Perry (1977, 1979), Kaplan (1980), Stich (1978a). (Among the many related discussions, see especially McDowell 1977 and Burge 1979.)

First there is Putnam's notorious thought experiment about Twin Earth. Briefly (since we will not pause now to explore the myriad objections that have been raised), the imagined case is this: there is a planet, Twin Earth, that is a near duplicate of Earth, right down to containing replicas or *Doppelgängers* of all the people, places, things, events, on Earth. There is one difference: lakes, rivers, clouds, water-pipes, bathtubs, living tissues . . . contain not H_2O but XYZ— something chemically different but indistinguishable in its normally observable macro-properties, from water, that is to say, H_2O. Twin Earthians *call* this liquid "water," of course, being atom-for-atom replicas of us (ignore the high proportion of water molecules in us, for the sake of the argument!). Now since my *Doppelgänger* and I are *physical* replicas (please, for the sake of the argument), we are surely *psychological* replicas as well: we instantiate all the same theories above the level at which H_2O and XYZ are distinguishable. We have all the same psychological states then. But where my beliefs are about water, my *Doppelgänger's* beliefs (though of exactly the same "shape") are not about water, but about XYZ. We believe different propositions. For instance, the belief I would express with the words "water is H_2O" is *about water*, and *true*; its counterpart in my *Doppelgänger*, which he would express with just the same sounds, of course, is *not* about water but about what he calls "water," namely XYZ, and it is *false*. We are psychological twins, but not propositional attitude twins. Propositional attitudes can vary independently of psychological state, so propositions (understood "classically" as meeting conditions (a) and (b)) are not graspable. As Putnam puts it, something must give: either meaning "ain't in the head" or meaning doesn't determine extension.

Stich (1978a) points out that it is instructive to compare this result with a similar but less drastic point often made about the state of *knowing*. It is often remarked that whereas "believes" is a psychological verb, "knows" is not—or not purely—a psychological verb, since *x knows that p* entails the truth of *p*, something that must in general be external to the psychology of *x*. Hence, it is said, while *believing that p* may be considered a pure psychological (or mental) state, *knowing that p* is a "mongrel" or "hybrid" state, partly psychological, partly something else—epistemic. In this case it is the verb component of the predicate of propositional attitude that renders the whole predicate psychologically impure and nonprojectible. (Note that it *is* nonprojectible: simple experiments involving deception or illusion would immediately show that "*x* will press the button when *x* knows that *p*" is a less reliable predictor than, say, "*x* will press the button when *x* is sure that *p*.") What Putnam's thought experiment claims to show, however, is that even when the verb is an apparently pure psychological verb, the mere fact that the propositional component (*any* propositional component) must meet conditions (a) and (b) renders the entire predicate psychologically impure.

Putnam's thought experiment is hardly uncontroversial. As it stands it rests on dubious doctrines of natural kinds and rigid designation, but easy variations on his basic theme can avoid at least some of the most common objections. For instance, suppose Twin Earth is just like Earth except that my wallet is in my coat pocket and my *Doppelgänger*'s wallet isn't in his coat pocket. I believe (truly) that my wallet is in my coat pocket. My *Doppelgänger* has the counterpart belief. His is false, mine is true; his is not about what mine is about—viz., *my* wallet. Different propositions, different propositional attitudes, same psychology.

In any event, Kaplan (1980) has produced an argument about a similar case, with a similar conclusion, which is perhaps more compelling since it does not rely on going along with outlandish thought experiments about near-duplicate universes or on the intuitions about natural kinds Putnam must invoke to support the claim that XYZ is not just "another kind of water."

Kaplan quotes Frege (1956):

If someone wants to say the same today as he expressed yesterday using the word "today," he must replace this word with "yesterday." Although the thought is the same its verbal expression must be different so that the sense, which would otherwise be affected by the differing times of utterance, is readjusted.

But he goes on to note what Frege missed:

If one says "Today is beautiful" on Tuesday and "Yesterday was beautiful" on Wednesday, one expresses the same thought according to the passage quoted. Yet one can clearly lose track of the days and not realize one is expressing the same thought [Fregean Thought, our proposition]. It seems then that thoughts are not appropriate bearers of cognitive significance.

Perry offers yet another argument, which will be discussed later, and there are still further arguments and persuasions to be found in the literature cited earlier.[3]

I do not want to endorse any of these arguments here and now, but I also want to resist the urge—which few can resist, apparently—to dig the trenches here and now and fight to the death on the terrain provided by reflections on Twin Earth, Natural Kinds, and What Frege Really Meant. I propose to yield a little ground and see where we are led.

Suppose these arguments are sound. What is their conclusion? One claim to be extracted from Kaplan (to which Putnam and Perry would assent, I gather) is this: If there is some indexical functor in my thought or belief, such as "now" or "today," the proposition I am "related to"—the proposition that fills the slot in the correct propositional attitude predicate applied to me—can depend crucially (but imperceptibly to me) on such events as the moving of a clock hand at the Greenwich Observatory. But it is frankly incredible to suppose that my psychological state (my behavior-predicting state) might depend not just on my internal constitution at the time but at the least also on such causally remote features as the disposition of the parts of some official timekeeper. That is not to say that my future behavior and psychology might not be *indirectly* a function of my actual propositional attitudes on occasion—however unknown to me they were. For instance, if I bet on a horse or deny an accusation under oath, the *long-range* effects of this action on me may be more accurately predicted from the proposition I *in fact* expressed (and even believed—see Burge 1979) than from the proposition I as it were took myself to be expressing—or believing.[4] This acknowledgment, however, only heightens the contrast between the unreliable or variable "accessibil-

---

3. One of the simplest and most convincing is due to Vendler (in conversation): suppose over a ten-year period I believe that Angola is an independent nation. Intuitively, this is a *constancy* of psychological state—something about me that does not change—and yet this one belief of mine can change in truth-value during the decade. Counting my state as one enduring belief, it cannot be a *propositional* attitude.

4. One could sum up the case Putnam, Kaplan, and Perry present thus: propositions are not *graspable* because they can *elude* us; the presence or absence of a particular proposition "in our grasp" can be psychologically irrelevant.

ity" of propositions and the built-in or constitutive accessibility of . . . *what*? If propositions in the Fregean mold are seen by these arguments to be psychologically inert (at least under certain special circumstances), what is the more accessible, graspable, effective object for the propositional role?

Sentential Attitudes

With what shall we replace propositions? The most compelling answer (if only to judge by the number of its sympathizers) is: something like *sentences in the head*. (See, e.g., Fodor 1975, 1980; Field 1978; Kaplan 1980; Schiffer 1978; Harman 1977—but for some eminent second thoughts, see Quine 1969.) In the end we shall find this answer unsatisfactory, but understanding its appeal is an essential preliminary, I think, to the task of finding a better retreat from propositions. There are many routes to *sentential attitudes*.

Here is the simplest: when one *figuratively* "grasps" a proposition, which is an abstract object, one must *literally* grasp something concrete but somehow proposition-like. What could this be but a sentence in the mind or brain—a sentence of Mentalese? (For those who already hold the view that propositions are sentence-like things, this is a short retreat indeed; it consists of giving up conditions (a) and (b) for propositions—but then, if propositions are to be something more than mere uninterpreted sentences, what more are they? Something must be put in place of (a) and (b).)

Here is another route to sentential attitudes. What are the actual *constituents* of belief-states about dogs and cats? Not real live dogs and cats, obviously, but . . . symbols for, or representations of, dogs and cats. The belief that the cat is on the mat consists somehow of a structured representation composed of symbols for the cat and the mat and the *on* relation—a sentence of sorts (or maybe a picture of sorts[5])—to which its contemplator says "Yes!" It is not that belief doesn't eventually have to tie the believer to the world, to real live dogs and cats, but the problem of that tying relation can be isolated and postponed. It is turned into the apparently more tractable and

---

5. The issues running in the mental-words-versus-mental-pictures controversies are largely orthogonal to the issues discussed here, which concern problems that must be solved before *either* mental images or mental sentences could be given a clean bill of health as theoretical entities.

familiar problem of the *reference* of the terms in sentences—in this case inner mental sentences. One imagines that the great horses of logical instruction—Frege, Carnap, Tarski—can be straightforwardly harnessed for this task. (See Field 1978 for the most explicit defense of this route.)

Here is the third route. We need a physical, causal explanation of the phenomenon of opacity; the fact that believing that it would be nice to marry Jocasta is a state with different psychological consequences, different effects in the world, from the state of believing that it would be nice to marry the mother of Oedipus, in spite of the now well-known identity. A tempting suggestion is that these two different states, in their physical realizations in a believer, have in effect a syntax, and the syntax of one state resembles and differs from the syntax of the other in just the ways the two sentences of attribution resemble and differ; and that the different effects of the two states can be traced eventually to these differences in physical structure. This can be viewed as an explanation of the opacity of *indirect* discourse by subsuming it under the *super*-opacity of a bit of *direct* discourse—the strict quotation, in effect, of different Mentalese sentences (Fodor 1980).

Here, finally, is the route to sentential attitudes of most immediate relevance to the problems we have discovered with propositional attitudes. Apparently what makes the Frege–Kaplan "today" and "yesterday" example work is what might be called the impermeability of propositions to indexicals. This impermeability is made explicit in Quine's surrogate for propositions, *eternal sentences,* which are equipped whenever needed with bound variables of time and place and person to remove the variable or perspectival effect of indexicals (Quine 1960). A psychologically perspicuous alternative to propositions would resist precisely this move and somehow build indexical elements in where needed. An obvious model is ready to hand: sentences—ordinary, external, concrete, uttered sentences of natural languages, spoken or written. Sentences are to be understood first and foremost as syntactically individuated objects—as strings of symbols of particular "shapes"—and it is a standard observation about sentences so individuated that tokens of a particular sentence type may "express" different propositions depending on "context." Tokens of the sentence type "I am tired" express different propositions in different mouths at different times; sometimes "I am tired" expresses a true proposition about Jones, and sometimes a false proposition about Smith. Perhaps there are, as Quine claims, some sentence types, the eternal sentences, all of whose tokens in effect express the same proposition. (Quine—no friend of propositions—must be more devious in making this claim.) But it is precisely the power of the other, *non*-eternal sentences to be context-*bound* that is needed, intuitively, for the role of individuating psychologically salient states and events. Indexicality of sentences appears to be the linguistic counterpart of that relativity to a subjective point of view that is a hallmark of mental states (Castañeda 1966, 1967, 1968; Perry 1977, 1979; Kaplan 1980; Lewis 1979).

If *what a sentence means* were taken to be *the proposition it expresses*, then different tokens of an indexical sentence type will mean different things, and yet there does seem both room and need for a sense of "meaning" according to which we can say that all tokens of a sentence type *mean the same thing*. A sentence *type*, even an indexical type such as "I am tired," means something—just one "thing"—and hence in this sense so do all its tokens. That same thing is no proposition, of course. Call it, Kaplan suggests, the sentence's *character*. "The character of an expression is set by linguistic conventions and, in turn, determines the content of the expression in every context." Kaplan's suggestion unfolds into a symmetrical two-stage picture of sentence interpretation:

Just as it was convenient to represent contents by functions from possible circumstances to extensions (Carnap's intensions), so it is convenient to represent characters by functions from possible contexts of utterance to contents. · · · This gives us the following picture:

Character: Contexts → Content
Content: Circumstances → Extensions

or in more familiar language,

Meaning + Context → Intension
Intension + Possible World → Extension

Although Kaplan is talking about public, external sentences—not sentences in the head, in Mentalese or brain writing—the relevance of this sort of linguistic meaning to psychology is immediately apparent. Kaplan comments: "Because character is what is set by linguistic conventions, it is natural to think of it as *meaning* in the sense of what is known by the competent language user." No mastery of my native tongue will ensure that I can tell *what proposition* I have expressed when I utter a sentence, but my competence as a native speaker does, apparently, give me access to the *character* of what I have said. Could we not generalize the point to the postulated language of thought and treat the character of Mentalese sentences as what is directly grasped when one "entertains" (mentally "utters") a Mentalese sentence? Couldn't the *objects* of belief be the characters of Mentalese sentences instead of the propositions they express?

Commenting on Kaplan, Perry (1977, 1979) develops this theme. Where Kaplan speaks of *expressions* of the same *character*, Perry moves the issue inside the mind and speaks of people *entertaining* the same *senses*, and where Kaplan speaks of *expressions* having the same *content*, Perry speaks of people *thinking* the same *thought*. (Perry's terms deliberately echo Frege, of course.) He nicely expresses the appeal of this theoretical move in a passage also cited by Kaplan:

> We use senses [Kaplan's *characters,* in essence] to individuate psychological states in explaining and predicting action. It is the sense entertained, and not the thought apprehended, that is tied to human action. When you and I entertain the sense of "A bear is about to attack me," we behave similarly. We both roll up in a ball and try to be as still as possible. Different thoughts apprehended, same sense entertained, same behavior. When you and I both apprehend the thought that I am about to be attacked by a bear, we behave differently. I roll up in a ball, you run to get help. Same thought apprehended, different sense entertained, different behavior. Again, when you believe that the meeting begins on a given day at noon by entertaining, the day before, the sense of "the meeting begins tomorrow at noon," you are idle. Apprehending the same thought the next day, by entertaining the sense of "the meeting begins now," you jump up from your chair and run down the hall. (1977, p. 494)

The idea, then, is that we postulate a language of thought, possibly entirely distinct from any natural language a believer may know, and adapt Kaplan's two-stage account of meaning (character + content), which was designed initially for the semantic interpretation of natural-language expressions, as a two-stage account of the semantic interpretation of psychological states. The first stage, Perry's *senses* (modeled on *characters*) would give us psychologically pure predicates with graspable objects; the second stage, Perry's *thoughts* (modeled on Kaplan's *contents*), would be psychologically impure but would complete the job of semantic interpretation by taking us all the way (via Carnapian intensions, in effect) to extensions—things in the world for beliefs to be about.

Here is the proposal from another perspective. Suppose we had begun with the question: what is it about a creature (about any entity with psychological states) that determines what it believes? That is, what features of the entity, considered all by itself in isolation from its embedding in the world, fix the propositions of its propositional attitudes? To this question the startling answer from Putnam is: nothing! Everything that is true about such an entity considered by itself is insufficient to determine its belief (its propositional attitudes). Facts about the environmental/causal/historical embedding of the entity—the "context of utterance" in effect—must be added before we have enough to fix propositions.

Why is the answer startling? To anyone with fond memories of Descartes's *Meditations* it ought to be startling, for in the *Meditations* it seemed unshakeably certain that the *only* matter that was fixed or determined solely within the boundaries of Descartes's mind was exactly which thoughts and beliefs he was having (which propositions he was entertaining). Descartes might bewail his inability to tell which of his beliefs or thoughts were true, which of his perceptions veridical, but which thoughts and beliefs they were, the identity of his own personal candidates for truth and falsehood, seemed to be fully determined by the internal nature of his own mind, and moreover clearly and distinctly graspable by him. If Putnam, Kaplan, and Perry are right, however, Descartes was worse off than he thought: he couldn't even be certain which propositions he was entertaining.

There are at least four ways of resolving this conflict. One could side with Descartes and search for a convincing dismissal of the Putnam line of thought. One could accept the Putnamian conclusion and dismiss Descartes. One could note that Putnam's case is not directly an attack on Descartes, since it presupposes the physicality of the mind, which of course Descartes would disavow; one could say that Descartes could grant that everything *physical* about me and my *Doppelgänger* underdetermines our propositional attitudes, but they are nevertheless "internally" determined by features of our nonphysical minds—which must be just dissimilar enough in their nature to fix our different propositional attitudes. Or one could try for a more irenic compromise, accepting Putnam's case against propositions understood as objects meeting conditions (a–c) and holding that what Descartes was in a privileged position to grasp were rather the *true* psychological objects of his attitudes, not propositions but Perry's senses.

Following the last course, we change our initial question: what, then, is the *organismic contribution* to the fixation of propositional attitudes? How shall we characterize what we get when we subtract facts about context or embedding from the determining whole? This remainder, however we ought to characterize it, is the proper domain of psychology, "pure" psychology, or in Putnam's phrase, "psychology in the narrow sense." Focusing on the organismic contribution in isolation is what Putnam calls *methodological solipsism*. When Fodor adopts the term and recommends methodological solipsism as a research strategy in cognitive psychology (1980), it is precisely this move he is recommending.

But how does one proceed with this strategy? How shall we characterize the organismic contribution? It ought to be analogous to Kaplan's notion of character, so we start, as Perry did, by psychologizing Kaplan's schema. When we attempt this we notice that Kaplan's schema is incomplete but can be straightforwardly extended in consonance with his supporting comments. Recall that Kaplan claimed that "linguistic conventions" determine the character of any particular expression type. So Kaplan's two-stage interpretation process is preceded in effect by an earlier stage (0), governed by linguistic conventions:

(0) Syntactic features + linguistic conventions → Character
(1) Character + Context → Content
(2) Content + Circumstances → Extension

When we psychologize the enlarged schema, what will we place in the first gap? What will be our analogue of the syntactic features of utterances which, given linguistic conventions, fix character? This is where our commitment to a language of thought comes in. The "expressions" in the language of thought are needed as the "raw material" for psychologico-semantic interpretation of psychological states.

This is just what we expected, of course, and at first everything seems to run nicely. Consider Putnam's thought experiment. When he introduces a *Doppelgänger* or physical replica, he is tacitly relying on our acquiescence in the claim that since two exact replicas—my *Doppelgänger* and I—have exactly the same structure of all levels of analysis from the microscopic on up, whatever syntactically defined systems one of us may embody the other embodies as well. If *I* think in brain writing or Mentalese, thoughts with exactly the same "shapes" occur in my *Doppelgänger* as well, and the further tacit corollary is that my thoughts and my *Doppelgänger's* will also be *character*-type identical, in virtue of their syntactic type identity. My

thoughts, though, are about me, while his thoughts are about him—
even though his names for himself are syntactically the same as my
names for myself: we both call ourselves "I" or "Dennett." Putnam's
case then apparently nicely illustrates Kaplan's schema in action. My
Doppelgänger and I have thoughts with the same character (sense, for
Perry), and all that is needed is context—Earth or Twin Earth—to
explain the difference in content (proposition, Perry's and Frege's
thought) expressed, and hence the difference in extension, given
circumstances.

What assumptions, though, permit the tacit corollary that syntactic
type identity is sufficient for character type identity? Why isn't it
possible that although a thought of the *shape* "I am tired" occurs in
both me and my *Doppelgänger*, in *him* the thought with that shape
means *snow is white*—and hence differs not only in proposition expressed, but in character as well? I grant that on any sane view of
Mentalese (if there is any), character type identity *should* follow from
physical replicahood, but why? It must be due to a difference between people and, say, books, for an atom-for-atom replica of *The
Autobiography of Malcolm X* on another planet (or just anywhere they
speak Schmenglish) might not be an autobiography of anyone; it
might be a monograph on epistemic logic or a history of warfare.[6] The
reason we can ignore this alternative in the case of Mentalese must
have to do with a more intimate relationship between form and function in the case of anything that could pass as Mentalese, in contrast
with a natural language. So the role played by linguistic conventions
in stage (0) will have to be played in the psychological version of the
schema by something that is not in any ordinary sense *conventional* at
all.

---

6. John McCarthy claims this is too strong: the purely formal patterns of repetition and
co-occurrence to be found in book-length strings of characters put a very strong constraint—which might be called the cryptographer's constraint—on anyone trying to
devise nontrivially different interpretations of a text. A number of "cheap tricks" will
produce different interpretations of little interest. For instance, declare first-person
singular in English to be a variety of third-person singular in Schmenglish, and (with a
little fussing), turn an autobiography into a biography. Or declare Schmenglish to have
very long words—English chapter length, in fact—and turn any ten-chapter book into
the ten-word sentence of your choice. The prospect of interestingly different interpretations of a text is hard to assess, but worth exploring, since it provides a boundary
condition for "radical translation" (and hence "radical interpretation"—see Lewis
1974) thought experiments.

In fact, when we turn to the attempt to fill in the details of stage (0) for the psychological schema, we uncover a host of perplexities. Whence come the syntactic features of Mentalese? Psychology is *not* literary hermeneutics; the "text" is not *given*. Which shapes of things in the head count? It appears that Kaplan has skipped over yet another prior stage in his schema.

(−1) physical features + design considerations (in other words: *minus* functional irrelevancies) → syntactic features

Differences in the typeface, color and size of written tokens, and in the volume, pitch, and timbre of spoken tokens don't count as syntactic differences, except when it can be shown that they *function* as syntactic differences by marking combinatorial "valences," possibilities of meaningful variation, etc. A syntactic characterization is a considerable abstraction from the physical features of tokens; Morse code tokens occurring in time can share their syntax with printed English sentence tokens.

By analogy then we can expect brain writing tokens to differ in many physical features and yet count as sharing a syntax. Our model grants us this elbow room for declaring physically quite different "systems of representation" to be mere "notational variants." This is in any case a familiar idea, being only a special case of the freedom of physical realization championed by functionalist theories of mind (e.g., Putnam 1960, 1975b; Fodor 1975). Surely the believer in sentential attitude psychology will be grateful for this elbow room, for the position beckoning at the end of this trail is startlingly strong. Let us call it *sententialism:*

(S) *x* believes what *y* believes if and only if (∃L) (∃s) (L is a language of thought and *s* is a sentence of *L* and there is a token of *s* in *x* and a token of *s* in *y*)

(We must understand that these tokens have to be in the functionally relevant and similar places, of course. One can't come to believe what Jones believes by writing his beliefs (in *L*) on slips of paper and swallowing them.)

On this view we must *share* a language of thought to believe *the same thing*—though we no longer mean by "the same thing" the same proposition. The idea is that from the point of view of psychology a different type-casting is more appropriate, according to which beliefs count as the same when they have the same sense (in Perry's usage) or when they consist in relations to internal sentences with the same character. In fleeing propositions, however, we have given up one of their useful features: language neutrality. The demand that we construe all like-believers (in the new, psychologically realistic typecasting) as thinking in the same language is apparently onerous, unless of course some way can be found either to defend this implication or to trivialize it.[7]

How might we defend sententialism? By declaring that it is an empirical question, and an interesting and important one at that, whether people do think in the same or different languages of thought. Perhaps dogs think in Doggish and people think in Peoplish. Perhaps we will discover "the brain writing which people have in common regardless of their nationality and other differences" (Zeman 1963). Such a discovery would certainly be a theoretical treasure. Or perhaps there will turn out to be nontrivially different Mentalese languages (not mere notational variants of each other) so that the implication we will have to live with is that if your brain speaks Mentallatin while mine speaks Mentalgreek, we cannot indeed *share the same psychological states.* Any comparison would "lose something in translation." This would not prevent us, necessarily, from sharing *propositional* attitudes (no longer considered "pure" psychological states); your way of believing that whales are mammals would just be different—in psychologically nontrivial ways—from mine. It would be a theoretical calamity to discover that each person thinks in a different, entirely idiosyncratic Mentalese, for then psychological generalization would be hard to come by; but if there turned out to be a smallish number of different languages of thought (with a few dialects thrown in), this might prove as theoretically fruitful as the monolingual discovery, since we might be able to explain important differences in cognitive styles by a multilingual hypothesis. (For example, people who think in Mentallatin do better on certain sorts of reasoning problems, while people who think in Mentalgreek are su-

---

7. Field (1978) notices this problem, but, astonishingly, dismisses it: "the notion of type-identity between tokens in one organism and tokens in the other is not needed for psychological theory, and can be regarded as a meaningless notion." (p. 58, note 34) His reasons for maintaining this remarkable view are no less remarkable—but too devious to do justice to explicitly here. There are many points of agreement and disagreement of importance between Field's paper and this one beyond those I shall discuss, but a discussion of them all would double the length of this paper. I discuss Fodor's (1975) commitment to sententialism in "A Cure for the Common Code" in *Brainstorms.*

perior analogy-discoverers. Recall all the old saws about English being the language of commerce, French the language of diplomacy, and Italian the language of love.)

In any event, there is a strategy of theory development available which will tend to replace multilingual hypotheses or interpretations with monolingual hypotheses or interpretations. Suppose we have tentatively fixed a level of functional description of two individuals according to which they are not colingual; their psychological states do not share a syntax. We can cast about for a somewhat higher level of abstraction at which we can redescribe their psychological states so that what had heretofore been treated as syntactic differences were now dismissed as physical differences *beneath syntax*. At the higher functional level we will discover *the same function* being subserved by what we had been considering syntactically different items, and this will entitle us to declare the earlier syntactic taxonomy too fine-grained (for distinguishing what are merely notational variants of rival tokening systems). Availing ourselves of this strategy will tend to blur the lines between syntax and semantics, for what we count as a syntactic feature at one level of analysis will depend on its capacity to figure in semantically relevant differences at the next higher level of functional analysis. Carried to a Pickwickian extreme, we would find ourselves at a *very* abstract level of functional analysis defending a version of monolingualism for Mentalese analogous to the following claim about natural language: French and English are just notational variants of one another or of some *ur*-language; "bouche" and "mouth" are different tokens of the same type (cf. Sellars 1974). Normally, and for good reasons, we consider these two words to share only *semantic* properties. Similar principles would presumably constrain our theorizing about Mentalese and its dialects. Anyone who thinks that there *has* to be a single Mentalese for human beings must be ignoring the existence of such principles and falling for the Pickwickian version of monolingualism.

Even if we acquiesced in multilingualism, and found it theoretically fruitful to conduct psychological investigations at such a fine-grained level that we could tolerate psychological state type-casting in syntactical terms, we would still want to have a way of pointing to important psychological *similarities* between counterpart states in people thinking in different languages of thought—analogous to the similarity between *"j'ai faim"* and "I'm hungry" and *"Ich habe Hunger,"* and between *"Es tut mir Leid"* and "I'm sorry." If we wish to view the claims we make at this level of abstraction as claims about *tokens of the same type*, the type-casting in question cannot be syntactic (for even at the grossest syntactic level, these expressions are grammatically different, having nouns where others have adjectives, for instance), nor can it be wholly semantic in the sense of *propositional*—since the expressions, with their indexicals, express different propositions on different occasions. What we will need is an intermediate taxonomy: the similar items will be similar in that they have similar *roles* to play within a functionalistic theory of the believers (cf. Sellars 1974).[8]

Kaplan is mute on the question of whether his notion of character can be applied interlinguistically. Does *"j'ai faim"* have just the same character as "I'm hungry"? We will want our psychological counterpart to character to have this feature if we are to use it to characterize psychological similarities that can exist between believers who think in different Mentalese languages. For recall that we are searching for a way of characterizing in the most general way the organismic contribution to the fixation of propositional attitudes, and since we want to grant that you and I can both believe the proposition that whales are mammals in spite of our Mentalese differences, we need to characterize that which is in common in us that can sometimes yield the same function from contexts—embeddings in the world—to propositions.

The value of a syntax-neutral level of psychological characterization emerges more clearly when one considers the task that faces the sentential attitude theorist who hopes to characterize a human being—more specifically a human nervous system—at a purely syntactical, utterly uninterpreted level of description. (This would provide the raw material, the "text," for subsequent semantic interpretation.) This would be methodological solipsism or psychology in the narrow sense with a vengeance, for we would be so narrowing our gaze as to lose sight of all the normal relations between things in the environment and the activities within the system. Part of the task would be to distinguish the subset of physical features and regularities inside the organism that betoken syntactic features and regularities—locating

8. Cf. also Field (1978, p. 47), who considers such claims as "He believes some sentence of his language which plays approximately the role in his psychology that the sentence 'there's a rabbit nearby' plays in mine." He decides that such claims involve introducing a "more-or-less semantic notion" into a psychological theory that was supposed to be liberated from semantic problems. Cf. also Stich 1982 on content ascription and content similarity.

and purifying the "text" midst the welter of scribbles and smudges. Since what makes a feature syntactic is its capacity to make a semantic difference, this purification of text cannot proceed innocent of semantic assumptions, however tentative. How might this work?

Our methodological solipsism dictates that we ignore the environment in which the organism resides—or has resided—but we can still locate a boundary between the organism and its environment and determine the input and output surfaces of its nervous system. At these peripheries there are the sensory *transducers* and motor *effectors*. The transducers respond to patterns of physical energy impinging on them by producing syntactic objects—"signals"—with certain properties. The effectors at the other end respond to other syntactic objects—"commands"—by producing muscle flexions of certain sorts. An idea that in various forms licenses all speculation and theorizing about the semantics of mental representation is the idea that the semantic properties of mental representations are at least partially determinable by their relations, however, indirect, with these transducers and effectors. If we know the stimulus conditions of a transducer, for instance, we can *begin* to interpret its signal—subject to many pitfalls and caveats. A similar tentative and partial semantic interpretation of "commands" can be given once we see what motions of the body they normally produce. Moving toward the center, downstream from the transducers and upstream from the effectors, we can endow more central events and states with representational powers, and hence at least a partial semantic interpretation (see e.g., Dennett 1969, 1978a).

For the moment, however, we should close our eyes to this information about transducer sensitivity and effector power and treat the transducers as "oracles" whose sources of information are hidden (and whose *obiter dicta* are hence uninterpreted by us) and treat the effectors as obedient producers of unknown effects. This might seem to be a bizarre limitation of viewpoint to adopt, but it has its rationale: it is the brain's-eye view of the mind, and it is the brain, in the end, that does all the work (see also Dennett 1978a, chapter 2 and 1978c). Brains are *syntactic engines*, so in the end and in principle the control functions of a human nervous system must be explicable at this level or remain forever mysterious.[9]

---

9. Fodor (1980) makes much the same point in arguing for what he calls the formality condition: mental states can be (type) distinct only if the representations which constitute their objects are formally distinct. See also Field 1978.

The alternative is to hold—most improbably—that *content* or *meaning* or *semantic value* could be independent, detectable causal properties of events in the nervous system. To see what I mean by this, consider a simpler case. There are two coins in my pocket, and one of them (only) *has spent exactly ten minutes on my desk.* This property is not a property causally relevant to how it will affect any entity it subsequently comes in contact with. There is no coin machine, however sophisticated, that could reject the coin by testing it for *that* property—though it might reject it for being radioactive or greasy or warmer than room temperature. Now if the coin had one of these properties just in virtue of having spent exactly ten minutes on my desk (the desk is radioactive, covered with grease, a combination desk and pottery kiln) the coin machine could be used to test indirectly (and of course not very reliably) for the property of having spent ten minutes on my desk. The brain's testing of *semantic* properties of signals and states in the nervous system must be similarly indirect testing, driven by merely syntactic properties of the items being discriminated—that is, by whatever structural properties the items have that are amenable to direct mechanical test. (A "direct" test is still not foolproof, of course, or absolutely direct.) Somehow, the syntactical virtuosity of our brains permits us to be interpreted at another level as *semantic engines*—systems that (indirectly) discriminate the significance of the impingements on them, that understand, mean, and believe.

This vantage point on brains as syntactic engines gives us a diagnosis of what is going on in Putnam's, Kaplan's, and Perry's arguments. If the meaning of anything—e.g., an internal information-storing state, a perceived change in the environment, a heard utterance—is a property that is only indirectly detectable by a system such as a person's brain, then meaning so conceived is *not* the property to use to build projectible predicates descriptive of the system's behavior. What we want is rather a property that is to meaning so conceived roughly as the property *guilt-beyond-a-reasonable-doubt* is to *guilt.* If you want to predict whether the jury will acquit or convict, the latter property is unfortunately but unavoidably a bit less reliable than the former.

But then we can see that Putnam et al. are driving an ancient wedge into a new crack—the distinction between *real* and *apparent* is being tailored to distinguish real and apparent propositions believed. Then it is not surprising, but also not very cheering, to note that the theoretical move many want to make in this situation is analogous to the move that earlier landed philosophers with sense data, or with qualia. What is *directly* accessible to the mind is not a feature of the surfaces of things *out there*, but a sort of inner copy that has a life of its own. Sentences of Mentalese are seen from this vantage point to be inner copies of the propositions we come to believe in virtue of our placement in the world. One must not argue guilt by association, however, so it remains an open question whether in this instance the theoretical move can yield us a useful model of the mind—whatever its shortcomings in earlier applications. We should persist with our earlier question: what could we understand about a brain (or a mind) considered just as a syntactic engine?

The strategy of methodological solipsism mates with the language of thought model of mentality to produce the tempting idea that one could in principle divide psychology into syntactic psychology (pursued under methodological solipsism) and semantic psychology (which would require one to cast one's glance out at the world). We have seen that the preliminary task of discovering which internal features ought to be considered syntactical depends on assumptions about the semantic roles to be played by events in the system, but it is tempting to suppose that the syntax of the system will not depend on particular details of these semantic roles, but just on assumptions about the existence and differentiation of these roles. Suppose, runs this tempting line of thought, we honor our methodological solipsism by *de-interpreting* the messages sent by the tranducers and the commands sent to the effectors: transducers are then taken to assert only that it is F now, getting G-er and G-er intermittently H—where these are uninterpreted sensory predicates; and effectors obediently turn on the X-er or the Y-er, or cause the Z to move. Might we not then be able to determine the *relative* semantic interpretation of more central states (presumably beliefs, desires, and such) in terms of these uninterpreted predicates? We would be able to learn that the system's past history had in one way or another brought it into the state of believing that all Fs are very GHs, and the X-ing usually leads to either a JK or a JL. The idea that we might do this is parallel to Field's suggestion (1972) that we might do Tarskian semantics for a (natural) language in two independently completable parts: the theory of reference for the primitives, and everything else. We can do the latter part first while temporizing by the use of such statements of primitive reference as

"snow" refers to whatever it refers to.

The enabling idea of sentential attitude psychology is that we might similarly be able to temporize about the ultimate reference of the predicates of Mentalese, while proceeding apace with their relative interpretation, as revealed in a systematic—and entirely internal— semantic edifice. Field (1978) proposes this division of the problem with the help of a technical term, "believe*".

(1) X believes that p if and only if there is a sentence S such that X believes* S and S means that p

. . . the effect of adopting (1) is to divide the problem of giving a materialistically adequate account of the belief relation into two subproblems:

subproblem (a): the problem of explaining what it is for a person to believe* a sentence (of his or her own language).

subproblem (b): the problem of explaining what it is for a sentence to mean that p.

. . . The rough idea of how to give an account of (a) should be clear enough: I believe* a sentence of my language if and only if I am disposed to employ that sentence in a certain way in reasoning, deliberating and so on. This is very vague of course . . . but I hope that even the vague remarks above are enough to predispose the reader to think that believing* is not a relation that should be a particular worry to a materialist (even a materialist impressed by Brentano's problem [of intentionality]). On the other hand, anyone impressed with Brentano's problem *is* likely to be impressed with subproblem (b), for unlike (a), (b) invokes a *semantic* relation (of *meaning that*). (1978, p. 13).

So believing* is supposed to be an entirely *non*semantic relation between a person and a syntactically characterized object. The "certain way" one must be disposed to employ the sentence is left unspecified, of course, but the presumption must be that its specification can in principle be completed in syntactic terms alone. Only thus could the relation not be a "worry" to a materalist.

So long as Field stays with sentences of natural language as the *relata* of believes*, he is on safe enough ground speaking in this way, for a sentence of a natural language can be identified independently of any person's dispositions to use it in various ways. But once Field turns to Mentalese sentences (or sentence-analogues, as he calls them)—as he must, for familiar reasons having to do with mute, animal, and prelinguistic believers, for instance—this first-approximation definition of "believe*" becomes highly problematic— although Field himself characterizes the shift as "only a minor modification" (p. 18).

Take just the simplest case: the "message" sent by a relatively peripheral reporter element near the retina. Let us call this element Rep. Let us suppose our first hypothesis is that Rep's signal is a token of the Mentalese sentence (in strict English translation) "There is now a small red spot in the middle of the visual field." De-interpreting the sentence, we see it to have the syntactical shape (for our purposes—and what other purposes could matter?) *there is now an FGH at J of K*. We take there to be this many terms in the message just because we suppose the message can contribute in this many different ways in virtue of its links. But perhaps we've misinterpreted its function in the system. Perhaps the Mentalese sentence to associate with it (again in strict English translation) is "There's a tomato in front of me" or merely "At least ten retinal cells of sort F are in state G" or perhaps "I am being appeared to redly." These sentences (at least their English translations as shown) have quite different syntactical analyses. But which syntactical form does the thing we have located in the brain have? We may be able to determine the "shape" of an item—an event type, for instance—in the brain, but we can't determine its syntactical form (as distinguished from its merely decorative—however, distinctive—properties) except by determining its particular powers of combination and cooperation with the other elements, and ultimately its *environmental* import via those powers of interaction.

A thought experiment will bring out the point more clearly. Suppose that our task were *designing* a language of thought rather than discovering an already existent language of thought in operation. We figure out what we want our system to believe (desire, etc.) and write down versions of all this information in sentences of some tentative variety of Mentalese. We inscribe each belief sentence in a separate box of a large map of the system we are designing. One belief box has the Mentalese translation of "snow is white" in it. Now just having the symbols written in the box cannot store the information that snow is white, of course. At the very least there must be machinery poised to utilize these symbols in this box in a way that makes a difference—the right sort of difference for believing that snow is white. This machinery must, for instance, somehow link the box with "snow is white" in it to all the boxes in which sentences with the Mentalese word for "white" occurs. These boxes are linked to each other, in some systematic ways, and ultimately somehow to the periphery of the system—to the machinery that could signal the presence of cold white stuff, cold green stuff, and so forth. The "snow is white" box is also linked to all the "snow" boxes, which are linked to all the "precipitation" boxes, and so forth. The imagined vast network of links would turn the collection of boxes into *something like* the taxonomic lattices or structural inheritance networks or semantic nets to be found in Artificial Intelligence systems (see, e.g., Woods 1975, 1981). Then there are all the links to the machinery, whatever it is, that relies on these boxes to contribute appositely to the control of the behavior of the whole system—or better, the creature in which the system is embedded. Without all these links, the inscriptions in the boxes are mere decoration—they don't store the information whatever they look like. But equally, once the links are in place, the inscriptions in the boxes are still mere decoration—or at best mnemonic labels encapsulating *for us* (more or less accurately) the information actually stored *for the system* at that node in virtue of the links from the node to other nodes of the system. The real "syntax," the structure in the system on which function depends, is all in the links. (I am using "links" as a wild card for whatever is needed to play this role; no one yet knows (so far as I know) how to solve this problem in detail.)

The separation imagined between the links and the inscriptions in the boxes in our example does not of course reflect the actual situation in Artificial Intelligence. The point of computer languages is that they are cleverly designed so that their inscriptions, properly entered in the system, *create* various links to elements in other inscriptions. It is this feature that makes computer languages so different from natural languages, and surely it is a feature that any language of thought would have to have—if its postulation is to avoid the fruitless epiphenomenalism or our imagined labels in boxes. And for any "language" having this feature, the relation between form and function is tight indeed—so tight that the distinction in Kaplan's enlarged schema at stage (0) between the contribution of syntactic features and the contribution of "linguistic conventions" has no counterpart in any plausible "language of thought" model for psychology. Getting the "text" independently of getting its interpretation is not a real prospect for psychology. So Field's proposed division of the problem of belief into subproblem (a), the syntactic problem, and subproblem (b), the semantic problem, if taken as a proposal for a research strategy, is forlorn.

Perhaps, however, Field's proposal can be recast, not as a recommendation for a research program, but as marking an important distinction of reason. Even if we cannot in fact *first* determine the syntax and *then* the semantics of a language of thought (for epistemological reasons), the distinction might still mark something real, so that, having bootstrapped our way to both a semantic and a syntactic theory of the language of thought, we could distinguish the system's syntactic properties from its semantic properties. No doubt a distinction rather like the distinction between semantics and syntax will be makeable in retrospect within any mature and confirmed psychology of belief, for there must be some way of describing the operation of the nervous system independently of its embedding in the world in virtue of which we fix its semantic characterization. But supposing that this distinction will have much in common with the distinction between syntax and semantics for a natural language is committing oneself to a gratuitously strong sententialism.

For a stronger moral can be drawn from the discussion of the problem of associating an *explicit message* with the contribution of Rep, the peripheral visual transducer. We supposed that we had isolated Rep as a functional component of the cognitive system, a component that could be seen to *inform* the system about some visual feature. Then we faced the problem of coming up with an apt *linguification* of that contribution—finding, that is, a *sentence* that explicitly and accurately expresses the message being asserted by Rep. And we saw that which sentence we chose depended critically on just what combinatorial powers Rep's message actually had. Even supposing we could determine this, even supposing that we could establish that we had a best functional description of the system of which Rep is a part, and could say *exactly* what functions Rep's signal can perform, there is no guarantee that those functions will be aptly and accurately referred to or alluded to by *any* claim to the effect that Rep's message inserts sentence S (in language L) as a premise in some deductive or inferential system. The conviction that it must be possible to linguify any such contribution seems to me to lie beneath a great deal of recent metatheoretical ideology, and I suspect it rests in part on a mistaken conflation of *determinateness* and *explicitness*.[10] Suppose Rep's semantic contribution, its *informing* of the system, is entirely determinate. That is, we can say exactly how its occurrence would produce effects that ramify through the system making differences to the content or semantic contribution of other subsystems. Still it would not follow that we could render this contribution *explicit* in the form of a sentence or sentences asserted. We might have some way of *describing*

---

10. Charles Taylor's discussions of explicitness and "explicitation" helped shape the claims in the rest of this section.

the semantic contribution perfectly explicitly, without describing it as any explicit assertion in any language.

 I am not merely alluding to the possibility that activity in one part of a cognitive system might have a systematic but noisy—or at any rate non-contentful—effect on another part. Such effects are quite possible. Smelling sulphur might just make someone think about baseball *for no reason*. That is, there could be no *informational* link, such as memories of odorous games behind the gasworks, but nevertheless a reliable if pointless *causal* link. I grant the possibility of such effects, but am urging something stronger: that there could be highly content-sensitive, informational, epistemically useful, designed relations between activities in different cognitive subsystems which nevertheless defied sententialist interpretation. Suppose, for instance, that Pat says that Mike "has a thing about redheads." What Pat means is, roughly, that Mike has a stereotype of a redhead which is rather derogatory and which influences Mike's expectations about and interactions with redheads. It's not just that he's prejudiced against redheads, but that he has a rather idiosyncratic and *particular* thing about redheads. And Pat might be right—more right than he knew! It could turn out that Mike does have a thing, a bit of cognitive machinery, that is *about redheads* in the sense that it systematically comes into play whenever the topic is redheads or a redhead, and that adjusts various parameters of the cognitive machinery, making flattering hypotheses about redheads less likely to be entertained, or confirmed, making relatively aggressive behavior *vis-à-vis* redheads closer to implementation than otherwise it would be, and so forth. Such a *thing about redheads* could be very complex in its operation or quite simple, and in either case its role could elude characterization in the format:

Mike believes that: (x) $(x$ is a redhead $\supset$ . . .$)$

no matter how deviously we piled on the exclusion clauses, qualifiers, probability operators, and other explicit adjusters of content. The contribution of Mike's thing about redheads could be perfectly determinate and also undeniably contentful and yet no linguification of it could be more than a mnemonic label for its role. In such a case we could say, as there is often reason to do, that various beliefs are *implicit* in the system. For instance, the belief that redheads are untrustworthy. Or should it be the belief that most redheads are untrustworthy; or "all the redheads I have met"? Or should it be

"(x) (x is a redhead $\supset$ the probability is 0.9 that x is untrustworthy)"? The concern with the proper form of the sentence is idle when the sentence is only part of a stab at capturing the implicit content of some nonsentential bit of machinery. (See "Propositional Attitudes" above on the futile debates occasioned by failure to distinguish propositions from sentences.)

It still might be argued that although *non*sentential semantic contributors of the sort I have just sketched could play a large role in the cognitive machinery of the human brain, explicitly sentential representational states are also required, if only to give the finite brain the compositionality it needs to represent indefinitely many different states of affairs with its finite resources. And for all I can see this may be so. Certainly some very efficient and elegant sort of compositionality accounts for the essentially limitless powers we have to perceive, think about, believe, intend . . . different things. The only examples we now have of (arguably) *universal* systems of representation with finite means are languages, and perhaps any possible universal system of representation must be recognizably sentential, in a sense yet to be settled, of course. Suppose this is so (and find yourself in good company). Then although a great deal of psychology might be both cognitive and *non*sentential, at the core of the person would be his sentential system. The theory of visual perception, for instance, might require Mentalese only at some relatively central "interface" with the sentential core. Initially we viewed the task of sentential attitude psychology as starting at the peripheral transducers and effectors and sententializing all the way in. Perhaps the mistake was just in supposing that the interface between the sentential system *and the world*—the overcoat of transducers and effectors worn by every cognitive system—was thinner than it is.

Thick or thin, the overcoat of tranducer–perceiver mechanisms and effector–actor mechanisms becomes an environment of sorts, a context, in which the postulated "utterances" of Mentalese occur. Ignoring that context, the predicates of Mentalese are *very* uninterpreted; even taking that context into account, the predicates of Mentalese would be only partially interpreted—not fully enough interpreted, for instance, to distinguish my propositional attitudes from my *Doppelgänger*'s. We can construct some bizarre variations on Putnam's thought-experiment using this notion. Suppose a physical duplicate of that part of my nervous system which is the sentential system were hooked up (right here on Earth) to a different overcoat of transducers and effectors. My sentential system can store the information that all *F*s are very *GH*s, and so can its replica, but in me, this sentential state subserves[11] my belief that greyhounds are very swift animals, while in the other fellow it subserves the belief that palaces are very expensive houses! These different tokens of the same *syntactic* type have the same *character* if we treat the transducer–effector overcoat as an undifferentiated part of the "external" context of utterance; if we draw a further boundary between the overcoat and the environment, then these tokens do not have the same character, but only the same syntax, and the different overcoats play the counterpart roles of the linguistic conventions of Kaplan's stage (0).

The point is that Kaplan's schema is a special case of something very general. Whenever we are describing a functional system, if we draw a boundary between the system "proper" and some context or environmental niche in which it resides, we find we can characterize a Kaplan-style schema

$$C + E \rightarrow I$$

where C is a character-like concept of narrow or intra-systemic application; E is the concept of an embedding context or environment of operation, and I is a *richer* semantic (or functional) characterization of the systemic role in question than that provided by C alone. Where the system in question is a representing or believing system, "richer" means closer to determining a (classical) proposition, or, if we include Kaplan's stage (2) as the ultimate step in this progression, richer in the sense of being closer to ultimate reference to things in the world. In other contexts—such as characterizations of functional components in biology or engineering (see Wimsatt 1974)—the "richer" characterization tells us more about the functional point of the item: what is narrowly seen as a spark-producer is seen, in context, to be a fuel-igniter, to take an overworked example.

Moving from stage to stage in such an interpretation schema, one sees that the richer the semantics of a particular stage, the more abstract or tolerant the syntax. Sentences with different physical properties can have the same syntax. Sentences with different syntax can have the same character. Sentences with different character can

---

11. "Subserves" is a useful hand-waving term for which we may thank the neurophysiologists. Putting two bits of jargon together, we can say a belief *supervenes* on the state that *subserves* it.

express the same proposition. Different propositions, finally, can attribute the same property to the same individual: that the Dean of Admissions is middle-aged is not identical with the proposition that the tallest Dean is middle-aged. Transplanted from the theory of natural language to the theory of psychological states, the part of the nesting of concern to us now looks like this: people believing the same proposition can be in different (narrow) psychological states; people in the same narrow psychological state can be in different fine-grained (i.e., syntactically characterized) states; people in the same syntactic states can implement those states in physically different ways. And, of course, looking in the other direction, we can see that two people narrowly construed as being in the same state can be reconstrued as being in different states if we redraw the boundaries between the people's states and the surrounding environment.[12]

Notional Attitudes

In the face of the objections of Putnam and others to "classical" propositional attitudes, we adverted to the question: what is the organismic contribution to the fixation of propositional attitudes? The answer would characterize psychological states "in the narrow sense." The attempt to capture these narrow psychological state types as sentential attitudes ran into a variety of problems, chief of which was that any sentential attitude characterization, being essentially a syntactical type-casting, would cut too fine. In Putnam's thought experiment we grant that *physical* replicahood is sufficient but not necessary for identity of organismic contribution; we could also grant that the weaker similarity captured by *syntactic* replicahood (at some level of abstraction) would be sufficient for identity of organismic contribution, but even though identity of organismic contribution—narrow-psychological twinhood—is a very stringent condition, it would not seem to require syntactic twinhood, at any level of description. Consider the somewhat analogous question: do all Turing machines that compute the same function share a syntactic (i.e., machine table) description? No, unless we adjust our levels of

---

12. Burge (1979) presents an extended thought experiment about beliefs about arthritis that can be seen as drawing the boundary between the system proper and its environment *outside* the biological individual entirely; the contextual variations involve *social* practices outside the experience of the subject. (For a criticism of Burge, see chapter 8.)

description of the machine table and the input–output behavior so that they coalesce trivially. What should count as equivalence for Turing machines (or computer programs) is a vexed question; it would not be if it weren't for the fact that nontrivially different descriptions in terms of internal "syntax" can yield the same "contribution"—at some useful level of description.

The analogy is imperfect, no doubt, and other considerations—e.g., biological considerations—might weigh in favor of supposing that *complete* narrow-psychological twinhood required syntactic twinhood at some level, but even if that were granted, it would not at all follow that *partial* psychological similarity can always be described in some general system of syntactic description applicable to all who share the psychological trait. People who are vain, or paranoid, for instance, are surely psychologically similar; a large part of the similarity in each case would seem well captured by talking of similar or shared beliefs. Even if one takes a self-defeatingly stringent line on belief-identity (according to which no two people ever really share a belief), these *similarities* in belief cry out for capturing within psychology. They could not plausibly be held to depend on monolingualism—vain people's brains all speaking the same Mentalese. Nor can we capture these similarities in belief-state via *propositional* attitudes, because of the indexicality of many of the crucial beliefs: "People admire *me*," "People are trying to ruin *me*."

These considerations suggest that what we are looking to characterize is an intermediate position—halfway between syntax and semantics you might say. Let us call it *notional attitude psychology*. We want it to work out that I and my *Doppelgänger*—and any other narrow-psychological twins—have exactly the same notional attitudes, so that our differences in propositional attitudes are due entirely to the different environmental contributions. But we also want it to work out that you and I, no psychological twins but "of like mind" on several topics, share a variety of notional attitudes.

A familiar idea that has occurred in many guises can be adapted for our purposes here: the idea of a person's subjective world, Helen Keller's *The World I Live In* or John Irving's *The World According to Garp*, for instance. Let us try to characterize the *notional world* of a psychological subject so that, for instance, although my *Doppelgänger* and I live in different real worlds—Twin Earth and Earth—we have the *same* notional world. You and I live in the same real world, but have different notional worlds, though there is a considerable overlap between them.

A notional world should be viewed as a sort of *fictional* world devised by a theorist, a third-party observer, in order to characterize the narrow-psychological states of a subject. A notional world can be supposed to be full of notional objects, and the scene of notional events—all the objects and events the subject believes in, you might say. If we relax our methodological solipsism for a moment, we will note that some objects in the real world inhabited by a subject "match" objects in the subject's notional world, but others do not. The real world contains many things and events having no counterparts in any subject's notional world (excluding the notional world of an omniscient God), and the notional worlds of gullible or confused or ontologically profligate subjects will contain notional objects having no counterparts in the real world. The task of describing the relations that may exist between things in the real world and things in someone's notional world is notoriously puzzle-ridden—that is one reason to retreat to methodological solipsism: to factor out those troublesome issues temporarily.

Our retreat has landed us in very familiar territory: what are notional objects but the *intentional objects* of Brentano? Methodological solipsism is apparently a version of Husserl's *ép;oché*, or bracketing. Can it be that the alternative to both propositional attitude psychology and sentential attitude psychology is . . . Phenomenology? Not quite. There is one major difference between the approach to be sketched here and the traditional approaches associated with Phenomenology. Whereas Phenomenologists propose that one can get to one's *own* notional world by some special somewhat introspectionist bit of mental gymnastics—called, by some, the phenomenological reduction—we are concerned with determining the notional world of *another*, from the outside. The tradition of Brentano and Husserl is *auto-phenomenology;* I am proposing *hetero-phenomenology* (see "Two Approaches to Mental Images" in *Brainstorms*). Although the results might bear a striking resemblance, the enabling assumptions are very different.

The difference can best be seen with the aid of a distinction recently resurrected by Fodor (1980) between what he calls, following James, *naturalistic* and *rational* psychology. Fodor quotes James:

On the whole, few recent formulas have done more service of a rough sort in psychology than the Spencerian one that the essence of mental life and of bodily life are one, namely, "the adjustment of inner to outer relations." Such a formula is vagueness incarnate; but because it takes into account the fact that minds inhabit environments which act on them and on which they in turn react; because, in short, it takes mind in the midst of all its concrete relations, it is immensely more fertile than the old-fashioned "rational psychology" which treated the soul as a detached existent, sufficient unto itself, and assumed to consider only its nature and its properties. (James 1890, p. 6)

James sings the praises of naturalistic psychology, psychology in the *wide* sense, but the moral from Twin Earth, drawn explicitly by Fodor, is that naturalistic psychology casts its net too wide to be doable. The Phenomenologists draw the same conclusion, apparently, and both turn to different versions of methodological solipsism: concern for the psychological subject "as a detached existent, sufficient unto itself," but when they "consider its nature and its properties," what do they find? The Phenomenologists, using some sort of introspection, claim to find a *given* in experience, which becomes the raw material for their construction of their notional worlds. If Fodor, using some sort of (imagined) internal inspection of the machinery, claimed to find a Mentalese text *given* in the hardware (which would become the raw material for construction of the notional attitudes of the subject) we would have as much reason to doubt the existence of the given in this case as in the case of Phenomenology (see chapter 8). James is right: you cannot do *psychology* (as opposed to, say, neurophysiology) without determining the *semantic* properties of the internal events and structures under examination, and you cannot uncover the semantic properties without looking at the relations of those internal events or structures to things in the subject's environment. But nowhere is it written that the environment relative to which we fix such a system's semantic properties must be a *real* environment, or the *actual* environment in which the system has grown up. A fictional environment, an idealized or imaginary environment, might do as well. The idea is that in order to do "mental representation" theory, you need to do the semantics of the representations from the beginning. (You can't first do the syntax, then the semantics.) But that means you need a model, in the sense of Tarskian semantics. A fictional model, however, might permit enough Tarskian semantics to get under way for us to determine the partial semantics, or proto-semantics, we need to characterize the organismic contribution.

The idea of a notional world, then, is the idea of a model—but not necessarily the actual, real, true model—of one's internal representations. *It does not consist itself of representations but of representeds.* It is the world "I live in," not the world of representations *in me*. (So far, this is pure Brentano, at least as I understand him. See Aquila 1977). The theorist wishing to characterize the narrow-psychological states of a creature, or, in other words, the organismic contribution of that creature to its propositional attitudes, *describes* a fictional world; the description exists on paper, the fictional world does not exist, but the inhabitants of the fictional world are treated as the notional referents of the subject's representations, as the intentional objects of that subject. It is hoped that by this ploy the theorist can get the benefits of James's and Spencer's naturalism without the difficulties raised by Putnam and the rest.

Now the question is: what guides our construction of an organism's notional world? Suppose, to dramatize the problem, we receive a box containing an organism from we know not where, alive but frozen (or comatose)—and hence cut off from any environment. We have a Laplacean snapshot of the organism—a complete description of its internal structure and composition—and we can suppose that this enables us to determine exactly how it *would* respond to any new environmental impacts were we to release it from its state of suspended animation and isolation. Our task is like the problem posed when we are shown some alien or antique gadget and asked: what is it for? Is it a needle-making machine or a device for measuring the height of distant objects or a weapon? What can we learn from studying the object? We can determine how the parts mesh, what happens under various conditions, and so forth. We can also look for telltale scars and dents, wear and tear. Once we have compiled these facts we try to imagine a setting in which given these facts it would *excellently* perform some imaginably useful function. If the object would be an equally good sail mender or cherry pitter we won't be able to tell what it *really* is—what it is *for*—without learning where it came from, who made it, and why. Those facts could have vanished without a trace. Such an object's true identity, or essence, could then be utterly undeterminable by us, no matter how assiduously we studied the object. That would not mean that there was no fact of the matter about whether the thing was a cherry pitter or a sail mender, but that the truth, whichever it was, no longer made a difference. It would be one of those idle or inert historical facts, like the fact that some of the gold in my teeth once belonged to Julius Caesar—or didn't.

Faced with our novel organism, we can easily enough determine what it is for—it is for surviving and flourishing and reproducing its kind—and we should have little trouble identifying its sense organs and modes of action and biological needs. Since *ex hypothesi* we can figure out what it would do if . . . (for all fillings in of the antecedent), we can determine, for instance, that it will eat apples but not fish, tends to avoid brightly lit places, is disposed to make certain noises under certain conditions, etc. Now what kind of an environment would these talents and proclivities fit it for? The more we learn about the internal structure, behavioral dispositions, and systemic needs of the organism, the more particular becomes our hypothetical ideal environment. By "ideal environment" I do not mean the best of all possible worlds for this organism ("with the lemonade spring where the bluebirds sing"), but the environment (or class of environments) for which the organism as currently constituted is best fitted. It might be a downright nasty world, but at least the organism is prepared to cope with its nastiness. We can learn something about the organism's enemies—real or only notional—by noting its protective coloration or its escape behavior or . . . how it would answer certain questions.

So long as the organism we are dealing with is very simple and has, for instance, little or no plasticity in its nervous system (so it cannot learn), the limit of specificity for the imagined ideal environment may fail to distinguish radically different but equally well-fitted environments, as in the case of the gadget. As the capacity to learn and remember grows, and as the richness and complexity of the possible relations with environmental conditions grows (see chapter 2), the class of equally acceptable models (hypothetical ideal environments) shrinks. Moreover, in creatures with the capacity to learn and store information about their world in memory, a new and more powerful exegetical principle comes into play. The scars and dents on the cherry pitter (or was it a sail mender?) may on occasion prove to be telltale, but the scars and dents on a learning creature's memory are *designed* to be telltale, to record with high fidelity both particular encounters and general lessons, for future use. Since the scars and dents of memory are for future use, we can hope to "read" them by exploiting our knowledge of the dispositions that depend on them, so long as we assume the dispositions so attached are in general appropriate. Such interpretations of "memory traces" yield more specific information about the world in which the creature lived and to which it had accommodated itself. But we will not be able to tell information about this world from misinformation, and thus the world we extrapolate as *constituted* by the organism's current state will be an ideal world, not in the sense of *best*, but in the sense of *unreal*.

The naturalists will rightly insist that the actual environment as encountered has left its mark on the organism and intricately shaped it; the organism is in its current state *because of the history it has had,* and only such a history could in fact have put it into its present state. But in a thought-experimental mood we can imagine creating a duplicate whose *apparent* history was not its actual history (as in the case of a faked antique, with its simulated "distress" marks and wear and tear). Such a complete duplication (which is only logically, thought-experimentally, possible) is the limiting case of something actual and familiar: any particular feature of current state may be misbegotten, so that the way the world ought to have been for the creature now to be in this state is not quite the way the world was. The notional world we describe by extrapolation from current state is thus not exactly the world we take to have created that state, even if we know that actual world, but rather the apparent world of the creature, the world apparent *to* the creature as manifested in the creature's current total dispositional state.

Suppose we apply this imaginary exercise in notional world formation to highly adaptive organisms like ourselves. Such organisms have internal structure and dispositional traits so rich in information about the environment in which they grew up that we could in principle say: this organism is best fitted to an environment in which there is a city called Boston, in which the organism spent its youth, in the company of organisms named . . . and so forth. We would not be able to distinguish Boston from Twin Earth Boston, of course, but except for such virtually indistinguishable variations on a theme, our exercise in notional world formation would end in a unique solution.

That, at any rate, is the myth. It is a practically useless myth, of course, but theoretically important, for it reveals the fundamental assumptions that are being made about the ultimate dependence of the organismic contribution on the physical constitution of the organism. (This dependence is otherwise known as the supervenience of (narrow) psychological traits on physical traits; see, e.g., Stich 1978a.) At the same time, the myth preserves the underdetermination of ultimate reference that was the acclaimed moral of the Putnamian considerations. If there is a language of thought, this is how you would have to bootstrap your way to discovering it and translating it—without so much as the benefit of bilingual interpreters or circumstantial evidence about the source of the text. If there is any third-person alternative to the dubious introspectionist (*genuinely*

solipsistic) method of the Phenomenologists, if hetero-phenomenology is possible at all, it will have to be by this method.

In principle, then, the ultimate fruits of the method, applied to a
human being under the constraints of methodological solipsism,
would be an exhaustive description of that person's notional world,
complete with its mistaken identities, chimaeras and personal bogey-
men, factual errors and distortions.[13] We may think of it as *the* notional world of the individual, but of course the most exhaustive
description possible would fail to specify a unique world. For instance, variations in a world entirely beyond the ken, or interests, of a
person would generate different possible worlds equally consistent
with the maximal determination provided by the constitution of the
person.

The situation is analogous to that of more familiar fictional worlds,
such as the world of Sherlock Holmes or Dickens's London. Lewis
(1978) provides an account of "truth in fiction," the semantics of the
interpretation of fiction, that develops the idea we need: "the" world
of Sherlock Holmes is formally better conceived of as a *set* of possible
worlds, roughly: all the possible worlds consistent with the entire
corpus of Sherlock Holmes texts by Conan Doyle.[14] Similarly, "the"

---

13. What about the objects of its fears, hopes, and desires? Are they denizens of the
subject's notional world, or must we add a desire world, a fear world, and so forth to
the subject's belief world? (Joe Camp and others have pressed this worry.) When
something the subject believes to exist is also feared, or desired, by him, there is no
problem: some denizen of his notional world is simply colored with desire or fear or
admiration or whatever. How to treat "the dream house I hope someday to build" is
another matter. Postponing the details to another occasion, I will venture some incautious general claims. My dream house is not a denizen of my notional world on a par
with my house or even the house I will end my days in; thinking about *it* (my dream
house) is not, for instance, to be analyzed in the same fashion as thinking about my
house or thinking about the house I will end my days in. (More on this theme in the
following section.) My dream house gets constituted indirectly in my notional world
via what we might call my *specifications*, which are perfectly ordinary denizens of my
notional world, and my general beliefs and other atttitudes. I believe in my specifications, which already exist in the world as items of mental furniture created by my
thinking, and then there are general beliefs and desires and the like involving those
specifications: to say my dream house is built of cedar is not to say my specification is
made of cedar, but to say that any house built to my specification would be made of
cedar. To say I plan to build *it* next year is to say that I plan to build a house to my specs
next year.

14. Special features of (literary) fiction lead Lewis to make substantial ingenious modifications to this idea, in order to account for the role of background assumptions,
narrator knowledge, and the like in the normal interpretation of fiction. For instance,
we assume that the map of Holmes's London is that of Victorian London except where

notional world we describe might better be viewed formally as the set of possible worlds consistent with the maximal description (see Hintikka 1962; Stalnaker 1984). Note that the description is the *theorist's* description; we do not *assume* that the structural features of the organism on which the theorist bases his description include elements which themselves are descriptions. (The features of the cherry pitter that lead us to describe a cherry (rather than a peach or an olive) are not themselves descriptions of cherries.) From this perspective, we can see that Putnam has devised Twin Earth and Earth both to be members of the set of possible worlds that *is* the notional world I share with my *Doppelgänger*. XYZ slakes thirst, dissolves wallpaper paste, and produces rainbows as well as H_2O does; its difference from H_2O is beneath all the thresholds of discrimination of both me and my *Doppelgänger*—provided, presumably, that neither of us is, or consults with, a wily chemist or microphysicist.

Given a notional world for a subject, we can talk about what the subject's beliefs are *about*, in a peculiar, but familiar, sense of "about." Goodman (1961) discusses sentences of Dickens that are "Pickwick-about," a semantic feature of these sentences that is not genuinely relational, there being no Mr. Pickwick for them to be about in the strong, relational sense. In a similar spirit, Brentano discusses the "relation*like*" status of mental phenomena whose intentional objects are nonexistent (see Aquila 1977). An enabling assumption of notional attitude psychology is that the theorist can use Pickwick-aboutness and its kin as the semantic properties one needs for the foundations of any theory of mental representation.

The strategy is not untried. Although notional attitude psychology has been concocted here as a response to the philosophical problems encountered in propositional attitude and sentential attitude psychology, it can be easily discerned to be the tacit methodology and ideology of a major branch of Artificial Intelligence. Consider, for instance, the now famous SHRDLU system of Winograd (1972). SHRDLU is a "robot" that "lives in" a world consisting of a table on which there are blocks of various colors and shapes. It perceives these and moves them about in response to typed commands (in English) and can answer questions (in English) about its activities and the state of its

---

overridden by Conan Doyle's inventions; the texts neither assert nor strictly imply that Holmes did not have a third nostril, but the possible worlds in which this is the case are excluded.

world. The scare-quotes above are crucial, for SHRDLU isn't really a robot, and there is no table with blocks on it for SHRDLU to manipulate. That world, and SHRDLU's actions in it, are merely simulated in the computer program of which SHRDLU the robot *simulation* is a part. Fodor (1980) makes the point we want, even anticipating our terminology:

> In effect, the machine lives in an entirely notional world; all its beliefs are false. Of course, it doesn't matter to the machine that its beliefs are false since falsity is a semantic property and, qua computer, the device satisfies the formality conditions; *viz.*, it has access only to formal (non-semantic) properties of the representation that it manipulates. In effect, the device is in precisely the situation that Descartes dreads: it's a mere computer which dreams that it's a robot.

To some critics, the fact that SHRDLU does not really perceive things in the world, touch them, and otherwise enter into causal relations with them, suffices to show that whatever else SHRDLU may have, SHRDLU certainly has no *beliefs* at all. What beliefs could SHRDLU have? What could their content be? What could they be about? SHRDLU is a purely formal system quite unattached to the world by bonds of perception, action, or indeed interest. The idea that such merely formal, merely syntactical states and processes, utterly lacking all semantic properties, could provide us with a model of belief is preposterous! (SHRDLU brings out the bluster in people.)

The gentle reply available in principle runs as follows. Indeed, as the critics proclaim, a genuine believer must be richly and intimately attached by perception and action to things in the world, the objects of his beliefs, but providing those bonds for SHRDLU by providing it with real TV-camera eyes, a real robotic arm, and a real table of blocks on which to live, would have been expensive, time consuming, and *of little psychological interest*. Clothed in a transducer–effector overcoat of robotics hardware, SHRDLU would have a notional world of blocks on a table top—which is to say, plunked into that *real* environment SHRDLU would make out very well; a blocks world is a good niche for SHRDLU. Stripped of the robotics overcoat, SHRDLU has a vastly less specific notional world; many more possible worlds are indistinguishable to it, but still, the functional structure of the core is the locus of the interesting psychological problems and their proposed solutions, so choosing the blocks world as an *admissible* notional world (it is in the set of Tarski models for the core system) is an innocent way of clothing the system in a bit of verisimilitude.

In the actual case of SHRDLU, this defense would be optimistic;

SHRDLU is not that good. It would *not* be trivial, or even an expensive but straightforward bit of engineering, to clothe SHRDLU in robotics, and the reasons why it would not are of psychological interest. By keeping SHRDLU's world merely notional, Winograd neatly excused himself from providing solutions to a wealth of difficult, deep, and important problems in psychology. It is far from clear that any improvements on SHRDLU, conceived in the same spirit within the same research program, could more justly avail themselves of this line of defense. But that it is the assumed ideal line of defense of such research is, I think, unquestionable. To Husserl's claim that bracketing the real world leaves you with the essence of the mental, Winograd and AI can add: Yes, and besides, bracketing saves you time and money.

The Husserlian themes in this AI research program are unmistakable, but it is important to remind ourselves as well of the differences. To the auto-phenomenologist, the relative inaccessibility of the real referents of one's beliefs—and hence, as Putnam argues, the relative inaccessibility of one's *propositional* attitudes—is presented as a point about the limits of introspective privileged access, a very Cartesian result: *I cannot discriminate for sure; I* am not *authoritative* about which proposition I am now entertaining, which real object I am now thinking about. But SHRDLU's "introspections" play no privileged role in Winograd's hetero-phenomenology: SHRDLU's notional world is fixed from the outside by appeal to objective and publicly accessible facts about the capacities and dispositions of the system, and hence its fate in various imagined environments. The counterpart to the Cartesian claim is that even the totality of these *public* facts underdetermines propositional attitudes. Even though the environments appealed to are imaginary, the appeal places hetero-phenomenology squarely on the naturalistic side of the Jamesian division.

The elaboration of imaginary ideal environments for purposes of comparison of internally different systems is a strategy of some currency, in engineering for instance. We can compare the power of different automobile engines by imagining them in pulling contests against a certain fictional horse, or we can compare their fuel efficiency by seeing how far they will push a car in a certain simulated environment. The use of an ideal environment permits one to describe *functional* similarities or competences independently of details of implementation or performance. Utilizing the strategy in psychology to elaborate notional worlds is just a particularly complex case. It enables us to describe partial similarities in the psychological "competences" of different subjects—for instance, their representational *powers*—in ways that are neutral about their implementation—for instance, their representational *means*.

The analogy with fiction is again useful in making this point. What exactly is the similarity between Shakespeare's *Romeo and Juliet* and Bernstein's *West Side Story?* The latter was "based on" the former, we know, but what do they actually have in common? Are they about the same people? No, for they are both fictions. Do they contain the same or similar representations? What could this mean? The same words or sentences or descriptions? The scripts of both happen to be written in English, but this is clearly irrelevant, for the similarity we are after survives translation into other languages, and—more dramatically— is evident in the film of *West Side Story* and in Gounod's opera. The similarity is independent of any particular means of representation— scripts, sketches, descriptions, actors on stages or before cameras— and concerns *what is represented*. It is not any kind of syntactic similarity. Since such similarities are as evident in fiction as in factual reporting, we must understand "what is represented" to take us to elements of a notional world, not necessarily the real world. We can compare different notional or fictional worlds with regard to matters large and small, just as we can compare different parts of the real world. We can compare a notional world with the real world. (The nearsighted Mr. Magoo's notional world only intermittently and par- tially resembles the real world, but just enough, miraculously, to save him from disaster.)

When, then, shall we say that two different people share a notional attitude or set of notional attitudes? When their notional worlds have a point or region of similarity. Notional worlds are agent-centered or egocentric (Perry 1977; Lewis 1979); when comparing notional worlds for psychological similarity it will typically be useful, therefore, to "superimpose" the centers—so that the origins, the intersection of the axes, coincide—before testing for similarity. In this way the psy- chological similarities between two paranoids will emerge, while the psychological difference between the masochist and his sadistic part- ner stands out in spite of the great similarity in the *dramatis personae* of their notional worlds viewed uncentered.[15]

---

15. The issues surrounding "I" and indexicality are much more complicated than this hurried acknowledgement reveals. See not only Perry and Lewis, but also Castañeda (1966, 1967, 1968). For illuminating reflections on a similar theme, see Hofstadter 1979, pp. 373–76.

The prospect of a rigorous method of notional world comparison—
a decision procedure for finding and rating points of coincidence, for
instance—is dim. But we have always known that, for the prospects
of setting conditions for propositional attitude identity are equally
dim. I believe that salt is sodium chloride, but my knowledge of
chemistry is abysmal; the chemist believes that salt is sodium chloride
as well, but there is not going to be any crisp way of capturing the
common core of our beliefs (Dennett 1969). The comparability of beliefs, viewed either as notional attitudes or as propositional attitudes,
is not going to be rendered routine by any theoretical stroke. The *gain
in precision* one might misguidedly have hoped to obtain by isolating
and translating "the language of thought"—if it exists—would not
improve the comparability of *beliefs,* such as mine and the chemist's
about salt, but only the comparability of a certain novel kind of sentence—sentences in the head. But sentences are already nicely com-
parable. The English-speaking chemist and I use exactly the same
words to express our belief about salt, and if perchance our brains do
as well, we will still have the problem of comparability for our beliefs.

A language of thought would give no more leverage in the vexed
case of irrational—and especially contradictory—beliefs, and for the
same reason. Suppose the hypothesis is bruited that Bill has a particular pair of contradictory beliefs: he believes both that Tom is to be
trusted and that Tom is not to be trusted. In any language worth its
salt nothing is more cut and dried than determining when one sentence contradicts another, so knowing Bill's language of thought, we
search in his brain for the relevant pair of sentences. And we find
them! What would this show? The question would still remain:
Which (if either) does he believe? We might find, on further investigation, that one of these sentences was vestigial and nonfunctional—
never erased from the cerebral blackboard, but never consulted
either. Or we might find that one sentence (the Mentalese for "Tom is
not to be trusted") was intermittently consulted (and acted upon)—
good evidence that Bill believes Tom is not to be trusted, but it keeps
slipping his mind. He forgets, and then his natural *bonhomie* takes
over and, believing that people in general are to be trusted, he be-
haves as if he believes Tom is to be trusted. Or perhaps we find truly
conflicting behavior in Bill; he goes on and on in conversation about
Tom's trustworthiness, but we note he never turns his back on Tom.
One can multiply the cases, filling gaps and extending the extremes,
but in none of the cases does the presence or absence of explicit

contradiction in the Mentalese play more than a peripheral supporting role in our decision to characterize Bill as vacillating, forgetful,
indecisive, or truly irrational. Bill's behavior counts for more, but
behavior will not *settle* the matter either (see chapter 4 and its
reflections).

People certainly do get confused and worse; sometimes they go
quite mad. To say that someone is irrational is to say (in part) that in
some regard he is ill equipped to deal with the world he inhabits; he
ill fits his niche. In bad cases we may be unable to devise any notional
world for him; no possible world would be a place where he fits right
in. One could leave the issue there, or one could attempt to be more
descriptive of the person's confusion.[16] One could compose an avow-
edly inconsistent description, citing chapter and verse from the subject's behavioral propensities and internal constitution in support of
the various parts of the description. Such an inconsistent description
could not be of *a* notional world, since notional worlds, as sets of
possible worlds, cannot have contradictory properties, but nothing
guarantees that a subject has a single coherent notional world. His
notional world may be shattered into fragmentary, overlapping, competing worlds.[17] When the theorist, the hetero-phenomenologist or
notional world psychologist, takes the course of offering an admittedly inconsistent description of a notional world, it counts not as a
settled, positive characterization of a notional world, but as a surren-
der in the face of confusion—giving up the attempt at (complete)
interpretation. It is analogous to lapsing into direct quotation when
conveying someone's remarks. "Well, what he *said* was: 'Nothing
noths.' "

Notional world hetero-phenomenology does not, then, settle the
disputes and indeterminacies, or even sharpen the boundaries of
everyday-folks' thinking about belief; it inherits the problems and
simply recasts them in a slightly new format. One might well wonder
what resources it has to recommend it. The prospect of constructing

---

16. "A man may think that he believes *p*, while his behavior can only be explained by
the hypothesis that he believes not-*p*, given that it is known that he wants *z*. Perhaps
the confusion in his mind cannot be conveyed by any simple [or complex—D.C.D.]
account of what be believes: perhaps only a reproduction of the complexity and confusion will be accurate." (Hampshire 1975, p. 123)

17. See the discussion of Phenomenology and "Feenomanology" in "Two Approaches
to Mental Images," in *Brainstorms*. See also Lewis's (1978) remarks on how to deal with
inconsistency in a work of fiction.

the notional world of an actual creature from an examination of its physical constitution is as remote as can be, so what value can there be in conceiving of a creature's notional world? Working in the other direction: starting with a description of a notional world and then asking how to design a "creature" with that notional world. Part of the allure of AI is that it provides a way of starting with what are essentially phenomenological categories and distinctions—features of notional worlds—and working backward to hypotheses about how to implement those competences. One starts with representational *powers,* and works toward *means.* Philosophers have also toyed with this strategy.

The recent philosophical literature on the distinction between *de re* and *de dicto* beliefs and other attitudes is replete with sketchy suggestions for various sorts of mental machinery that might play a crucial role in drawing that distinction: Kaplan's (1968) *vivid names,* the *modes of presentation* of Schiffer (1978) and various other authors, and Searle's (1979) *aspects,* to name a few. These are typically supposed to be definable purely in terms of narrow psychology,[18] so notional attitude psychology should, in principle, be able to capture them. When we turn to that literature in the next section, we will explore the prospects for such machinery, but first there are some more grounds for skepticism about notional worlds to bring into the open.

The theme of a notional world, a world *constituted* by the mind or experience of a subject, has been a recurrent *leitmotif* in philosophy at least since Descartes. In various forms it has haunted idealism, phenomenalism, verificationism, and the coherence theory of truth, and in spite of the drubbing it typically takes, it keeps getting resurrected in new, improved versions: in Goodman's (1978) *Ways of Worldmaking* and in Putnam's (1978) recent revaluation of realism, for instance. The ubiquity of the theme is no proof of its soundness in any guise; it may be nothing more than an eternally tempting mistake. In its present guise it runs headlong into an equally compelling intuition about reference. If notional attitudes are to play the intermediary role assigned to them, if they are to be the counterpart for psychology of Kaplan's concept of the character of a linguistic expression, then it should follow that when a psychological subject or creature, with its

---

18. Kaplan (1968) is explicit: "The crucial feature of this notion [Ralph's vivid names] is that it depends only on Ralph's current mental state, and ignores all links whether by resemblance or genesis with the actual world. . . . It is intended to go to the purely internal aspects of individuation." (p. 201)

notional world fixed by its internal constitution, is placed in different contexts, different real environments, this should determine different propositional attitudes for the subject:

notional attitude + environment → propositional attitude.

That means that if I and my *Doppelgänger* were to be switched, instantaneously (or in any case without permitting any change of internal state to occur during the transition—the interchange could take a long time so long as I and my *Doppelgänger* were comatose throughout), I would wake up with propositional attitudes *about the things on Twin Earth,* and my *Doppelgänger* would have propositional attitudes *about things on Earth.*[19] But that is highly counterintuitive (to many people, I discover, but not to all). For instance, I have many beliefs and other attitudes about my wife, a person on Earth. When my *Doppelgänger* first wakes up on Earth after the switch, and thinks "I wonder if Susan has made the coffee yet," *surely* he isn't thinking thoughts about *my wife*—he has never met her or heard of her! His thoughts, surely, are about *his* Susan, light years away, though he hasn't an inkling of the distance, of course. The fact that he'd never know the difference, nor would anyone else except the Evil Demon that pulled off the switch, is irrelevant; what no one could verify would nevertheless be true; his thoughts are not about my wife—at least not until he has had some causal commerce with her.

That is the essence of the causal theory of reference (see, e.g., Kripke 1972; Evans 1973; Donnellan 1966, 1970, 1974) and the thought experiment nicely isolates it. But intuitions provoked in such wildly

---

19. My *Doppelgänger* would not, however, have thoughts *about me* when he thought "I'm sleepy" and so forth. The reference of the first-person pronoun is not affected by world switching, of course (see Putnam 1975a; Perry 1977, 1979; Lewis 1979). But one must be careful not to inflate this point into a metaphysical doctrine about personal identity. Consider this variation on a familiar science-fiction theme in philosophy. Your space ship crashes on Mars, and you want to return to Earth. Fortunately, a Teleporter is available. You step into the booth on Mars and it does a complete microphysical analysis of you, which requires dissolving you into your component atoms, of course. It beams the information to Earth, where the receiver, stocked with lots of atoms the way a photocopier is stocked with fresh white paper, creates an exact duplicate of you, which steps out and "continues" your life on Earth with your family and friends. Does the Teleporter "murder to dissect," or has it transported you home? When the newly arrived Earth-you says "I had a nasty accident on Mars," is what he says true? Suppose the Teleporter can obtain its information about you without dissolving you, so that you continue a solitary life on Mars. On your mark, get set, go. . . (Some who have taken up this philosophical party game: Hofstadter and Dennett 1981; Nozick 1981; Parfit 1984; Nagel 1986.)

science-fictional circumstances are a poor test. Consider the same issue as it could arise in a perfectly possible train of events right here on Earth. In Costa Mesa, California, there is, or at any rate used to be, an establishment called Shakey's Pizza Parlor, a garish place featuring an ill-tuned player piano with fluorescent keys and with various "funny" hand-painted signs on the walls: "Shakey's has made a deal with the bank: we don't cash checks, and the bank doesn't make pizza," and so forth. Oddly enough, very oddly in fact, in Westwood Village, California, some fifty miles away, there was another Shakey's Pizza Parlor, and it was eerily similar: built to the same blueprint, same ill-tuned player piano, same signs, same parking lot, same menu, same tables and benches. The obvious practical joke occurred to me when first I noticed this, but sad to say I never carried it out. It could easily have been done, however, so let me tell you the tale as if it actually happened.

The Ballad of Shakey's Pizza Parlor

Once upon a time, Tom, Dick, and Harry went to Shakey's in Costa Mesa for beer and pizza, and Dick and Harry played a trick on Tom, who was new to the area. After they had ordered their food and begun eating, Tom went to the men's room, whereupon Dick slipped a mickey into Tom's beer. Tom returned to the table, drained his mug, and soon fell sound asleep at the table. Dick gathered up the uneaten pizzas, Harry got Tom's hat off the peg behind his head, and then they dragged Tom out to the car and sped to Westwood Village, where they re-established themselves, with a new pitcher of beer and some mugs, at the counterpart table. Then Tom woke up. "I must have dozed off," he commented, and the evening proceeded, noisily, as before. The conversation turned to the signs and other decorations, and then to graffiti; to the delight of Dick and Harry, Tom pointed toward the men's room and confessed that although he isn't really that sort of guy, tonight he was inspired to carve his initials on the door of the leftmost stall in that men's room. Dick and Harry doubted his word, whereupon Tom offered a wager. He announced he was prepared to bet that his initials were carved on that door. Dick took the wager, with Harry to referee, and a paper and pencil were produced, on which the explicit expression of the proposition at issue was to be written. At his point, the suspense was high, for whether or not Dick won the wager depended on the exact wording. If Tom wrote "I wager $5 that on the leftmost stall door in the men's room in the Costa Mesa Shakey's my initials appear," Tom would win the wager. But if Tom wrote "I wager $5 that my initials appear on the leftmost stall of the men's room of the pizza parlor in which we currently are seated"—or words to *that* effect—Dick would win. A third possibility was that Tom would compose a sentence that *failed to express a proposition* because it contained a vacuous name or vacuous description: "the Costa Mesa Shakey's, in which we are now sitting" or "the men's room of the place wherein I bought and entirely consumed an anchovy pizza on the night of February 11, 1968." In that case Harry would be forced to declare the wager ill formed and return the stakes. (If Harry is a strict Russellian about definite descriptions, he may declare Tom's sentence false in these instances, and award the money to Dick.)

But Tom played into their hands, committed himself on paper to the Westwood Village door (though not under *that* description, of course), and lost the bet. The practical joke was explained to him, and Tom, though he admitted he'd been tricked, agreed that he had committed himself to a false proposition and had fairly lost the bet. But which door had he "had in mind"? Well, in some regards, he could rightly insist, he'd had the Costa Mesa door in mind. He'd vividly recalled the episode of his penknife digging into that door. But also he'd vividly "pictured" the door as being just a few feet away and eagerly anticipated, in his imagination, the triumph to ensue when the three of them walked into the adjacent men's room to settle the bet. So there was also a lot to be said in favor of his having had the Westwood Village door in mind. Such a puzzle! Clearly this was a job for sober philosophers with a technical vocabulary at their disposal!

There is a distinction, the philosophers say, between belief *de re* and belief *de dicto*. Everyone knows this distinction in his heart, but like many important philosophical distinctions, it is hard to characterize precisely and uncontroversially. We're working on it. In the meantime, we mark the distinction, which tends to get lost in the ambiguities of casual talk, by always using the awkward but at least arguably grammatical "of" style of attribution, when speaking of beliefs *de re*, reserving the "that" style for attributions of belief *de dicto*.[20] Thus

(1) Bill believes *that* the captain of the Soviet Ice Hockey team is a man

but it is not the case that

(2) Bill believes *of* the captain of the Soviet Ice Hockey Team that he is a man

since Bill is utterly unacquainted with that stalwart Russian, whoever he is. In contrast,

---

20. Connoisseurs of the literature will note that this sentence delicately reproduces a familiar equivocation that marks the *genre:* does *"de re"* modify "speaking" or "beliefs"; does *"de dicto"* modify "attributions" or "belief"?

(3)   Bill believes *of* his own father that he is a man.

Surely we all know *that* distinction, the distinction ostended by the example, so now we can proceed to apply it in the case of Shakey's Pizza Parlor. In virtue of Tom's rich causal intercourse with the Costa Mesa Shakey's and the things within it, Tom is entitled to *de re* beliefs relating him to those things. When he wakes up in Westwood Village, as his eyes dart about the room he swiftly picks up the obligatory causal relations with *many* of the objects in Westwood Village as well, including the Westwood Village Shakey's itself. Thus we can catalogue some of the true and false *de re* beliefs on Tom shortly after waking.

Tom believes *of* the Costa Mesa Shakey's:

True	False
that he bought a pizza in it tonight	that he is in it now
that he dozed off in it	that he woke up in it
that he put his hat on a peg in it	that his hat is on a peg in it

Tom believes *of* the Westwood Village Shakey's:

True	False
that he is in it now	that he bought a pizza in it tonight
that he woke up in it	that he dozed off in it
that his hat is on a peg in it	that he puts his hat on a peg in it

Where in the normal course of things a person would have a single list of *de re* beliefs, Tom, because of the trick dislocation we have produced, has a dual list of *de re* beliefs; every true *de re* belief has a false twin about a different object. Of course this doubling up of Tom's beliefs is entirely unrecognized by Tom; there is still *something unitary* about his *psychological state*. (We could say: there is unity in his notional world, where there is duality in the real world. Each single notional attitude of his spawns a pair of propositional attitudes, given his peculiar circumstances.)

But problems emerge when we attempt to continue the list of Tom's *de re* beliefs. Tom presumably believes *of* his hat both that it is on a peg in Costa Mesa and that it is on a peg right behind his head. Having noticed the Costa Mesa peg, however casually, Tom can also be said to believe *of* the Costa Mesa peg that his hat is on it (or, putting the two together: he believes *of* his hat and that peg that the former is on the latter). But can he believe *of* the peg behind his head,

with which his only causal interaction to date has been an infin-
itesimally weak mutual gravitational attraction, that his hat is on it?
The causal theorist must deny it. One would think that Tom's psychological state *vis-à-vis* his hat and its location was quite simple (and
so it seems to Tom), but in fact it is quite wonderfully complex, when
subjected to philosophical analysis. Tom believes *that* his hat is on a
peg behind his head (and that is a true belief); he also believes truly
that the peg behind his head on which his hat is resting is made of
wood. He does not believe *of* that peg, however, that it is made
of wood or behind his head. Moreover, Tom believes truly *that* there
is a leftmost stall door in the adjacent men's room and believes falsely
that the leftmost stall door in the adjacent men's room has his initials carved on it. So he believes that the leftmost stall door has his
initials on it, but he does not believe of the leftmost stall door that it
has his initials on it.

Some philosophers would disagree. Some (e.g., Kaplan 1968)
would say Tom's rapport with the Costa Mesa peg was too *casual*
(though causal) to qualify Tom for *de re* beliefs about it. Pushing in the
other direction, some (e.g., Kaplan 1978) would hope to weaken the
causal requirement (and replace it with something else, still to be
determined) so that Tom could have *de re* beliefs about the unseen
peg and the unmarked door. And some would stick to their guns and
claim that the admittedly bizarre distinctions drawn in the preceding
paragraph were nothing more than the tolerable implications of a
good theory put *in extremis* by highly unusual conditions.

The point of pursuing these disagreements, of settling the philosophical dispute, might well be lost on a psychologist. It is tempting
to hold that the *philosophical* problems encountered here, even if they
are serious, real problems whose solution is worth pursuing, are not
problems for psychology at all. For note that the different schools of
thought about Tom's *de re* beliefs fail to differ in the predictions they
would make of Tom's behavior under various circumstances. Which
sentences he can be enticed to bet on, for instance, does not depend
on which *de re* beliefs he *really* has. No school can claim predictive
superiority based on its more accurate catalogue of Tom's beliefs.
Those who hold he does not have any *de re* beliefs about the unseen
door will *retrospectively* describe those cases in which Tom makes a
losing bet as cases in which he willy-nilly asserts something he does
not mean to assert, while those of the opposite persuasion will count
him on those occasions as having (willy-nilly) expressed exactly what

he believed. In the imagined case, if not perhaps in other, more normal cases, the presence or absence of a particular *de re* belief plays no predictive, hence no explanatory, role. But if in the imagined case it plays no role, should we not abandon the concept in favor of some concept which can characterize the crucial variables in both the normal and the abnormal cases?

The apparent failure of the philosophical distinctions to mesh with any useful psychological distinction may be due, however, to our looking in the wrong place, focusing too narrowly on a contrived *local* indiscernibility and thus missing an important psychological difference that emerges somehow in a broader context. The family of outlandish cases concocted by participants in the literature, involving elaborate practical jokes, tricks with mirrors, people dressed up like gorillas, identical twins, and the rest of the theatrical gimmicks designed to produce cases of *mistaken identity*, succeed in producing only momentary or at best unstable effects of the desired sort. One cannot easily sustain the sort of illusion required to ground the anomalous verdicts or other puzzles. Drawing verdicts based on short-lived anomalies in a person's psychological state provides a seriously distorted picture of the way people are related to things in the world; our capacity to keep track of things through time is not well described by any theory that atomizes psychological processes into successive moments with certain characteristics.[21] This is all, I think, very plausible, but what conclusion should be drawn from it? Perhaps this: formal semantics requires us to *fix* an object to be evaluated, at a particular time and in a particular context, for truth-value or reference, and while overt linguistic behavior provides the theorist with candidate objects—utterances—for such a role, *moving the game inside* and positing analogous "mental" objects or states for such fixing must do violence to the psychological situation. Anyone who imports the categories required for a formal semantic theory and presses them into service in a psychological theory is bound to create a monster. Such a conclusion is, as James might say, "vagueness incarnate." In particular, it is not yet clear whether it might be so strong a conclusion as to threaten *all* versions of "mental representation" theory, all

---

21. Evans, in lectures in Oxford in 1979, developed the theme of the *process* of keeping track of things in the world (see Evans 1982). It echoes a central theme in Neisser's (1976) apostatic renunciation of two-dimensional, tachistoscopic experiments in the psychology of perception, in favor of a Gibsonian "ecological" approach to perception.

theories that suppose there are syntactic objects in the head for which a principled semantic interpretation can be given.

I find it very difficult to put a crisper expression to this worry, but can for the moment render it more vivid with the aid of an analogy. One of the most inspired skits featured regularly on the television show *Laugh-In* was "Robot Theater," in which Arte Johnson and Judy Carne played a pair of newlywed robots. They would appear in some mundane circumstance, making breakfast or hubby-home-from-the-office, and would move about in a slightly jerky simulacrum of human action. But things never worked quite right; Arte would reach out to open a door, grasp just short of the knob, turn wrist, swing arm, and crash headlong into the still closed door; Judy would pour coffee for Arte, but the coffee would miss the cup—no matter, since Arte would not notice, and would "drain" the cup, turn lovingly to Judy and say "Delicious!" And so forth. The "problem," one saw, was that their *notional worlds didn't quite "match" the real world;* one had the impression that if they had been moved over about a half an inch before they were "started," everything would have gone swimmingly; then their beliefs would have had a chance of being *about* the things in the world around them. Their behavior was to be explained, presumably, by the fact that each of them contained an internal representation of the world, by consultation with which they governed their behavior. That's how robots work. This internal representation was constantly updated, of course, *but not continuously.* Their perceptual machinery (and their internal records of their actions) provided them with a succession of snapshots, as it were, of reality, which provoked revisions in their internal representations, but not fast enough or accurately enough to sustain a proper match of their notional world, their world-as-represented, and the real world.[22] Hence the behavioral infelicity. The "joke" is that *we are not at all like that.*

Well, are we or aren't we? The hope of cognitive science is that we *are* like that, only much, much better. In support of this conviction, cognitive science can point to precisely the anomalous cases envisaged in the literature on *de re* and *de dicto* beliefs: these are nothing

---

22. The problem of preserving that match has as its core the "frame problem" of Artificial Intelligence which arises for planning systems that must reason about the effects of contemplated actions. See McCarthy and Hayes 1969, and Dennett 1978a, chapter 7, and 1984c. It is either the most difficult problem AI must—and can eventually—solve, or the *reductio ad absurdum* of mental representation theory.

more than experiments, in effect, that induce pathology in the machinery, and hence are rich sources of clues about the design principles of that machinery. That one must work so hard to contrive cases of actual pathology just shows how very good we are at updating our internal representations. The process of keeping track of things is practically continuous, but it will still have a perspicuous description in terms of swift revision of an internal model. Besides, as the pathological cases often show, when one adds *verbal* informing to purely *perceptual* informing of the system, the possibilities of serious dislocation, the creating of notional objects with no real counterparts, and the like, are dramatically increased. Beliefs acquired through the medium of language create problems when they must be meshed with perceptually induced beliefs, but these are problems soluble within the domain of cognitive science (Dennett, forthcoming c).

This suggests that the problems encountered in the story of Shakey's Pizza Parlor come from the attempt to apply a single set of categories to two (or more) very different styles of cognitive operation. In one of these styles, we do have internal representations of things in the world, the content of which in some way guides our behavior. In the other style we have something like procedures for keeping track of things in the world, which permit us to minimize our *representations* of those things by letting us consult the things themselves, rather than their representatives, when we need more information about them. Reflections on this theme are to be found in the literature of philosophy (e.g., Burge 1977; Kaplan 1968, 1978, 1980; Morton 1975; Nelson 1978), psychology (e.g., Gibson 1966; Neisser 1976) and Artificial Intelligence (e.g., Pylyshyn 1979), but no one has yet succeeded in disentangling the goals and assumptions of the various different theoretical enterprises that converge on the topic: the semantics of natural language, the semantics and metaphysics of modal logic, the narrow cognitive psychology of individuals, the broad or naturalistic psychology of individuals in environments and social groups. Armed, tentatively, with the idea of notional worlds, which provides at least a picturesque, if not demonstrably sound, way of describing those matters that belong within the domain of narrow psychology and distinguishing them from matters requiring a different perspective, perhaps some progress can be made by considering the origins of the problematic distinctions in the context of the theoretical problems that gave birth to them.

De re and *de dicto* Dismantled

Unless we are prepared to say that "the mind cannot get beyond the circle of its own ideas," we must recognize that some of the things in the world may in fact become objects of our intentional attitudes. One of the facts about Oliver B. Garrett is that he once lived in Massachusetts; another is that the police have been seeking him for many years; another is that I first learned of his existence in my youth; and another is the fact that I believe him still to be in hiding. (Chisholm 1966)

These are facts *about* Oliver B. Garrett, and they are not trivial. In general, the relations that exist between things in the world in virtue of the beliefs (and other psychological states) of believers are relations we have very good reasons to talk about, so we must have *some* theory or theories capable of asserting that such relations hold. No methodologically solipsistic theory will have that capacity, of course.

The same conclusion is borne in on Quine, the founding father of the contemporary literature on the so called *de re* and *de dicto* distinction, and it requires him to give up, reluctantly, the program of treating *all* attribution of belief (and other psychological states) as "referentially opaque." Nonrelationality is the essence of Quine's concept of referential opacity; a context in a sentence is referentially opaque if the symbols occurring within it are not to be interpreted as playing their normal role; are not, for instance, terms denoting what they normally denote, and hence cannot be bound by quantifiers. Frege maintained a similar view, saying that terms in such contexts had an *oblique* occurrence, and referred not to their ordinary denotations, but to their *senses*. Quine's ontological scruples about Fregean senses and their many kin (propositions, concepts, intensions, attributes, intentional objects . . .) force him to seek elsewhere for an interpretation of the semantics of opaque contexts (see, e.g., Quine 1960, p. 151). In the end, he handles the myriads of different complete belief-predicates (one for each attributable belief) by analogy with *direct quotation;* to have a belief (nonrelationally construed) is to be related to no object or objects in the world save a closed sentence. To believe is to be in an otherwise unanalyzed state captured by a lumpy predicate distinguished from others of its kind by containing an inscription of a sentence which it in effect quotes.

We might try using, instead of the intensional objects, the sentences themselves. Here the identity condition is extreme: notational identity. . . . The plan has its recommendations. Quotation will not fail us in the way abstraction did. Moreover, conspicuously opaque as it is, quotation is a vivid form to which to reduce other opaque constructions. (1960, p. 212; see also p. 216 and Quine 1969)

Such lumpy predicates are not much use, but Quine has long professed his skepticism about the possibility of making any sense of the refractory idioms of intentionality,[23] so he needs opacity only to provide a quarantine barrier protecting the healthy, extensional part of a sentence from the infected part. What one gives up by this tactic. Quine thinks, is nothing one cannot live without: "A *maxim of shallow analysis* prevails: *expose no more logical structure than seems useful* for the deduction or other inquiry at hand. In the immortal words of Adolf Meier, where it doesn't itch, don't scratch." (1960, p. 160) With persistence and ingenuity, Quine staves off most of the apparent demands for relational construals of intentional idioms, but, faced with the sort of case Chisholm describes, he recognizes an itch that must be scratched.

The need of cross-reference from inside a belief construction to an indefinite singular term outside is not to be doubted. Thus see what urgent information the sentence "There is someone whom I believe to be a spy" imparts, in contrast to "I believe that someone is a spy" (in the weak sense of "I believe there are spies"). (1960, p. 148)

This then sets the problem for Quine and subsequent authors: "Belief contexts are referentially opaque; therefore it is prima facie meaningless to quantify into them; how then to provide for those indispensable relational statements of belief, like 'There is someone whom Ralph believes to be a spy'?" (Quine 1956)

Quine is led to acknowledge a distinction between two kinds of belief attribution: *relational* attributions and *notional* attributions, in his terms, although others speak of *de re* and *de dicto* attributions, and Quine acknowledges that it comes to the same thing. (It *does* come to the same thing in the literature, but if Quine had meant what he ought to have meant by "relational" and "notional" it would not have come to the same thing, as we shall see.) This sets in motion the cottage industry of providing an adequate analysis of these two dif-

---

23. "One may accept the Brentano thesis either as showing the indispensability of intentional idioms and the importance of an autonomous science of intention, or as showing the baselessness of intentional idioms and the emptiness of a science of intention. My attitude, unlike Brentano's, is the second." (Quine 1960, p. 221)

ferent kinds of belief attribution. Unfortunately, three different strains of confusion are fostered by Quine's setting of the problem, though Quine himself is not clearly prey to any of them, nor of course is he entirely responsible for the interpretation of his views that solidified the confusions in the subsequent literature. First, like Chisholm, Quine is struck by only one variety of important relation between believers and the things of the world: cases in which the believer is related to a particular concrete individual (almost exclusively in the examples in the literature, another *person*) in virtue of a belief; focus on these cases has led to a sort of institutional blindness to the importance of other relations. Second, by following Adolf Meier's advice and avoiding explicitly relational construals except when the situation demanded it, Quine helps create the illusion that there are two different *types of belief*, two different sorts of mental phenomena, and not just two different styles or modes of belief attribution. Quine's acknowledgment that there are times when one is obliged to make an explicitly relational assertion (and then there are times when one can get by with a merely notional assertion) becomes transformed into an imagined demonstration that there are two different sorts of belief: relational beliefs and nonrelational beliefs. Third, putting the first two confusions together, the identification of relational beliefs as beliefs about particular single individuals leaves it tempting to conclude that *general* beliefs (beliefs that are not, intuitively, about any *one* particular thing) are an entirely nonrelational variety of beliefs. This subliminal conclusion has permitted an unrecognized vacillation or confusion about the status of general beliefs to undermine otherwise well-motivated projects. I shall treat these three sources of confusion in turn, showing how they conspire to create spurious problems and edifices of theory to solve them.

Chisholm draws our attention to some interesting facts about Garrett, and Quine acknowledges the "urgent information" imparted by the assertion that there is someone Ralph believes to be a spy.[24] But consider as well a rather different sort of interesting and important fact.

(1) Many people (wrongly) believe that snakes are slimy.

---

24. Quine (1969) contrasts this "portentous" belief with "trivial" beliefs, such as the belief that the shortest spy is a spy—but later in the same piece is led to a view that "virtually annuls the seemingly vital contrast between [such beliefs]. . . . At first this seems intolerable, but it grows on one." It does, with suitable cultivation, which I shall try to provide.

This is a fact about people, but also about snakes. That is to say,

(2) Snakes are believed by many to be slimy.

This is a property that snakes have, and it is about as important a property as their scaliness. For instance, it is an important *ecological* fact about snakes that many people believe them to be slimy; if it were not so, snakes would certainly be more numerous in certain ecological niches than they are, for many people try to get rid of things they think to be slimy. The ecological relevance of this fact about snakes does not "reduce" to a conjunction of cases of particular snakes being mistakenly believed to be slimy by particular people; many a snake has met an untimely end (thanks to snake traps or poison, say) as a result of someone's *general* belief about snakes, without ever having slithered into rapport with its killer. So the relation snakes bear to anyone who believes *in general* that snakes are slimy is a relation we have reason to want to express in our theories. So too is the relation any particular snake (in virtue of its snakehood) bears to such a believer. Here are some other interesting facts chosen to remind us that not all belief is about particular people.

(3) Snow is believed by virtually everyone to be cold.
(4) It is a fact about charity that some think it superior to faith and hope.
(5) Not having many friends is believed by many to be worse than not having any money.
(6) Democracy is esteemed over tyranny.

What the Quinian quarantine of opaque construal tends to hide from us is that you really cannot make these claims (in a form that allows you to use them in arguments in the obvious ways) unless you can make them in a way that permits explicit relations to be expressed. It will help us to consider a single case in more detail.

Sam is an Iranian living in California, and Herb believes that all Iranians in California should be deported immediately, but he doesn't know Sam from Adam and in fact has no inkling of his existence, though he knows there are Iranians in California, of course. Supposing Herb is an authority or even just an influential citizen, this belief of his is one that Sam, who enjoys California, would regret. A world in which people have this belief is worse, for Sam, than a world in which no one has this belief. Let us say Sam is *jeopardized* by this belief of Herb's. Who else is jeopardized? All Iranians living in California.

Suppose Herb also believes that all marijuana smokers should be publicly whipped. Does this belief also jeopardize Sam? It depends, of course, on whether Sam is a marijuana smoker. Now something follows from

(7) Sam is an Iranian living in California

and

(8) Herb believes all Iranians living in California should be deported immediately

that does not follow from (7) and

(9) Herb believes all marijuana smokers should be publicly whipped.

What follows is something that licenses the conclusion that Sam is jeopardized by Herb's belief cited in (8), but we can agree that what follows is *not*

(10) Herb believes *of Sam* that he should be deported immediately.

That is, no belief of the sort that impresses Quine and Chisholm follows from (7) and (8). Rather, we are looking for something more like

(11) Sam is a member of the set of Iranians in California, and *of that set* Herb believes that all its members should be deported immediately.

Some might shudder at the idea of having sufficient *acquaintance* with a set to enable one to have *de re* beliefs about it, but sets in any case will not do the job. Sam, learning of his jeopardy, may wish to get out of it, e.g., by leaving California *or* by changing Herb's belief. His leaving California changes the membership of the relevant set—changes which set is relevant—but surely does not alter Herb's belief. In short, it is not set membership that jeopardizes Sam, but attribute-having.

(12) There is an attribute (Iranicalifornihood) such that Sam has it, and Herb believes *of* it that anything having it should be deported immediately.

Not just quantifying in, but quantifying over attributes! One might attempt to soften the ontological blow by fiddling around with circumlocutory devices along the lines of

(13) (∃α) (∃c) (α denotes c & Sam is a member of c & Herb believes-
    true ⌜(x) (x is a member of α ⊃ x should be deported
    immediately)⌝)

but they won't work without *ad hoc* provisos of various sorts. If one is
going to take belief talk seriously at all, one might as well let it all
hang out and permit quantification over attributes and relations, as
well as individuals and classes, in all positions within belief contexts.[25] See Wallace (1972) for a proposal in a similar spirit.

The brief for this course has been before us from the outset, for it is
an implication of the Putnamian arguments that even general propositional attitudes, if they are genuinely *propositional* in meeting Frege's
first two conditions, must imply a relation between the believer and
things in the world. *My* belief that all whales are mammals is *about
whales;* my *Doppelgänger's* counterpart belief might not be (if his Twin
Earth had large fish called "whales," for instance). It is whales I
believe to be mammals, and I could not truly be said to believe *that*
whales are mammals unless it could also be said *of* whales that I
believe them to be mammals.

Should we say entirely general beliefs are about anything? One can
read our Fregean condition (b) as requiring it, but there are ways of
denying it (see e.g., "What do General Propositions Refer to?" and
"Oratio Obliqua" in Prior 1976). For instance, can one note that the
logical form of general beliefs such as the belief that all whales are
mammals is $(x) (Fx ⊃ Gx)$, which says, in effect, each thing is such
that if it is a whale, it is a mammal. Such a claim is as much about
cabbages and kings as about whales. By being about everything, it is
about nothing (cf. Goodman 1961; Ullian and Goodman 1977; Donnellan 1974). This does little to still the intuition that when someone
believes whales are fishes he is *wrong about whales,* not *wrong about
everything.* But here is another troublesome challenge: if general beliefs are always about the things mentioned in their expression, what
is the belief that there are no unicorns about? Unicorns? There aren't
any. If we are prepared, as I have urged we should be, to quantify
over attributes, we can say this belief is about *unicornhood,* to the

---

25. Quine explicitly renounces this course, while still hoping to capture whatever
useful, important inferences there are (1960, p. 221; 1969). For further arguments in
favor of viewing some cases of psychological states as *de re* attitudes toward properties
and relations, see Aquila 1977, especially pp. 84–92.

effect that it is nowhere instantiated.[26] If there were unicorns, the belief would be a false belief about unicorns in just the same way the belief that there are no blue whales is (today) a false belief about blue whales. Pointing to a pod of blue whales we could say: these creatures are believed not to exist by Tom.

In any event a tug-of-war about "about" does not strike me as a fruitful strategy to pursue (cf. Donnellan 1974), and yet a bit more must be said about this troublesome but practically indispensable term—mentioned once and used twice within this very sentence. "The term 'about' is notoriously vague and notoriously not to be confused with 'denotes'." (Burge 1978, p. 128) Perhaps there is a sense of "about" that must be carefully distinguished from "denotes"—much of the literature on *de re* belief is after all a quest to explicate just such a *strong* sense of "about"—but there is undeniably another, weaker (and in fact much clearer) sense of "about" of which denotation is the essence. Suppose I believe the shortest spy is a woman. (I have no one in mind, as one says, but it seems a good bet.) Now since I have no one in mind, as one says, there may indeed be a sense in which my belief is not *about* anyone. Yet my belief is either true or false. Which it is depends on the gender of some actual person, the shortest spy, whoever that is. That person is the verifier or falsifier of my belief, the satisfier of the definite description I used to express the belief. There is *that* much relation between me and the shortest spy in virtue of my belief, and paltry and uninteresting as some might find that relation, it is a relation I bear to just one person in virtue of my belief, and we could hardly give it a better name than aboutness—*weak* aboutness, we may call it, allowing for the possible later discovery of stronger, more interesting sorts of aboutness. Suppose Rosa Klebb is the shortest spy. Then it might be misleading to say I was thinking about her when it occurred to me that the shortest spy was probably a woman, but in this weak sense of "about" it would nevertheless be true.[27]

---

26. Kripke's views on unicorns require that not only are there no unicorns, but there could not be any. Could there then be the attribute of unicornhood? See the Addendum to Kripke 1972, pp. 763–69.

27. It would thus also be true that *you* are talking *about her* (in this weak sense) when you assert that I was thinking about the shortest spy. Thus I must disagree with Kripke: "If a description is embedded in a *de dicto* (intensional) context, we cannot be said to be talking *about* the thing described, either *qua* its satisfaction of the description or *qua* anything else. Taken *de dicto*, 'Jones believes that the richest debutante in Dubuque will

The second confusion, of which Quine himself is apparently innocent, is promoted by some misdirection in his "Quantifiers and Propositional Attitudes" (1956), the chief problem-setter for the subsequent
literature. Quine illustrates the difference between two senses of
"believes" with a brace of examples.

Consider the relational and notional senses of believing in spies:

(14) $(\exists x)$ (Ralph believes that x is a spy),
(15) Ralph believes that $(\exists x)$ (x is a spy).

. . . The difference is vast; indeed, if Ralph is like most of us, (15) is true and
(14) is false. (p. 184) [I have changed Quine's numbering of his examples to
conform to my sequence.]

The examples certainly do illustrate two different attribution styles:
Quine's (14) is ontologically committing where (15) is reticent; but
they also illustrate very different sorts of psychological state; (14) is
about what we may call a *specific* belief, while (15) is about a *general*
belief (cf. Searle 1979). It has proven irresistible to many to draw the
unwarranted conclusion that (14) and (15) illustrate a relational kind
of belief and a notional kind of belief respectively. What people ignore is the possibility that *both* beliefs can be attributed in *both* the
relational and notional styles of attribution. On the one hand, some
other relational claim (other than (14)) may be true in virtue of (15),
e.g.,

(16) $(\exists x)$ (x is spyhood & Ralph believes x to be instantiated),

and on the other hand perhaps there are other merely notional readings (other than (15)) that follow from (14). Many have thought so; all
who have tried to isolate a "*de dicto* component" in *de re* belief have
thought so, in effect, though their efforts have typically been confounded by misunderstandings about what *de dicto* beliefs might be.
In contrasting (14) with (15), Quine is comparing apples and oranges,
a mismatch concealed by the spurious plausibility of the idea that the
lexically simple change effected by moving the quantifier takes you
back and forth between a relational claim and its closest notional

---

marry him', can be asserted by someone who thinks (let us suppose, wrongly) that
there are no debutantes in Dubuque; certainly then, he is *in no way* [my italics] talking
about the richest debutante, even 'attributively'." (1977) Imagine Debby, who knows
quite well she is the richest debutante in Dubuque, overhearing this remark; she might
comment: "You may not know it, buster, but you're talking about me, and you've
given me a good laugh. For though Jones doesn't know me, I know who he is—the
social climbing little jerk—and he hasn't a prayer."

counterpart. The true notional counterpart claim of the relational

(17) $(\exists x)$ (x is believed by Tommy to have filled his stocking with toys)

is not

(18) Tommy believes that $(\exists x)$ (x has filled his stocking with toys),

but something for which we do not have a formal expression, although its intended force can be expressed with scare-quotes:

(19) Tommy believes "of Santa Claus" that he has filled his stocking with toys.[28]

Tommy's notional world is inhabited by Santa Claus, a fact we want to express in describing Tommy's current belief-state without committing ourselves to the existence of Santa Claus, which the relational claim (17) would do. That is the job for which we introduced notional world talk. Similarly, but moving in the other direction, when we want to distinguish my general belief that all water is H_2O from its notional twin in my *Doppelgänger,* we will have to say, relationally, that *water* is what I believe to be H_2O.

This is not meant in itself to show that there are two importantly different sorts of belief, or more than two, but only that a certain familiar alignment of the issues is a misalignment. A further particularly insidious symptom of this misalignment is the myth of the non-relationality of "pure *de dicto*" beliefs. (What could be more obvious, one might say: if *de re* beliefs are relational beliefs, then *de dicto* beliefs must be nonrelational beliefs!) The orthodox position is succinctly summarized—not defended—by Sosa (1970):

(20) "Belief *de dicto* is belief that a certain *dictum* (or proposition) is true, whereas belief *de re* is belief about a particular *res* (or thing) that it has a certain property."

One might pause to wonder whether the following definition would be an acceptable substitute:

(21) Belief *de dicto* is belief *of* a certain *dictum* (or proposition) that it is true, whereas belief *de re* is belief *that* a particular *res* (or thing) has a certain property.

---

28. Sellars (1974) discusses the formula: "Jones believes with respect to someone (who may or may not be real) that he is wise."

and if not why not. But instead of pursuing that wonder, I want to focus instead on the wedding of words *"dictum* (or proposition),*"* and what can be conjured from them. The Latin is nicely ambiguous; it means *what is said,* but does that mean *what is uttered* (the words themselves) or *what is expressed* (what the words are used to assert)? The *OED* tells us that a dictum is "a saying," which provides yet another version of the equivocation. We saw at the outset that there were those who viewed propositions as sentence-like things and those who viewed them rather as the (abstract) *meanings* of (*inter alia*) sentence-like things. These are importantly different conceptions, as we have seen, but they are often kept conveniently undistinguished in the literature on *de re* and *de dicto*. This permits the covert influence of an incoherent picture: propositions as *mental sayings,* entirely internal goings on that owe their identities to nothing but their intrinsic properties, and hence are entirely nonrelational.[29] At the same time, these mental sayings are not mere *sentences,* mere syntactic objects, but *propositions.* The idea is fostered that a *de dicto* propositional attitude attribution is an entirely internal or methodologically solipsistic determination of content that is independent of how the believer is situated in the world. The subconscious metaphysics of this reliance on "*de dicto*" formulations as content specifiers is the idea that somehow the mental embrace of a *sentence* causes the *proposition* the sentence *expresses* to be *believed.*[30] (Details of the embracing machinery are left to the psychologist. What is mildly astonishing to me is the apparent willingness of many psychologists and theorists in AI to accept this setting of their task without apparent misgivings.)

No one is clearer than Quine about the difference between a sentence and a proposition, and yet the legerdemain with which he attempts to spirit propositions off the scene and get by with just sentences may have contributed to the confusion. In *Word and Object*

---

29. In this regard mental sayings are seen to be like qualia: *apparently* intrinsic features of minds to be contrasted with relational, functionalistically characterizable features. I argue for the incoherence of this vision of qualia in "Quining Qualia" (forthcoming d). For a clear expression of the suspect view, consider Burge (1977, p. 345: "From a semantical viewpoint, a *de dicto* belief is a belief in which the believer is related only to a completely expressed proposition (*dictum*)."

30. Kaplan (1980) makes disarmingly explicit use of this image in proposing to "use the distinction between direct and indirect discourse to match the distinction between character and content" (of thoughts or beliefs, now, not sentences); this, in spite of his equally disarming concession that "there is no real syntax to the language of thought."

(1960), after introducing the various problems of belief contexts and toying with a full-blown system of propositions, attributes, and relations-in-intension to handle them, Quine shows how to renounce these "creatures of darkness" in favor of the lumpy predicates of direct quotation of sentences. Earlier (1956) he had given a curious defense of this move:

> How, where, and on what grounds to draw a boundary between those who believe or wish or strive that p, and those who do not quite believe or wish or strive that p, is undeniably a vague and obscure affair. However, if anyone does approve of speaking of belief of a proposition at all and of speaking of a proposition in turn as meant by a sentence, then certainly he cannot object to our semantical reformulation "w believes-true S" on any special grounds of obscurity; for "w believes-true S" is explicitly definable in *his* terms as "w believes the proposition meant by S". (pp. 192–93)

This tells us how the believer in propositions, attributes, and the like is to make sense of Quine's new predicates, but it does not tell us how Quine makes sense of them. He never tells us, but given the "flight from intension" he advocates for us all, one can suppose that he doesn't think they really make much sense. They are just a device for getting over a bad bit of material that other people keep insisting on inserting into the corpus of serious utterance. The function of Quine's paraphrases is to permit the imaginary civil servant who translates the corpus into the "canonical notation" to get to the end of the sentence "safely," and on the next sentence—confident that he has made *at least* enough new predicates to ensure that he never uses the same predicate to translate two differently intended propositional attitude claims. If sense is ever made of such claims, they can be recovered without loss of distinctness from canonical deep freeze. In the meantime, Quine's predicates are notional to a fault, but also inert. The problem with this emerges in three quotations:

(A) In the . . . opaque sense "wants" is not a relative term relating people to anything at all, concrete or abstract, real or ideal. (1960, pp. 155–56)

(B) If belief is taken opaquely then [*Tom believes that Cicero denounced Catiline*] expressly relates Tom to no man. (p. 145)

(C) (1) "Tully was a Roman" is trochaic.
(2) The commissioner is looking for the chairman of the hospital board.

Example (2), even if taken in the not purely referential way, differs from (1) in that it still seems to have far more bearing on the chairman of the hospital board, dean though he be, than (1) has on Tully. Hence my cautious phrase "not purely referential," designed to apply to all such cases and to affirm no distinction among them. If I omit the adverb, the motive will be brevity. (p. 142)

(A) is unbending: there is *nothing* relational in the opaque sense of "want"; in (B) the opaque claim does not *expressly* relate Tom to anyone; in (C) it is acknowledged that example (2) "has a bearing on" a particular person, and hence it is to be taken as somewhat referential, but not purely referential. In fact, in all these cases there is clear evidence of what we might call *impure referentiality*. Wanting a sloop "in the notional sense" does not relate one preeminently to any particular sloop, but this wanting relief from slooplessness, as Quine calls it, nevertheless has a bearing on sloops; if no one wanted relief from slooplessness, sloops would not be as numerous, or expensive, as they are. One cannot believe *that* Cicero denounced Catiline without believing *of* Cicero that he denounced Catiline. And it is fact about the chairman of the hospital board that he is being sought by the commissioner, in virtue of the truth of (2).

This impure referentiality has been noted by several authors, and Quine himself provides the paradigm for the later analyses with his example

(22) Giorgione was so-called because of his size (1960, p. 153)

in which, as Quine notes, "Giorgione" does double duty; the perspicuous expansion of (22) is

(23) Giorgione was called "Giorgione" because of his size.

Castañeda (1967), Kiteley (1968), Loar (1972), and Hornsby (1977) develop the theme of the *normally* dual role of singular terms within the clauses of sentences of propositional attitude—for instance to explain the apparent role of the pronoun in such sentences as

(24) Michael thinks that that masked man is a diplomat, but he obviously is not (Loar 1972, p. 49).

This gets part of the story right, but misses the extension of the doctrine from singular terms to general terms. When we quantify over attributes, as in (12) and (16), we complete the picture. A general term within a propositional clause in a sentence of propositional attitude *normally* plays a dual role—as suggested by such sentences as

(25) Herb believes that all Iranians in California should be deported, but none of them have anything to fear from him.[31]

Once we distinguish notional from relational attributions, and distinguish *that* distinction from the distinction between specific and general beliefs, we can see that many of the claims that have been advanced in the effort to characterize *"de re* belief" apply across the board and fail to distinguish a special sort of belief. First, consider the distinction between notional and relational attributions that emerges when we tackle the problem of relating a subject's narrow-psychological states to his broad, propositional states. We start with the myth that we have determined the subject's notional world, and now must line up his notional attitudes with a set of propositional attitudes. This is a matter of looking for the best fit. As we have seen, in the case of seriously confused subjects, there may be no good fit at all. In the case of an irrational subject, there will be no flawless fit because there is no *possible* world in which the subject could be happily situated. In the case of a badly misinformed subject, there will simply be an area of mismatch with the *actual* world. For instance, the child who "believes in Santa Claus" has Santa Claus in his notional world, and no one in the real world is a suitable counterpart, so some of the child's notional attitudes about Santa Claus (Santa-Claus-about) cannot be traded in for *any* propositional attitudes at all. They are like sentence tokens whose character is such that in the context in which they occur they fail to determine *any* content. As Donnellan claims, when such a child *says* "Santa Claus is coming tonight," what he says does not express any proposition (1974, p. 234). We can add: the child's psychological state at that time is a notional attitude that determines no propositional attitude. McDowell (1977) and Field (1978) also endorse different versions of this claim, which can be made to appear outrageous to anyone who insists on viewing beliefs as (nothing but) propositional attitudes. For one must say in that case that no one has beliefs about Santa Claus, and no one could; some people just think they do! Santa-believers have many propositional attitudes, of course, but also some psychological states that are not any propositional attitudes at all. What do they have in their place? (Cf. Blackburn 1979.) Notional attitudes. The attribution of notional attitudes to the child who believes in Santa Claus will provide us with

31. When Burge (1977) doubts the existence of any "pure" *de dicto* beliefs he is best read, I think, as expressing an appreciation of this point. See also Field 1978, pp. 21–23.

all the understanding and all the theoretical leverage we need to account for the child's behavior. For instance, we may derive genuine propositional attitudes from the child's merely notional attitudes when the world occasionally obliges (House, unpublished). Tommy believes the man in the department store with the phony beard will bring him presents because he believes that the man is Santa Claus. That's why Tommy tells *him* what he wants.

On other occasions, e.g., at Shakey's Pizza Parlor, there is an embarrassment of riches: too many objects in the real world as candidate *relata* when we go relational and trade in notional attitude claims for propositional attitude claims. This possibility is not restricted to specific beliefs about individuals. Putnam's (1975a) discussions of natural kind terms reveals that the same problem arises when we must decide which general proposition someone believes when he believes something he would express with the words "All elms are deciduous," when we know he cannot tell an elm from a beech. In such a case different properties or attributes are the candidate *relata* for the beliefs.

The distinction between general and specific beliefs has not yet been made clear, but only ostended, but in the meantime we can note that when we go relational, we will trade in specific notional attitude claims for specific relational—that is, propositional attitude—claims, and general notional attitude claims for general relational—that is, propositional attitude—claims. Ralph's banal belief cited notionally in (15) can also be cited relationally as (16), while Ralph's portentous belief, cited relationally in (14), could also be cited notionally if there were a reason—for instance if Ralph had been duped into his urgent state by pranksters who had convinced him of the existence of a man who never was. The necessary conditions for sustaining a relational attribution are entirely independent of the distinction between specific and general attitudes. This can be seen if we insert examples of general beliefs into the familiar arenas of argument.

(26) Tom believes that whales are mammals.

This is a general belief of Tom's, if any is, but earlier we suggested that Tom cannot truly be said to believe *that* whales are mammals unless we are prepared to say as well *of whales* that they are believed by Tom to be mammals. Formally, such a belief claim would license quantifying in as follows:

(27) $(\exists x)\ (x = $ whalehood & Tom believes of x that whatever instantiates it is a mammal)

If so, then must Tom not have a *vivid name* of whalehood? (Kaplan 1968).

Contrast (26) with

(28) Bill believes that the largest mammals are mammals.

If all Bill knows about whales is that they are the largest mammals, he has a very unvivid name of whalehood. Most of us are in closer rapport with whales, thanks to the media, but consider

(29) Tom believes that dugongs are mammals.

There is certainly an intuitive pull against saying that dugongs are believed by Tom to be mammals, for Tom, like most of us, is cognitively remote from dugongs. He could get closer by learning (in the dictionary) that dugongs are of the order Sirenia, large aquatic herbivores that can be distinguished from manatees by their bilobate tail. Now is Tom equipped to believe *of* dugongs that they are mammals? Are you? It is one thing to believe, as a monolingual German might, that the sentence "Dugongs are mammals" is true; that does not count at all as believing dugongs are mammals; it is another thing to know English and believe that the sentence "Dugongs are mammals" is true, and hence believe (in a very minimal sense) that dugongs are mammals—this is roughly the state most of us are in.[32] If you have read a book about dugongs or seen a film or—even better—seen a dugong in a zoo or had a dugong as a pet, then you are much more secure in your status as a believer that dugongs are mammals. This is not a question of the conditions for believing some particular dugong

---

32. Hornsby (1977) discusses the case of "Jones, an uneducated individual, who has . . . found 'Quine' on a list of names of philosophers. He knows nothing whatsoever about that man, but comes simply to believe that one could assert something true with the words 'Quine is a philosopher.' In such circumstances as these a relational reading . . . cannot be right. But in these circumstances Jones really believes no more than that the properties of being called 'Quine' and being a philosopher are somewhere coinstantiated." (p. 47) The last sentence is *a* relational reading, however, and depending on circumstances further relational readings are likely: e.g., the property of being the person named "Quine" whom the authors of this list intended to include on the list is uniquely instantiated by someone who also instantiates the property of being a philosopher.

to be a mammal, but just of believing in general that (all) dugongs are mammals.[33]

Kaplan initially proposed vivid names as a condition of genuine *de re* belief, but maintained that there was no threshold of vividness above which a name must rise for one to believe *de re* with it. He has since abandoned vividness as a condition of *de re* belief, but why was the idea so appealing in the first place? Because vividness, or what amounts to vividness as Kaplan characterized it (1968), is a condition on *all* belief; one must be richly informed about, intimately connected with, the world at large, its occupants and properties, in order to be said with any propriety to have beliefs. All one's "names" must be somewhat vivid. The idea that some beliefs, *de dicto* beliefs, have no vividness requirement is a symptom of the subliminal view of *de dicto* beliefs as mere mental sayings—not so different from the monolingual German's state when he has somehow acquired "Dugongs are mammals" as a true sentence.

Yet another theme in the literature concerns the admissibility or inadmissibility of substitution of co-designative expressions within the propositional clauses of belief attributions. It is said that when one is attributing a belief *de re*, substitution is permissible, otherwise not. But if all general beliefs have relational renderings (in which they are viewed as beliefs *of* certain attributes, in the manner of (12) and (27)), do these admit of substitution? Yes, under the same sorts of pragmatic constraints for securing reference without misleading that have been noted in the literature for beliefs about individuals (Sosa 1970; Boër and Lycan 1975; Hornsby 1977; Searle 1979—to name a few).

(30) My wife wants me to buy her a sweater the color of your shirt.
(31) Your grandfather thought that children who behave the way you're behaving should be sent to bed without supper.

---

33. Richmond Thomason, in conversation, suggests that the problems raised by these cases (by (1), (2), (25), and (29)) are actually problems about the logic of plurals. He would distinguish believing that dugongs are mammals from believing that all dugongs are mammals. Perhaps we must make this distinction—and if so, it's a pity, since Thomason claims no one has yet devised a trouble-free account of plurals—but even if we make the distinction, I think nothing but naturalness is lost if we recast my examples explicitly as cases of believing all snakes are slimy, all whales are mammals and so forth.

and of course Russell's famous

(32) I thought your yacht was longer than it is.

In (30) and (31) the attributes are referred to by description (cf. Aquila 1977, p. 91). Sometimes reference to *objects* is secured by something like direct ostension, often with the aid of demonstratives, and Donnellan (1966, 1968, 1970, 1974), Kaplan (1978, 1980), and others have claimed that there is a fundamental difference between *direct* reference and the somehow indirect reference obtainable via definite description. Again postponing consideration of the merits of these claims, note that the presumed distinction fails to mark a special feature of specific belief about particular objects. We can say, in an act of direct reference

(33) *This* is the Eiffel Tower and *that* is the Seine.

We can also say, in the same spirit:

(34) An English horn sounds *thus,* while an oboe sounds *thus.*
(35) To get a good vibrato, do *this.* (See Jackendoff, 1985.)

A Frenchman says that something has a certain *je ne sais quoi;* what he means is that *il sait* perfectly well *quoi,* he just can't *say quoi,* for the property in question is a *quale* like the taste of pineapple or the way you look tonight (see Dennett, forthcoming d). He can predicate the property of something only by making an identifying reference to the property by such a definite description, and if this occurs within an intensional context, it often must be read transparently, as in (30) and (31) or

(36) Rubens believed that women who look like you are very beautiful.

With relationality, vividness, substitutability, and direct demonstrative reference set behind us, we can return to the postponed question: what is the distinction between general and specific belief? We should be able to draw the distinction independently of genuinely relational attributions, hence at the level of notional attitude attributions—since we want to distinguish specific Santa-Claus-about states of mind from general states of mind, for instance.

There are two opposing views in the philosophical literature that must be disentangled from their usual involvement with referential and attributive uses of definite descriptions in public speech acts, and with problems arising in attempts to capture a specifically *causal* theory of reference. One can be called the Definite Description view and the other, its denial, which takes various forms, can be noncommittally called the Special Reference view. On the former view, the only distinction to mark is that between believing *all* Fs are Gs on the one hand (general beliefs), and believing *just one* F is G on the other (specific belief), where such specific beliefs are viewed as adequately captured by Russell's theory of definite descriptions. The latter view, while not denying the existence of that distinction in logical form, insists that even the beliefs the former view calls specific, the beliefs expressed with Russellian definite descriptions, are properly general, while there is a further category of truly specific beliefs, which are more strongly *about* their objects, because they pick out their objects by some sort of *direct* reference, unmediated by (the sense of) descriptions of any sort.

To the great frustration of anyone attempting to address the issue as, say, a psychologist or AI theorist, neither view as typically expressed in the philosophical literature makes much plausible contact with what must be, in the end, the empirical issue: what it is, *literally* in the heads of believers, that makes a psychological state a belief about a particular object. The Definite Description view, if taken at literal face value, would be preposterous sententialism; recognizing that, its adherents gesture in the direction of recognitional mechanisms, procedures, and criterial tests as ways of capturing the effect of definite descriptions in more psychologically realistic (if only because vaguer and hence less unrealistic) terms. On the other side, the critics of all such proposals have their own gestures to make in the direction of unspecified causal intimacies and genealogical routes between psychological states and their true objects. Since no progress can be made at those levels of metaphoricalness, perhaps it is best to revert to the traditional philosophical terms (ignoring psychology for a while) to see what the issue might be.

In favor of the Definite Description view it can be noted that a Russellian definite description does indeed manage to cull one specific object from the domain of discourse when all goes well. Against this, the Special Reference view can hold that the Russellian expansion of a definite description reveals its disguised generality: asserting that *the man who killed Smith is insane* is, on Russellian analysis, asserting that *some* person x has a certain property (some F is G): some x has the property of being identical with any person who killed Smith and being insane. This generality is also revealed to intuition (it is claimed) by the "whoever" test: "the man who killed Smith," if it means "*whoever* killed Smith" (as it must, on Russellian analysis) makes no specific reference. Intuitively, "whoever killed Smith" does not *point at* anyone in particular, but rather *casts a net* into the domain. A genuine specific belief points directly to its object, which is identified not by its being the unique bearer of some property, but by its being . . . the object of the belief. Why should we suppose there are any such beliefs? There are two different motivations entangled here, one metaphysical, having to do with essentialism, and the other psychological, having to do with differences in psychological state that we dimly appreciate but have yet to describe. First we must expose the metaphysical issue, and then, at long last, we can address the psychological issue.

Consider what we should say about the identity conditions of the belief cited in

(37) Tom believes that the shortest spy is a woman.

If we treat this attribution relationally, as we must if we want to know whether Tom's belief is true or false, then the proposition he believes, given the world he is embedded in, is about (in the weak sense) some actual person, Rosa Klebb, let us suppose, so his belief is true. Were someone else, Tiny Tim Traitor, the shortest spy, then in *that* world, Tom would have had a false belief. Would we say, though, that in *that* world Tom would have had the same belief, or a different belief? Here we must be careful to distinguish narrow-psychological state or notional attitude from propositional attitude. We must also be careful to distinguish reflections about what *could have been* the case from what *may become* the case. For note that Tom's narrow-psychological state could stay constant in the relevant regards for, say, a year, during which time the "title" of shortest spy changed hands—entirely unbeknownst to Tom of course. For months Rosa Klebb was shortest spy, until Tiny Tim took the KGB's ruble. For those first few months Tom believed something true, and then, when Tiny Tim took over, Tom believed something false. Different propositions, it must be. In fact, as many different propositions in that year as you like, depending on how finely you slice the specious present. The changes in Tom, however, as each evanescent proposition flashes by, as a series of true propositions (the shortest spy on January 1 is a woman, etc.) is followed, suddenly, by a series of false propositions, are what Geach would call Cambridge changes—like that change that befalls you when you suddenly cease to have the property of being nearer the North Pole than the oldest living plumber born in Utah. Not all notional attitudes are thus related to propositional attitudes, of course.

(38) Tom believes that the youngest member of the Harvard class of
     1950 graduated with honors.

Which proposition he believes in this case does not change from day to day; moreover, whoever this belief is about (in the weak sense), it is about that person for all eternity. We cannot say that someone else might in the future *come to be* the object (in the weak sense) of that belief, but *perhaps* we can make sense of the suggestion that, counterfactually, someone else *could have been* the object of *that very belief*. To see just what this involves, let us review the possibilities. Fix Tom's *notional* attitude. First there are possible worlds in which Tom, with his notional attitude or narrow-psychological state, *believes no proposition at all;* these are worlds, for instance, without Harvard, and without any Twin Harvard either. Second, there are possible worlds in which Tom believes a proposition not about Harvard but about some Twin Harvard and its youngest graduate of Twin 1950. Third, there are worlds in which Tom believes the very same proposition he believes in the actual world, but in which someone else is the youngest graduate. The identity of the proposition is tied to the attribute, youngest-graduatehood, not to its bearer. And in (37) the propositions believed are tied to shortest-spyhood, not the bearers of the title. That, at any rate, is the doctrine that must be sustained if (37) and (38) are to be distinguished by the Special Reference view from genuinely specific beliefs. This doctrine requires us to make sense of the claims that it is possible that someone else could have been the shortest spy (on January first, on January second, . . .), and it is possible that someone else could have been the youngest graduate of the Harvard class of 1950. Now consider

(39) Tom believes the person who dropped the gum wrapper (whoever it might be) is a careless slob.

Suppose (since some say it makes a difference) that Tom did not see this person but just the discarded gum wrapper. Now Tom's belief in this instance is, as it happens, about (in the weak sense) some one individual, whoever dropped the gum wrapper, and the belief will be about that one individual through eternity; but had history been just a bit different, had someone else dropped the gum wrapper, then the very same belief of Tom's (the very same notional attitude *and* the very same propositional attitude) could have been about someone else. Could it have been about someone else if Tom had seen the wrapper being dropped? Why not? What difference could it make if Tom sees the person? If Tom sees the person, no doubt

(40) Tom believes that the person he saw drop the gum wrapper (whoever it might be) is a careless slob

will also be true. This belief is weakly about the same careless individual, but had history been just a bit different, it too would have been about someone else. It is at just this point that the believer in the Special Reference view of *de re* belief intervenes to insist that on the contrary, had history been just a bit different, had Tom seen someone else drop the gum wrapper, *he would have had a different belief.* It would have been a different belief because it would have been about (in the *strong* sense) a different person. It is easy to confuse two different claims here. It is tempting to suppose that what the *de re* theorist has in mind is this: had history been a little different, had a tall, thin person been seen dropping the gum wrapper instead of a short, fat person, Tom's perceptions would have been quite different, so he would have been in quite a different narrow-psychological state. But although this would normally be true, this is not what the *de re* theorist has in mind; the *de re* theorist is not making a claim about Tom's narrow state, but about Tom's propositional attitude: had history been a little different, had the short, fat person's twin brother dropped the gum wrapper under indistinguishable circumstances, Tom's notional attitude could have been just the same, we can suppose, but he would have had a different belief, a different propositional attitude altogether, because—just because—his notional state was directly caused (in some special way) by a different individual.[34]

---

34. Not all believers in the causal theory carve up the cases the same way. Vendler (1981) would insist that even in the case where I do not see the dropping of the gum wrapper, *since only one person could have dropped that gum wrapper*—since only one person could have made that Kripkean "insertion into history"—my belief is rigidly and strongly *about* that person. "Are we not acquainted, in a very real sense, with the otherwise unknown slave who left his footprint in King Tut's tomb? Or with the scribe who carved *that* particular hieroglyph into *that* stone four thousand years ago?" (p. 73) I suspect that Vendler's apparently extreme position is the only stable position for a causal theorist to adopt. But perhaps I have misinterpreted Vendler; perhaps *someone else* could have dropped *that* gum wrapper, but *no one else* could have left *that* footprint.

The metaphysics of the view can be brought into sharp focus with a contrived example. Suppose Tom has been carrying a lucky penny around for years. Tom has no name for this penny, but we can call it Amy. Tom took Amy to Spain with him, keeps Amy on his bedside table when he sleeps, and so forth. One night, while Tom sleeps, an evil person removes Amy from the bedside table and replaces Amy with an imposter, Beth. The next day Tom fondles Beth lovingly, puts Beth in his pocket, and goes to work.

(41) Tom believes he once took the penny in his pocket to Spain.

This true sentence about Tom asserts that he has a particular false belief about Beth, but had history been a little different, had the evil person not intervened, this very belief would have been a true belief about Amy. But according to the Special Reference theory of *de re* beliefs, there are some other beliefs to consider:

(42) Tom believes of Amy that she is in his pocket.
(43) Tom believes of Amy that he once took her to Spain.

These are beliefs strongly about Amy, the first false, the second true, and their being about Amy is *essential* to them. About them we cannot say: had history been a bit otherwise *they* would have been about Beth. If so, then one must also consider:

(44) Tom believes of Beth that she is in his pocket.
(45) Tom believes of Beth that he once took her to Spain.

These are beliefs strongly about Beth, the first true, the second false, and their being about Beth is *essential* to them. About them we cannot say: had history been a bit otherwise *they* would have been about Amy. Why should we adopt this vision? It cannot be because we need to grant that Tom has beliefs about both pennies, for in (41) his belief is (weakly) about Beth and

(46) Tom believes that the penny he took to Spain is in his pocket

attributes to Tom a belief (weakly) about Amy. Let us grant that in all cases of beliefs that are *weakly* about objects in virtue of those objects

---

Then Tom's belief about whoever made the footprint in the wet concrete, to the effect that he is a careless slob, is directly about *that* individual in a way his belief about the dropper of the gum wrapper is not directly about *him*. Not for nothing have several wits called the causal theory the Doctrine of Original *Sinn*.

being the lone satisfiers of a description, we can insert, to mark this, the phrase "whoever it might be." This will often have a very odd ring, as in

(47) Tom believes that his wife (whoever she might be) is an excellent swimmer

but only because the pragmatic implication of the inserted phrase suggests a very outlandish possibility—unless it merely is taken to suggest that the *speaker* of (47) is unable to pick Tom's wife out of a lineup.

Is there then another reason we should adopt this view? It cannot be because we need to distinguish a special class of *de re* beliefs strongly about objects in order to mark a distinguished class of cases where we may *quantify in*, for we may quantify in whenever a belief is only weakly about an individual, although such a practice would often be very misleading. It would be very misleading, for instance, to say, pointing to Rosa Klebb during her reign as shortest spy: "Tom believes her to be a woman," It would also be very misleading, though, for the evil person to hold up Amy and say "Tom believes he once took this penny to Spain." These claims would be misleading because the normal pragmatic implication of a relational claim of this sort is that the believer can identify or reidentify the object (or property) in question. But nothing about the manner of acquisition of a belief could *guarantee* this against all future misadventures, so *any* theory of "*de re* belief" would license potentially misleading relational claims (cf. Schiffer 1978, pp. 179, 188).

If it still seems that there is an elusive *variety of belief* that has not been given its due, this is probably because of a tempting misdiagnosis of the sorts of examples found in the literature. Dragging out a few more examples may serve to lay the ghost of *de re* belief (in this imagined sense that distinguishes it as a subvariety) once and for all. Suppose I am sitting in a committee meeting, and it occurs to me that the youngest person in the room (whoever that is—half dozen people present are plausible candidates) was born after the death of Franklin D. Roosevelt. Call that thought of mine Thought *A*. Now in the weak sense of "about," Thought *A* is about one of the people present, but I know not which. I look at each of them in turn and wonder, e.g., "Bill, over there—is it likely that Thought *A* is *about him?*" Call *this* thought of mine Thought *B*. Now *surely* (one feels) Thought *B* is *about Bill* in a much more direct, intimate, strong sense than Thought *A* is, even if Thought A does turn out to be about Bill. For one thing, I *know* that Thought B is about Bill. This is, I think, an illusion. There is only a difference in degree between Thought A and Thought B and their relation to Bill. Thought B is (weakly) about whoever is the only person I am looking at and whose name I believe to be Bill and . . . for as long as you like. Bill, no doubt, is the lone satisfier of that description, but had his twin brother taken his place unbeknownst to me, Thought B would not have been about Bill, but about his brother. Or more likely, in that eventuality, I would be in a state of mind like poor Tom's in Shakey's Pizza Parlor, so that *no* psychologically perspicuous rendition of my *propositional* attitudes is available.

Another example, with a different flavor. George is Smith's murderer (as Gracie well knows), and she rushes in to tell him that Hoover thinks he did it. Alarmed, George wants to know how Hoover got on to him. Gracie reasons: Hoover knows that the one and only person who shot Smith with a .38, left three unrecordable fingerprints on the window, and is currently in possession of the money from Smith's wallet is Smith's murderer; since George is the lone satisfier of Hoover's description, Hoover believes of George that he did it. "No, Gracie," George says, "Hoover knows only that *whoever* fits this description is Smith's murderer. He doesn't know that *I* fit the description, so he doesn't know that I am Smith's murderer. Wake me up when you learn that *I* am suspected." (Cf. Sosa 1970.) George has misdiagnosed his situation, however, for consider the case in which Poirot gathers all the houseparty guests into the drawing room and says "I do not yet know *who the murderer is;* I do not even have a suspect, but I have deduced that the murderer, whoever he is, is the one and only person in the drawing room with a copy of the pantry key on his person." Search, identification, and arrest follow. It is not true that George is safe so long as Hoover's beliefs are of the form *whoever fits description D is Smith's murderer,* for if description D is something like "the only person in Clancy's bar with yellow mud on his shoes," the jig may soon be up.[35] One is a (minimal) suspect if

---

35. Consider the contrast between

(a) I enter a telephone booth and find a dime in the coin return box; I believe that whoever used the booth last left a dime in the box.

(b) I enter a telephone booth, make a call and deliberately leave a dime in the coin box; I believe that whoever uses the booth next will find a dime in the coin return box.

Is my belief in (b) *already* about some particular person? But I haven't the faintest idea who that is or will be! (Cf. Harman 1977.) So what? (Cf. Searle 1979.) I don't have the

one satisfies *any* definite description Hoover takes to pick out Smith's murderer. It follows trivially that Smith's murderer is a minimal suspect (because he satisfies the description "Smith's murderer") even in the situation when Hoover is utterly baffled, but merely believes the crime has been committed by a single culprit. This would be an objectionable consequence only if there were some principled way of distinguishing minimal suspects from genuine, or true or *de re* suspects, but there is not. Thus as Quine suggests, the apparently sharp psychological distinction between

(48) Hoover believes that someone (some *one*) murdered Smith

and

(49) Someone is believed by Hoover to have murdered Smith

collapses (the logical difference in the ontological commitment of the speaker remains). It remains true that in the case in which Hoover is baffled he would naturally deny to the press that there was anyone he believed to be the murderer. What he would actually be denying is that he knows more than anyone knows who knows only that the crime has been committed. He is certainly not denying that he has a *de re* belief directly about some individual to the effect that he is the murderer, a belief he has acquired by some intimate cognitive rapport with that individual, for suppose Hoover wrestled with the murderer at the scene of the crime, in broad daylight, but has no idea who the person was with whom he wrestled; surely on anyone's causal theory of *de re* belief, that person is believed by him to be the murderer, but it would be most disingenuous for Hoover to claim to have a suspect (cf. Sosa 1970, pp. 894ff).

The tying of belief identity and belief reference to a causal condition is a plausible proposal because, in most instances, varying degrees of causal intimacy in the past can be used to distinguish weaker from stronger relations between believers and their objects, such that the stronger relations have implications for future conduct, but in unusual situations the normal implications do not hold. From the fact that we can produce dislocations, we see that the causal requirement

faintest idea whom my belief in (a) is about either, and in fact it is much likelier that I can discover the object of my belief in (b) than in (a). If I believe whoever left the dime kidnapped Jones, the kidnapper is probably quite safe; if I believe whoever finds the dime is the kidnapper (it's a signal in the ransom exchange scheme) capture is more likely.

is not in itself necessary or sufficient; effects are as important as causes. What is necessary is the creation of a notional object in the subject's notional world. This will not typically happen in the absence of causal commerce; it is unlikely for something to "get into position" for someone to have beliefs about it without having been in causal interaction of *some* sort with the believer, but we can force this result (the Westwood Village peg, the door, Poirot's culprit) in special cases. The special cases draw attention to an independence in principle—if seldom in practice—between psychologically salient states and their metaphysical credentials.

The believer in *de re* belief must decide whether or not the concept at issue is supposed to play a marked role in behavioral explanations (see, e.g., Morton 1975; Burge 1977). One view of *de re* belief would not suppose that anything at all about Tom's likely behavior follows from the truth of

(50) Tom believes *of* the man shaking hands with him that he is a heavily armed fugitive mass murderer.

This view acquiesces in what might be called the psychological opacity of semantic transparency (we may not know at all what our beliefs are about), and while I can see no obstacle to defining such a variety of propositional attitude, I can see no use for such a concept, since nothing of interest would seem to follow from a true attribution of such a belief. Suppose, on this view, that something, *a*, is believed by me to be *F*. It does not follow that *a* is not also believed by me to be *not-F*; and if *a* is also believed by me to be *G*, it does not follow that *a* is believed by me to be *F and G*; it does not even follow from the fact that *a* is believed by me to be *the only F*, that no other object *b* is also believed by me to be *the only F*. The premise of the quest for *de re* belief was that there were interesting and important relations between believers and the objects of their beliefs—relations we had reason to capture in our theories—but this termination of the quest lands us with relations that are of only intermittent and unprojectible interest. That being so, there is no longer any motivation I can see for denying that one believes *of* the shortest spy that he is a spy. The formal apparatus for making such relational claims is available, and once one has asserted that two objects are related, however minimally, as believer and object, one can go on to assert whatever other facts about the believer's state of mind or the object's situation might be relevant to plotting and explaining the relevant future careers of both.

If, shunning this view, one seeks a view of *de re* belief as somehow a psychologically distinguished phenomenon, then it cannot be a theory well named, for it will have to be a theory of distinctions within *notional* attitude psychology. If *a* is an object *in my notional world* that I believe to be *F* it *does* follow that I do not also believe *a* to be *not-F*, and the other implications cited above fall into place as well, but only because notional objects are the "creatures" of one's beliefs (cf. Schiffer 1978, p. 180). Having created such creatures, we can then see what real things (if any) they line up with, but not from any position of privileged access in our own cases. There is a very powerful intuition that we can have it both ways: that we can define a sort of aboutness that is *both* a real relation between a believer and something in the world *and* something to which the believer's access is perfect. Evans calls this Russell's Principle: *it is not possible to make a judgment about an object without knowing what object you are making a judgment about.* In Russell's case, the attempt to preserve this intuition in the face of the sorts of difficulties encountered here led to his doctrine of knowledge by acquaintance and hence inevitably to his view that we could only judge *about* certain abstract objects or certain of our own internal states. The Principle becomes:

Whenever a relation of supposing or judging occurs, the terms to which the supposing or judging mind is related by the relation of supposing or judging must be terms with which the mind in question is acquainted. (Russell 1959, p. 221)

Here the term "term" nicely bridges the gap and prepares the way for precisely the sort of theory Chisholm abhors in the opening quotation of this section: a theory that supposes "the mind cannot get beyond the circle of its own ideas." The way out is to give up Russell's Principle (cf. Burge 1979), and with it the idea of a special sort of *de re* belief (and other attitudes) intimately and strongly *about* their objects. There still remains a grain of truth, however, in Russell's idea of a special relation between a believer and some of the *things he thinks with*, but to discuss this issue, one must turn to notional attitude psychology and more particulary to the "engineering" question of how to design a cognitive creature with the sort of notional world we typically have. In that domain, now protected from some of the misleading doctrines about the mythic phenomena of *de re* and *de dicto* beliefs, phenomenological distinctions emerge that cut across the attempted boundaries of the recent philosophical literature and hold some promise of yielding insights about cognitive organization.

Since this paper has already grown to several times its initially intended size, I will save a detailed examination of these distinctions for other occasions, and simply list what I consider the most promising issues.

Different ways of thinking of something. This is a purely notional set of distinctions—none of the ways entails the existence of something of which one is thinking. Vendler (1976, 1984) has some valuable reflections on this topic (along with his unintended *reductio ad absurdum* of the causal theory of reference for belief).

The difference between (episodic) thinking and believing. At any time we have *beliefs* about many things we are unable to *think* about not because the beliefs are unconscious or tacit or unthinkable, but just because we are temporarily unable to *gain access* to that to which we may want to gain access. (Can you *think* about the person who taught you long division? If you can "find the person in your memory," you will no doubt discover a cache of beliefs about that person.) Any plausible psychological theory of action must have an account of how we recognize things, and how we keep track of things (cf. Morton 1975), and this will require a theory of the strategies and processes we use in order to exploit our beliefs in our thoughts.

The difference between explicit and virtual representation (see chapter 6). When I hop into a rental car and drive off, I expect the car to be in sound working order, and hence I expect the right front tire to have a safe tread—I would be surprised if I discovered otherwise. Not only have I not *consciously* thought about the right front tire, I almost certainly have not *unconsciously* (but still explicitly) represented the tread of the right front tire as a separate item of belief. The difference that *having attended to something* (real or merely notional) makes is not the difference between *de re* and *de dicto;* it is a real difference of some importance in psychology.

The difference between linguistically infected beliefs and the rest—what I call opinions and beliefs in "How to Change Your Mind" (in *Brainstorms*). No dog could have the opinion that it was Friday or that the shortest dog was a dog. Some people have supposed that this means that animals without language are incapable of *de dicto* belief. It is important to recognize the independence of this distinction from the issues at stake in the *de re/de dicto* debates.

The difference between artifactual or transparently notional objects and other notional objects. We can conjure up an imaginary thing—just to daydream about, or in order to solve a problem, e.g., to design a dream house or figure out what kind of car to buy. It is not always our intent that the notional worlds we construct within our notional worlds be *fiction*. For instance, coming upon Smith's corpse, we might reconstruct the crime in our imagination—a different way of thinking about Smith's murderer.

That ignoring these distinctions has contributed to the confusion in the discussions of *de re* and *de dicto* is clear, I trust. Just consider the infamous case of believing that the shortest spy is a spy. It is commonly presumed that we all know what state of mind is being alluded to in this example, but in fact there are many quite different possibilities undistinguished in the literature. Does Tom believe that the shortest spy is a spy in virtue of nothing more than a normal share of logical acumen, or does he also have to have a certain sort of idleness and a penchant for reflecting on tautologies? (Should we say we all believe this, and also that the tallest tree is a tree, and so forth ad infinitum?) Does Tom believe that the shortest dugong is a dugong? Or, to pursue a different tack, what is the relation between believing that that man is a spy and thinking that that man is a spy? Sincere denial is often invoked as a telling sign of disbelief. What is it best viewed as showing? And so forth. When good psychological accounts of these notional attitude phenomena are in hand, some of the puzzles about reference will be solved and others will be discredited. I doubt if there will be any residue.[36]

---

36. I am grateful to all the patient souls who have tried to help me see my way out of this project. In addition to all those mentioned in the other notes and bibliography, I want to acknowledge the help of Peter Alexander, David Hirschmann, Christopher Peacocke, Pat Hayes, John Haugeland, Robert Moore, Zenon Pylyshyn, Paul Benacerraf, and Dagfinn Føllesdal. This research was supported by an N.E.H. Fellowship, and by the National Science Foundation (BNS 78-24671) and the Alfred P. Sloan Foundation.

Reflections:
About Aboutness

Fodor begins his pioneering book *Psychological Explanation* (1968a) with some self-mockery:

> I think many philosophers secretly harbor the view that there is something deeply (i.e., conceptually) wrong with psychology, but that a philosopher with a little training in the techniques of linguistic analysis and a free afternoon could straighten it out.
>
> Several years ago I found myself with a free afternoon. (p. vii)

In 1978 Stich and I, participating in Woodfield's Fulbright workshop on the philosophy of psychology at the University of Bristol, had a similar hunch: it was obvious to us that there was something deeply (i.e., conceptually) wrong with the whole edifice of *de re/de dicto* belief/desire theory in philosophy, and we thought we might spend a few weeks working together on the dirty job of setting everyone straight. We found during those few weeks that in spite of our shared dismay, we had residual and unresolvable differences about how to treat the issues. After more than a year of work, we contributed separate papers to Woodfield's 1981 anthology: "Beyond Belief" from me, and Stich's "On the Ascription of Content," which several years later became the heart of his vision in *From Folk Psychology to Cognitive Science: The Case Against Belief* (1983).

Despite a year's work, "Beyond Belief" is undeniably an unfinished project, and even some of its admirers have been uncertain about just what its messages are. So I will list what I take to be its four chief claims, discuss each in turn, and then say a bit more about where I think this leaves matters.

(1) *Propositions:* at this time there is no stable, received view of propositions or propositional attitudes on which one can rely. The two chief schools of thought, propositions as sentence-like things and proposi-

tions as sets of possible worlds, are strongly incompatible, appealing to quite different intuitions.

(2) *Notional worlds:* the well-trodden path from "propositional attitude psychology" to "language of thought psychology" is a route to fantasyland. A more realistic psychology does not use "propositions" (or their near kin) to characterize psychological mechanisms directly; rather, it uses them to characterize the mechanisms indirectly—by directly characterizing the "world" those mechanisms are designed to cope with.

(3) *Russell's Principle:* the common assumption that *it is not possible to make a judgment about an object without knowing what object you are making a judgment about*—called Russell's Principle by Evans—must be abandoned. For all its intuitive, introspective appeal, it is the source of a lion's share of the theorists' misfortunes.

(4) *De re/de dicto:* there is no stable, coherent view of the so-called *de re/de dicto* distinction. Accounts that appeal to such a supposed distinction are vitiated by an elusive ambiguity between a psychologically salient and projectible distinction and a metaphysically crisp but psychologically inert distinction.

These predominantly negative theses were intended to upset the complacency of those philosophers who have thought the puzzles (about Ortcutt, the shortest spy, Twin Earth) could be handled within the presumably orthodox—shall we say *Russellian*—tradition. In my view this orthodoxy is an illusion, a by-product of the sociology of the discipline: when experts write for experts, they tend to err on the side of presupposing more agreement about basics than actually exists. The philosophical literature on propositions has from the outset been the work of philosophers of language and logic, in the main, whose concerns have been only tangentially related to psychology. For them (until recently) the puzzles about propositional attitudes were apparently peripheral snags in otherwise handsome fabrics, and they dealt with them by inventing just enough plausible psychology to cover them. It might have worked, but it didn't; philosophy of psychology driven by the concerns of philosophy of language does not fall happily into place. So now we have theorists, their intuitions sullied by a makeshift but authoritative tradition, who have been talking past each other for a generation, falsely presupposing that there was common understanding of what the central concept of a proposition was supposed to do.

Propositions

There is still widespread belief in the imaginary stable orthodoxy, but mine is hardly the only iconoclastic vision; the mix of contention and invention in the literature (which has grown apace since I completed "Beyond Belief" in 1980) puts it practically off limits to all but the hardy specialists, which is probably just as well. Others are encouraged to avert their gaze until we get our act together.

And yet, these others might provide an important infusion of reality into an increasingly inbred and artifactual subdiscipline. After all, if there is one thing the rest of academia really seems to need from philosophers, it is a theory of propositions, or at least a theory of something like propositions. The term "information" is commonly used as a mass noun, as if information were some kind of substance that could be moved, stored, compressed, chopped up. Theorists in disciplines as diverse as neuroscience, ethology, economics, and literary criticism pretend to know how to measure and characterize batches of this stuff we call information. According to the mass media, we now live in the Information Age, but in fact we have no sound and mutually recognized understanding of what information is and what kinds of parcels it should be measured in.

The information characterized by formal information theory, measured in bits or bytes (1 byte = 8 bits), underlies all information transfer and processing, and this is indeed a well-understood commodity that can be broken up and then stored or moved in clearly individuated portions. But this is hardly the concept we must appeal to when we worry about the leakage of (important) information in government, the cost of obtaining information in administrative decision-making, the flood of information in which we and our projects seem to be drowning (Dennett 1986b)—or when we speak of information-processing models of the nervous system or in cognitive psychology (Dennett 1969, pp. 185–89). The information measured in bits is content-neutral. A graphic reminder of this: a single videodisc can store enough gigabytes of information to record the entire Grolier Encyclopedia—or three hours of Bugs Bunny. There is roughly the same *amount of information* in each. When we want to know *what information* (on what topics, with what content) was transferred when Philby talked to the Russians, or when the frog's eye talked to the frog's brain, we need a different concept. We have a name for it— *semantic information*—but despite ingenious (if unsuccessful) attempts to develop the requisite concept as an extension of the information-theoretic concept (Dretske 1981, Sayre 1986, Dennett 1986a), we still have no better way of individuating portions of the wonderful stuff than by talking in one way or another of propositions.

Propositions, as the ultimate medium of information transfer, as logically distinct, observer-independent, language-neutral morsels of fact (or fiction), continue to play a foundational role as atomic elements in many different theoretical investigations and practical projects. As the *p*s and *q*s of the propositional calculus and its heirs, propositions wear their unanalyzed atomicity on their sleeves. The structured objects of the predicate calculus and its heirs and relations presuppose a canonical—if imaginary—language and hence tend to confer spurious respectability on some form of sententialism. Meanwhile, cognitive and social psychologists take themselves to be cataloguing the *beliefs* of their subjects by listing their responses on questionnaires; and in artificial intelligence, the use of the predicate calculus to capture the putative beliefs of the subject being modeled is a well-entrenched tradition with no serious, articulated rivals. (For a critical overview of the problems of propositions in artificial intelligence, see Dennett, "Cognitive Wheels, the Frame Problem of AI" (1984c) and "The Logical Geography of Computational Approaches: A View from the East Pole" (1986e). If the philosophical theory of propositions is as bad off as I claim, are these enterprises all in jeopardy, or are all the philosophical puzzles *safely* submersible under a wave of "for all practical purposes" clauses?

My defense of the intentional stance bespeaks my own reliance on propositions and propositional attitude attributions and at the same time shows the limits of the weight I think can be placed on them. Propositions would be much better behaved if we didn't try to harness them so tightly to "propositional attitude psychology." That is, the main source of the problems with propositions is the fund of intuition about the graspability of propositions. Once one relaxes the grip of graspability by treating propositions as only indirectly and approximately "measuring" psychological states (as Churchland recommends), they play their limited role rather well. So long as one recognizes that proposition talk is only a *heuristic overlay* (Dennett 1969, p. 80), a useful—if sometimes treacherous—approximation that is systematically incapable of being rendered precise, one can get away with what is in essence the pretense that all informing can be modeled on *telling*—sending a *dictum* from *A* to *B*. What the frog's eye tells the frog's brain is not anything that one can capture whole in a sentence, and if some spy sells a set of secret blueprints in Geneva, the information thereby transmitted may be just as incapable of "explicitation" in any formula of the predicate calculus.[1] But one can typically find a sentence that usefully distills the gist (not the essence in any stronger sense) of the informing to which one is referring. This sentence can be held to express, to a first approximation, the proposition at issue.

What is the proposition itself, and how can it be precisely identified? The proposition-as-canonical-sentence avenue is blocked by the fact that any informing is relative to a particular intentional system— frog, frog's brain, national defense establishment, spymaster—and in virtue of the different predicaments of such intentional systems, their capacities for uptake can differ in incommensurable ways that defy any *lingua franca* of transmission. The alternative avenue, the proposition-as-set-of-possible-worlds, has the great virtue of recognizing and building on precisely this agent relativity.[2]

Treating the proposition as nothing more than a particular exhaustive sorting of agent-detectable possibilities permits in principle a more precise and realistic determination of the "actual proposition believed by the agent," but given the incommensurability, such precision as is thereby obtained limits the generality of the inter-agent claims that can be expressed. What Tom, Pierre, Sherlock, and Boris have in common (see chapter 3) cannot be precisely stated in possible worlds terms, since they will inevitably partition their sets of possible

---

1. See Dennett 1983b for a further development of the analogy between cognitive science and counterespionage.

2. Stalnaker (1984) is the most insightful and systematic exploration of the prospect. The standard and presumably crushing objection to the possible worlds treatment of believed propositions is that, possibility being what it is, there can be (for any one believer) only one logically true or necessary proposition—true in *all* possible worlds— whereas mathematicians, for instance, would certainly seem to believe and disbelieve many different logical truths. Stalnaker argues that this phenomenon can be handled by distinguishing mathematicians' various beliefs *about particular formulae* to the effect that they are "expressions" of the solitary logical truth. While this ploy seems to some to be a desperate stratagem, I find it has independent motivation. Fine-grained distinctions between logical truths are accessible to (are graspable by, make a difference to) language-using intentional systems only; the psychological states at issue, then, are those verbally infected states I call *opinions*, and Stalnaker's semantic ascent is a promising way of making that point.

worlds via somewhat different idiosyncratic concepts of *Frenchman,* *murder,* and *Trafalgar Square.*[3] There is nothing, I claim, that is *precisely* in common between Tom, Pierre, Sherlock, and Boris.

If this is so, then the quest for a stable theory of propositions should be slightly reconceived. Any useful parceling of semantic information will set a somewhat arbitrary and potentially distorting standard, so we must complicate Churchland's appealing proposal that we treat propositions the same way physicists treat numbers. Propositions, as ways of "measuring" semantic information by the topic-ful, *turn out to be more like dollars than like numbers.* Just as "what is that worth in U. S. dollars?" asks a usefully unifying question in spite of the frequent occasions when the answer distorts the reality in which we are interested, so "what proposition (in Standard Scheme *P*) does that store/transmit/express?" might exploit a valuable, somewhat systematic if often procrustean testbed. Only naive Americans confuse the former question with "what is that worth in *real* money?" and it would be similarly naive to consider a proposition-fixing standard, however well established, to be even an approximation of the way semantic information is *really* parceled out. *There are no real, natural, universal units of either economic value or semantic information.*

Presumably we are neither dismayed nor perplexed by the discovery that there are no natural, universal units of economic value. What is a live goat worth? Well, where and when? In rural France today it has considerable value, but is it more or less than its current value in China, or the value of a secondhand Chevy pickup in Louisiana in 1972? What is the same live goat worth today, delivered to the private office of a Wall Street broker? One can work out an estimate of "the value" of the goat (in 1968 dollars, let us say) at various times and places, to various people, by working through the exchange rates, inflation rates, market prices, etc. (Who earned more in an average year: one of Caesar's generals or a Supreme Court Justice?) I take it no one supposes such exercises home in on unique, real economic values. Why should one persist in thinking that there are unique real contents of psychological states, uniquely well-jointed units of semantic information?

---

3. Curiously, the same morals can be drawn from the consideration of a different fictional Frenchman in London—Kripke's Pierre, who may or may not believe that London is pretty (Kripke 1979; among the many responses to Kripke, see especially Marcus 1983).

Notional Worlds

Notional world psychology, attempting to capture the organismic contribution to belief in isolation, is one approach to what has come to be called "narrow conceptual role semantics" (Field 1977, 1978; Loar 1981; Fodor 1987. For illuminating criticisms of the approach, see Harman, forthcoming a; Stalnaker, unpublished). We want to do justice to the intuition that the information we are speaking of—the semantic information—is *in* the organism in a way that makes a difference (see, e.g., Stich 1983). This can be dramatized by the requirement that the information can be sent from A to B by sending the organism (in isolation) from A to B and counting on those who receive it to do the best possible job of radical interpretation. This they will do by reconstructing the organism's notional world. To the extent that the result is undetermined—to the extent, that is, that rival notional worlds are equally well supported by all the facts about the organism available at B—the information at issue is simply *not there.*

Some (see especially Stalnaker, unpublished) have doubted that this method of reconstruction would be as fecund as I have claimed. Would Martian interpreters, on receiving a comatose human body by interplanetary mail, be able to piece out its notional world as well as I claim? Note that the Martians' task is officially no harder than—indeed just a special case of—the familiar imaginary task of Quinian radical translation (or Davidson's (1973) or Lewis's (1974) "radical interpretation"). What makes the case special is that the body is effectively cut off from any environmental influences (either on Mars or on Earth), but *ex hypothesi* the Martians can determine how the body, once awake, *would* respond to any stimulus any environment might provide, so they can conduct, hypothetically, as many *gavagai?*-experiments as they like, and reap the benefits. Presumably they would use their calculations to induce the body, hypothetically, to recount in its native tongue as much of its biography as it could muster. (The exercise is described in detail by Hofstadter in "A Conversation with Einstein's Brain" in Hofstadter and Dennett 1981). Supposing the Martians take the available steps to control for lying and forgetfulness, their examination should yield, as I claimed, a description of a notional world that fails to distinguish Boston from Twin Boston but is otherwise remarkably specific.

Once again, I am not proposing notional world psychology as an actual methodology to be assiduously followed by empirical psychologists, but just as a way of getting explicit, when the rare dislocation cases occur, about the commitments and presuppositions of theory. The indirectness of descriptions of possible worlds has its utility, then, in characterizing the commonality among those who believe in Santa Claus without committing the theorist to either a Santa Claus in the world or a "Santa Claus" in each brain. And the notional world format reminds us that, as Jackendoff (1985) has put it, "information is in the mind of the beholder."

Russell's Principle

The pernicious role of Russell's Principle has gradually come into better focus for me, thanks in large measure to the sustained attack on it (under the broader label of "meaning rationalism") by Millikan (1984, 1986). For instance, in "Beyond Belief" I took myself to be describing a counterfactual Fodor when I imagined him claiming to "find a Mentalese text *given* in the hardware" and hence thought I was being merely hypothetical when I said we "would have as much reason to doubt the existence of the given in this case as in the case of Phenomenology." But as chapter 8 shows, I was closer to the truth than I supposed in putting this claim in Fodor's mouth, and Fodor is far from alone in wanting to preserve first-person privileged access for some form of Fregean *grasping* of propositions.

De re/de dicto

The attempts to define this distinction in terms of causal ancestry fail in instructive ways. We might rebaptize the concept of strong (*de re*) aboutness as *original direct reference* to help us see that it is one of a family of perennially attractive concepts, including *original intentionality* and *original functionality* (see chapter 8), all of which founder on the possibility of what I call inert historical facts. Origins are important, but so are current propensities or dispositions, and if one is interested in usefully projectible properties of things, one must treat all the backward-looking conditions as only normally highly reliable signs—symptoms—rather than as criteria. As I granted in "Beyond Belief," it is quite possible to define a version of *de re* belief in causal terms; it is just as easy, as we shall see in chapter 8, to define a version of *original intentionality* so that some things *really* have states with (cer-

tain) contents and other, behaviorally identical things do not—
because of the illegitimacy of their ancestry. In neither case does one
capture anything of value by the test, unless one puts a somewhat
mystical value on brute genealogical fact. The standard way of defending such mysticism is by attacking the opposition for its verificationism ("what no one could *verify* would nevertheless be *true*"),
but this improperly deflects my criticism. I am quite prepared to
acknowledge the existence of idle, unverifiable truths—I call them
inert facts, after all—but insist that they cannot have the theoretical
importance invested in them by their defenders; what is unverifiable
cannot "make a difference" anymore, and we mislead ourselves
when we make much of theoretical distinctions that cannot be relied
upon to make a difference.

"Beyond Belief" closes with a somewhat wistful look at some
unfinished tasks for philosophy of psychology that take on a different
guise once one shakes off the trance of the tradition, and several new
works seem to me to provide signposts to follow, at least, on how to
make headway on these residual perplexities. In addition to the
philosophical work by Millikan and Stalnaker already cited, I highly
recommend two books by psychologically and philosophically acute
linguists: Jackendoff (1983) and Fauconnier (1985).

6   Styles of Mental Representation

More than thirty years ago, in *The Concept of Mind* (1949), Gilbert Ryle attacked a vision of the mind he called the intellectualist myth. This is the idea that minds are composed mainly of such episodes as the thinking of private thoughts, the consultation of rules and recipes, the application of general truths to particular circumstances, and the subsequent deduction of implications about those particulars. This vision of the mind was no less preposterous for being traditional, in Ryle's opinion, and his attack was a vigorous—if not rigorous—combination of ridicule and *reductio*. Of course he knew perfectly well that there really are such phenomena as the memorization of rules, the later consultation of those rules, the self-conscious deduction of conclusions from premises, and the like, but he thought that viewing these schoolroom activities as the model for all intelligent behavior was getting matters just backward. In fact, he argued, the very existence of such public human practices as the deliberate self-conscious consideration of stated maxims and the deduction of conclusions from sets of premises on blackboards *depends* on the agents in question having full-blown sets of mental talents. If one attempted to explain these prior and more fundamental competences as based in turn upon yet another intellectual process, this time an *inner* process of calculation, involving looking up propositions, deducing conclusions from them, and the like, one would be taking the first step on an infinite regress.

It was a powerful and rhetorically winning attack, but not so many years later it was roundly and bluntly rejected by those philosophers

"Styles of Mental Representation" originally appeared in Proceedings of The Aristotelian Society, Vol. LXXXIII 1982/83. Reprinted by courtesy of the Editor of The Aristotelian Society.

and other theorists who saw the hope of a cognitive psychology, or more broadly, a "cognitive science," a theory of the mind that was very close in spirit to the view Ryle was lampooning. In fact the reigning ideology of cognitive science sets itself so defiantly against Ryle that it might with some justice be called *intellectualist science*. It seems to be just the sort of thing Ryle claimed was wrongheaded. Cognitive science speaks openly and unabashedly of inner mental representations and of calculations and other operations performed on these inner representations. The mind, it proclaims, is a computing device, and as Jerry Fodor, a leading ideologue of cognitive science has put it, "no computation without representation." (Fodor 1975)

How did this new movement shrug off Ryle's attack so blithely? Part of the answer is that what Ryle was attacking was not one view but a mishmash of several views. Many of his slings and arrows can be so easily dodged by sophisticated cognitive scientists that perhaps their respect for the rest of his arsenal has been unduly diminished. Ryle danced quite a jig on the corpse of Cartesian dualism, for instance, but cognitive science is openly materialistic or physicalistic, in a sophisticated way Ryle apparently underestimated and maybe never even considered. So cognitive science has no worries about "ghosts in the machine." Its hypotheses are frankly mechanical, not, as Ryle would have it, "paramechanical"—mysteriously pseudomechanical. And cognitive science has no allegiance to "privileged access," another of Ryle's bugbears. Indeed most of the mental representations that it talks of are presumed to be utterly inaccessible to the consciousness of the agent. It is a doctrine of *unconscious* mental representations for the most part. So this is not the intellectualism of the inner Cartesian theater, with everything happening on the stage of consciousness; this is "backstage" intellectualism—and in the view of these new theorists, so much the better for it.

But there was more to Ryle's attack than that. He was deeply suspicious—and I think for good reason—of *any* claims made on behalf of inner representations, whether they were supposed to be materially embodied, mechanistically manipulated, outside of consciousness or not, because he thought that in all their forms such postulations of inner representations were incoherent.

This feature of Ryle's view has certainly not gone unnoticed. Why then has it been so widely disregarded? Surely the main contribution to the conviction that Ryle must be wrong on this point is the growing influence of the computer metaphor in the field. The mind is like a computer, runs the slogan, and a computer is indeed a mindless manipulator of internal explicit representations—no infinite regresses there, surely, for there the computers sit. Whatever is actual is possible, so internal-representation-manipulators are not the perpetual motion machines Ryle would have us think. Cognitive scientists have thus felt comfortable speaking about information processing systems and subsystems that utilize sorts of internal representation. These representations are like words and sentences, and like maps and pictures; they're just enough like these familiar representations for it to be appropriate to call them representations, but they are also just enough unlike words and pictures and so forth to evade Ryle's infinite regress machine. That is at any rate the common understanding, not that it has yet received its proper defense.

I propose to look more closely at the issue, for while I think that the computer metaphor, properly used, *can* liberate the theorist from Ryle's worries, it is often abused by ideologues of cognitive science. It is obvious, let us grant, that computers *somehow* represent things by using internal representations of those things. So it is *possible* (somehow) that brains represent things by using internal representations of those things. But if we are to move beyond that modest bit of metaphysical elbow room and actually understand *how* the brain might represent by analogy with computer representation, we had best be clear about just how it is computers represent. There are several ways, or styles, of computer representation, and only some of them are plausible models for ways, or styles, of mental representation in the brain.

When cognitive scientists have talked about representations, they typically have committed themselves to some view about syntax—to use the shorthand term. That is, they have supposed themselves to be talking about representations about which the following sorts of distinctions can be made: there are structural elements that are symbols; there are multiple *tokens* of *types* of representation (where these types are individuated syntactically, not semantically); there are rules of formation or composition rules—something like a grammar—so one can form big representations out of little representations; and the meaning of the larger representations is a function of the meanings of their parts.

This heavy commitment to a syntactical picture is often made willingly enough, but if it is made, it is solely on the basis of aprioristic reasoning, for so far as I can see, while there has been plenty of interesting speculation, there is almost no empirical evidence yet that tends to confirm any substantive hypothesis about the nature of this supposed syntax of mental representation (see Stabler 1983). This is not at all to deny that excellent and telling evidence has been obtained by cognitivist research, but rather to claim that this evidence to date has been evidence at the semantic level only. That is, it has been evidence about what information is being somehow relied upon by various cognitive processes, not evidence about how this reliance is effected (Dennett 1983b).

We cannot yet say, for instance, whether various pieces of information that have been implicated one way or another in various cognitive activities and competences are represented "explicitly" or "implicitly" in the human cognitive system. One reason we cannot say this is the confusion about how to use the terms "explicit" and "implicit." People working in the field have meant quite different things by these terms, and here I will try to clarify the situation somewhat by offering some definitions—not of the terms as they are used, but of some terms as they should be used.

Let us say that information is represented *explicitly* in a system if and only if there actually exists in the functionally relevant place in the system a physically structured object, a *formula* or *string* or *tokening* of some members of a system (or "language") of elements for which there is a semantics or interpretation, and a provision (a mechanism of some sort) for reading or parsing the formula. This definition of explicit representation is exigent, but still leaves room for a wide variety of representation systems. They need not be linear, sequential, sentence-like systems, but might, for instance, be "map-reading systems" or "diagram interpreters."

Then let us have it that for information to be represented *implicitly*, we shall mean that it is *implied* logically by something that is stored explicitly. Now "implicitly" defined thus does not mean what one might take it to mean: "potentially explicit." All the theorems of Euclid are implicit in the axioms and definitions. And if you have a mechanical Euclid machine—if you have the axioms and definitions explicitly stored in the machine and it can churn out theorems—then the theorems it churns out and hence renders explicit were implicit in the system all along—they were implied by the axioms. But so were lots of other theorems the machine may *not* be able to churn out. They are all implicit in the system, given its explicit representation of the axioms, but only a proper subset of them are potentially explicit. (This is not a point about "incompleteness"; I have in mind the more mundane limitations of middle-sized pieces of hardware obeying the Einsteinian speed limit during relatively brief life spans.)

It is an interesting question whether the concept of *potentially explicit* representations is of more use to cognitive science than the concept of (merely) implicit representations. Put another way, can some item of information that is *merely* implicit in some system ever cited (to any explanatory effect) in a cognitive or intentional explanation of any event? There is a strong but tacit undercurrent of conviction, I think, to the effect that only by being rendered explicit, only by being actually *generated* by something like the Euclid machine, can an item of information *play a role*. The idea, apparently, is that in order to have an effect, in order to throw its weight around, as it were, an item of information must weigh something, must have a physical embodiment, and what could that be but an explicit representation or expression of it? I suspect, on the contrary, that this is almost backwards. Explicit representations, by themselves (considered in isolation from the systems that can use them), may be admirably salient bits of the universe, off which to bounce photons or neurotransmitter molecules or marbles, but they are by themselves quite inert as information bearers in the sense we need. They *become* information bearers only when given roles in larger systems, at which time those of their features in virtue of which we call them explicit play problematic roles at best.

One might well say that implicit representation isn't representation at all; only explicit representation is representation. But then one should go on to note that if this is what we are to understand by "representation," there are ways of holding or even sending information in a system that do not involve representing it. After all, a spy can send a message from A to B indirectly by sending explicit premises from which the intended message, the information-to-be-sent follows.[1] Another important point to remember about implicit storage of information is that it has no upper bound. It needn't take more space to store more implicit information.

So *implicit* depends on *explicit*. But in the sense of "tacit" I will use, it is the other way round: *explicit* depends on *tacit*. This is what Ryle

---

1. This possibility is ingeniously exploited by Jorge Luis Borges in his classic short story "The Garden of Forking Paths" in *Labyrinths: Selected Stories and Other Writings* edited by Donald A. Yates and James E. Irby (New York: New Directions, 1962).

was getting at when he claimed that explicitly proving things (on blackboards and so forth) depended on an agent's having a lot of *know-how*, which could not itself be explained in terms of the explicit representation in the agent of any rules or recipes, because to be able to manipulate *those* rules and recipes there would have to be an inner agent with the know-how to handle those explicit items—and that would lead to an infinite regress. At the bottom, Ryle saw, there has to be a system that *merely* has the know-how. If it can be said to *represent* its know-how at all, it must represent it not explicitly and not implicitly—in the sense just defined—but tacitly. The know-how has to be built into the system in some fashion that does not require it to be represented (explicitly) in the system. People often use the word "implicit" to describe such information-holding; what they mean is what I mean by "tacit."

Ryle thought that the regress of representers had to stop somewhere, with systems having merely tacit know-how. He was right about that. But he also thought it was obvious that whole people weren't composed of smaller subsystems that themselves represented anything explicitly, and he was wrong about that. It isn't *obvious*—as several decades of cognitive psychology show. It might still be true—or at any rate much closer to the truth than the current ideology supposes.

All these terms—"explicit," "potentially explicit," "implicit," and "tacit"—are to be distinguished from "conscious" and "unconscious." Thus what you consciously represent to yourself is at best indirect evidence of what might be explicitly represented in you unconsciously. So far as cognitive science is concerned, the important phenomena are the explicit unconscious mental representations. Thus when Chomsky (1980a) talks about the explicit representation of one's grammar in one's head, he certainly doesn't mean the conscious representation of that grammar. It is presumed to be unconscious and utterly inaccessible to the subject. But he also means that it is not merely tacit in the operation or competence of the system, and it is also not merely implicit in something "more basic" that is explicit in the head. He means to take the hard line: the grammar is itself unconsciously but explicitly represented in the head (see Chomsky 1980a, 1980b).

We can understand the hard line by comparing it to a paradigm case of *conscious* explicit rule-following. Consider bridge players, and their relation to a familiar rule of thumb in bridge:

Third Hand High!

There, right on this page, is an explicit representation of the rule. It is often explicitly represented (in just these three English words) in books and articles on bridge; one can also often hear tokens of it yelled across bridge tables. The rule enjoins the third of the four players to any trick to play his highest card in the suit led. (This is a tactical rule—not a rule of the game. You can play bridge and not know the rule; you can play *good* bridge and not "know" the rule.)

Consider the most extreme case. This is the person who consciously and even self-consciously and explicitly consults the rule, who when his turn comes to play a card thinks to himself (perhaps he even moves his lips!): "Let's see, now, I think there's a rule here. Yes. 'Third Hand High!' Am I third hand? One-two-three, yes, I'm third. I'm supposed to play the highest card in the suit led. That would be my jack."—and then he plays his jack. That would be a case of explicitly following a rule: getting the rule out of memory, putting it up in the "workspace" of consciousness, examining it, checking to see if its conditions are met, and on seeing that they are, "firing off" the activity. Now Ryle's claim was that anyone who thinks that this is a good model for human mentation of all sorts, from tying one's shoes to understanding a sentence in one's native language, is—shall we say—benighted. But that's just what the cognitive scientists, at least some of them, think. We can see what their point is by comparing our first bridge player with some other familiar types.

Consider next the "intuitive" bridge player. Let us suppose that our intuitive bridge player never heard the rule in his life, and the words of the rule have never occurred to him in any language he knows. He's never "reflected" on it, so when he thinks about which card to play he certainly does not consciously, explicitly follow the rule. That leaves him only the position that most of us are in with respect to the rules of our native language. It doesn't follow that he's not *un*consciously following some explicit version of that rule. Let us suppose in any case that his dispositions to card-playing behavior (card-*choosing* behavior—we are to ignore the accompanying frowns, delays, and *sotto voce* mumblings) are indistinguishable from those of the first bridge player. The hard-line hypothesis is that the backstage-processing account of this player's "intuitive" card-choosing bears a very strong resemblance to the "introspective" account our first player might give.

Finally, look at a third case: a player who combines the features of the first two—and hence is a much better bridge player than our first, and maybe better than our second as well. This person knows the rule, but is smart enough to realize that there are exceptions to it, that it shouldn't be slavishly followed. He can think about the rationale of the rule and about whether this is a good opportunity to apply the rule.

This third player would be a much worse model for cognitive psychology to adopt (and I suspect Ryle had this sort of rule-consulter in mind when he dismissed the prospect), because he lacks a very important property the first player had: stupidity. A systematically important feature revealed by our first player's rule-following is the possibility of storing and "acting on" something without really understanding it. It is the *worst sort* of classroom activity, the rote memorization, that supplies the best model for cognitive science, because it has the nice feature of decoupling memory from understanding. Memory of this sort is just brute storage (like a singer memorizing the lyrics of a Russian song without having the faintest idea what they mean).

This is just what we want, it seems, if we're trying to explain understanding in terms of storage and manipulation. For we want our storers and manipulators to be stupider than our understander (of which they are proper parts); otherwise we'll get into a Rylean regress. The storers and manipulators must indeed have *some* know-how—even our first bridge player knows enough to know how to apply the rule, and this is not nothing; just think of the bridge players who can't seem to get this simple rule into their thick heads. This know-how in turn might be merely tacit, *or* based on some further internal rule-following process of even narrower horizons and greater stupidity (see *Brainstorms*, chapters 5 and 7). The possibility in principle of terminating this regress in a finite number of steps is a fundamental guiding insight of cognitive science. But will the regress actually be used? It must terminate in the end with merely tacit know-how, but could Ryle turn out to be right after all about the "size" of the largest merely tacit knowers: whole people? Could virtually all the *backstage* know-how be merely tacit in the organization of the system? How powerful can a system of tacit "representation" be?

This is a hard question to answer, in part because the critical term, "tacit," still has been given only an impressionistic, ostensive definition. We haven't really pinned down what it should mean. Consider a benchmark question: does a pocket calculator represent the "truths of arithmetic" explicitly, implicitly, or tacitly? A tiny hand calculator *gives one access to* a virtual infinity of arithmetical facts, but in what sense are *any* arithmetical facts "stored" in it? If one looks closely at the hardware, one finds no numerical propositions written in code in its interior. The only obvious explicit representation of numbers is either printed on the input buttons or, during output, displayed in liquid crystal letters in the little window.

But surely there is further explicit representation hidden from the user? Consider what happens when one gives the calculator the problem: 6 × 7 = ? Let us suppose the calculator does the multiplication by swiftly adding (in binary notation) 7 + 7 + 7 + 7 + 7 + 7, and during the actual process it holds in its accumulator or buffer the interim totals of each successive sum. Thus we can clearly distinguish the process it goes through when multiplying 6 × 7 from the process it goes through in multiplying 7 × 6. In the former case the interim results are 14, 21, 28, 35, while in the latter case they are 12, 18, 24, 30, 36. Surely this is explicit and systematic representation of *numbers*, but where does the calculator represent any true arithmetical *propositions*? Its inner machinery is so arranged that it has the fancy dispositional property of *answering arithmetical questions correctly.* It does this without ever *looking up* any arithmetical facts or rules of operation stored in it. It was designed, of course, by engineers who knew the truths of arithmetic and the rules of arithmetical calculation, and who saw to it that the device would operate so as to "honor" all those truths and rules. So the calculator is a device with the dispositional competence to produce explicit answers to explicit questions (so these truths are *potentially explicit* in it), but it does this without relying on any explicit representations within it—except the representations of the questions and answers that occur at its input and output edges and a variety of interim results. The truths of arithmetic potentially explicit in it are thus not *implicit* in it, for there are no explicit truths in it of which these are the implications.

Outlandish as it may seem at first, it is worth comparing this view of the pocket calculator with Ryle's view of human beings. Ryle is the foe of internal representation, certainly, but he has the good sense to acknowledge what might be called *peripheral* explicit representation— at the input and output boundaries of people (!), as instanced by such familiar Rylean categories as *sotto voce* rehearsings, talking to oneself without moving one's lips, reminding oneself of interim results before getting on with the task at hand. Ryle's view, I take it, is that just as there is no deeper, covert-but-explicit representation of anything in the pocket calculator in virtue of which these conceded representations are manipulated, so there is no covert-but-explicit representation in us in virtue of which we are enabled to say and think the things we do.

An interesting feature of the design process that yields such things as hand calculators as products is that the designers typically *begin* with a perfectly explicit specification of truths to be honored and rules to be followed. They eventually succeed in creating a device that "obeys" the rules and "honors" the truths without itself representing them explicitly at all. Does this process have an analogue in human mental development? Occasionally human beings learn skills that are *first* governed (or so "introspection" strongly assures us) by quite explicit consultation of explicitly rehearsed rules—as with our first bridge player—but these skills, with practice, eventually become *somehow* "automatized": the tennis player no longer mutters directions to herself as she prepares for a backhand stroke, the newly "fluent" speaker of a second language no longer *consciously* checks to make sure the adjective agrees in gender with the noun it modifies.[2] What is going on in these probably related phenomena? One possibility, most vividly sketched by Fodor (1968b), is that such automatization is a matter of merely *hiding* the explicit-recipe-following beneath normal conscious access. (His example is tying one's shoes; he supposes that submerged beneath conscious access is an explicit recipe, called "How to Tie Your Shoes"; it is retrieved by an equally hidden recipe-reading-and-following subsystem, which governs the actual shoe-tying process in the manner of our first bridge player.) Another possibility, suggested by the example of the calculator design process, is that practicing is somehow an analogous process of partial self-design: it yields, like its analogue, a "device" that "obeys" the rules without consulting any expression of them.

This latter possibility may seem probable only for systems whose tasks—and hence whose rules of operation—are as static and unchanging as those "hard-wired" into a calculator. But it is entirely possible to design systems that can change mode, switching from "following" one set of tacit rules to "following" another. An automatic elevator, for instance, can be made to follow one set of rules

---

2. One of the most fascinating cases of this move to automaticity is the self-training of a calculating prodigy reported in Hunter 1962.

from nine to five on weekdays and a different set of rules during off-peak and weekend hours. And of course it can be made to do this without either set of rules being explicitly represented in it; all it needs is a clock-controlled switch to take it back and forth between two different control systems, each of which tacitly represents a set of rules of operation. This gives us a simple example of what we may call *transient tacit representation*. All the rules are tacitly represented all the time, but depending on the state of the system, only one set of rules is tacitly represented *as being followed* at any time. Or one might equally well say that the whole system tacitly and permanently represents the rule "Follow rule system R on weekdays from nine to five and rule system R' at other times," and the state of the system at any time transiently and tacitly represents the time of the week—a way of providing a vehicle (but not a vehicle of *explicit* representation) for such indexical propositions as "Now it is weekend time."

We can imagine similar systems in animals. We can imagine, for instance, an animal that is both aquatic and terrestrial, and when it is on the land it obeys one set of rules, and when it is in the water it obeys another. Simply *getting wet* could be the trigger for changing internal state from one set of rules to the other.

So far the systems I have described are switched from one state to another by a simple switch—an uncomplicated "transducer" keying on some feature of the environment (or the mere passage of time if the transducer is a clock), but we could have more elaborate switching machinery, so that which system of rules was transiently tacitly represented depended on complex distal features of the environment. If elaborate perceptual analysis machinery drives the system into its various states, then there is no apparent limit to the specificity or complexity of the state of the world, for instance, that could be tacitly represented by the current state of such a system. Not just "Now it is weekend time" but "Now I'm in grandmother's house" or "Now there is a distinct danger of being attacked by a predator approaching from the north-northeast." Such systems of tacit representation would need no *terms* to be "translated by" the various terms in the theorists' attempts to capture the information tacitly represented by such states (such as the attempts appearing between quotation marks in the previous sentence). For the whole point of tacit representation is that it is tacit! States of such a system get their semantic properties directly and only from their globally defined functional roles.

But as the number of possible different states (each with its distinctive set of tacitly represented rules) grows, as a system becomes versatile enough to be driven into a great many significantly different control states, this profligacy demands that the design rely in one way or another on economies achieved via multiple use of resources. For instance, where the different states are variations on a theme (involving only minor changes in the tacitly followed rules) it becomes useful—virtually mandatory—to design the whole system to change states not by switching control from one physically distinct subsystem to another near-duplicate subsystem, but by changing some one or more features of the current subsystem, leaving the rest intact—changing states by *editing* and *revising*, one might say, instead of by *discarding* and *replacing*. Economies of this sort require systematicity; the loci into which substitutions can be made have to have fixed ways of changing their functions as a function of the identity of the substituends. The whole system thus does begin to look *somewhat* like a language, with counterparts for all the syntactical features mentioned at the outset.

Should we say that such a system finally emerges as a truly explicit system of internal representation? There will certainly be uses for that view of such systems. But it is important to note that the "syntactical" elements of such systems are to be viewed first as having an entirely internal semantics—"referring" to memory addresses, internal operations, other states of the system, and so forth, not to things and events in the outer world.[3] If these internal state components are cunningly interanimated, the states achievable by them can bear delicate informational relations to events and things in the outer world, but then, insofar as the states of such systems can be interpreted as having external semantic properties, they obtain their semantic properties in just the same way—for just the same reasons—as the merely tacitly representing states. It is only the globally defined role of such a state (the role that is characterized in terms of the rules of operation the whole system "follows" when it goes into that state) that fixes its informational or external semantic properties.

In an extended usage, then, it might be profitable to grant indirect

3. In "Tom Swift and his Procedural Grandmother" (1981c), Fodor sees clearly that the internal semantics of programming languages and their kin do not *in themselves* solve the problem of mental reference or intentionality. My claim here is that we have not yet been given compelling reasons for supposing that any of the "syntactical" elements of internal states that do have external semantic properties will themselves admit of any straightforward external semantic interpretation.

external semantic properties to some of the elements of such a system of states. So it *might* be found that the state of someone responsible for his believing that snow is white has components identifiable as the "snow" component and the "white" component. But such "sentences in the language of thought," if we decide it is wise to call them that, are in striking contrast to the sentences of natural languages. Given what the English sentences "snow is white" and "snow is cold" and "milk is white" mean, we can say what "milk is cold" means (whether or not some speaker or audience realizes it); but given the counterpart cases in Mentalese, we won't be able to *tell* what the "milk is cold" state means—it may not mean anything at all—until we've determined its global role.

My goal in this essay has been simply to explore—and perhaps improve our view of—some open, empirically researchable territory. Ryle said, aprioristically, that we *couldn't* be mental-representation-manipulators; Fodor and others have said, aprioristically, that we *must* be. Some of the details of the computer metaphor suggest what we *might* be, and in so doing may eventually shed some light on what we are.

Reflections:
The Language of Thought
Reconsidered

The idea of a language of thought is ancient. In its most recent guise, provocatively championed by Fodor (1975), it has now received more than a decade of scrutiny as the dominant theoretical slogan of cognitive science. This is a good time to review its prospects and see what alternatives might be discernible. It began its recent career as a fine stab in the dark, inspired by relatively aprioristic arguments about the only way the demands of cognition could be met rather than by any very compelling empirical clues. As more light has been shed on the mechanisms and methods of various psychological and neural systems, it is emerging neither vindicated nor entirely discredited.[1]

It would have been vindicated with fanfare had it led to detailed and testable hypotheses about the organization of cognitive processes, but nothing like that has happened. It may help us to understand the current state of the art, however, if we pause to imagine what that triumph would have been like.

Recall Marr's (1975) three levels of explanation in cognitive science (see above, pp. 74–75). We can describe the imaginary vindication of the language of thought hypothesis in terms of a triumphant cascade through Marr's three levels.

Suppose, then, that thanks to the efforts of propositional attitude task forces, the principles of folk-psychological calculation have come to be as rigorously specified as those of arithmetic. And suppose that these principles have proven to work as well as arithmetic works as a competence model for calculators. We would have the computational level well in hand.

---

1. These reflections summarize themes developed in recent papers, reviews, and commentaries I deemed too specialized to include in this volume: 1984a, b, c; 1986c; forthcoming e.

Then, as we descend from this pure, infinitely extensible level of belief attribution (at which, for instance, we mark the difference between believing that one third is .33333333333 and believing that one third is .333333333333), to the finite, approximating, algorithmic level, suppose we didn't have to change categories radically; the actual states—drawn from a finite set of possible states—through which the algorithms pass bear a striking resemblance to the states referred to at the computational level. And finally, suppose the mapping of algorithms onto neural hardware goes smoothly; we discover the location, duration, and other physical parameters of the actual symbol manipulations postulated at the algorithmic level.

Suppose all this were so; then Fodor and the other Realists would be in heaven, for this would be the reduction of propositional attitude psychology to High Church Computationalism (Dennett 1984b, 1986e). Beliefs and other propositional attitudes, we would have confirmed, are perfectly real; having a propositional attitude turns out to be, as Fodor originally put it, "being in some *computational* relation to an internal representation." (1975, p. 198).

But now suppose it doesn't turn out that way. Suppose something rather big has to give way as we move from our idealized computational level model—which itself turns out not to be rigorous—down through algorithm to hardware. This is not an idle supposition, for as Fodor himself notes, the great progress in cognitive science has been in uncovering the modes of action of the *peripheral* sensory, perceptual, and motor systems, and here the progress has been largely a matter of showing how these systems can do their work *without* any recourse to a level of computations involving explicit representations (Fodor 1983; see also Dennett 1984a; and Akins, unpublished).

If we probably do not need a language of thought, then, to get to and from the peripheries, do we need a language of thought to handle the most central control processes of higher animals (or just human beings)? Such "higher cognitive functions" as planning, problem solving, and "belief fixation" are intuitively the functions that involve *thinking* (as opposed to "mere" perceiving and acting). Here, if anywhere, the intellectualist vision should triumph. Here we might well still expect inferential processes in which "the postulates . . . are internally represented and etiologically involved." (Fodor 1981, p. 120) But in fact there has been almost no advance on the empirical theory of these most central psychological activities. Fodor savors the gloom:

We have, to put it bluntly, no computational formalisms that show us how to do this, and we have no idea how such formalisms might be developed. . . . If someone—a Dreyfus, for example—were to ask us why we should even suppose that the digital computer is a plausible mechanism for the simulation of global cognitive processes, the answering silence would be deafening. (1983, p. 129)

The problem is not that sententialist models of such thinking do not lead to plausible testable hypotheses. Worse, they seem to lead quite systematically down recognizable dead ends: hopelessly brittle, inefficient, and unversatile monstrosities of engineering that would scarcely guide an insect through life unscathed. At the heart of the difficulties lies the Frame Problem of artificial intelligence, as Fodor recognizes (1983, pp. 112ff), and it has proven so resistant to solution by the orthodox techniques of cognitive science that a strong case can be made that it spells the doom of propositional attitudes as computational relations to internal representations (Dennett 1984c).

The idea of a language of thought would be entirely discredited if a clear alternative to it had been formulated and shown to handle the tasks it was postulated to perform. Fodor threw down this gauntlet in 1975, acknowledging that the idea of a language of thought was hard to swallow but defying the skeptics to find an alternative. His epigraph was from Lyndon B. Johnson: "I'm the only President you've got." (p. 27) The recent wave of Connectionist models (McClelland and Rumelhart 1986) has been seen by some enthusiasts as just such an alternative, but tempting as Connectionism is as a response to Fodor's challenge, it is too early for verdicts. A summary description of this recent trend (drawn from Dennett 1984b, 1986e) may serve, however, to give at least an impression of what an alternative to the language of thought *might be like.*

The Connectionist networks so far developed are (at best) *fragments* of cognitive systems composed of richly interconnected, relatively simple units. Such a network typically differs from the traditional (High Church Computationalist) models of cognitive science in that it has

(1) "distributed" memory and processing, in which units play multiple, drastically equivocal roles, and in which disambiguation occurs only "globally" (in short, there aren't "propositions" located at "addresses" in the memory);

(2) no central control but rather a partially anarchic system of somewhat competitive elements;

(3) no complex message-passing between units;

(4) a reliance on statistical properties of ensembles to achieve effects;

(5) the relatively mindless and inefficient making and unmaking of many partial pathways or solutions, until the system settles down after a while—not necessarily on a predesignated "right" answer.

The models are still computational in one important sense: they are implemented on computers and the behavior of each node or unit is a clearly defined (and computed) function of the behavior of (some of) the other nodes. How then, do these models differ so strikingly in flavor from traditional cognitive science models?

For one thing, the level at which the modeling is computational is much closer to neuroscience than to psychology. *What is computed* is not (for instance) an implication of some predicate-calculus "proposition" *about Chicago* or a formal description *of a grammatical transformation*, but (for instance) the new value of some threshold-like parameter of some element *which all by itself has no univocal external-world semantic role*. At such a low level of description, the semantics of the symbolic medium of computation refers only to events, processes, states, addresses within the brain—within the computational system itself.

How then do we ever get anything happening in such a system that is properly *about Chicago?* There must indeed be a higher level of description at which we can attribute external-semantical properties to relatively global features of the network's activities, but at such a level the interactions and relationships between semantic elements are not computational but—and here we lapse temporarily into metaphor and handwaving—statistical, emergent, holistic. The "virtual machine" that is recognizably psychological in its activity is not a *machine* in one familiar sense: its behavior is not formally specifiable *in the psychological-level vocabulary* as the computation of some high-level algorithm. Thus in this vision, the algorithmic level is importantly *un*like a normal machine language in that there is no supposition of a direct translation or implementation relation between the high-level phenomena that do have an external-world semantics and the phenomena at the low, algorithmic level. If there were, then the usual methodological precept of computer science would be in order: ignore the hardware since the idiosyncracies of its particular implementation add nothing to the phenomenon, provided the phenomenon is rigorously described at the higher level. In Connectionist models, the (typically stimulated) hardware does add something: just which content-relative effects actually occur (something that is only statistically describable at the high-level) depends on low-level features of the history of operations. The different flavors of cognition emerge from the activity, without being specifically designed to emerge.

Such Connectionist networks have been shown to be capable of performing a variety of cognitive subtasks that heretofore were presumed to require elaborate rule-based computational machinery—all without the explicit, designed representation of rules. To cite perhaps the most accessible instance, Sejnowski's NETtalk (1986) "learns" how to pronounce written English, starting with an entirely random set of dispositions to pronounce the text elements and being "corrected" as it proceeds. It soon exhibits just the sort of behavior that has heretofore been seen as symptomatic of rule-based computation: it generalizes from what it has seen, but comes to recognize exceptions to its generalizations—and generalizes on those exceptions. Yet nowhere in NETtalk are any rules *explicitly* represented; they are, of course, *tacitly* represented in the emergent dispositional structure of the network, but nothing happens in the network which is anything like *checking to see if a rule applies* or *looking up the target term in a table of exceptions*—paradigms of the covert intellectualist activities Ryle disparaged.

There are still abundant grounds for skepticism about Connectionism. All of the existing networks achieve their striking effects with the aid of ominously unrealistic props, such as the "teacher" that stands by to pump corrections into NETtalk, and, at a lower level, varieties of two-way traffic between nodes that are so far unknown to neuroscience. And as with earlier false hopes in artificial intelligence (see *Brainstorms*, chapter 7), there are worries about *scaling up:* models that work impressively when restricted to a few dozens or hundreds of elements sometimes stop dead in their tracks when expanded to realistic dimensions. Plausible avenues of escape from these problems have already been identified, but it will take some years of exploration to see where they lead.

If Cognitive Science were Aeronautical Science, we could describe the current situation as follows. The first great step in the attempt to create Flying Machines was the insistence by the Founders that mystical appeals to *wonder tissue* (Dennett 1984c) were hopeless: designs had to be based on sound, well-understood, mechanistic principles. Years of brilliant design efforts followed, and a variety of promising—

but hapless—machines were built out of the then well-understood materials: bricks, mortar, and wood. Nothing really flew. Then along came the Connectionists with what appeared to be a variety of new, synthetic wonder tissues. It has yet to be shown how these exciting fabrics can be sewn into whole, working Flying Machines; perhaps some of the earlier design work will be adaptable to the new materials.[2]

The problems still unaddressed by the Connectionists are acknowledged by McClelland and Rumelhart (1986) and Smolensky (forthcoming). One of these remains the problem of generativity. The best argument for the language of thought is still the claim that *somehow* the whole system, at least in human beings, must be capable of a virtually unlimited capacity to differentiate and then to base its behavior on features of those differentiations. No differentiation without representation, to paraphrase Fodor's battle cry. We still have only one clear example of a method of *indefinitely extendable and articulate* representation: a natural language. The system of generativity of whatever serves to represent the world in us will thus almost surely be interpretable in retrospect as if composed of terms and sentences in a language, but that would not in itself vindicate the idea of linguistic objects as the basic building blocks of cognition. It may well be that this linguistic level will appear as an innocently emergent property of the distributed activities of other units rather the way a picture is discernible in a mosaic composed of elements held together by principles that ignore the boundaries of the picture elements.

How closely tied are the fates of the language of thought hypothesis on the one hand and Realism with regard to propositional attitudes on the other? Fodor has always maintained that they stand or fall together, and he has been joined by many others, including Stich and the Churchlands. In the eventuality that our folk-psychological competence model is forever only an idealized competence model, bearing scant relation to the underlying mechanisms—and this would be the case if Connectionism is triumphant—what should we say in the end about the categories of folk psychology? Stich (1983, pp. 221–28), still finding the idea of a language of thought attractive, holds out some hope for a "modified Panglossian prospect" in which mature psychology "cleaves reasonably closely to the

---

2. For a pioneering sketch, see, for example, Touretzky and Hinton's (1985) demonstration of how to build a *production system* (one of the architectures of High Church Computationalism) out of a Boltzmann machine (one of the new Connectionist fabrics).

pattern presupposed by folk psychology," but "in more pessimistic moments" he anticipates just this negative outcome. So, more cheerily, does Churchland (1981). They both declare that this would show that there are no such states as beliefs after all; they would announce the death of folk psychology and all its spruced-up versions as propositional attitude psychology.

What would they put in its place? Stich, whenever optimism overwhelms him and he anticipates that Fodor will prove *almost* right, would replace folk psychology with a purely "syntactic" theory; he would hang on to versions of the folk categories—belief-states, for instance—but de-interpret them. In his pessimistic moments, he would join Churchland and do just the opposite: cling to the contentfulness or intentionality of inner something-or-others but drop the presupposition that these inner vehicles of meaning behaved, syntactically, in the ways Realists have supposed beliefs to behave. Belief dis-contented versus content dis-believed.

There is something to be said for each of these positions. Indeed they could both be "vindicated" at once by future triumphs in empirical psychology! For if I am right, there are really two sorts of phenomena being confusedly alluded to by folk-psychological talk about beliefs: the verbally infected but only problematically and derivatively contentful states of language-users ("opinions") and the deeper states of what one might call animal belief (frogs and dogs have beliefs, but no opinions). Stich, with his syntactic theory, can be recommending more or less the right way to go with opinions, while Churchland can be the methodological guru for those theorizing about the others, the internal behavior-guiding, information-sensitive states, which are not at all "sentential" in structure.

I choose not to follow either eliminativist branch, however. My inability to join either camp is not, like the immobility of Buridan's ass, a matter of my seeing equally the attractions of both and being unable to choose. For although I acknowledge these attractions, I see a shared problem in their extreme eliminativism: until the rest of the world catches up with them and shares their world view, what will they tell the judge? That is, when called on to give sworn testimony in a court of law, and asked by the judge whether they *believe* they have ever seen the defendant before, what will they say? Surely they must deny that they are saying what they believe, since they believe (uh-oh) that there is no such thing as belief. That is to say, they are *of the opinion* (will that do?) that there is no such thing as belief. What they mean is, the theory they, um, espouse or champion has no room in its ontology for beliefs.

This is a familiar line of attack, and no news to Stich and Churchland. Skinner's earlier brand of eliminativism has often been claimed to be systematically self-refuting for such reasons. I am sure that none of the *a priori* arguments purporting to render these categories of the manifest image immune to scientific discredit is sound, and I do not endorse any of them. I take the problem to be not directly doctrinal but tactical (see "Quining Qualia," forthcoming d, and chapter 1 of *Content and Consciousness*). When I say the choice is tactical, I am not just calling discretion the better part of valor and counseling a decorous retreat before the big battalions of outraged common sense. That would be craven and dishonest (though one could make a pretty good case for it in the courtroom: which do you prefer, that justice be done the defendant or that you spend your precious day in court annoying the judge with an unconvincing philosophy lesson?) Of more importance to the philosopher of science, tactically, is not losing sight of the tremendous—if flawed—predictive power of the intentional stance. The judge may be a ceremonial figure, but he is not a witch doctor; his official desire to learn what you believe is not irrational; his method is, beyond any doubt, the best way we know of getting at the truth. Is there any reason to believe that in the Golden Age of Eliminative Psychosyntax or Eliminative Neurobiology a serious rival method of truth-seeking will arise?

Churchland offers optimistic speculations on just this point, and he might, for all anyone can say now, turn out to be prophetic. But in the meantime he has to have some line on the status of the (apparent) predictive and explanatory powers of not only humble folk psychology, but the academic social sciences. What is going on in economic models that presuppose rational agents? How can he explain the power of cognitive psychologists to design fruitful experiments that require assumptions about the beliefs their subjects have about the test situation, the desire they have inculcated in their subjects to attend to the message in the left ear, and so forth? (Dennett 1985c) That power is perfectly real, and requires an explanation. He might say, might he not, that, pending the Golden Age, there is a sort of instrumentalistic calculus available, of humble parentage but a certain effectiveness withal?

Suppose, for the sake of drama, that it turns out that the subpersonal cognitive psychology of some people turns out to be dramatically different from that of others. One can imagine the newspaper headlines: "Scientists Prove Most Left-handers Incapable of Belief" or "Startling Discovery—Diabetics Have No Desires." But this is not what we would say, no matter how the science turns out.

And our reluctance would not be just conceptual conservatism, but the recognition of an obvious empirical fact. For let left- and right-handers (or men and women or any other subsets of people) be as internally different as you like, we already know that there are reliable, robust patterns in which all behaviorally normal people participate—the patterns we traditionally describe in terms of belief and desire and the other terms of folk psychology. What spread around the world on July 20, 1969? The belief that a man had stepped on the moon. In no two people was the effect of the receipt of that information the same, and the causal paths eventuating in the state they all had in common were no doubt almost equally various, but the claim that therefore they all had nothing in common—nothing importantly in common—is false, and obviously so. There are indefinitely many ways one could reliably distinguish those with the belief from those without it, and there would be a high correlation between the methods. That is not something science should—or could—turn its back on.

How then do I see the Golden Age? Very much as Churchland does, with some shifts in emphasis. In chapter 3 I laid out the kinds. First there will be our old, reliable friend, folk psychology, and second, its self-consciously abstract idealization; intentional system theory. Finally there will be a well-confirmed theory at a level between folk psychology and bare biology, sub-personal cognitive psychology. We can now say a bit more about what it might be like: it will be "cognitive" in that it will describe processes of information-transformation among content-laden items—mental representations—but their style will not be "computational"; the items will not look or behave like sentences manipulated in a language of thought.

7   Intentional Systems in Cognitive Ethology: The "Panglossian Paradigm" Defended

The Problem

The field of cognitive ethology provides a rich source of material for the philosophical analysis of meaning and mentality, and even holds out some tempting prospects for philosophers to contribute fairly directly to the development of the concepts and methods of another field. As a philosopher, an outsider with only a cursory introduction to the field of ethology, I find that the new ethologists, having cast off the straightjacket of behaviorism and kicked off its weighted over-shoes, are looking about somewhat insecurely for something presentable to wear. They are seeking a theoretical vocabulary that is powerfully descriptive of the data they are uncovering and at the same time a theoretically fruitful method of framing hypotheses that will *eventually* lead to information-processing models of the nervous system of the creatures they are studying (see Roitblat 1982). It is a long way from the observation of the behavior of, say, primates in the wild to the validation of neurophysiological models of their brain activity, and finding a sound interim way of speaking is not a trivial task. Since the methodological and conceptual problems confronting the ethologists appear to me to bear striking resemblances to problems I and other philosophers have been grappling with recently, I am tempted to butt in and offer, first, a swift analysis of the problem; second, a proposal for dealing with it (which I call intentional system theory); third, an analysis of the continuity of intentional system theory with the theoretical strategy or attitude in evolutionary theory often called *adaptationism*; and, finally, a limited defense of adapta-

Originally published in *The Behavioral and Brain Sciences* 6 (1983): 343–90, and reprinted with permission.

tionism (and its cousin, intentional system theory) against recent criticisms by Stephen J. Gould and Richard C. Lewontin.

The methodology of philosophy, such as it is, includes as one of its most popular (and often genuinely fruitful) strategies the description and examination of entirely imaginary situations, elaborate thought experiments that isolate for scrutiny the presumably critical features in some conceptual domain. In *Word and Object*, W.V.O. Quine (1960) gave us an extended examination of the evidential and theoretical tasks facing the "radical translator," the imaginary anthropologist-linguist who walks into an entirely alien community—with no string of interpreters or bilingual guides—and who must figure out, using whatever scientific methods are available, the language of the natives. Out of this thought experiment came Quine's thesis of the "indeterminacy of radical translation," the claim that it must always be possible in principle to produce nontrivially different translation manuals, equally well supported by all the evidence, for any language. One of the most controversial features of Quine's position over the years has been his uncompromisingly behaviorist scruples about how to characterize the task facing the radical translator. What happens to the task of radical translation when you give up the comitment to a behavioristic outlook and terminology? What are the prospects for fixing on a unique translation of a language (or a unique interpretation of the "mental states" of a being) if one permits oneself the vocabulary and methods of "cognitivism"? The question could be explored via other thought experiments, and has been in some regards (Bennett 1976; Dennett 1971; Lewis 1974), but the real-world researches of Seyfarth, Cheney, and Marler (1980) with vervet monkeys in Africa will serve us better on this occasion. Vervet monkeys form societies, of sorts, and have a language, of sorts, and of course there are no bilingual interpreters to give a boost to the radical translators of Vervetese. This is what they find.

Vervet monkeys give different alarm calls to different predators. Recordings of the alarms played back when predators were absent caused the monkeys to run into the trees for leopard alarms, look up for eagle alarms, and look down for snake alarms. Adults call primarily to leopards, martial eagles, and pythons, but infants give leopard alarms to various mammals, eagle alarms to many birds, and snake alarms to various snakelike objects. Predator classification improves with age and experience. (Abstract of Seyfarth, Cheney, and Marler 1980, p. 801)

This abstract is couched, you will note, in almost pure Behaviorese—the language of *Science* even it if is no longer exclusively the language of science. It is just informative enough to be tantalizing. How much of a language, one wants to know, do the vervets really have? Do they *really* communicate? Do they *mean what they say*? Just what interpretation can we put on these activities? What, if anything, do these data tell us about the cognitive capacities of vervet monkeys? In what ways are they—must they be—like human cognitive capacities, and in what ways and to what degree are vervets more intelligent than other species by virtue of these "linguistic" talents? These loaded questions—the most natural ones to ask under the circumstances—do not fall squarely within the domain of any science, but whether or not they are the right questions for the scientist to ask, they are surely the questions that we all, as fascinated human beings learning of this apparent similarity of the vervets to us, want answered.

The cognitivist would like to succumb to the temptation to use ordinary mentalistic language more or less at face value and to respond directly to such questions as: What do the monkeys *know*? What do they *want*, and *understand* and *mean*? At the same time, the primary point of the cognitivists' research is not to satisfy the layman's curiosity about the relative IQ, as it were, of his simian cousins, but to chart the cognitive *talents* of these animals on the way to charting the cognitive *processes* that explain those talents. Could the everyday language of belief, desire, expectation, recognition, understanding and the like also serve as the suitably rigorous abstract language in which to describe cognitive competences?

I will argue that the answer is yes. Yes, if we are careful about what we are doing and saying when we use ordinary words like "believe" and "want," and understand the assumptions and implications of the strategy we must adopt when we use these words.

The decision to conduct one's science in terms of beliefs, desires, and other "mentalistic" notions, the decision to adopt "the intentional stance," is not an unusual sort of decision in science. The basic strategy of which this is a special case is familiar: changing levels of explanation and description in order to gain access to greater predictive power or generality—purchased, typically, at the cost of submerging detail and courting trivialization on the one hand and easy falsification on the other. When biologists studying some species choose to call something in that species' environment *food* and leave it at that, they ignore the tricky details of the chemistry and physics of nutrition, the biology of mastication, digestion, excretion, and the rest. Even supposing many of the details of this finer-grained biology are still ill understood, the decision to leap ahead in anticipation of fine-grained biology, and rely on the well-behavedness of the concept of food at the level of the theory appropriate to it is likely to meet approval from the most conservative risk takers.

The decision to adopt the intentional stance is riskier. It banks on the soundness of some as yet imprecisely described concept of information—not the concept legitimized by Shannon-Weaver information theory (Shannon 1949), but rather the concept of what is often called *semantic information*. (A more or less standard way of introducing the still imperfectly understood distinction between these two concepts of information is to say that Shannon-Weaver theory measures the *capacity* of information-transmission and information-storage vehicles, but is mute about the *contents* of those channels and vehicles, which will be the topic of the still-to-be-formulated theory of semantic information (see Dretske 1981 for an attempt to bridge the gap between the two concepts). Information, in the semantic view, is a perfectly real but very abstract commodity, the storage, transmission, and transformation of which is informally—but quite sure-footedly—recounted in ordinary talk in terms of beliefs and desires and the other states and acts philosophers call *intentional*.

Intentional System Theory

Intentionality, in philosophical jargon, is—in a word—*aboutness*. Some of the things, states, and events in the world have the interesting property of *being about* other things, states, and events; figuratively, they point to other things. This arrow of reference or aboutness has been subjected to intense philosophical scrutiny and has engendered much controversy. For our purposes, we can gingerly pluck two points from this boiling cauldron, oversimplifying them and ignoring important issues tangential to our concerns.

First, we can mark the presence of intentionality—aboutness—as the topic of our discussions by marking the presence of a peculiar *logical* feature of all such discussion. Sentences attributing intentional states or events to systems use idioms that exhibit *referential opacity*: they introduce clauses in which the normal, permissive, substitution rule does not hold. This rule is simply the logical codification of the maxim that a rose by any other name would smell as sweet. If you have a true sentence, so runs the rule, and you alter it by replacing a term in it by another, different term that still refers to exactly the same thing or things, the new sentence will also be true. Ditto for false sentences—merely changing the means of picking out the objects of the sentence is about cannot turn a falsehood into a truth. For instance, suppose Bill is the oldest kid in class; then if it is true that

(1) Mary is sitting next to Bill,

then, substituting "the oldest kid in class" for "Bill," we get

(2) Mary is sitting next to the oldest kid in class,

which *must* be true if the other sentence is.

A sentence with an *intentional idiom* in it, however, contains a clause in which such substitution can turn truth into falsehood and vice versa. (This phenomenon is called *referential opacity* because the terms in such clauses are shielded or insulated by a barrier to logical analysis, which normally "sees through" the terms to the world the terms are about.) For example, Sir Walter Scott wrote *Waverly*, and Bertrand Russell (1905) assures us

(3) George IV wondered whether Scott was the author of *Waverly*,

but it seems unlikely indeed that

(4) George IV wondered whether Scott was Scott.

(As Russell remarks, "An interest in the law of identity can hardly be attributed to the first gentleman of Europe." [1905, p. 485]) To give another example, suppose we decide it is true that

(5) Burgess fears that the creature rustling in the bush is a python

and suppose that in fact the creature in the bush is Robert Seyfarth. We will not want to draw the conclusion that

(6) Burgess fears that Robert Seyfarth is a python.

Well, in one sense we do, you say, and in one sense we also want to insist that, oddly enough, King George *was* wondering whether Scott was Scott. But that's not how he put it to himself, and that's not how Burgess conceived of the creature in the bush, either—that is, *as* Seyfarth. It's the sense of conceiving *as*, seeing *as*, thinking of *as* that the intentional idioms focus on.

One more example: Suppose you think your next-door neighbor would make someone a good husband and suppose, unbeknownst to you, he's the Mad Strangler. Although in one, very strained, sense you could be said to believe that the Mad Strangler would make someone a good husband, in another more natural sense you don't, for there is another—very bizarre and unlikely—belief that you surely don't have which could better be called the belief that the Mad Strangler would make a good husband.

It is this resistance to substitution, the insistence that for *some* purposes how you call a rose a rose makes all the difference, that makes the intentional idioms ideally suited for talking about the ways in which information is represented in the heads of people—and other animals. So the first point about intentionality is just that we can rely on a marked set of idioms to have this special feature of being sensitive to the *means of reference* used in the clauses they introduce. The most familiar of such idioms are "believes that," "knows that," "expects (that)," "wants (it to be the case that)," "recognizes (that)," "understands (that)." In short, the "mentalistic" vocabulary shunned by behaviorists and celebrated by cognitivists is quite well picked out by the logical test for referential opacity.

The second point to pluck from the cauldron is somewhat controversial, although it has many adherents who have arrived at roughly the same conclusion by various routes: the use of intentional idioms carries a presupposition or assumption of *rationality* in the creature or system to which the intentional states are attributed. What this amounts to will become clearer if we now turn to the intentional stance in relation to the vervet monkeys.

Vervet Monkeys as Intentional Systems

To adopt the intentional stance toward these monkeys is to decide—tentatively, of course—to attempt to characterize, predict, and explain their behavior by using intentional idioms, such as "believes" and "wants," a practice that assumes or presupposes the rationality of the vervets. A vervet monkey is, we will say, an intentional system, a thing whose behavior is predictable by attributing beliefs and desires (and, of course, rationality) to it. *Which* beliefs and desires? Here there are many hypotheses available, and they are testable in virtue of the rationality requirement. First, let us note that there are different grades of intentional systems.

A *first-order* intentional system has beliefs and desires (etc.) but no beliefs and desires *about* beliefs and desires. Thus all the attributions we make to a merely first-order intentional system have the logical form of

(7) x believes that p
(8) y wants that q

where p and q are clauses that themselves contain no intentional idioms. A *second-order* intentional system is more sophisticated; it has beliefs and desires (and no doubt other intentional states) about beliefs and desires (and other intentional states)—both those of others and its own. For instance

(9) x *wants* y to *believe* that x is hungry
(10) x *believes* y expects x to jump left
(11) x *fears* that y *will discover* that x has a food cache.

A *third-order* intentional system is one that is capable of such states as

(12) x *wants* y to *believe* that x *believes* he is alone.

A fourth-order system might *want* you to *think* it *understood* you to be *requesting* that it leave. How high can we human beings go? In principle, forever, no doubt, but in fact I suspect that you wonder whether I realize how hard it is for you to be sure that you understand whether I mean to be saying that you can recognize that I can believe you to want me to explain that most of us can keep track of only about five or six orders, under the best of circumstances. See Cargile (1970) for an elegant but sober exploration of this phenomenon.

How good are vervet monkeys? Are they really capable of third-order or higher-order intentionality? The question is interesting on several fronts. First, these orders ascend what is *intuitively* a scale of intelligence; higher-order attributions strike us as much more sophisticated, much more human, requiring much more intelligence. There are some plausible diagnoses of this intuition. Grice (1957, 1969) and other philosophers (see especially Bennett 1976) have developed an elaborate and painstakingly argued case for the view that genuine *communication*, speech acts in the strong, human sense of the word, depend on *at least* three orders of intentionality in both speaker and audience.

Not all interactions between organisms are communicative. When I swat a fly I am not communicating with it, nor am I if I open the window to let it fly away. Does a sheep dog, though, communicate with the sheep it herds? Does a beaver communicate by slapping its tail, and do bees communicate by doing their famous dances? Do human infants communicate with their parents? At what point can one be sure one is really communicating with an infant? The presence of specific linguistic tokens seems neither sufficient nor necessary. (I can use English commands to get my dog to do things, but that is at best a pale form of communication compared to the mere raised eyebrow by which I can let someone know he should change the topic of our conversation.) Grice's theory provides a better framework for answering these questions. It defines intuitively plausible and formally powerful criteria for communication that involve, at a minimum, the correct attribution to communicators of such third-order intentional states as

(13) Utterer *intends* Audience to *recognize* that Utterer *intends* Audience to produce response *r*.

So one reason for being interested in the intentional interpretation of the vervets is that it promises to answer—or at least help answer—the questions: Is this behavior really linguistic? Are they really communicating? Another reason is that higher-orderedness is a conspicuous mark of the attributions speculated about in the sociobiological literature about such interactive traits as reciprocal altruism. It has even been speculated (by Trivers 1971), that the increasing complexity of mental representation required for the maintenance of systems of reciprocal altruism (and other complex social relations) led, in evolution, to a sort of brain-power arms race. Humphrey (1976) arrives at similar conclusions by a different and in some regards less speculative route. There may then be a number of routes to the conclusion that higher-orderedness of intentional characterization is a deep mark—and not just a reliable symptom—of intelligence.

(I do not mean to suggest that these orders provide a uniform scale of any sort. As several critics have remarked to me, the first iteration—to a *second-order* intentional system—is the crucial step of the recursion; once one has the principle of *embedding* in one's repertoire, the complexity of what one can then in some sense entertain seems plausibly more a limitation of a memory or attention span or "cognitive workspace" than a fundamental measure of system sophistication. And thanks to "chunking" and other, artificial, aids to memory, there seems to be no *interesting* difference between, say, a fourth-order and a fifth-order intentional system. But see Cargile 1970 for further reflections on the natural limits of iteration.)

But now, back to the empirical question of how good the vervet monkeys are. For simplicity's sake, we can restrict our attention to a single apparently communicative act by a particular vervet, Tom, who, let us suppose, gives a leopard alarm call in the presence of another vervet, Sam. We can now compose a set of competing intentional interpretations of this behavior, ordered from high to low, from romantic to killjoy. Here is a (relatively) romantic hypothesis (with some variations to test in the final clause):

Fourth order

Tom *wants* Sam to *recognize* that Tom *wants* Same to *believe* that
   there is a leopard
   there is a carnivore
   there is a four-legged animal
   there is a live animal bigger than a breadbox.

A less exciting hypothesis to confirm would be this third-order version (there could be others):

Third order

Tom *wants* Sam to *believe* that Tom *wants* Sam to run into the trees.

Note that this particular third-order case differs from the fourth-order case in changing the speech act category: on this reading the leopard call is an imperative (a request or command) not a declarative (informing Sam of the leopard). The important difference between imperative and declarative interpretations (see Bennett 1976, sections 41, 51) of utterances can be captured—and then telltale behavioral differences can be explored—at any level of description above the second order, at which, *ex hypothesi*, there is no intention to utter a speech act of either variety. Even at the second order, however, a related distinction in effect-desired-in-the-Audience is expressed, and is in principle behaviorally detectable, in the following variations:

Second order

Tom *wants* Sam to *believe* that
   there is a leopard
   he should run into the trees.

This differs from the previous two in not supposing Tom's act involves ("in Tom's mind") any recognition by Sam of Tom's own role in the situation. If Tom could accomplish his end equally well by growling like a leopard, or just somehow attracting Sam's attention to the leopard without Sam's recognizing Tom's intervention, this would be only a second-order case. (Cf. I *want* you to *believe* I am not in my office; so I sit very quietly and don't answer your knock. That is not communicating.)

First order

Tom *wants* to cause Sam to run into the trees (and he has this noisemaking trick that produces that effect; he uses the trick to induce a certain response in Sam).

On this reading the leopard cry belongs in the same general category with coming up behind someone and saying "Boo!" Not only does its intended effect not depend on the victim's recognition of the perpetrator's intention; the perpetrator does not need to have any conception at all of the victim's mind: making loud noises behind certain things just makes them jump.

Zero order

Tom (like other vervet monkeys) is prone to three flavors of anxiety or arousal: leopard anxiety, eagle anxiety, and snake anxiety.[1] Each has its characteristic symptomatic vocalization. The effects on others of these vocalizations have a happy trend, but it is all just tropism, in both utterer and audience.

We have reached the killjoy bottom of the barrel: an account that attributes no mentality, no intelligence, no communication, no intentionality at all to the vervet. Other accounts at the various levels are possible, and some may be more plausible; I chose these candidates for simplicity and vividness. Lloyd Morgan's canon of parsimony enjoins us to settle on the most killjoy, least romantic hypothesis that will account systematically for the observed and observable behavior, and for a long time the behaviorist creed that the curves could be made to fit the data well at the lowest level prevented the exploration of the case that can be made for higher-order, higher-level systemati-

---

1. We can probe the boundaries of the stimulus-equivalence class for this response by substituting for the "normal" leopard such different "stimuli" as dogs, hyenas, lions, stuffed leopards, caged leopards, leopards dyed green, firecrackers, shovels, motorcyclists. Whether these independent tests are tests of *anxiety specificity* or of the *meaning* of one-word sentences of Vervetese depends on whether our tests for the other components of our nth-order attribution, the nested intentional operators, come out positive.

zations of the behavior of such animals. The claim that *in principle* a lowest-order story can always be told of any animal behavior (an entirely physiological story, or even an abstemiously behavioristic story of unimaginable complexity) is no longer interesting. It is like claiming that in principle the concept of food can be ignored by biologists—or the concept of cell or gene for that matter—or like claiming that in principle a purely electronic-level story can be told of any computer behavior. Today we are interested in asking what gains in perspicuity, in predictive power, in generalization, might accrue if we adopt a higher-level hypothesis that takes a risky step into intentional characterization.

The question is empirical. The tactic of adopting the intentional stance is not a matter of *replacing* empirical investigations with aprioristic ("armchair") investigations, but of using the stance to suggest which brute empirical questions to put to nature. We can test the competing hypotheses by exploiting the rationality assumption of the intentional stance. We can start at either end of the spectrum; either casting about for the depressing sorts of evidence that will *demote* a creature from a high-order interpretation, or hunting for the delighting sorts of evidence that *promote* creatures to higher-order interpretations (cf. Bennett 1976). We are delighted to learn, for instance, that lone male vervet monkeys, traveling between bands (and hence out of the hearing, so far as they know, of other vervets) will, on seeing a leopard, *silently* seek refuge in the trees. So much for the killjoy hypothesis about leopard-anxiety yelps. (No hypothesis succumbs quite so easily, of course. Ad hoc modifications can save any hypothesis, and it is an easy matter to dream up some simple "context" switches for leopard-anxiety yelp mechanisms to save the zero-order hypothesis for another day.) At the other end of the spectrum, the mere fact that vervet monkeys apparently have so few different things they can say holds out little prospect for discovering any real theoretical utility for such a fancy hypothesis as our fourth-order candidate. It is only in contexts or societies in which one must rule out (or in) such possibilities as irony, metaphor, storytelling, and illustration ("second-intention" uses of words, as philosophers would say)[2] that we must avail ourselves of such high-powered interpretations. The evidence is not yet in, but one would have to be romantic indeed to have high expectations here. Still, there are encouraging anecdotes.

---

2. See Quine 1960, pp. 48–49, on second-intention cases as "the bane of theoretical linguistics."

Seyfarth reports (in conversation) an incident in which one band of vervets was losing ground in a territorial skirmish with another band. One of the losing-side monkeys, temporarily out of the fray, seemed to get a bright idea: it suddenly issued a leopard alarm (in the absence of any leopards), leading *all* the vervets to take up the cry and head for the trees—creating a truce and regaining the ground his side had been losing. The intuitive sense we all have that this is *possibly* (barring killjoy reinterpretation) an incident of great cleverness is amenable to a detailed diagnosis in terms of intentional systems. If this act is not just a lucky coincidence, then the act is truly devious, for it is not simply a case of the vervet uttering an *imperative* "get into the trees" in the expectation that *all* the vervets will obey, since the vervet (being rational—our predictive lever) should not *expect* a rival band to honor *his* imperative. So either the leopard call is *considered* by the vervets to be informative—a *warning*, not a *command*—and hence the utterer's credibility but not authority is enough to explain the effect, or our utterer is more devious still: he *wants* the rivals to *think* they are *overhearing* a command *intended* (of course) only for his own folk, and so on. Could a vervet possibly have that keen a sense of the situation? These dizzying heights of sophistication are strictly implied by the higher-order interpretation taken with its inevitable presupposition of rationality. Only a creature capable of appreciating these points could properly be said to have those beliefs and desires and intentions.

Another observation of the vervets brings out this role of the rationality assumption even more clearly. When I first learned that Seyfarth's methods involved hiding speakers in the brush and playing recorded alarm calls, I viewed the very success of the method as a seriously demoting datum, for if the monkeys really were Gricean in their sophistication, when playing their audience roles they should be perplexed, unmoved, somehow disrupted by disembodied calls issuing from no known utterer. If they were oblivious to this problem, they were no Griceans. Just as a genuine Communicator typically checks the Audience periodically for signs that it is getting the drift of the communication, a genuine Audience typically checks out the Communicator periodically for signs that the drift it is getting is the drift being delivered.

To my delight, however, I learned from Seyfarth that great care had been taken in the use of the speakers to prevent this sort of case from arising. Vervets can readily recognize the particular calls of their band—thus they recognize Sam's leopard call *as* Sam's, not Tom's.

Wanting to give the recordings the best chance of "working," the experimenters took great care to play, say, Sam's call only when Sam was neither clearly in view and close-mouthed or otherwise occupied, nor "known" by the others to be far away. Only if Sam could be "supposed" by the audience to be actually present and uttering the call (though hidden from their view), only if the audience could *believe* that the noisemaker in the bush was Sam, would the experimenters play Sam's call. While this remarkable patience and caution are to be applauded as scrupulous method, one wonders whether they were truly necessary. If a "sloppier" scheduling of playbacks produced just as "good" results, this would in itself be a very important *demoting* datum. Such a test should be attempted; if the monkeys are baffled and unmoved by recorded calls except under the scrupulously maintained circumstances, the necessity of those circumstances would strongly support the claim that Tom, say, *does* believe that the noisemaker in the bush is Sam, that vervet monkeys are not only capable of believing such things, but *must* believe such things for the observed reaction to occur.

The rationality assumption thus provides a way of taking the various hypotheses seriously—seriously enough to test. We expect at the outset that there are bound to be grounds for the verdict that vervet monkeys are believers only in some attenuated way (compared to us human believers). The rationality assumption helps us look for, a measure, the signs of attenuation. We frame conditionals such as

(14) If x believed that p, and *if x was rational*, then since "p" implies "q" x would (have to) believe that q.

This leads to the further attribution to x of belief that q,[3] which, coupled with some plausible attribution of desire, leads to a prediction of behavior, which can be tested by observation or experiment.[4]

Once one gets the knack of using the rationality assumption for leverage, it is easy to generate further telling behaviors to look for in

---

3. "I shall always treasure the visual memory of a very angry philosopher, trying to convince an audience that 'if you believe that A and you believe that if A then B then you *must* believe that B.' I don't really know whether he had the moral power to coerce anyone to believe that B, but a failure to comply does make it quite difficult to use the word 'belief,' and that is worth shouting about." (Kahnemann, unpublished)

4. The unseen normality of the rationality assumption in any attribution of belief is revealed by noting that (14), which explicitly assumes rationality, is virtually synonymous with (plays the same role as) the conditional beginning: if x *really* believed that p, then since "p" implies "q" . . . .

the wild or to provoke in experiments. For instance, if anything as sophisticated as a third- or fourth-order analysis is correct, then it ought to be possible, by devious (and morally dubious!) use of the hidden speakers to create a "boy who cried wolf."[5] If a single vervet is picked out and "framed" as the utterer of false alarms, the others, being rational, should begin to lower their trust in him, which *ought* to manifest itself in a variety of ways. Can a "credibility gap" be created for a vervet monkey? Would the potentially nasty results (remember what happened in the fable) be justified by the interest such a positive result would have?

How to Use Anecdotal Evidence: The Sherlock Holmes Method

One of the recognized Catch 22s of cognitive ethology is the vexing problem of anecdotal evidence. On the one hand, as a good scientist, the ethologist knows how misleading and, officially, unusable anecdotes are, and yet on the other hand they are often so telling! The trouble with the canons of scientific evidence here is that they virtually rule out the description of anything but the oft-repeated, oft-observed, stereotypic behavior of a species, and this is just the sort of behavior that reveals no particular intelligence at all—all this behavior can be more or less plausibly explained as the effects of some humdrum combination of "instinct" or tropism and conditioned response. It is the *novel* bits of behavior, the acts that couldn't plausibly be accounted for in terms of prior conditioning or training or habit, that speak eloquently of intelligence; but if their very novelty and unrepeatability make them anecdotal and hence inadmissible evidence, how can one proceed to develop the cognitive case for the intelligence of one's target species?

Just such a problem has bedeviled Premack and Woodruff (1978), for instance, in their attempts to demonstrate that chimps "have a theory of mind"; their scrupulous efforts to force their chimps into nonanecdotal, repeatable behavior that manifests the intelligence they believe them to have engenders the frustrating side effect of providing prolonged training histories for the behaviorists to point to in developing their rival, conditioning hypotheses as putative explanations of the observed behavior.

We can see the way out of this quandary if we pause to ask our-

---

5. I owe this suggestion to Susan Carey, in conversation.

selves how we establish our *own* higher-order intentionality to the satisfaction of all but the most doctrinaire behaviorists. We can concede to the behaviorists that any single short stretch of human behavior can be given a relatively plausible and not obviously ad hoc demoting explanation, but as we pile anecdote upon anecdote, apparent novelty upon apparent novelty, we build up for each acquaintance such a biography of *apparent* cleverness that the claim that it is *all* just lucky coincidence—or the result of hitherto undetected "training"—becomes the more extravagant hypothesis. This accretion of unrepeatable detail can be abetted by using the intentional stance to provoke one-shot circumstances that will be particularly telling. The intentional stance is in effect an engine for generating or designing anecdotal circumstances—ruses, traps, and other intentionalistic litmus tests—and predicting their outcomes.

This tricky tactic has long been celebrated in literature. The idea is as old as Odysseus testing his swineherd's loyalty by concealing his identity from him and offering him temptations. Sherlock Holmes was a master of more intricate intentional experiments, so I shall call this the *Sherlock Holmes method*. Cherniak (1981) draws our attention to a nice case:

In "A Scandal in Bohemia," Sherlock Holmes' opponent has hidden a very important photograph in a room, and Holmes wants to find out where it is. Holmes has Watson throw a smoke bomb into the room and yell "fire" when Holmes' opponent is in the next room, while Holmes watches. Then, as one would expect, the opponent runs into the room and takes the photograph from where it was hidden. Not everyone would have devised such an ingenious plan for manipulating an opponent's behaviour; but once the conditions are described, it seems very easy to predict the opponent's actions. (p. 161)

In this instance Holmes simultaneously learns the location of the photograph and confirms a rather elaborate intentional profile of his opponent, Irene Adler, who is revealed to *want* the photograph; to *believe* it to be located where she goes to get it; to *believe* that the person who yelled "fire" *believed* there was a fire (note that if she believed the yeller wanted to deceive her, she would take entirely different action); to *want* to retrieve the photograph without letting anyone *know* she was doing this, and so on.

A variation on this theme is an intentional tactic beloved of mystery writers: provoking the telltale move. All the suspects are gathered in the drawing room, and the detective knows (and he alone knows) that the guilty party (and only the guilty party) *believes* that an incriminating cuff link is under the gateleg table. Of course the culprit *wants* no one else to *believe* this, or to *discover* the cuff link, and *believes* that in due course it will be discovered unless he takes covert action. The detective arranges for a "power failure"; after a few seconds of darkness the lights are switched on and the guilty party is, of course, the chap on his hands and knees under the gateleg table. What else on earth could conceivably explain this novel and bizarre behavior in such a distinguished gentleman?[6]

Similar stratagems can be designed to test the various hypotheses about the beliefs and desires of vervet monkeys and other creatures. These stratagems have the virtue of provoking novel but interpretable behavior, of *generating anecdotes* under controlled (and hence scientifically admissible) conditions. Thus the Sherlock Holmes method offers a significant increase in investigative power over behaviorist methods. This comes out dramatically if we compare the actual and contemplated research on vervet monkey communication with the efforts of Quine's imagined behavioristic field linguist. According to Quine, a necessary preliminary to any real progress by the linguist is the tentative isolation and identification of native words (or speech acts) for "Yes" and "No," so that the linguist can enter into a tedious round of "query-and-assent"—putting native sentences to cooperative natives under varying conditions and checking for patterns in their yes and no responses (Quine 1960, chapter 2). Nothing just like Quine's game of query-and-assent can be played by ethologists

---

6. It is a particular gift of the playwright to devise circumstances in which behavior—verbal and otherwise—speaks loudly and clearly about the intentional profiles ("motivation," beliefs, misunderstandings, and so forth) of the characters, but sometimes these circumstances grow too convoluted for ready comprehension; a very slight shift in circumstance can make all the difference between utterly inscrutable behavior and lucid self-revelation. The notorious "get thee to a nunnery" speech of Hamlet to Ophelia is a classic case in point. Hamlet's lines are utterly bewildering until we hit upon the fact (obscured in Shakespeare's minimal stage directions) that while Hamlet is speaking to Ophelia, he *believes* not only that Claudius and Polonius are listening behind the arras, but that they *believe* he doesn't *suspect* that they are. What makes this scene particularly apt for our purposes is the fact that it portrays an intentional experiment: Claudius and Polonius, using Ophelia as decoy and prop, are attempting to provoke a particularly telling behavior from Hamlet in order thereby to discover just what his beliefs and intentions are; they are foiled by their failure to design the experiment well enough to exclude from Hamlet's intentional profile the belief that he is being observed, and the desire to create false beliefs in his observers. See, for example, Dover Wilson (1951). A similar difficulty can bedevil ethologists: "Brief observations of avocet and stilt behavior can be misleading. Underestimating the bird's sharp eyesight, early naturalists believed their presence was undetected and misinterpreted distraction behavior as courtship." (Sordahl 1981, p. 45)

studying animals, but a vestige of this minimalist research strategy is evident in the patient explorations of "stimulus substitution" for animal vocalizations—to the exclusion, typically, of more manipulative (if less intrusive) experiments (see note 1). So long as one is resolutely behavioristic, however, one must miss the evidential value of such behavior as the lone vervet quietly taking to the trees when a "leopard stimulus" is presented. But without a goodly amount of such telling behavior, no mountain of data on what Quine calls the "stimulus meaning" of utterances will reveal that they are communicative acts, rather than merely audible manifestations of peculiar sensitivities. Quine of course realizes this, and tacitly presupposes that his radical translator has already informally satisfied himself (no doubt by using the powerful, but everyday, Sherlock Holmes method) of the richly communicative nature of the natives' behavior.

Of course the power of the Sherlock Holmes method cuts both ways; failure to perform up to expectations is often a strongly demoting datum.[7] Woodruff and Premack (1979) have tried to show that chimpanzees in their lab can be full-fledged *deceivers*. Consider Sadie, one of four chimps used in this experiment. In Sadie's sight food is placed in one of two closed boxes she cannot reach. Then either a "cooperative" or a "competitive" trainer enters, and Sadie has learned she must point to one of the boxes in hopes of getting the food. The competitive trainer, if he discovers the food, will take it all himself and leave. The cooperative trainer shares the food with Sadie. Just giving Sadie enough experience with the circumstances to assure her appreciation of these contingencies involves training sessions that give the behaviorist plenty of grist for the "mere reinforcement" mill. (In order to render the identities of the trainers sufficiently distinct, there was strict adherence to special costumes and rituals; the competitive trainer always wore sunglasses and a bandit's mask, for instance. Does the mask then become established as a simple "eliciting stimulus" for the tricky behavior?)

Still, setting behaviorists' redescriptions aside, will Sadie rise to the

---

7. I do not wish to be interpreted as *concluding* in this paper that vervet monkeys, or laboratory chimpanzees, or any nonhuman animals have *already been shown* to be higher-order intentional systems. Once the Sherlock Holmes method is applied with imagination and rigor, it may very well yield results that will disappoint the romantics. I am arguing in favor of a method of raising empirical questions and explaining the method by showing what the answers *might be* (and why); I am not giving those answers in advance of the research.

occasion and do the "right" thing? Will she try to decieve the competitive trainer (and only the competitive trainer) by *pointing to the wrong box*? Yes, but suspicions abound about the interpretation.[8] How could we strengthen it? Well if Sadie *really* intends to deceive the trainer, she must (being rational) start with the belief that the trainer does not already know where the food is. Suppose, then, we introduce all the chimps in an entirely different context to transparent plastic boxes; they *should* come to *know* that since they—and anyone else—can see through them, anyone can see, and hence come to *know*, what is in them. Then on a one-trial, novel behavioral test, we can introduce a plastic box and an opaque box one day and place the food in the plastic box. The competitive trainer then enters and lets Sadie see him looking right at the plastic box. If Sadie *still* points to the opaque box, she reveals, sadly, that she really doesn't have a grasp of the sophisticated ideas involved in deception. Of course this experiment is still imperfectly designed. For one thing, Sadie might point to the opaque box out of despair, seeing no better option. To improve the experiment, an option should be introduced that would appear better to her only if the first option was hopeless, as in this case. Moreover, shouldn't Sadie be puzzled by the competitive trainer's curious behavior? Shouldn't it bother her that the competitive trainer, on finding no food where she points, just sits in the corner and "sulks" instead of checking out the other box? Shouldn't she be puzzled to discover that her trick keeps working? She *should* wonder: Can the competitive trainer be that stupid? Further, better-designed experiments with Sadie, and other creatures, are called for.[9]

---

8. It is all too easy to stop too soon in our intentional interpretation of a presumably "lower" creature. There was once a village idiot who, whenever he was offered a choice between a dime and a nickel, unhesitatingly took the nickel—to the laughter and derision of the onlookers. One day someone asked him if he could be so stupid as to continue choosing the nickel after hearing all that laughter. Replied the idiot, "Do you think that if I ever took the dime they'd ever offer me another choice?"

The curiously unmotivated rituals that attended the training of the chimps as reported in Woodruff and Premack (1979) might well have baffled the chimps for similar reasons. Can a chimp wonder why these human beings don't just eat the food that is in their control? If so, such a wonder could overwhelm the chimps' opportunities to understand the circumstance in the sense the researchers were hoping. If not, then this very limit in their understanding of such agents and predicaments undercuts somewhat the attribution of such a sophisticated higher-order state as the desire to deceive.

9. This commentary on Premack's chimpanzees grew out of discussion at the Dahlem conference on animal intelligence with Sue Savage-Rumbaugh, whose chimps, Austin and Sherman, themselves exhibit apparently communicative behavior (Savage-Rumbaugh, Rumbaugh, and Boysen 1978) that cries out for analysis and experimentation via the Sherlock Holmes method.

Not wanting to feed the galling stereotype of the philosopher as an armchair answerer of empirical questions, I will nevertheless succumb to the temptation to make a few predictions. It will turn out on further exploration that vervet monkeys (and chimps and dolphins, and all other higher nonhuman animals) exhibit mixed and confusing symptoms of higher-order intentionality. They will pass some higher-order tests and fail others; they will in some regards reveal themselves to be alert to third-order sophistications, while disappointing us with their failure to grasp some apparently even simpler second-order points. No crisp, "rigorous" set of intentional hypotheses of any order will be clearly confirmed. The reason I am willing to make this prediction is not that I think I have special insight into vervet monkeys or other species but just that I have noted, as any one can, that much the same is true of us human beings. We are not ourselves unproblematic exemplars of third- or fourth- or fifth-order intentional systems. And we have the tremendous advantage of being voluble language users, beings that can be plunked down at a desk and given lengthy questionnaires to answer, and the like. Our very capacity to engage in linguistic interactions of this sort seriously distorts our profile as intentional systems, by producing illusions of much more definition in our operative systems of mental representation than we actually have (*Brainstorms*, chapters 3, 16; see also chapter 3 in this volume). I expect the results of the effort at intentional interpretations of monkeys, like the results of intentional interpretations of small children, to be riddled with the sorts of gaps and foggy places that are inevitable in the interpretation of systems that are, after all, only imperfectly rational (see chapters 2 and 3).

Still, the results, for all their gaps and vagueness, will be valuable. How and why? The intentional stance profile or characterization of an animal—or for that matter, an inanimate system—can be viewed as what engineers would call a set of specs—specifications for a device with a certain overall information-processing *competence*. An intentional system profile says, roughly, *what information* must be receivable, usable, rememberable, transmittable by the system. It alludes to the ways in which things in the surrounding world must be represented—but only in terms of distinctions drawn or drawable, discriminations makeable—and not at all in terms of the actual machinery for doing this work (cf. Johnston 1981 on "task descriptions"). These intentional specs, then, set a design task for the next sort of theorist, the representation-system designer.[10] This division of labor is already familiar in certain circles within artificial intelligence (AI); what I have called the intentional stance is what Newell (1982) calls "the knowledge level." And, oddly enough, the very defects and gaps and surd places in the intentional profile of a less than ideally rational animal, far from creating problems for the system designer, point to the shortcuts and stopgaps Mother Nature has relied upon to design the biological system; they hence make the system designer's job easier.

Suppose, for example, that we adopt the intentional stance toward bees, and note with wonder that they seem to *know* that dead bees are a hygiene problem in a hive; when a bee dies its sisters *recognize* that it has died, and, *believing* that dead bees are a health hazard and *wanting*, rationally enough, to avoid health hazards, they *decide* they must remove the dead bee immediately. Thereupon they do just that. Now if that fancy an intentional story were confirmed, the bee-system designer would be faced with an enormously difficult job. Happily for the designer (if sadly for bee romantics), it turns out that a much lower-order explanation suffices: dead bees secrete oleic acid; the smell of oleic acid turns on the "remove it" subroutine in the other bees; put a dab of oleic acid on a live, healthy bee, and it will be dragged, kicking and screaming, out of the hive (Gould and Gould 1982; Wilson, Durlach, and Roth 1958).

Someone in artificial intelligence, learning that, might well say: "Ah how familiar! I know *just* how to design systems that behave like that. Shortcuts like that are my stock in trade." In fact there is an eerie resemblance between many of the discoveries of cognitive ethologists working with lower animals and the sorts of prowess mixed with stupidity one encounters in the typical products of AI. For instance, Roger Schank (1976) tells of a "bug" in TALESPIN, a story-writing program written by James Meehan in Schank's lab at Yale, which produced the following story: "Henry Ant was thirsty. He walked over to the river bank where his good friend Bill Bird was sitting. Henry slipped and fell in the river. Gravity drowned." Why did "gravity drown"? (!) Because the program used a usually reliable shortcut of treating gravity as an unmentioned *agent* that is always

10. In the terms I develop in chapter 3, intentional system theory specifies a semantic engine which must then be realized—mimicked, in approximation—by a syntactic engine designed by the sub-personal cognitive psychologist.

around pulling things down, and since gravity (unlike Henry in the tale) had no friends (!), there was no one to pull it to safety when it was in the river pulling Henry down.

Several years ago, in "Why Not the Whole Iguana?" (Dennett 1978d), I suggested that people in AI could make better progress by switching from the modeling of human microcompetences (playing chess, answering questions about baseball, writing nursery stories, etc.) to the whole competences of much simpler animals. At the time I suggested it might be wise for people in AI just to *invent* imaginary simple creatures and solve the whole-mind problem for them. I am now tempted to think that truth is apt to be both more fruitful, and, surprisingly, more tractable, than fiction. I suspect that if some of the bee and spider people were to join forces with some of the AI people, it would be a mutually enriching partnership.

A Broader Biological Perspective on the Intentional Stance

It is time to take stock of this upbeat celebration of the intentional stance as a strategy in cognitive ethology before turning to some lurking suspicions and criticisms. I have claimed that the intentional stance is well suited to describe, in predictive, fruitful, and illuminating ways, the cognitive prowess of creatures in their environments and that, moreover, it nicely permits a division of labor in cognitive science of just the right sort: field ethologists, given both their training and the sorts of evidence derivable by their methods, are in no position to frame—let alone test—positive hypotheses about actual representational machinery in the nervous systems of their species. That sort of hardware and software design is someone else's specialty.[11] The intentional stance, however, provides just the right interface between specialties: a "black box" characterization of behavioral and cognitive competences observable in the field, but couched in language that (ideally) heavily constrains the design of machinery to put in the black box.[12]

---

11. I should acknowledge, though, that in the case of insects and spiders and other *relatively* simple creatures, there are some biologists who have managed to bridge this gap brilliantly. The gap is much narrower in nonmammalian creatures, of course.

12. In "How to Study Human Consciousness Empirically: Or, Nothing Comes to Mind" (Dennett 1982b), I describe in more detail how purely "semantic" descriptions constrain hypotheses about "syntactic" mechanisms in cognitive psychology.

This apparently happy result is achieved, however, by the dubious decision to throw behaviorist scruples to the winds and commit acts of mentalistic description, complete with assumptions of rationality. Moreover, one who takes this step is apparently as unconcerned with details of physiological realization as any (shudder) dualist! Can this be legitimate? I think it will help to answer that question if we postpone it for a moment and look at adopting the intentional stance in the broader context of biology.

A phenomenon that will nicely illustrate the connection I wish to draw is "distraction display," the well-known behavior, found in many very widely separated species of ground-nesting birds, of feigning a broken wing to lure a predator that aproaches the nest away from its helpless inhabitants (Simmons 1952; Skutch 1976). This seems to be *deception* on the bird's part, and of course it is commonly called just that. Its point is to *fool* the predator. Now if the behavior is *really* deceptive, if the bird is a real deceiver, then it must have a highly sophisticated representation of the situation. The rationale of such deception is quite elaborate, and adopting Dawkins's (1976) useful expository tactic of inventing "soliloquies," we can imagine the bird's soliloquy:

I'm a low-nesting bird, whose chicks are not protectable against a predator who discovers them. This approaching predator can be *expected* soon to discover them unless I distract it; it could be distracted by its *desire* to catch and eat me, but only if it *thought* there was a *reasonable* chance of its actually catching me (it's no dummy); it would contract just that *belief* if I *gave it evidence that* I couldn't fly anymore; I could do that by feigning a broken wing, etc.

Talk about sophistication! It is unlikely in the extreme that any feathered "deceiver" is an intentional system of this intelligence. A more realistic soliloquy for any bird would probably be more along the lines of: "Here comes a predator; all of a sudden I feel this tremendous urge to do that silly broken-wing dance. I wonder why?" (Yes, I know, it would be wildly romantic to suppose such a bird would be up to such a metalevel wondering about its sudden urge.) Now it is an open and explorable empirical question just how sensitive a bird's cognitive control system is to the relevant variables in the environment; if birds engage in distraction display even when there is a manifestly better candidate for the predator's focus of attention (another, actually wounded bird or other likely prey, for instance), the behavior will be unmasked as very low order indeed (like the bees' response to oleic acid). If, on the other hand, birds—some birds anyway—exhibit considerable sophistication in their use of the stratagem (distinguishing different sorts of predators, or, perhaps, revealing appreciation of the fact that you can't fool the same predator with the same trick again and again), our higher-order interpretation of the behavior as genuinely deceptive will be promoted or even confirmed.

But suppose it turned out that the killjoy interpretation was closest to the truth; the bird has a dumb tropism of sorts and that's all. Would we thereupon discard the label "deception" for the behavior? Yes and no. We would no longer *credit the individual bird* with a rationale of deception, but that rationale won't just go away. It is too obvious that the raison d'être of this instinctual behavior is its deceptive power. That's why it evolved. If we want to know why this strange dance came to be provokable on just these occasions, its power to deceive predators will have to be distilled from all the myriad of other facts, known and unknown and unknowable, in the long ancestry of the species. But who *appreciated* this power, who *recognized* this rationale, if not the bird or its individual ancestors? Who else but Mother Nature herself? That is to say: nobody. Evolution by natural selection "chose" this design for this "reason."

Is it unwise to speak this way? I call this the problem of *free-floating rationales*. We start, sometimes, with the hypothesis that we can assign a certain rationale to (the "mind" of) some individual creature, and then we learn better; the creature is too stupid to harbor it. We do not necessarily discard the rationale; if it is no coincidence that the "smart" behavior occurred, we pass the rationale from the individual to the evolving genotype. This tactic is obvious if we think of other, nonbehavioral examples of deception. No one has ever supposed that individual moths and butterflies with eye spots on their wings figured out the bright idea of camouflage paint and acted on it. Yet the deceptive rationale is there all the same, and to say it is *there* is to say that there is a domain within which it is *predictive* and, hence, explanatory. (For a related discussion, see Bennett 1976, sections 52, 53, 62.) We may fail to notice this just because of the obviousness of what we can predict. For example, in a community with bats but not birds for predators we don't expect moths with eye spots (for as any rational deceiver knows, visual sleight-of-hand is wasted on the blind and myopic).

The transmission of the rationale from the individual back to the genotype is of course an old trick. For a century now we have spoken, casually, of species "learning" how to do things, "trying out" various strategies; and of course the figurative practice has not been restricted to cognitive or behavioral traits. Giraffes stretched their necks, and ducks had the wisdom to grow webs between their toes. All just figurative ways of speaking, of course—at best merely dramatic expository shortcuts, one would think. But surprisingly, these figurative ways of speaking can sometimes be taken a lot more seriously than people had thought possible. The application of ideas from game theory and decision theory—for example, Maynard Smith's (1972, 1974) development of the idea of *evolutionarily stable strategies*—depended on taking seriously the fact that the long-term patterns in evolution figuratively described in intentional terms bore a sufficient resemblance to the patterns in short-term interactions between (rational) (human) agents to warrant the application of the same normative-descriptive calculi to them. The results have been impressive.

The "Panglossian Paradigm" Defended

The strategy that unites intentional system theory with this sort of theoretical exploration in evolutionary theory is the deliberate adoption of *optimality models*. Both tactics are aspects of *adaptationism*, the "programme based on the faith in the power of natural selection as an optimizing agent" (Gould and Lewontin 1979). As Lewontin (1978b) observes, "optimality arguments have become extremely popular in the last fifteen years, and at present represent the dominant mode of thought."

Gould has joined his Harvard colleague Lewontin in his campaign against adaptationism, and they call the use of optimality models by evolutionists "the Panglossian paradigm," after Dr. Pangloss, Voltaire's biting caricature, in *Candide*, of the philosopher Leibniz, who claimed that this is the best of all possible worlds. Dr. Pangloss could rationalize any calamity or deformity—from the Lisbon earthquake to venereal disease—and show, no doubt, that it was all for the best. Nothing *in principle* could prove that this was not the best of all possible worlds.

The case leveled against adaptationist thinking by Gould and Lewontin has been widely misinterpreted, even by some of those who have espoused it, perhaps because of the curious mismatch between the rhetoric of Gould and Lewontin's attack and the mildness of their explicit conclusions and recommendations. They heap scorn on the supposed follies of the adaptationist mind set, which leads many to suppose that their conclusion is that adaptationist thinking should be shunned altogether. Their work was drawn to my attention, in fact, by critics of an earlier version of this paper who claimed that my position was a version of adaptationism, "which Gould and Lewontin have shown to be completely bankrupt." But when I turned to this supposed refutation of my fundamental assumptions, I found that the authors' closing summation finds a legitimate place in biology for adaptationist thinking. Theirs is a call for "pluralism," in fact, a plaint against what they see as an exclusive concentration on adaptationist thinking at the cost of ignoring other important avenues of biological thought. But still, the arguments that precede this mild and entirely reasonable conclusion seem ill suited to support it, for they are clearly presented as if they were attacks on the fundamental integrity of adaptationist thinking, rather than support for the recommendation that we should all try in the future to be more careful and pluralistic adaptationists.

Moreover, when I looked closely at the arguments, I was struck by a feeling of *déjà vu*. These arguments were not new, but rather a replay of B. F. Skinner's long-lived polemical campaign against "mentalism." Could it be, I wondered, that Gould and Lewontin have written the latest chapter of Postpositivist Harvard Conservatism? Could it be that they have picked up the torch that Skinner, in retirement, has relinquished? I doubt that Gould and Lewontin view the discovery of their intellectual kinship with Skinner with unalloyed equanimity,[13] and I do not at all mean to suggest that Skinner's work is the conscious inspiration for their own, but let us survey the extent of their agreement.

One of the main troubles with *adaptationism*, Lewontin (1978b) tells us, is that it is too easy: "optimality arguments dispense with the

---

13. For all their manifest differences, Lewontin and Skinner do share a deep distrust of cognitive theorizing. Lewontin closes his laudatory review of Gould's *The Mismeasure of Man* (1981) in the *New York Review of Books* (October 22, 1981) with a flat dismissal of cognitive science, a verdict as sweeping and undiscriminating as any of Skinner's obiter dicta: "It is not easy, given the analytic mode of science, to replace the clockwork mind with something less silly. Updating the metaphor by changing clocks into computers has got us nowhere. The wholesale rejection of analysis in favor of obscurantist holism has been worse. Imprisoned by our Cartesianism, we do not know how to think about thinking" (p. 16).

tedious necessity of knowing anything concrete about the genetic basis of evolution," he remarks caustically; a healthy imagination is the only requirement for this sort of speculative "storytelling," and plausibility is often the sole criterion of such stories (Gould and Lewontin 1979, pp. 153–54).

One of the main troubles with *mentalism*, Skinner (1964) tells us, is "[mentalistic] way stations are so often simply invented. It is too easy." One can always dream up a plausible mentalistic "explanation" of any behavior, and if your first candidate doesn't work out, it can always be discarded and another story found. Or, as Gould and Lewontin (1979, p. 153) say about adaptationism, "Since the range of adaptive stories is as wide as our minds are fertile, new stories can always be postulated. And if a story is not immediately available, one can always plead temporary ignorance and trust that it will be forthcoming."[14]

Gould and Lewontin object that adaptationist claims are unfalsifiable; Skinner claims the same about mentalist interpretations. And both object further that these all too easy to concoct stories *divert attention* from the nitty-gritty hard details that science should look for: Gould and Lewontin complain that adaptationist thinking distracts the theorist from the search for evidence of nonadaptive evolution via genetic drift, "material compensation," and other varieties of "phyletic inertia" and architectural constraints; in Skinner's case mentalism distracts the psychologist from seeking evidence of histories of reinforcement. As Skinner (1971) complains, "The world of the mind steals the show" (p. 12).

Both campaigns use similar tactics. Skinner was fond of trotting out the worst abuses of "mentalism" for derision—such as psychoanalytic "explanations" (in terms of unconscious beliefs, desires, intentions, fears, etc.) of syndromes that turn out to have simple hormonal or mechanical causes. These are cases of gratuitous and incautious overextension of the realm of the intentional. Gould and Lewontin give as a bad example some sloppy jumping to conclusions by an adaptationist, Barash (1976), in his attempt to explain aggression in mountain bluebirds—the invention of an "anticuckoldry" tactic,

---

14. This objection is familiar to E. O. Wilson, who notes: "Paradoxically, the greatest snare in sociobiological reasoning is the ease with which it is conducted. Whereas the physical sciences deal with precise results that are usually difficult to explain, sociobiology has imprecise results that can be too easily explained by many different schemes." (1975, p. 20) See also the discussion of this in Rosenberg 1980.

complete with rationale, where a much simpler and more direct account was overlooked (Gould and Lewontin 1979, p. 154). They also "fault the adaptationist programme for its failure to distinguish current utility from reasons of origin," a criticism that is exactly parallel to the claim (which I have not found explicitly in Skinner, though it is common enough) that mentalistic interpretation often confuses post hoc rationalization with a subject's "real reasons"—which must be reformulated, of course, in terms of a prior history of reinforcement.

Finally, there is the backsliding, the unacknowledged concessions to the views under attack, common to both campaigns. Skinner notoriously availed himself of mentalistic idioms when it suited his explanatory purposes, but excused this practice as shorthand, or as easy words for the benefit of laymen—never acknowledging how much he would have to give up saying if he forswore mentalistic talk altogether. Gould and Lewontin are much subtler; they espouse "pluralism" after all, and both are very clear about the utility and probity—even the necessity—of *some* adaptationist explanations and formulations.[15] Anyone who reads them as calling for the extirpation, root and branch, of adaptationism seriously misreads them—though they decline to say how to tell a good bit of adaptationism from the bits they deplore. This is indeed a sharp disanalogy with Skinner, the implacable foe of "mentalism." But still, they seem to me not to acknowledge fully their own reliance on adaptationist thinking, or indeed its centrality in evolutionary theory.

This comes out very clearly in Gould's (deservedly) popular book of essays, *Ever since Darwin* (1977). In "Darwin's Untimely Burial" Gould deftly shows how to save Darwinian theory from that old bugbear about its reducing to a tautology, via a vacuous concept of fitness: "certain morphological, physiological, and behavioral traits should be superior *a priori* as designs for living in new environments. These traits confer fitness by an engineer's criterion of good design, not by the empirical fact of their survival and spread" (1977, p. 42).[16] So we

---

15. Lewontin, for instance, cites his own early adaptationist work, "Evolution and the Theory of Games"(1961), in his recent critique of sociobiology, "Sociobiology as an Adaptationist Program" (1979). And in his *Scientific American* article "Adaptation," he concludes: "To abandon the notion of adaptation entirely, to simply observe historical change and describe its mechanisms wholly in terms of the different reproductive success of different types, with no functional explanation, would be to throw out the baby with the bathwater." (1978a, p. 230)

16. For a more rigorous discussion of how to define fitness so as to evade tautology, see Rosenberg 1980, pp. 164–75.

can look at designs the way engineers do and rate them as better or worse, on a certain set of assumptions about conditions and needs or purposes. But that is adaptationism. Is it Panglossian? Does it commit Gould to the view that the designs selected will always yield the *best* of all possible worlds? The customary disclaimer in the literature is that Mother Nature is not an optimizer but a "satisficer" (Simon 1957), a settler for the near-at-hand *better*, the good enough, not a stickler for the *best*. And while this is always a point worth making, we should remind ourselves of the old Panglossian joke: the optimist says this is the best of all possible worlds; the pessimist sighs and agrees.

The joke reveals vividly the inevitable existence of a trade-off between constraints and optimality. What appears far from optimal on one set of constraints *may* be seen to be optimal on a larger set. The ungainly jury-rig under which the dismasted sailboat limps back to port may look like a mediocre design for a sailboat until we reflect that given the conditions and available materials, what we are seeing may just be the best possible design. Of course it also may not be. Perhaps the sailors didn't know any better, or got rattled, and settled for making a distinctly inferior rig. But what if we allow for such sailor ignorance as a boundary condition? "Given their ignorance of the fine points of aerodynamics, this is probably the best solution *they* could have recognized." When do we—or must we—stop adding conditions? There is no principled limit that I can see, but I do not think this is a *vicious* regress, because it typically stabilizes and stops after a few moves, and for however long it continues, the discoveries it provokes are potentially illuminating.

It doesn't *sound* Panglossian to remind us, as Gould often does, that poor old Mother Nature makes do, opportunistically and short-sightedly exploiting whatever is at hand—until we add: she isn't perfect, but *she does the best she can*. Satisficing itself can often be shown to be the *optimal* strategy when "costs of searching" are added as a constraint (see Nozick 1981, p. 300 for a discussion). Gould and Lewontin are right to suspect that there is a tautology machine in the wings of the adaptationist theater, always ready to spin out a new set of constraints that will save the Panglossian vision—but they are, I think, committed to playing on the same stage, however more cautiously they check their lines.

Skinner is equally right when he insists that *in principle* mentalistic explanations are unfalsifiable; their logical structure *always* permits revision ad lib in order to preserve rationality. Thus if I predict that Joe will come to class today because he wants to get a good grade, and believes important material will be presented, and Joe fails to show up, there is nothing easier than to decide that he *must*, after all, have had some more pressing engagement or not have known today's date or simply have forgotten or—a thousand other hypotheses are readily available. Of course maybe he was run over by a truck, in which case my alternative intentional interpretations are so much wheel spinning. The dangers pointed out by Skinner, and by Gould and Lewontin, are real. Adaptationists, like mentalists, do run the risk of building the theoretical edifices out of almost nothing—and making fools of themselves when these card castles tumble, as they occasionally do. That is the risk one always runs whenever one takes the intentional stance, or the adaptationist stance, but it can be wise to take the risk since the payoff is often so high, and the task facing the more cautious and abstemious theorist is so extraordinarily difficult.

Adaptationism and mentalism (intentional system theory) are not *theories* in one traditional sense. They are stances or strategies that serve to organize data, explain interrelations, and generate questions to ask Nature. Were they theories in the "classical" mold, the objection that they are question begging or irrefutable would be fatal, but to make this objection is to misread their point. In an insightful article, Beatty (1980) cites the adaptationists Oster and Wilson (1978): " 'The prudent course is to regard optimality models as provisional guides to future empirical research and not as the key to deeper laws of nature'." (p. 312) Exactly the same can be said about the strategy of adopting the intentional stance in cognitive ethology.

The criticism of ever-threatening vacuity, raised against both adaptationism and mentalism, would be truly telling if in fact we always, or even very often, availed ourselves of the slack that is available in principle. If we were forever revising, post hoc, our intentional profiles of people when they failed to do what we expected, then the practice would be revealed for a sham—but then, if that were the case the practice would have died out long ago. Similarly, if adaptationists were always (or very often) forced to revise their lists of constraints post hoc to preserve their Panglossianism, adaptationism would be an unappealing strategy for science. But the fact about both tactics is that, in a nutshell, *they work*. Not always, but gratifyingly often. We are actually pretty good at picking the right constraints, the right belief and desire attributions. The bootstrapping evidence for the claim that we have in fact located all the important constraints relative to which an optimal design should be calculated is that we make that optimizing calculation, and it turns out to be predictive in the real world. Isn't this arguing in a circle? One claims to have located all the genuinely important constraints on the ground that

(1) the optimal design given those constraints is *A*
(2) Mother Nature optimizes
(3) *A* is the observed (that is, apparent) design.

Here one *assumes* Pangloss in order to infer the completion of one's list of constraints. What other argument could ever be used to convince ourselves that we had located and appreciated all the relevant considerations in the evolutionary ancestry of some feature? As Dawkins (1980, p. 358) says, an adaptationist theory such as Maynard Smith's evolutionarily stable strategy theory

as a whole is not intended to be a testable hypothesis which may be true and may be false, empirical evidence to decide the matter. It is a tool which we may use to find out about the selection pressures bearing upon animal behavior. As Maynard Smith (1978) said of optimality theory generally: "we are *not* testing the general proposition that nature optimizes, but the specific hypotheses about constraints, optimization criteria, and heredity. Usually we test whether we have correctly identified the selective forces responsible."

The dangers of blindness in adaptationist thinking, pointed out so vividly by Gould and Lewontin, have their mirror image in any approach that shuns adaptationist curiosity. Dobzhansky (1956) says, in much the spirit of Gould and Lewontin, "The usefulness of a trait must be demonstrated, it cannot just be taken for granted." But, as Cain (1964) observes, "Equally, its uselessness cannot be taken for granted, and indirect evidence on the likelihood of its being selected for and actually adaptive cannot be ignored . . . . Where investigations have been undertaken, trivial characters have proved to be of adaptive significance in their own right." Cain slyly compares Dobzhansky's attitude with Robert Hooke's curiosity about the antennae of insects in *Micrographia* (1665):

What the use of these kind of horned and tufted bodies should be, I cannot well imagine, unless they serve for smelling or hearing, though how they are adapted for either, it seems very difficult to describe: they are in almost every several kind of Flies of so various a shape, though certainly they are some very essential part of the head, and have some very notable office assigned them by Nature, since in all Insects they are to be found in one or other form.

"Apparently," Cain concludes, "the right attitude to enigmatic but widely occurring organs was fully understood as long ago as the middle of the seventeenth century, at least in England." (1964, p. 50)

Finally, I would like to draw attention to an important point Gould makes about the *point* of biology, the ultimate question the evolutionist should persistently ask. This occurs in his approving account of the brilliant adaptationist analysis (Lloyd and Dybas 1966) of the curious fact that cicada reproductive cycles are prime-numbered-years long—thirteen years, for instance, and seventeen years: "As evolutionists, we seek answers to the question, why. Why, in particular, should such striking synchroneity evolve, and why should the period between episodes of sexual reproduction be so long?" (Gould 1977, p. 99) As his own account shows, one has not *yet* answered the "why" question posed when one has abstemiously set out the long (and in fact largely inaccessible) history of mutation, predation, reproduction, selection—with no adaptationist gloss. Without the adaptationist gloss, we won't *know why*.[17]

The contrast between the two sorts of answers, the scrupulously nonadaptationist historic-architectural answer Gould and Lewontin *seem* to be championing and the frankly Panglossian adaptationist answer one can also try to give, is vividly captured in one final analogy from the Skinnerian war against mentalism. I once found myself in a public debate with one of Skinner's most devout disciples, and at one point I responded to one of his more outrageously implausible Skinnerisms with the question, "Why do you say *that*?" His instant and laudibly devout reply was, "Because I have been reinforced for saying that in the past." My "why" question asked for a justification, a rationale, not merely an account of historical provenance. It is just possible, of course, that any particular such "why" question will have the answer: "no *reason* at all; I just happened to be caused to make that utterance," but the plausibility of such an answer drops to near zero as the complexity and *apparent* meaningfulness of the utterance rises. And when a supportable rationale for such an act is found, it is a mistake—an anachronistic misapplication of positivism—to insist

---

17. Boden (1981) advances the claims for "the cognitive attitude" (in essence, what I have called the intentional stance) in a different biological locale: the microstructure of genetics, enzyme "recognition" sites, embryology, and morphogenesis. As she says, the cognitive attitude "can encourage biologists to ask empirically fruitful questions, questions that a purely physico-chemical approach might tend to leave unasked." (p. 89)

that "the real reason" for the act *must* be stated in terms that make no allusion to this rationale. A purely causal explanation of the act, at the microphysical level, say, is *not in competition* with the rationale-giving explanation. This is commonly understood these days by post-behaviorist psychologists and philosophers, but the counterpart point is apparently not quite so well received yet among biologists, to judge from the following passage, in *Science*, reporting on the famous 1980 Chicago conference on macroevolution:

> Why do most land vertebrates have four legs? The seemingly obvious answer is that this arrangement is the optimal design. This response would ignore, however, the fact that the fish that were ancestral to terrestrial animals also have four limbs, or fins. Four limbs may be very suitable for locomotion on dry land, but *the real reason* [my emphasis] that terrestrial animals have this arrangement is because their evolutionary predecessors possessed the same pattern. (Lewin 1980, p. 886)

When biologists ask the evolutionists' "why" question, they are, like mentalists, seeking the rationale that explains why some feature was selected. The more complex and apparently meaningful the feature, the less likely it is that there is *no* sustaining rationale; and while the historical and architectonic facts of the genealogy may in many cases loom as the most salient or important facts to uncover, the truth of such a nonadaptationist story does not *require* the falsehood of all adaptationist stories of the same feature. The *complete* answer to the evolutionists' question will almost always, in at least some minimal way, allude to *better* design.

Is this the best of all possible worlds? We shouldn't even try to answer such a question, but adopting Pangloss's assumption, and in particular the Panglossian assumption of rationality in our fellow cognizers, can be an immensely fruitful strategy in science, if only we can keep ourselves from turning it into a dogma.

Reflections:
Interpreting Monkeys,
Theorists, and Genes

Four years of discussion and exploration, in both the field and the library, have greatly expanded my perspective on the issues raised in the preceding essay. In these reflections, after tying off some loose ends concerning the setting of the essay and its reception, I will recount what I learned firsthand about the practical problems of adopting the intentional stance toward vervet monkeys in Kenya, then review the state of the controversy surrounding adaptationism and the intentional stance, and finally draw out some further implications about their intimate relationship.

Ancestry and Progeny

In "Conditions of Personhood" (1976) I argued that our higher-order intentions marked a critical difference between us and other beasts and speculated about the empirical question of just how one could confirm the presence of such intentions in nonhuman animals. I had discussed the issue with David Premack in 1975 and later commented (1978b) on his article in *Behavioral and Brain Sciences (BBS)* "Does the Chimpanzee have a Theory of Mind?" (Premack and Woodruff 1978), but the Dahlem Conference on "Animal Mind—Human Mind" in March 1981 (Griffin 1982) was my first wide-ranging introduction to the problems and possibilities of interpretation in ethology, ecology, and animal psychology. At that conference I was put on the spot and invited—or perhaps challenged—to show how the self-conscious adoption of the intentional stance could actually help scientists design experiments or interpret their data. I was pleased to discover that my impromptu exercises in applying the intentional stance to their research problems did in fact generate some novel testable hypotheses, designs for further experiments, and methods of developing interpretations. I was urged by participants at the conference to write an introduction to the intentional stance accessible to non-philosophers, and the preceding chapter, reprinted from *BBS,* is the result.

Like all "target articles" in that journal, this one was accompanied by a wide range of commentary and a reply by the author (see also "Continuing Commentary," *BBS* 8 (1985b), pp. 758–66). The several dozen commentators include philosophers, ethologists, psychologists, and evolutionary theorists, and their criticisms probe the strengths and weaknesses of my case from many angles, a valuable resource to anyone who wants to pursue the issues raised here more carefully. I particularly recommend the commentaries by Bennett, Menzel, and Lewontin, the three most vehement critics—from three entirely different vantage points—but I also particularly recommend my replies to them. The comments of Skinner and Rachlin usefully provide the behaviorists' perspective, while Dawkins, Eldredge, Ghiselin, and Maynard Smith illuminate the debate among evolutionary theorists.

Developments since the piece appeared in 1983 make its strengths and weaknesses stand out more clearly. Cheney and Seyfarth have extended their analyses of the vervets' communication system in a series of papers (1982, 1985) and most recently have succeeded in running a good variation on the "boy who cried wolf" experiment. As it happens, the vervets have two acoustically very different calls with (apparently) the same meaning: a rival band of vervets is approaching. Not surprisingly, repeated playings of a recording of an individual vervet's call produces habituation in the audience, as measured by a gradual decrease in reactions of vigilance and the like, but since there are two "synonymous" calls, it has proved possible to get evidence of habituation not to the *sound* but to the *import* of the call and, moreover, habituation that is speaker-relative. Thus a particular vervet can indeed lose credibility with the group on a particular topic, thanks to being "framed" by experimenters (Seyfarth and Cheney, personal communication).

Ristau, meanwhile, has produced a series of experimental studies of the distraction displays of piping plovers (Ristau, forthcoming, unpublished) and Marler has investigated sensitivity to appropriate "audience" in domestic chickens (Marler et al. 1986a, 1986b). Byrne and Whiten (forthcoming) survey a wide variety of experimental studies with and observations of primates. Among other reactions by ethologists to my proposals, I have found Heyes (forthcoming) and

McFarland (1984) particularly useful. The psychologists Wimmer and Perner (1983) have used a variation on the experiment I proposed to test for higher-order beliefs in Sarah, Premack's chimpanzee, to show the marked onset of such beliefs about beliefs in young children. And Premack has conducted a host of further experiments shedding light on the extent and limits of chimpanzee understanding of other creatures and of artificial sign systems (Premack 1986).

Other ethologists and psychologists have exploited the methods I recommended with more enthusiasm than care, I am sorry to say. A few, I gather, have mistaken my advocacy of the Sherlock Holmes method of *creating* (and *controlling*) "anecdotes" for a wholesale defense of casually obtained anecdotes as evidence! So I should reiterate and emphasize the point I was trying to make: a unique or one-off bit of behavior is useless *as evidence* for an attribution of intentional state (however valuable to the researcher as a hint for further experiments) unless it can be *shown* to be an otherwise unlikely behavior, provoked just by the conditions that would provoke, in a rational agent, beliefs and desires which would render the unlikely behavior rational. *Showing this always requires running controlled experments.* The method I was extolling was not a substitute for experimentation, but a way of seeing which experiments needed to be done.

Another shortcoming in my attempt to impart philosophical niceties to students of animal behavior has emerged from my continuing discussions with ethologists: by and large they persist in conflating the philosophical notion (Brentano's notion—the concept of *aboutness,* in a word) and the more or less everyday notion of intentionality: the capacity to perform intentional actions or frame intentions to act. There are few scolds more tiresome than the philosopher trying to reform the linguistic habits of others, and I have been sorely tempted to drop the issue, especially since the closer one looks at the empirical question of whether or when an organism is capable of framing an intention to act, the more it merges, in the way it gathers and treats the data, with the empirical question of whether or when an organism has states ("of mind") that require characterization via intentional idioms. But it is important, I still think, to keep these two ways of raising questions distinct. In particular, it is otherwise all too easy to think one has eliminated appeals to intentionality when one has traded in talk of intentions, hopes, and expectations for the apparently more scientific talk of information storage and goal structures.

In *Content and Consciousness* (1969), I proposed enforcing heightened consciousness of this distinction by always capitalizing the philosopher's term "Intentionality." I persisted with this policy in "Intentional Systems" (1971), but I was unable to get the bandwagon moving; so when I reprinted that piece in *Brainstorms* (1978a), I reluctantly abandoned my lonely orthographic idiosyncrasy. Since then Searle (1983) has reinvented the capitalization scheme, but since his views on intentionality are not at all mine, I have decided to let him keep the capital "I" all to himself. What Searle calls Intentionality is something I utterly disbelieve in. (See chapters 8 and 9, and my commentary on Searle in "The Milk of Human Intentionality" (1980b). For an encyclopedia entry on the philosophers's concept of intentionality, see Dennett and Haugeland (1987) in *The Oxford Companion to the Mind*.)

Out of the Armchair

In June of 1983 I had a brief introduction to ethological fieldwork, as I observed Seyfarth and Cheney observing the vervet monkeys in Kenya. (This is described in detail in Dennett, forthcoming b and c, from which the rest of this section is excerpted.)

Once I got in the field and saw firsthand some of the obstacles to performing the sorts of experiments I had recommended, I found some good news and some bad news. The bad news was that the Sherlock Holmes method, in its classical guise, has very limited applicability to the vervet monkeys—and, by extrapolation, to other "lower" animals. The good news was that by adopting the intentional stance, one can generate some plausible and indirectly testable hypotheses about why this should be so and thereby learn something important about the nature of the selection pressures that probably have shaped the vervets' communication systems.

A vocalization that Seyfarth and Cheney were studying during my visit had been dubbed the Moving Into the Open (or MIO) grunt. Shortly before a monkey in a bush moves out into the open, it often gives a MIO grunt. Other monkeys in the bush will often repeat it; spectrographic analysis has not (yet) revealed a clear mark of difference between the initial grunt and this response. If no such echo is made, the original grunter will often stay in the bush for five or ten minutes and then repeat the MIO. When the MIO is echoed by one or more other monkeys, the original grunter often will move cautiously into the open.

But what does the MIO grunt mean? We listed the possible translations to see which we could eliminate or support on the basis of evidence already at hand. I started with what seemed to be the most straightforward and obvious possibility:

"I'm going."
"I read you. You're going."

But what would be the use of saying this? Vervets are in fact a taciturn lot—they keep silent most of the time—and are not given to anything that looks like passing the time of day by making obvious remarks. Then could it be a request for permission to leave?

"May I go, please?"
"Yes, you have my permission to go."

This hypothesis could be knocked out if higher-ranking vervets ever originated the MIO in the presence of their subordinates. In fact, higher-ranking vervets do tend to move into the open first, so it doesn't seem that MIO is a request for permission. Could it be a command, then?

"Follow me!"
"Aye, Aye, Cap'n."

Not very plausible, Cheney thought. "Why waste words with such an order when it would seem to *go without saying* in vervet society that low-ranking animals follow the lead of their superiors? For instance, you would think that there would be a vocalization meaning 'May I?' to be said by a monkey when approaching a dominant in hopes of grooming it. And you'd expect there to be two responses: 'You may' and 'You may not,' but there is no sign of any such vocalization. Apparently such interchanges would not be useful enough to be worth the effort. There are gestures and facial expressions which may serve this purpose, but no audible signals." Perhaps, Cheney mused, the MIO grunt served simply to acknowledge and share the fear:

"I'm really scared."
"Yes. Me too."

Another interesting possibility is that the grunt helped with coordination of the group's movements:

"Ready for me to go?"
"Ready whenever you are."

A monkey that gives the echo is apt to be the next to leave. Or perhaps even better:

"Coast clear?"
"Coast is clear. We're covering you."

The behavior so far observed is compatible with this reading, which would give the MIO grunt a robust purpose, orienting the monkeys to a task of cooperative vigilance. The responding monkeys do watch the leave-taker and look in the right directions to be keeping an eye out. "Suppose then, that this is our best candidate hypothesis," I said. "Can we think of anything to look for that would particularly shed light on it?" Among males, competition overshadows cooperation more than among females. Would a male bother giving the MIO if its only company in a bush was another male? Seyfarth had a better idea: suppose a male originated the MIO grunt; would a rival male be devious enough to give a dangerously misleading MIO response when he saw that the originator was about to step into trouble? The likelihood of ever getting any good evidence of this is miniscule, for you would have to observe a case in which Originator didn't see and Responder did see a nearby predator *and* Responder saw that Originator didn't see the predator. (Otherwise Responder would just waste his credibility and incur the wrath and mistrust of Originator for no gain.) Such a coincidence of conditions must be extremely rare. This was an ideal opportunity, it seemed, for a Sherlock Holmes ploy.

Seyfarth suggested that perhaps we could spring a trap with something like a stuffed python that we could very slyly and surreptitiously reveal to just one of two males who seemed about to venture out of a bush. The technical problems would clearly be nasty, and at best it would be a long shot, but with luck we might just manage to lure a liar into our trap. But on further reflection, the technical problems looked virtually insurmountable. How would we establish that the "liar" had actually seen (and been taken in by) the "predator" and wasn't just innocently and sincerely reporting that the coast was clear? I found myself tempted (as often before in our discussions) to indulge in a fantasy: "If only I were small enough to dress up in a vervet suit, or if only we could introduce a trained vervet, or a robot or puppet vervet who could . . ." and slowly it dawned on me that this recurring escape from reality had a point: there is really no substitute, in the radical translation business, for going in and *talking with the natives*. You can test more hypotheses in half an hour of attempted chitchat than you can in a month of observation and unobtrusive manipulation. But to take advantage of this you have to become obtrusive: you—or your puppet—have to enter into communicative encounters with the natives, if only in order to go around pointing to things and asking "Gavagai?" in an attempt to figure out what "Gavagai" means. Similarly, in your typical mystery-story caper, some crucial part of the setting up of the "Sherlock Holmes method" trap is—*must be*—accomplished by imparting some (mis)information verbally. Maneuvering your subjects into the right frame of mind— and knowing you've succeeded—without the luxurious efficiency of words can prove to be arduous at best, and often next to impossible.

In particular, it is often next to impossible in the field to establish that particular monkeys have been shielded from a particular bit of information. And since many of the theoretically most interesting hypotheses depend on just such circumstances, it is very often very tempting to think of moving the monkeys into a lab, where a monkey can be physically *removed* from the group and given opportunities to acquire information that the others don't have *and that the test monkey knows they don't have*. Just such experiments are being done by Seyfarth and Cheney with a group of captive vervets in California and by other researchers with chimpanzees. The early results are tantalizing but equivocal (of course), and *perhaps* the lab environment, with its isolation booths, will be just the tool we need to open up the monkeys' minds, but my hunch is that being isolated in that way is such an unusual predicament for vervet monkeys that they will prove to be unprepared by evolution to take advantage of it.

The most important thing I think I learned from actually watching the vervets is that they live in a world in which secrets are virtually impossible. Unlike orangutans, who are solitary and get together only to mate and when mothers are rearing offspring, and unlike chimps, who have a fluid social organization in which individuals come and go, seeing each other fairly often but also venturing out on their own a large proportion of the time, vervets live in the open in close proximity to the other members of their groups and have no solitary projects of any scope. So it is a rare occasion indeed when one vervet is in a position to learn something that it alone knows *and knows that it alone knows*. (The knowledge of the others' ignorance, and of the possibility of maintaining it, is critical. Even when one monkey is the first to see a predator or a rival group, and knows it, it is almost never in a position to be sure the others won't very soon make the same discovery.) But without such occasions in abundance, there is little to impart to others. Moreover, without frequent opportunities to *recognize* that one knows something that the others don't know, devious reasons for or against imparting information cannot even exist—let alone be recognized and acted upon. I can think of no way of describing this critical simplicity in the *Umwelt* of the vervets, this missing ingredient, that does not avail itself explicitly or implicitly of higher-order intentional idioms.

In sum, the vervets couldn't really make use of most of the features of a human language, for their world—or you might even say their lifestyle—is too simple. Their communicative needs are few but intense, and their communicative opportunities are limited. Like honeymooners who have not been out of each other's sight for days, they find themselves with not much to say to each other (or to decide to withhold). But if they couldn't make use of a fancy, human-like language, we can be quite sure that evolution hasn't provided them with one. Of course *if* evolution provided them with an elaborate language in which to communicate, the language itself would radically change their world and permit them to create and pass secrets as profusely as we do. And then they could go on to use their language, as we use ours, in hundreds of diverting and marginally "useful" ways. But without the original information-gradients needed to prime the evolutionary pump, such a language couldn't get established.

So we can be quite sure that the MIO grunt, for instance, is not crisply and properly translated by *any* familiar human interchange. It can't be a (pure, perfect) command or request or question or exclamation because it isn't part of a system that is elaborate enough to make room for such sophisticated distinctions. When you say "Wanna go for a walk?" to your dog and he jumps up with a lively bark and expectant wag of the tail, this is not really a question and answer. There are only a few ways of "replying" that are available to the dog. It can't do anything tantamount to saying "I'd rather wait till sundown" or "Not if you're going to cross the highway" or even "No thanks." Your utterance is a question *in English* but a sort of melted-together mixture of question, command, exclamation, and mere *harbinger* (you've made some of those going-out noises again) to your dog (Bennett 1976, 1983). The vervets' MIO grunt is no doubt a similar mixture, but while that means we shouldn't get our hopes too high about learning Vervetese and finding out all about monkey life by having conversations with the vervets, it doesn't at all rule out the utility of these somewhat fanciful translation hypotheses as ways of interpreting—and uncovering—the actual informational roles or funtions of these vocalizations. When you think of the MIO as "Coast clear?" your attention is directed to a variety of testable hypotheses about further relationships and dependencies that ought to be discoverable if that is what MIO means, or even just "sort of" means.

The Panglossian Paradigm Reconsidered

In the context of *BBS*, my coda defending the use of optimality assumptions by adaptationists and discussing the relationship of that tactic to the intentional stance seemed to be a digression, raising side issues that might better have been left for another occasion. As these reflections and the next chapter will make clear, however, it introduced a central theme in my analysis of the intentional stance: the problems of interpretation in psychology and the problems of interpretation in biology are *the same problems,* engendering the same prospects—and false hopes—of solution, the same confusions, the same criticisms and arguments. That is a voluminous claim, true or false, and there is a tendency to underestimate its ramifications. Some view it as a relatively superficial and obvious truth and endorse it without seeing what they must then give up to remain consistent; others dismiss it just as prematurely, failing to recognize that the "obvious" premises from which their criticisms flow are themselves put in doubt by the claim. The most telling misapprehensions were well represented in the commentaries in *BBS*, and corrected in my reply, from which the following comments are drawn, with additions and revisions.

The most important parallel I wished to draw is this: psychologists can't do their work without the rationality assumption of the intentional stance, and biologists can't do their work without the optimality assumptions of adaptationist thinking—though some in each field are tempted to deny and denounce the use of these assumptions. Optimality assumptions are popular ploys in many disciplines, and it is hardly controversial to claim that for better or for worse, the social sciences are overrun with adoptions of the intentional stance, some much more problem-ridden than others. Debates over the constraints of *Verstehen* in *Geisteswissenschaft*, false consciousness and ideology in anthropology and political theory, methodological individualism and the anthropologists' brand of functionalism, the proper role of idealization in economics, the "principle of charity" in interpretation and translation—all these controversies and more are problems about the justification for particular adoptions of the intentional stance, and the curious role of the optimality or rationality assumption figures in all of them.

In biology, the adaptationists assume optimality of design in the organisms they study, and this practice is viewed askance by some other biologists, since it seems to them to invoke a doctrinaire optimism. Why should anyone today suppose that an organism, just because it has evolved, is in any way optimally designed? There is now a mountain of evidence and good theory in population genetics, for instance, to show that under many conditions maladaptations are fixed and that developmental constraints limit phenotypic plasticity. But this challenge is ill posed; the critics who remind the adaptationists of these complications are already talking past the opposition.

This comes out most clearly in Ghiselin's commentary (1983). "The alternative" to Panglossianism, he says, "is to reject such teleology altogether. Instead of asking 'What is good?' we ask, 'What has happened?' The new question does everything we could expect the old one to do, and a lot more besides." (p. 362) This is an illusion exactly parallel to Skinner's familiar claim that the question "What is the history of reinforcement?" is a vast improvement over "What does this person believe, want, intend?" We cannot hope to answer either sort of historical question with a "pure" (utterly non-interpretational) investigation, without, that is to say, a healthy helping of adaptationist (or intentionalist) assumptions. This is because without answers to "why" questions, we cannot begin to categorize *what has happened* into the right sorts of parts. The biologist who helps himself to even such an obviously safe functional category as *eye, leg,* or *lung* is already committed to assumptions about what is good, just as the psychologist who helps himself to the bland categories of *avoidance* or *recognition* is committed to assumptions about what is rational. (This is argued in detail in the next chapter.)

We take on optimality assumptions not because we naively think that evolution has made this the best of all possible worlds, but because we must be interpreters, if we are to make any progress at all, and interpretation requires the invocation of optimality.[1] As Maynard Smith (1983) says in his commentary, "in using optimisation, we are not trying to confirm (or refute) the hypothesis that animals always optimise; we are trying to *understand* [emphasis added] the selective forces that shaped their behaviour."

The adaptationist strategy in biology seeks to answer "why" questions in exactly the same way the intentional strategy in psychology does. Why, asks the folk psychologist, did John decline the invitation to the party? The presumption is that there is a (good) reason, at least in John's eyes. Why, asks the adaptationist, do these birds lay four eggs? The adaptationist starts with the supposition that there is a (good) reason: that four eggs are better, somehow, than two or three or five or six. Looking for possible answers to that "why" question opens up an exploration. One asks, in effect: if five were too many and three were too few, what would have to be the case? Hypothetical calculations suggest themselves—about energy expenditure, probability of survival, scarcity of food and so forth—and soon enough, in fine Panglossian fashion, one has a candidate explanation of why indeed it turns out to be for the best that these birds lay exactly four eggs—if in fact that is what they do. Of course, it may turn out that due to developmental constraints, the alternatives to four eggs—like the alternative to four legs for horses—are prohibitively costly, and hence virtually "unthinkable" options, but even this discovery would be illuminated by the adaptationist's raising the issue.

As Gould and Lewontin insist, one can always contrive such a story, so creation of a plausible story is no proof that it is true. But like lies, such stories ramify, and either they lead to falsified predictions in other quarters or they do not. If they ramify without recalcitrance, this actually tells the biologists very little. "Isn't nature wonderful!"

---

1. Kitcher (1987) notes that "it is a major achievement to divide up the stream of animal behavior into meaningful units, to describe what the animal did" but then goes on to ask: "To what extent are descriptions that are backed by optimality analyses more likely to be true, *in virtue of that fact alone?*" This is already, subtly, the wrong question to ask. Its dual in psychology would be: To what extent is an intentional attribution backed by a rational justification more likely to be true, in virtue of that fact alone?—as if there were the prospect of keeping the issues of attribution and rational justification separate. Kitcher asks when an optimality argument could succeed in "boosting the prior probability of some functional descriptions," but—to continue the parallel in a slightly different perspective—Quine (1960) would insist that it would be a mistake to ask under what conditions a finding of logical consistency might "boost the prior probability" of a hypothesized radical translation.

they may mutter disconsolately, but they will not have learned much. If on the other hand one of their predictions proves false, the adaptationists can hypothesize that something important has been left out of account. What perturbing factor could be added to the Panglossian tale so that what the organisms *actually* do is wisest for them after all? One starts with a naive understanding of the "problem" faced by some organism and in the terms of that naive understanding works out how the organism ought to be designed. This suggests experiments that show that the organism is not so designed. Instead of shrugging and concluding "second-rate design," the adaptationist asks whether the results point to a more sophisticated understanding.

Psychologists, starting from the intentional stance, can do likewise. A good illustration can be found in recent research by Kahneman and Tversky (1983). They put a question to their pool of subjects: Suppose you had bought a ticket to the theater for ten dollars and when you got to the theater you found you had lost the ticket. But there are more tickets for sale, and you have money enough in your wallet. Would you spend ten dollars to replace the ticket you lost? More than half the subjects express the conviction that they would not buy another ticket. Other subjects are asked to consider this variation. You plan to go to the theater and when you get up to the window to buy your ticket, you discover you have lost a ten-dollar bill. Would you go ahead and buy a ticket? Only twelve percent of the subjects say that the loss of the ten dollars would have any effect on their decision to purchase a ticket.

There is a sharp difference in the responses to the two questions, but, Kahneman and Tversky point out, the two circumstances are equivalent. In each case, if you go to the theater, you have ten dollars less at the end of the day than if you don't. Surely it is irrational to treat the two cases differently! There is no doubt that such a bias is rationally indefensible if all we consider are the costs and benefits mentioned so far. But should we then conclude that this is *nothing more* than a sign of pitiable human frailty? Or is there some other perspective from which this bias is defensible? Kahneman and Tversky suggest that if we factor in the "bookkeeping costs" we may discover gains in efficiency and lucidity of planning if we partition our wealth into separate "accounts" and distinguish sharply between such categories as "losses" and "costs of doing business" (for instance). These gains may far outweigh the occasional losses we suffer when that bookkeeping policy dictates a suboptimal decision. The hypothesis that such bookkeeping costs could matter that much suggests something about the internal organization of our cognitive systems. Nothing is proved (yet), but the discovery of this *systematic* weakness in our normal mode of reasoning about such matters suggests that its elimination would be more costly than we might have imagined.

The foregoing exemplifies the parallel I wanted to draw between adaptationist and intentionalist theorizing, but there is another way of lining up the disciplines that has suggested to several authors that I have got the analogy exactly backward. Dahlbom (1985) takes the bird's-eye view:

> Romanticism is the fashion in science these days. Deep-rooted ideas central to our Enlightenment tradition are being questioned. There is a trend away from atomism, empiricism, functionalism (adaptationism), and gradualism toward holism, innatism, structuralism, and saltationism . . . . Chomsky's critical review of Skinner's *Verbal Behavior* (Chomsky 1959) was an admirable, early press release announcing the new trend.
>
> The recent commotion in evolutionary theory brought about by Eldredge, Gould, Lewontin, Stanley and others . . . is only another instance of this Romantic trend. . . . So why does Dennett choose to place Gould and Lewontin in a camp with Skinner, of all people, rather than with Chomsky, Kuhn, and the like, where they clearly belong? (p. 760)

Amundson (unpublished) describes the same line of battle in terms of theories that "explain existing characters as environmentally selected results of randomly generated variation" versus theories according to which the "environment may *shape* the expressed outcome of development, but the shaping effects are significantly constrained by internal structure."

> Theories of the first sort (let us call them "environmentalist") include behaviorist learning theories and selectionist-adaptationist biology. Theories of the second sort ("structuralist") include nativist and cognitive psychology, and evolutionary theories which stress, for example, morphological and embryological constraints on evolution.

The pivotal figure in this analogy, as Dahlbom suggests, is Chomsky, whose extreme nativism, tantamount to the denial that there is any such thing as learning, represents the dark—Romantic—side of cognitive science. (I once suggested to Chomsky that on his view no one ever *learned* quantum mechanics, but that some people, thanks to the structure of their innate endowment, happened to "imprint" on quantum mechanics. He agreed.) And, curiously enough, this extreme structuralism does have one thing in common with extreme behaviorism: a premature willingness to stop asking "why" questions. Why do all grammars have such-and-such a feature? Because that's the way language-users are built. End of explanation. Why are they built that way? Why did those constraining structures arise? That is not a question for linguists or psychologists to answer, on Chomsky's view.

All that structure has to be given some explanation, however, and as I argued in "Passing the Buck to Biology" (1980a), it is an entirely reasonable strategy to canvass the nearby, accessible processes before opting for more distant alternatives. "The more the infant brain can be viewed as a *tabula rasa*, the more accessible to *experimental* research the *ultimate* mysteries of learning will be; if the facts constrain psychologists to pass the buck to the evolutionary biologists, we will have to settle for more abstract and speculative answers to the ultimate questions." (p. 19)

To whom, however, can the "structuralist" theorists in evolutionary biology pass the buck? What accounts for the existence of the constraining *Baupläne* relative to which adaptations are only so much fine tuning? One can say: the biosphere is just built that way. End of explanation? Perhaps, but those of us looking for Enlightenment will always be ready to ask, one more time, why? It is the puritanical distaste for this teleological and functional thinking that unites—in this regard—not just Skinner and Ghiselin, but Lewontin and Chomsky, leaving Kahneman, Tversky, Dawkins, Maynard Smith, and other intentionalists on the other side of the fence.

Gould and Lewontin's attack on adaptationist thinking, and the controversy that ensued, has been instructive in spite of—and indeed sometimes because of—the way the participants have been tempted to talk past each other. As Kitcher (1985) notes in his summary of the episode:

Gould and Lewontin campaign for attention to rival forms of evolutionary hypotheses, but they distort their point by suggesting that the unfalsifiability of adaptationist claims is an insuperable obstacle. If I am right, the correct position is that the successful pursuit of adaptationist hypotheses about traits of organisms already presupposes just that attention to rival possibilities that Gould and Lewontin urge upon their colleagues. (p. 232)

Mayr (1983), delivers a concurring verdict:

It would seem obvious that little is wrong with the adaptationist program as such, contrary to what is claimed by Gould and Lewontin, but that it should not be applied in an exclusively atomistic manner. There is no better evidence for this conclusion than that which Gould and Lewontin themselves have presented. Aristotelian "why" questions are quite legitimate in the study of adaptations, provided one has a realistic conception of natural selection and understands that the individual-as-a-whole is a complex genetic and developmental system and that it will lead to ludicrous answers if one smashes this system and analyzes the pieces of the wreckage one by one. (p. 332)

Encouraged, then, by what I take to be good company (see also Rosenberg 1985), I stick to my guns:

(1) Adaptationist thinking in biology is precisely as unavoidable, as wise, as fruitful—and as risky—as mentalist thinking in psychology and cognitive science generally.
(2) Proper adaptationist thinking just *is* adopting a special version of the intentional stance in evolutionary thinking—uncovering the "free-floating rationales" of designs in nature.[2]

Adaptationism as Retrospective Radical Interpretation

This view is not in fact as radical as it appears to some; it may be surprising, but it has been implicit all along in the uncontested triumphs of Darwinian (and neo-Darwinian) biology, as Dawkins shows in detail in *The Blind Watchmaker* (1986). In spite of the orthodoxy of this position, however, it continues to trouble some people. The sources of resistance to this view include a surprising variety of ideologies and phobias, in addition to those scouted in this chapter: and in chapter 8 I will show how a curious constellation of philosophers—Searle, Fodor, Dretske, Burge, and Kripke—are united by their antipathy to some of its implications. In preparation for that, I want to point out a special problem of evidence faced by evolutionary theory. As many commentators have noted, evolutionary explanations are essentially historical narratives. Mayr (1983) puts it this way: "When one attempts to explain the features of something that is the product of evolution, one must attempt to reconstruct the

---

2. Illuminating discussions of other facets of the relationship between evolutionary theory and psychology—discussions with which I do not always agree—are found in Patricia Kitcher (1984), Sober (1985), and Rosenberg (1986a, b).

evolutionary history of this feature." (p. 325) But particular historical facts, as we shall see, play an elusive role in such explanations.

The theory of natural selection shows how every feature of the natural world *can* be the product of a blind, unforesightful, non-teleological, ultimately mechanical process of differential reproduction over long periods of time. But of course some features of the natural world—the short legs of dachshunds and Black Angus beef cattle, the thick skins of tomatoes—are the product of artificial selection, in which the goal of the process, and the rationale of the design aimed for, played an explicit role in the etiology, by being "represented" in the minds of the breeders who did the selecting. So of course the theory of natural selection must allow for the existence of such products, and such historical processes, as special cases. But can such special cases be distinguished in retrospective analysis? Consider a thought experiment extracted from my reply to commentary in *BBS*.

Imagine a world in which *actual* hands supplemented the "hidden hand" of natural selection, a world in which natural selection had been aided and abetted over the eons by tinkering, farsighted, reason-representing, organism designers, like the animal and plant breeders of our actual world, but not restricting themselves to "domesticated" organisms designed for human use. These bioengineers would have actually formulated and represented and acted on the rationales of their designs—just like automobile engineers. Now would their handiwork be detectable by biologists in that world? Would their products be distinguishable from the products of an agentless, unrepresenting, purely Darwinian winnowing where all the rationales were free floating? They might be, of course (e.g., if some organisms came with service manuals attached), but they might not be, if the engineers chose to conceal their interventions as best they could.[3]

---

3. NovaGene, a biotechnology company in Houston, has adopted the policy of "DNA branding": writing the nearest codon rendering of their company trademark in amino acids in the "extra" or "junk" DNA of their products (according to the standard abbreviations, asparagine-glutamine-valine-alanine-glycine-glutamic acid-asparagine-glutamic acid = NQVAGENE) (*Scientific American*, June 1986, pp. 70–71). This suggests a new exercise in radical translation for philosophers: how could we confirm or disconfirm the hypothesis that trademarks—or service manuals—were discernible in the bulk of DNA that is apparently uninvolved in the direction of the formation of the phenotype? Dawkins's gene's-eye view predicts, and hence could explain, the presence of this meaningless "selfish DNA" (see Dawkins 1982, chapter 9: "Selfish DNA, Jumping Genes, and a Lamarckian Scare") but that doesn't show that it *couldn't* have a more dramatic source—and hence a meaning after all.

Would a closer look at the designs reveal some telltale discontinuities? Natural selection, lacking foresight, cannot see the wisdom in *reculer pour mieux sauter*—step back in order to jump forward better. If there are designs that cannot be approached by a gradual, stepwise redesign process in which each step is at least no worse for the gene's survival chances than its predecessor, then the existence of such a design in nature would seem to require, at some point in its ancestry, a helping hand from a foresightful designer—either a gene splicer, or a breeder who somehow preserved the necessary succession of intermediate backsliders until they could yield their sought progeny. But couldn't such a leap forward—a "saltation" in the terms of evolutionary theorists—be a mere lucky leap? At what point do we dismiss the hypothesis of cosmic accident as too improbable and settle for the hypothesis of interventionist engineers? (See the discussions of gradualism, saltation, and probability in Dawkins 1986.)

These questions suggest—but do not prove, of course—that there may be no foolproof marks of natural (as opposed to artificial) selection. Would this conclusion, if proven, be a terrible embarrassment to the evolutionists in their struggle against creationists? One can imagine the hubbub: "Scientists Concede: Darwinian Theory Cannot Disprove Intelligent Design!" But this is to mistake the status of orthodox evolutionary theory. It would be most foolhardy for any defender of the theory of natural selection to claim that it gives one the power to read history so finely from present data as to rule out, absolutely, the earlier historical presence of rational designers. It may be a wildly implausible fantasy, but it is a possibility after all.

In our world today, there are organisms we *know* to be the result of foresighted, goal-seeking redesign efforts, but that knowledge depends on our direct knowledge of recent historical events (we've actually watched the breeders at work), and these special events might not cast any fossily shadows into the future. To take a simpler variation on our thought experiment, suppose we were to send Martian biologists a laying hen, a Pekingese dog, a barn swallow, and a cheetah and ask them to determine which designs bore the mark of intervention by artificial selectors. What could they rely on? How would they argue? They might note that the hen did not care "properly" for her eggs; some varieties of hen have had their instinct for broodiness bred right out of them and would soon become extinct were it not for the environment of artificial incubators human beings have provided for them. They might note that the Pekingese was pathetically ill suited for fending for itself in any demanding environment. The barn swallow's fondness for carpentered nest sites might fool them into the view that it was some sort of pet, and whatever features of the cheetah convinced them that it was a creature of the wild might also be found in greyhounds and have been patiently encouraged by breeders. Artificial environments are themselves a part of nature, after all.

Prehistoric fiddling by intergalactic visitors with the DNA of earthly species cannot be ruled out, except on grounds that it is an entirely gratuitous fantasy. Nothing we have found (so far) on earth so much as hints that such a hypothesis is worth further exploration. (And note—I hasten to add, lest creationists take heart—that even if we were to discover and translate such a "trademark message" in our spare DNA, this would do nothing to rescind the claim of the theory of natural selection to explain all design in nature without invocation of a foresighted Designer-Creator *outside the system*. If the theory of evolution by natural selection can account for the existence of the people at NovaGene who dreamed up DNA branding, it can also account for the existence of any predecessors who may have left their signatures around for us to discover.) The power of the theory of natural selection is not the power to prove exactly how (pre-)history was, but only the power to prove how it could have been, given what we know about how things are.

Adaptationist thinking, then, may often be unable to answer particular questions about specific features of the historical mechanisms, the actual etiology, of a natural design development, even while it can succeed in formulating and even confirming—insofar as confirmation is ever possible—a functional analysis of the design. The difference between a design's having a free-floating (unrepresented) rationale in its ancestry and its having a represented rationale may well be indiscernible in the features of the design, but this uncertainty is independent of the confirmation of that rationale for that design. Moreover, as we shall see in the next chapter, the historical facts about the process of design development, even when we can discover them, are equally neutral when we move in the other direction: they are unable to resolve questions about the rationale of the design on which our interpretation of its activities depends. We should still hope science will eventually uncover the historical truth about these etiological details, but not because it will resolve all our Aristotelian "why" questions, even when they are cautiously and appropriately posed.

8   Evolution, Error, and Intentionality

Sometimes it takes years of debate for philosophers to discover what it is they really disagree about. Sometimes they talk past each other in long series of books and articles, never guessing at the root disagreement that divides them. But occasionally a day comes when something happens to coax the cat out of the bag. "Aha!" one philosopher exclaims to another, "so that's why you've been disagreeing with me, misunderstanding me, resisting my conclusions, puzzling me all these years!"

In the fall of 1985 I discovered what I took to be just such a submerged—perhaps even repressed—disagreement and guessed that it might take some shock tactics to push this embarrassing secret into the harsh glare of philosophical attention. There are few things more shocking to philosophers than strange bedfellows, so, in an earlier draft of this chapter which circulated widely in 1986, I drew up some deliberately oversimplified battle lines and picked sides—the good guys versus the bad guys. It worked. I was inundated with detailed, highly revealing responses from those I had challenged and from others who rose to the bait. By and large these reactions confirmed both my division of the field and my claims for its unacknowledged importance.

So constructive were the responses, however, even from those I had treated rather roughly—or misrepresented—in the earlier draft, that instead of just crowing "I told you so!" I should acknowledge at the outset that this heavily revised and expanded offspring of my

All but the last section of this chapter appears under the same title, in Y. Wilks and D. Partridge, eds., *Source Book on the Foundations of Artificial Intelligence* (Cambridge: Cambridge University Press, 1987), and is reprinted with permission.

earlier act of provocation owes a special debt to the comments of Tyler Burge, Fred Dretske, Jerry Fodor, John Haugeland, Saul Kripke, Ruth Millikan, Hilary Putnam, Richard Rorty, and Stephen Stich, and to many others, including especially Fred Adams, Peter Brown, Jerome Feldman, D. K. Modrak, Carolyn Ristau, Jonathan Schull, Stephen White, and Andrew Woodfield.

The Great Divide I want to display resists a simple, straightforward formulation, not surprisingly, but we can locate it by retracing the steps of my exploration, which began with a discovery about some philosophers' attitudes toward the interpretation of artifacts. The scales fell from my eyes during a discussion with Jerry Fodor and some other philosophers about a draft of a chapter of Fodor's *Psychosemantics* (1987). Scales often fall from my eyes when discussing things with Fodor, but this was the first time, so far as I can recall, that I actually found myself muttering "Aha!" under my breath. The chapter in question, "Meaning and the World Order," concerns Fred Dretske's attempts (1981, especially chapter 8; 1985; 1986) to solve the problem of misrepresentation. As an aid to understanding the issue, I had proposed to Fodor and the other participants in the discussion that we first discuss a dead simple case of misrepresentation: a coin-slot testing apparatus on a vending machine accepting a slug. "That sort of case is irrelevant," Fodor retorted instantly, "because after all, John Searle is right about one thing; he's right about artifacts like that. They don't have any intrinsic or original intentionality—only derived intentionality."

The doctrine of original intentionality is the claim that whereas some of our artifacts may have intentionality derived from us, we have original (or intrinsic) intentionality, utterly underived. Aristotle said that God is the Unmoved Mover, and this doctrine announces that we are Unmeant Meaners. I have never believed in it and have often argued against it. As Searle has noted, "Dennett . . . believes that nothing *literally* has any *intrinsic intentional* mental states" (1982, p. 57), and in the long-running debate between us (Searle 1980b, 1982, 1984, 1985; Dennett 1980b; Hofstadter and Dennett 1981; Dennett 1982c, 1984b, forthcoming f), I had assumed that Fodor was on my side on this particular point.

Did Fodor really believe that Searle is right about this? He said so. Dretske (1985) goes further, citing Searle's attack on artificial intelligence (Searle 1980) with approval, and drawing a sharp contrast between people and computers:

I lack specialized skills, knowledge and understanding, but nothing that is essential to membership in the society of rational agents. With machines, though, and this includes the most sophisticated modern computers, it is different. They *do* lack something that is essential. (p. 23)

Others who have recently struggled with the problem of misrepresentation or error also seemed to me to fall on Searle's side of the fence: in particular, Tyler Burge (1986) and Saul Kripke (1982, especially p. 34ff). In fact, as we shall see, the problem of error impales all and only those who believe in original or intrinsic intentionality.

Are *original intentionality* and *intrinsic intentionality* the same thing? We will have to approach this question indirectly, by pursuing various attempts to draw a sharp distinction between the way our minds (or mental states) have meaning and the way other things do. We can begin with a familiar and intuitive distinction discussed by Haugeland. Our artifacts

. . . only have meaning because we give it to them; their intentionality, like that of smoke signals and writing, is essentially borrowed, hence *derivative*. To put it bluntly: computers themselves don't mean anything by their tokens (any more than books do)—they only mean what we say they do. Genuine understanding, on the other hand, is intentional "in its own right" and not derivatively from something else. (1981, pp. 32–33)

Consider an encyclopedia. It has derived intentionality. It contains information about thousands of things in the world, but only insofar as it is a device designed and intended for our use. Suppose we "automate" our encyclopedia, putting all its data into a computer and turning its index into the basis for an elaborate question-answering system. No longer do we have to look up material in the volumes; we simply type in questions and receive answers. It might seem to naive users as if they were communicating with another person, another entity endowed with original intentionality, but we would know better. A question-answering system is still just a tool, and whatever meaning or aboutness we vest in it is just a by-product of our practices in using the device to serve our own goals. It has no goals of its own, except for the artificial and derived goal of "understanding" and "answering" our questions correctly.

But suppose we endow our computer with somewhat more autonomous, somewhat less slavish goals. For instance, a chess-playing computer has the (artificial, derived) goal of defeating its human opponent, of concealing what it "knows" from us, of tricking us perhaps. But still, surely, it is only our tool or toy, and although many of its internal states have a sort of aboutness or intentionality—e.g., there are states that represent (and hence are about) the current board positions, and processes that investigate (and hence are about) various possible continuations of the game—this is just derived intentionality, not original intentionality.

This persuasive theme (it is not really an argument) has convinced more than a few thinkers that no artifact could have the sort of intentionality we have. Any computer program, any robot we might design and build, no matter how strong the illusion we may create that it has become a genuine agent, could never be a truly autonomous thinker with the same sort of original intentionality we enjoy. For the time being, let us suppose that this is the doctrine of original intentionality, and see where it leads.

The Case of the Wandering Two-Bitser

I will now press my vending machine example—the example Fodor insisted was irrelevant—explicitly, for it makes vivid exactly the points of disagreement and casts several recent controversies (about "individualistic psychology" and "narrow content," about error, about function) in a useful light. Consider a standard soft-drink vending machine, designed and built in the United States, and equipped with a transducer device for accepting and rejecting US quarters.[1] Let's call such a device a two-bitser. Normally, when a quarter is inserted into a two-bitser, the two-bitser goes into a state, call it Q, which "means" (note the scare-quotes) "I perceive/accept a genuine US quarter now." Such two-bitsers are quite clever and sophisticated, but hardly foolproof. They do "make mistakes" (more scare-quotes). That is, unmetaphorically, sometimes they go into state Q when a slug or other foreign object is inserted in them, and sometimes they reject perfectly legal quarters—they fail to go into state Q when they are *supposed to*. No doubt there are detectable patterns in the cases of "misperception." No doubt at least some of the cases of "misidentification" could be predicted by someone with enough knowledge of the relevant laws of physics and design parameters of the two-bitser's transducing machinery, so that it would be just as

---

1. This tactic is hardly novel. Among earlier discussions of intentionality drawing on such examples of simple discriminating mechanisms are MacKenzie, unpublished (1978), Ackermann 1972, and Enc 1982.

much a matter of physical law that objects of kind K would put the device into state Q as that quarters would. Objects of kind K would be good "slugs"—reliably "fooling" the transducer.

If objects of kind K became more common in the two-bitser's normal environment, we could expect the owners and designers of two-bitsers to develop more advanced and sensitive transducers that would reliably discriminate between genuine US quarters and slugs of kind K. Of course trickier counterfeits might then make their appearance, requiring further advances in the detecting transducers, and at some point such escalation of engineering would reach diminishing returns, for there is no such thing as a *foolproof* mechanism. In the meantime, the engineers and users are wise to make do with standard, rudimentary two-bitsers, since it is not cost effective to protect oneself against negligible abuses.

The only thing that makes the device a quarter-detector rather than a slug-detector or a quarter-*or*-slug-detector is the shared intention of the device's designers, builders, owners, users. It is only in the environment or context of those users and their intentions that we can single out some of the occasions of state Q as "veridical" and others as "mistaken." It is only relative to that context of intentions that we could justify calling the device a two-bitser in the first place.

I take it that so far I have Fodor, Searle, Dretske, Burge, Kripke, et al. nodding their agreement: that's just how it is with such artifacts; this is a textbook case of derived intentionality, laid bare. And so of course it embarrasses no one to admit that a particular two-bitser, straight from the American factory and with "Model A Two-Bitser" stamped right on it, might be installed on a Panamian soft-drink machine, where it proceeded to earn its keep as an accepter and rejecter of quarter-balboas, legal tender in Panama, and easily distinguished from US quarters by the design and writing stamped on them, but not by their weight, thickness, diameter, or material composition.

(I'm not making this up. I have it on excellent authority—Albert Erler of the Flying Eagle Shoppe, Rare Coins—that Panamanian quarter-balboas minted between 1966 and 1984 are indistinguishable from US quarters by standard vending machines. Small wonder, since they are struck from US quarter stock in American mints. And—to satisfy the curious, although it is strictly irrelevant to the example—the current official exchange rate for the quarter-balboa is indeed $.25!)

Such a two-bitser, whisked off to Panama (the poor man's Twin Earth), would still normally go into a certain physical state—the state with the physical features by which we used to identify state Q—whenever a US quarter or an object of kind K or a Panamanian quarter-balboa is inserted in it, but now a different set of such occasions count as the mistakes. In the new environment, US quarters count as slugs, as inducers of error, misperception, misrepresentation, just as much as objects of kind K do. After all, back in the United States a Panamanian quarter-balboa is a kind of slug.

Once our two-bitser is resident in Panama, should we say that the state we used to call Q still occurs? The physical state in which the device "accepts" coins still occurs, but should we now say that we should identify it as "realizing" a new state, QB, instead? Well, there is considerable freedom—not to say boredom—about what we should say, since after all a two-bitser is just an artifact, and talking about its perceptions and misperceptions, its veridical and nonveridical states—its intentionality, in short—is "just metaphor." The two-bitser's internal state, call it what you like, doesn't *really* (originally, intrinsically) mean either "US quarter here now" or "Panamanian quarter-balboa here now." It doesn't *really* mean anything. So Fodor, Searle, Dretske, Burge, and Kripke (*inter alia*) would insist.

The two-bitser was originally designed to be a detector of US quarters. That was its "proper function" (Millikan 1984), and, quite literally, its *raison d'être*. No one would have bothered bringing it into existence had not this purpose occurred to them. And given that this historical fact about its origin licenses a certain way of speaking, such a device may be primarily or originally characterized as a two-bitser, a thing whose function is to detect quarters, so that *relative to that function* we can identify both its veridical states and its errors.

This would not prevent a two-bitser from being wrested from its home niche and pressed into service with a new purpose—whatever new purpose the laws of physics certify it would reliably serve—as a K-detector, a quarter-balboa-detector, a doorstop, a deadly weapon. In its new role there might be a brief period of confusion or indeterminacy. How long a track record must something accumulate before it is no longer a two-bitser, but rather a quarter-balboa-detector (a q-balber)—or a doorstop or a deadly weapon? On its very debut as a q-balber, after ten years of faithful service as a two-bitser, is its state already a *veridical* detection of a quarter-balboa, or might there be a sort of force-of-habit error of nostalgia, a mistaken identification of a quarter-balboa *as* a US quarter?

As described, the two-bitser differs strikingly from us in that it has no provision for memory of its past experiences—or even "memory" (in scare-quotes) for its past "experiences." But the latter, at least, could easily be provided, if it was thought to make a difference. To start with the simplest inroad into this topic, suppose the two-bitser (to refer to it by the name of its original baptism) is equipped with a counter, which after ten years of service stands at 1,435,792. Suppose it is not reset to zero during its flight to Panama, so that on its debut there the counter turns over to 1,435,793. Does this tip the balance in favor of the claim that it has not yet switched to the task of correctly identifying quarter-balboas? Would variations and complications on this theme drive your intuitions in different directions?

We can assure ourselves that nothing *intrinsic* about the two-bitser considered narrowly all by itself and independently of its prior history would distinguish it from a genuine q-balber, made to order on commission from the Panamanian government. Still, given its ancestry, is there not a problem about its function, its purpose, its meaning, on this first occasion when it goes into the state we are tempted to call *Q?* Is this a case of going into state *Q* (meaning "US quarter here now") or state *QB* (meaning "Panamanian quarter-balboa here now")? I would say, along with Millikan (1984), that whether its Panamanian debut counts as going into state *Q* or state *QB* depends on whether, in its new niche, it was *selected for* its capacity to detect quarter-balboas—literally selected, e.g., by the holder of the Panamanian Pepsi-Cola franchise. If it was so selected, then even though its new proprietors might have forgotten to reset its counter, its first "perceptual" act would count as a correct identification by a q-balber, for that is what it would *now* be *for.* (It would have acquired quarter-balboa detection as its proper function.) If, on the other hand, the two-bitser was sent to Panama by mistake, or if it arrived by sheer coincidence, its debut would mean nothing, though its utility might soon—immediately—be recognized and esteemed by the relevant authorities (those who could press it into service in a new role), and thereupon its *subsequent* states would count as tokens of *QB.*

Presumably Fodor et al. would be content to let me say this, since, after all, the two-bitser is just an artifact. It has no intrinsic, original intentionality, so there is no "deeper" fact of the matter we might try to uncover. This is just a pragmatic matter of how best to talk, when talking metaphorically and anthropomorphically about the states of the device.

But we part company when I claim to apply precisely the same morals, the same pragmatic rules of interpretation, to the human case. In the case of human beings (at least), Fodor and company are sure that such deeper facts do exist—even if we cannot always find them. That is, they suppose that, independently of the power of any observer or interpreter to discover it, there is always a fact of the matter about what a person (or a person's mental state) *really means.* Now we might call their shared belief a belief in *intrinsic* intentionality, or perhaps even *objective* or *real* intentionality. There are differences among them about how to characterize, and name, this property of human minds, which I will continue to call *original intentionality,* but they all agree that minds are unlike the two-bitser in this regard, and this is what I now take to be the most fundamental point of disagreement between Fodor and me, between Searle and me, between Dretske and me, between Burge and me, etc. Once it was out in the open many things that had been puzzling me fell into place. At last I understood (and will shortly explain) why Fodor dislikes evolutionary hypotheses almost as much as he dislikes artificial intelligence (see, e. g., "Tom Swift and his Procedural Grandmother" in Fodor 1981a and the last chapter of Fodor 1983); why Dretske must go to such desperate lengths to give an account of error; why Burge's "anti-individualism" and Kripke's ruminations on rule-following, which strike some philosophers as deep and disturbing challenges to their complacency, have always struck me as great labors wasted in trying to break down an unlocked door.

I part company with these others because although they might agree with me (and Millikan) about what one should say in the case of the transported two-bitser, they say that we human beings are not just fancier, more sosphisticated two-bitsers. When we say that we go into the state of believing that we are perceiving a US quarter (or some genuine water as opposed to XYZ, or a genuine twinge of arthritis) this is no metaphor, no mere manner of speaking. A parallel example will sharpen the disagreement.

Suppose some human being, Jones, looks out the window and thereupon goes into the state of thinking he sees a horse. There may or may not be a horse out there for him to see, but the fact that he is in the mental state of thinking he sees a horse is not just a matter of interpretation (these others say). Suppose the planet Twin Earth were just like Earth, save for having schmorses where we have horses. (Schmorses look for all the world like horses, and are well-nigh indistinguishable from horses by all but trained biologists with special apparatus, but they aren't horses, any more than dolphins are fish.) If we whisk Jones off to Twin Earth, land of the schmorses, and confront him in the relevant way with a schmorse, then either he really is, still, provoked into the state of believing he sees a horse (a mistaken, nonveridical belief) or he is provoked by that schmorse into believing, for the first time (and veridically), that he is seeing a schmorse. (For the sake of the example, let us suppose that Twin Earthians call schmorses *horses* (*chevaux, Pferde,* etc.) so that what Jones or a native Twin Earthian *says to himself*—or others—counts for nothing.) However hard it may be to determine exactly which state he is in, he is really in one or the other (or perhaps he really is in neither, so violently have we assaulted his cognitive system). Anyone who finds this intuition irresistible believes in original intentionality and has some distinguished company: Fodor, Searle, Dretske, Burge, and Kripke, but also Chisholm (1956, 1957), Nagel (1979, 1986), and Popper and Eccles (1977). Anyone who finds this intuition dubious if not downright dismissible can join me, the Churchlands (see especially Churchland and Churchland 1981), Davidson, Haugeland, Millikan, Rorty, Stalnaker, and our distinguished predecessors, Quine and Sellars, in the other corner (along with Douglas Hofstadter, Marvin Minsky, and almost everyone else in AI).

There, then, is a fairly major disagreement. Who is right? I cannot hope to refute the opposing tradition in the short compass of a chapter, but I will provide two different persuasions on behalf of my side: I will show what perplexities Fodor, Dretske, et al. entangle themselves in by clinging to their intuition, and I will provide a little thought experiment to motivate, if not substantiate, my rival view. First the thought experiment.

Designing a Robot

Suppose you decided, for whatever reasons, that you wanted to experience life in the twenty-fifth century, and suppose that the only known way of keeping your body alive that long required it to be placed in a hibernation device of sorts, where it would rest, slowed down and comatose, for as long as you liked. You could arrange to climb into the support capsule, be put to sleep, and then automatically awakened and released in 2401. This is a time-honored science-fiction theme, of course.

Designing the capsule itself is not your only engineering problem, for the capsule must be protected and supplied with the requisite energy (for refrigeration or whatever) for over four hundred years. You will not be able to count on your children and grandchildren for this stewardship, of course, for they will be long dead before the year 2401, and you cannot presume that your more distant descendants, if any, will take a lively interest in your well-being. So you must design a supersystem to protect your capsule and to provide the energy it needs for four hundred years.

Here there are two basic strategies you might follow. On one, you should find the ideal location, as best you can foresee, for a fixed installation that will be well supplied with water, sunlight, and whatever else your capsule (and the supersystem itself) will need for the duration. The main drawback to such an installation or "plant" is that it cannot be moved if harm comes its way—if, say, someone decides to build a freeway right where it is located. The second alternative is much more sophisticated, but avoids this drawback: design a mobile facility to house your capsule along with the requisite sensors and early-warning devices so that it can move out of harm's way and seek out new energy sources as it needs them. In short, build a giant robot and install the capsule (with you inside) in it.

These two basic strategies are obviously copied from nature: they correspond roughly to the division between plants and animals. Since the latter, more sophisticated strategy better fits my purposes, we shall suppose that you decide to build a robot to house your capsule. You should try to design it so that above all else it "chooses" actions designed to further your best interests, of course. "Bad" moves and "wrong" turns are those that will tend to incapacitate it for the role of protecting you until 2401—which is its sole *raison d'être*. This is clearly a profoundly difficult engineering problem, calling for the highest level of expertise in designing a "vision" system to guide its locomotion, and other "sensory" and locomotory systems. And since you will be comtaose throughout and thus cannot stay awake to guide and plan its strategies, you will have to design it to generate its own plans in response to changing circumstances. It must "know" how to "seek out" and "recognize" and then exploit energy sources, how to move to safer territory, how to "anticipate" and then avoid dangers.

With so much to be done, and done fast, you had best rely whenever you can on economies: give your robot no more discriminatory prowess than it will probably need in order to distinguish what needs distinguishing in its world.

Your task will be made much more difficult by the fact that you cannot count on your robot being the only such robot around with such a mission. If your whim catches on, your robot may find itself competing with others (and with your human descendents) for limited supplies of energy, fresh water, lubricants, and the like. It would no doubt be wise to design it with enough sophistication in its control system to permit it to calculate the benefits and risks of cooperating with other robots, or of forming alliances for mutual benefit. (Any such calculation must be a "quick and dirty" approximation, arbitrarily truncated. See Dennett, forthcoming e.)

The result of this design project would be a robot capable of exhibiting self-control, since you must cede fine-grained real-time control to your artifact once you put yourself to sleep.[2] As such it will be capable of deriving its own subsidiary goals from its assessment of its current state and the import of that state for its ultimate goal (which is to preserve you). These secondary goals may take it far afield on century-long projects, some of which may be ill advised, in spite of your best efforts. Your robot may embark on actions antithetical to your purposes, even suicidal, having been convinced by another robot, perhaps, to subordinate its own life mission to some other.

But still, according to Fodor et al., this robot would have no original intentionality at all, but only the intentionality it derives from its artifactual role as your protector. Its simulacrum of mental states would be just that—not *real* deciding and seeing and wondering and planning, but only *as if* deciding and seeing and wondering and planning.

We should pause, for a moment, to make sure we understand what this claim encompasses. The imagined robot is certainly vastly more sophisticated than the humble two-bitser, and perhaps along the path to greater sophistication we have smuggled in some crucial new capacity that would vouchsafe the robot our kind of original intentionality. Note, for instance, that our imagined robot, to which we have granted the power to "plan" new courses of actions, to "learn" from past errors, to form allegiances, and to "communicate" with its com-

---

2. For more on control and self-control, see my *Elbow Room: The Varieties of Free Will Worth Wanting* (1984), chapter 3, "Control and Self-Control"; and forthcoming a.

petitors, would probably perform very creditably in any Turing Test to which we subjected it (see Dennett 1985a). Moreover, in order to do all this "planning" and "learning" and "communicating" it will almost certainly have to be provided with control structures that are rich in self-reflective, self-monitoring power, so that it will have a human-like access to its own internal states and be capable of reporting, avowing, and commenting upon what it "takes" to be the import of its own internal states. It will have "opinions" about what those states mean, and we should no doubt take those opinions seriously as very good evidence—probably the best evidence we can easily get— about what those states "mean" *metaphorically speaking* (remember: it's only an artifact). The two-bitser was given no such capacity to sway our interpretive judgments by issuing apparently confident "avowals."

There are several ways one might respond to this thought experiment, and we will explore the most promising in due course, but first I want to draw out the most striking implication of standing firm with our first intuition: no artifact, no matter how much AI wizardry is designed into it, has anything but derived intentionality. If we cling to this view, the conclusion forced upon us is that our own intentionality is exactly like that of the robot, for the science-fiction tale I have told is not new; it is just a variation on Dawkins's (1976) vision of us (and all other biological species) as "survival machines" designed to prolong the futures of our selfish genes. We are artifacts, in effect, designed over the eons as survival machines for genes that cannot act swiftly and informedly in their own interests. Our interests as we conceive them and the interests of our genes may well diverge—even though were it not for our genes' interests, we would not exist: their preservation is our original *raison d'être*, even if we can learn to ignore that goal and devise our own *summum bonum*, thanks to the intelligence our genes have installed in us. So our intentionality is derived from the intentionality of our "selfish" genes! *They* are the Unmeant Meaners, not us!

Reading Mother Nature's Mind

This vision of things, while it provides a satisfying answer to the question of whence came our own intentionality, does seem to leave us with an embarrassment, for it derives our own intentionality from entities—genes—whose intentionality is surely a paradigm case of mere *as if* intentionality. How could the literal depend on the metaphorical? Moreover, there is surely this much disanalogy between my science-fiction tale and Dawkins's story: in my tale I supposed that there was conscious, deliberate, foresighted engineering involved in the creation of the robot, whereas even if we are, as Dawkins says, the product of a design process that has our genes as the primary beneficiary, that is a design process that utterly lacks a conscious, deliberate, foresighted engineer.

The chief beauty of the theory of natural selection is that it shows us how to eliminate this intelligent Artificer from our account of origins. And yet the process of natural selection is responsible for designs of great cunning. It is a bit outrageous to conceive of genes as clever designers; genes themselves could not be more stupid; *they* cannot reason or represent or figure out anything. They do not do the designing themselves; they are merely the beneficiaries of the design process. But then who or what does the designing? Mother Nature, of course, or more literally, the long, slow process of evolution by natural selection.

To me the most fascinating property of the process of evolution is its uncanny capacity to mirror *some* properties of the human mind (the intelligent Artificer) while being bereft of others. While it can never be stressed enough that natural selection operates with no foresight and no purpose, we should not lose sight of the fact that the process of natural selection has proven itself to be exquisitely sensitive to rationales, making myriads of discriminating "choices" and "recognizing" and "appreciating" many subtle relationships. To put it even more provocatively, when natural selection selects, it can "choose" a particular design *for one reason rather than another*, without ever consciously—or unconsciously!—"representing" either the choice or the reasons. (Hearts were chosen for their excellence as blood circulators, not for the captivating rhythm of their beating, though that *might* have been the reason something was "chosen" by natural selection.)

There is, I take it, no representation at all in the process of natural selection. And yet it certainly seems that we can give principled explanations of evolved design features that invoke, in effect, "what Mother Nature had in mind" when that feature was designed.[3]

---

3. "There must, after all, be a finite number of general principles that govern the activities of our various cognitive-state-making and cognitive-state-using mechanisms and there must be explanations of why these principles have historically worked to aid

Just as the Panamanian Pepsi-Cola franchise-holder can select the two-bitser *for* its talent at recognizing quarter-balboas, can adopt it *as* a quarter-balboa-detector, so evolution can select an organ *for* its capacity to oxygenate blood, can establish it *as* a lung. And it is only relative to just such design "choices" or evolution-"endorsed" purposes—*raisons d'être*—that we can identify behaviors, actions, perceptions, beliefs, or any of the other categories of folk psychology. (See Millikan 1984, 1986, for a forceful expression of this view.)

The idea that we are artifacts designed by natural selection is both compelling and familiar; some would go so far as to say that it is quite beyond serious controversy. Why, then, it is resisted not just by Creationists, but also (rather subliminally) by the likes of Fodor, Searle, Dretske, Burge, and Kripke? My hunch is because it has two rather unobvious implications that some find terribly unpalatable. First, if we are (just) artifacts, then what our innermost thoughts mean—and whether they mean anything at all—is something about which we, the very thinkers of those thoughts, have no special authority. The two-bitser turns into a q-balber without ever changing its inner nature; the state that used to mean one thing now means another. The same thing could in principle happen to us, if we are just artifacts, if our own intentionality is thus not original but derived. Those—such as Dretske and Burge—who have already renounced this traditional doctrine of privileged access can shrug off, or even welcome, that implication; it is the second implication that they resist: if we are such artifacts, not only have we no guaranteed privileged access to the deeper facts that fix the meanings of our thoughts, but *there are no such deeper facts*. Sometimes functional interpretation is obvious, but when it is not, when we go to read Mother Nature's mind, there is no text to be interpreted. When "the fact of the matter" about proper function is controversial—when more than one interpretation is well supported—there is no fact of the matter.

The tactic of treating evolution itself from the intentional stance needs further discussion and defense, but I want to approach the task indirectly. The issues will come into better focus, I think, if first we diagnose the resistance to this tactic—and its Siamese twin, the tactic of treating ourselves as artifacts—in recent work in philosophy of mind and language.

our survival. To suppose otherwise is to suppose that our cognitive life is an accidental epiphenomenal cloud hovering over mechanisms that *evolution devised with other things in mind*." (Millikan 1986, p. 55; my emphasis)

Error, Disjunction, and Inflated Interpretation

Dretske's attempt (1981, 1985, 1986) to deal with these issues invokes a distinction between what he calls *natural meaning* and *functional meaning*. Natural meaning (*meaning$_n$*) is defined in such a way as to rule out misrepresentation; what a particular ringing of the doorbell means$_n$ depends on the integrity of the circuit that causes the ringing. "When there is a short-circuit, the ring of the doorbell (regardless of what it was designed to indicate, regardless of what it normally indicates) does not indicate that the doorbutton is being depressed." "This is what is it *supposed* to mean$_n$, what it was *designed* to mean$_n$, what (perhaps) tokens of that type *normally* mean$_n$, but not what it *does* mean$_n$." (1986, p. 21)

It then falls to Dretske to define *functional meaning*, what it is for something to *mean$_f$* that such-and-such, in such a way as to explain how a sign or state or event in some system can, on occasion, misrepresent something or "say" something false. But "if these functions are (what I shall call) *assigned* functions, then meaning$_f$ is tainted with the purposes, intentions and beliefs of those who assign the function from which meaning$_f$ derives its misrepresentational powers." (p. 22) Clearly, the meaning of the two-bitser's acceptance state Q is just such an assigned functional meaning, and Dretske would say of it: "That is the function we assign it, the reason it was built and the explanation for why it was built the way it was. Had our purposes been otherwise, it might have meant$_f$ something else." (p. 23)

Since merely *assigned* functional meaning is "tainted," Dretske must seek a further distinction. What he must characterize is the *natural* functions of the counterpart states of organisms, "functions a thing has which are independent of *our* interpretive intentions and purposes" (p. 25), so that he can then define natural functional meaning in terms of those functions.

We are looking for what a sign is *supposed* to mean$_n$ where the "supposed to" is cashed out in terms of the function of that sign (or sign system) in the organism's *own* cognitive economy. (p. 25)

The obvious way to go, as we saw in the last section, is to substitute for our interpretive intentions and purposes the intentions and purposes of the organism's designer, Mother Nature—the process of natural selection—and ask ourselves what, in *that* scheme, any particular type of signal or state is designed to signal, supposed to mean.

Just as we would ultimately appeal to the engineers' rationales when deciding on the best account of representation and misrepresentation in our imagined survival-machine robot, so we can appeal to the discernible design rationales of natural selection in assigning content, and hence the power of *mis*representation, to event types in natural artifacts—organisms, ourselves included.

But although Dretske pays homage to those who have pursued that evolutionary path, and warily follows it some distance himself, he sees a problem. The problem is none other than the biological version of our question about what principled way there is to tell whether the state of the two-bitser (in some particular environment) means "quarter here now" or "quarter-balboa here now" or "thing of kind F or kind G or kind K here now." We must find an interpretation principle that assigns content, Dretske says, "without doing so by artificially *inflating* the natural functions of these systems"—while at the same time avoiding the too-deflationary principle which resolves all functional meaning into brute natural meaning, where misrepresentation is impossible.

Consider the classic case of what the frog's eye tells the frog's brain (Lettvin et al. 1959). Suppose we provoke a frog into catching and swallowing a lead pellet we toss at it (cf. Millikan 1986). If we interpret the signal coming from the eye as "telling" the frog that there is a fly flying toward it, then it is the eye that is passing mistaken information to the frog, whereas if we interpret that signal as merely signaling a dark moving patch on the retina, it is "telling the truth" and the error must be assigned to some later portion of the brain's processing (see Dennett 1969, p. 83). If we are strenuously minimal in our interpretations, the frog never makes a mistake, for every event in the relevant pathway in its nervous system can always be *de-interpreted* by adding disjunctions (the signal means something less demanding: fly *or* pellet *or* dark moving spot *or* slug of kind K or . . .) until we arrive back at the brute meaning$_n$ of the signal type, where misrepresentation is impossible. No matter how many layers of transducers contribute to a signal's specificity, there will always be a deflationary interpretation of its meaning as meaning$_n$ unless we relativize our account to some assumption of the normal (Normal, in Millikan's sense) function (see Dennett 1969, section 9, "Function and Content").

Dretske is worried about overendowing event types with content, attributing a more specific or sophisticated meaning to them than the facts dictate. But given the stinginess of Mother Nature the engineer, this otherwise laudable hermeneutical abstemiousness puts one at risk of failing to appreciate the "point," the real genius, of her inventions. A particularly instructive instance of the virtues of "inflationary" functional interpretation is Braitenberg's (1984) speculative answer to the question of why so many creatures—from fish to human beings—are equipped with special-purpose hardware that is wonderfully sensitive to visual patterns exhibiting symmetry around a vertical axis. There can be little doubt about what the deflationary description is of the content of these intricate transducers: they signal "instance of symmetry around vertical axis on the retina." But why? What is this for? The provision is so common that it must have a very general utility. Braitenberg asks what in the natural world (before there were church facades and suspension bridges) presents a vertically symmetrical view? Nothing in the plant world, and nothing in the terrain. Only this: other animals, *but only when they are facing the viewer!* (Rear views are often vertically symmetrical, but generally less strikingly so.) In other words, what a vertical-symmetry transducer tells one is (roughly) "someone is looking at you." Needless to say, this is typically a datum well worth an animal's attention, for the other creature, in whose cross-hairs the animal currently sits, may well be a predator—or a rival or a mate. And so it is not surprising that the normal effect of the symmetry detector's being turned ON is an immediate orientation reaction and (in the case of fish, for instance) preparation for flight. Is it inflationary to call this transducer a predator-detector? Or a predator-or-mate-or-rival-detector? If you were hired to design a fish's predator-detector, would you go for a more foolproof (but cumbersome, slow) transducer, or argue that this is really the very best sort of predator-detector to have, in which the false alarms are a small price to pay for its speed and its power to recognize relatively well-hidden predators?

Ecologically insignificant vertical symmetries count as *false* alarms only if we suppose the special-*purpose* wiring is *supposed* to "tell" the organism (roughly) "someone is looking at you." What *exactly* is the content of its deliverance? This quest for precision of content ascription, and for independence of interpretation, is the hallmark not only of Dretske's research program, but also of much of the theoretical work in philosophy of language and mind (the philosophical theory of meaning, broadly conceived). But at least in the case of the symmetry-detector (or whatever we want to call it) there is no "principled" answer to that, beyond what we can support by appeal to the functions we can discover and make sense of in this way, in the normal operation of the transducer in nature.

We saw in the case of human-designed artifacts that we could use our appreciation of the costs and benefits of various design choices to upgrade our interpretation of the two-bitser's discriminatory talent from mere disk-of-weight-w-and-thickness-t-and diameter-d-and material-m detection to quarter detection (or quarter-balboa detection, depending on the user's intentions). This is, if you like, the fundamental tactic of artifact hermeneutics. Why should Dretske resist the same interpretive principle in the case of natural functional meaning? Because it is not "principled" enough, in his view. It would fail to satisfy our yearning for an account of what the natural event *really* means, what it means under the aspect of "original" or "intrinsic" intentionality.[4]

In "Machines and the Mental" (1985) Dretske claims that the fundamental difference between current computers and us is that while computers may process information by manipulating internal symbols of some sort, they have "no access, so to speak, to the *meaning* of these symbols, to the things the representations represent." (p. 26) This way of putting it suggests that Dretske is conflating two points: something's meaning something *to* or *for* a system or organism, and that system or organism's being in a position to know or recognize or intuit or introspect that fact from the inside.

---

4. Dretske happens to discuss the problem of predator detection in a passage that brings out this problem with his view: "If (certain) bacteria did not have something inside that meant that *that* was the direction of magnetic north, they could not orient themselves so as to avoid toxic surface water. They would perish. If, in other words, an animal's internal sensory states were not rich in information, intrinsic natural meaning, about the presence of prey, predators, cliffs, obstacles, water and heat, it could not survive." (1985, p. 29) The trouble is that, given Dretske's conservative demands on information, the symmetry-detector wouldn't count as sending a signal with information (intrinsic natural meaning) about predators but only about patterns of vertical symmetry on the retina, and while no doubt it could be, and normally would be, supplemented by further transducers designed to make finer-grained distinctions between predators, prey, mates, rivals, and members of ignorable species, these could be similarly crude in their actual discriminatory powers. If, as Dretske suggests, some bacteria can survive with only north-detectors (they don't need toxic-water-detectors, as it happens), other creatures can get by with mere symmetry-detectors, so the last sentence quoted above is just false: most animals survive and reproduce just fine without the benefit of states that are rich enough in (Dretskean) information to inform their owners about prey, predators, cliffs, and the like.

Unless these symbols have what we might call an *intrinsic* [my emphasis] meaning, a meaning they possess which is independent of our communicative intentions and purposes, then this meaning *must* be irrelevant to assessing what the machine is doing when it manipulates them. (p. 28)

Dretske quite correctly insists that the meaning he is seeking for mental states must *make a real difference* in, and to, the life of the organism, but what he fails to see is that the meaning he seeks, while it is, in the case of an organism, independent of *our* intentions and purposes, is not independent of the intentions and purposes of Mother Nature, and hence is, in the end, just as derived and hence just as subject to indeterminacy of interpretation, as the meaning in our two-bitser.

Dretske attempts to escape this conclusion, and achieve "functional determination" in the face of threatened "functional indeterminacy," by devising a complicated story of how *learning* could make the crucial difference. According to Dretske, a learning organism can, through the process of repeated exposures to a variety of stimuli and the mechanism of associative learning, come to establish an internal state type that has a *definite, unique* function and hence functional meaning.

Confronted with our imagined robotic survival machine, Dretske's reaction is to suppose that in all likelihood some of its states do have natural (as opposed to merely assigned) functional meaning, in virtue of the learning history of the survival machine's first days or years of service. "I think we could (logically) create an artifact that *acquired* original intentionality, but not one that (at the moment of creation, as it were) *had* it" (personal correspondence). The functions dreamed of, and provided for, by its engineers are only *assigned* functions— however brilliantly the engineers anticipated the environment the machine ends up inhabiting—but once the machine has a chance to respond to the environment in a training or learning cycle, its states have at least the opportunity of acquiring natural (definite, unique) functional meaning—and not just the natural meaning in which misrepresentation is ruled out.

I will not present the details of this ingenious attempt because, for all its ingenuity, it won't work. Fodor (1987), in the chapter with which we began, shows why. First, it depends, as Fodor notes, on drawing a sharp line between the organism's learning period, when the internal state is developing its meaning, and the subsequent period when its meaning is held to be fixed. Misrepresentation is possible, on Dretske's view, only in the second phase, but any line we draw must be arbitrary. (Does a whistle blow, Fodor wonders, signaling the end of the practice session and the beginning of playing for keeps?) Moreover, Fodor notes (not surprisingly), Dretske's account cannot provide for the fixed natural functional meaning of any innate, unlearned representative states.

Dretske does not view this as a shortcoming. So much the worse for innate concepts, he says. "I don't think there are, or can be, innate concepts or beliefs. . . . Beliefs and desires, *reasons* in general (the sort of thing covered by the intentional stance), are (or so I would like to argue) invoked to explain patterns of behavior that are acquired during the life history of the organism exhibiting the behavior (i.e., learned)" (personal correspondence).

The motivation for this stand can be brought out by considering an example. The first thing a baby cuckoo does when it hatches is to look around the nest for other eggs, its potential competitors for its adoptive parents' attention, and attempt to roll them over the edge. It surely has no inkling of the functional meaning of its activity, but that meaning is nevertheless there—*for* the organism and *to* the organism—unless we suppose by the latter phrase that the organism has to "have access" to that meaning, has to be in a position to reflect on it, or avow it, for instance. The rationale of the cuckoo's chillingly purposive activity is not in question; what remains to be investigated is to what extent the rationale is the fledgling's rationale and to what extent it is free-floating—merely what Mother Nature had in mind (see chapter 7). For Dretske, however, this is an all-or-nothing question, and it is tied to his intuition that there must be unique and unequivocal (natural functional) meanings for mental states.

Dretske seems to be trying to do two things at one stroke: first, he wants to draw a principled (and all-or-nothing) distinction between free-floating and—shall we say?—"fully appreciated" rationales; and second, he wants to remove all interpretive slack in the specification of the "actual" or "real" meaning of any such appreciated meaning-states. After all, if we appeal to our introspective intuitions, that is just how it seems: not only is there something we mean by our thoughts—something utterly determinate even if sometimes publicly ineffable—but it is our recognition or appreciation of *that meaning* that explains what we thereupon do. There certainly is a vast difference between the extremes represented by the fledgling cuckoo and, say, the cool-headed and cold-blooded human murderer who "knows just what he is doing, and why," but Dretske wants to turn it into the wrong sort of difference. Echoing Searle, Dretske would sharply distinguish between syntax and semantics: in the human murderer, he would say, "it is the structure's having this meaning (its semantics), not just the structure that has this meaning (the syntax), which is relevant to explaining behavior" (personal correspondence; cf. Dretske 1985, p. 31). Even supposing Dretske could motivate the placement of such a threshold, dividing the spectrum of increasingly sophisticated cases into those where syntax does all the work and those where semantics comes unignorably into play, it is out of the question that the rigors of a learning history could break through *that* barrier, and somehow show an organism what its internal states "really meant."

Furthermore, *if* Dretske's learning-history move worked for learned representations, the very same move could work for innate representations "learned" by the organism's ancestors via natural selection over the eons. That is, after all, how we explain the advent of innate mechanisms—as arising out of a trial-and-error selection process over time. If, as Dretske supposes, "soft"-wiring can acquire natural functional meaning during an organism's lifetime, thanks to its relations to environmental events, "hard"-wiring could acquire the same natural functional meaning over the lifetime of the species.

And again, when do we blow the whistle and freeze, for all future time, the meaning of such a designed item? What started out as a two-bitser can become a q-balber; what started out as a wrist bone can become a panda's thumb (Gould 1980), and what started out as an innate representation meaning one thing to an organism can come, over time in a new environment, to mean something else to that organism's progeny. (There are further problems with Dretske's account, some well addressed by Fodor, but I will pass over them.)

What, then, does Fodor propose in place of Dretske's account? He too is exercised by the need for an account of how we can pin an error on an organism. ("No representation without misrepresentation" would be a good Fodorian motto.) And like Dretske, he draws the distinction between derivative and original intentionality:

I'm prepared that it should turn out that smoke and tree rings represent only relative to our interests in predicting fires and ascertaining the ages of trees, that thermostats represent only relative to our interest in keeping the room warm, and that English words represent only relative to our intention to use them to communicate our thoughts. I'm prepared, that is, that only mental states (hence, according to RTM [the Representational Theory of Mind], only mental representations) should turn out to have semantic properties *in the first instance;* hence, that a naturalized semantics should apply, strictu dictu, to mental representations only. (Fodor 1987, p. 99)

And then, like Dretske, he faces what he calls the disjunction problem. What principled or objective grounds can we have for saying the state means "quarter here now" (and hence is an error, when it occurs in perceptual response to a slug) instead of meaning "quarter *or* quarter-balboa *or* slug of kind *K or* . . ." (and hence, invariably, is not an error at all)? Fodor is no more immune than Dretske (or anyone else) to the fatal lure of teleology, of discovering what the relevant mechanism is "supposed to do," but he manfully resists:

I'm not sure that this teleology/optimality account is false, but I do find it thoroughly unsatisfying. . . . I think maybe we can get a theory of error without relying on notions of optimality or teleology; and if we can, we should. All else being equal, the less Pop-Darwinism the better, surely. (Fodor 1987, pp. 105–6)

I appreciate the candor with which Fodor expresses his discomfort with appeals to evolutionary hypotheses. (Elsewhere he finds he must help himself to a bit of "vulgar Darwinism" to buttress an account he needs of the functions of transducers.) Why, though, should he be so unwilling to follow down the path? Because he sees (I gather) that the most one can ever get from any such story, however well buttressed by scrupulously gathered facts from the fossil record, etc., is a story with all the potential for indeterminacy that we found in the tale of the transported two-bitser. And Fodor wants real, original, intrinsic meaning—not for the states of artifacts, heaven knows, for Searle is right about them!—but for our own mental representations.

Does Fodor have an account that will work better than Dretske's? No. His is equally ingenious, and equally forlorn. Suppose, Fodor says, "I see a cow which, stupidly, I misidentify. I take it, say, to be a horse. So taking it causes me to effect the tokening of a symbol; viz., I say 'horse'." There is an asymmetry, Fodor argues, between the causal relations that hold between horses and "horse" tokenings on the one hand and between cows and "horse" tokenings on the other:

In particular, misidentifying a cow as a horse wouldn't have led me to say 'horse' *except that there was independently a semantic relation between 'horse' tokenings and horses.* But for the fact that the word 'horse' expresses the property of *being a horse* (i.e., but for the fact that one calls *horses* 'horses'), it would not have been *that* word that taking a cow to be a horse would have caused me to utter. Whereas, by contrast, since 'horse' does mean *horse*, the fact that horses cause me to say 'horse' does not depend upon there being semantic—or, indeed, any—connection between 'horse' tokenings and cows. (Fodor 1987, pp. 107–8)

This doctrine of Fodor's then gets spelled out in terms of counterfactuals that hold under various circumstances. Again, without going into the details (for which see Akins, unpublished), let me just say that the trouble is that our nagging problem arises all over again. How does Fodor establish that, in his mental idiolect, "horse" means *horse*—and not *horse-or-other-quadruped-resembling-a-horse* (or something like that)? Either Fodor must go Searle's introspective route and declare that this is something he can just tell, from the inside, or he must appeal to the very sorts of design considerations, and the "teleology/optimality story" that he wants to resist. Those of us who have always loved to tell that story can only hope that he will come to acquire a taste for it, especially when he realizes how unpalatable and hard to swallow the alternatives are.

This brings me to Burge, who has also constructed a series of intuition pumps designed to reveal the truth to us about error. Burge has been arguing in a series of papers against a doctrine he calls *individualism*, a thesis about what facts settle questions about the content or meaning of an organism's mental states. According to individualism,

an individual's intentional states and events (types and tokens) could not be different from what they are, given the individual's physical, chemical, neural, or functional histories, where these histories are specified nonintentionally and in a way that is independent of physical or social conditions outside the individual's body. (1986, p. 4)

Or in other words:

The meaning or content of an individual's internal states could not be different from what it is, given the individual's *internal* history and constitution (considered independent of conditions outside its "body").

The falsehood of this thesis should not surprise us. After all, individualism is false of such simple items as two-bitsers. We changed the meaning of the two-bitser's internal state by simply moving it to Panama and giving it a new job to perform. Nothing structural or physical inside it changed, but the meaning of one of its states changed from Q to QB in virtue of its changed embedding in the world. In order to attribute meaning to functional states of an artifact, you have to depend on assumptions about what it is supposed to do, and in order to get any leverage about that, you have to look to the wider world of purposes and prowesses. Burge's anti-individualistic thesis is then simply a special case of a very familiar observation: functional characterizations are relative not only to the embedding environment, but also to assumptions about optimality of design. (See, e.g., Wimsatt 1974. Burge seems to appreciate this in footnote 18 on p. 35.)

Moreover, Burge supports his anti-individualism with arguments that appeal to just the considerations that motivated our treatment of the two-bitser. For instance, he offers an extended argument (pp. 41ff) about a "person P who normally correctly perceives instances of a particular objective visible property O" by going into state O' and it turns out that in some circumstances, a different visible property, C, puts P into state O'. We can substitute "two-bitser" for "P", "Q" for "O", "quarter" for "O", and "quarter-balboa" for "C", and notice that his argument is our old friend, without addition or omission.

But something is different: Burge leaves no room for indeterminacy of content; his formulations always presume that there is a fact of the matter about what something *precisely* means. And he makes it clear that he means to disassociate himself from the "stance-dependent" school of functional interpretation. He chooses to "ignore generalized arguments that mentalistic ascriptions are deeply indeterminate" (1986, p. 6) and announces his Realism by noting that psychology seems to presuppose the reality of beliefs and desires, and it seems to work. That is, psychology makes use of interpreted that-clauses, "—or what we might loosely call 'intentional content'." He adds, "I have seen no sound reason to believe that this use is merely heuristic, instrumentalistic, or second class in any other sense." (p. 8) That is why his thesis of anti-individualism seems so striking; he seems to be arguing for the remarkable view that *intrinsic* intentionality, *original* intentionality, is just as context sensitive as derived intentionality.

Although Burge, like Dretske and Fodor, is drawn inexorably to evolutionary considerations, he fails to see that his reliance on those very considerations must force him to give up his uncomplicated Realism about content. For instance, he champions Marr's (1982) theory of vision as a properly anti-individualistic instance of successful psychology without noticing that Marr's account is, like "engineering" accounts generally, dependent on strong (indeed too strong—

see Ramachandran, 1985a,b) optimality assumptions that depend on making sense of *what Mother Nature had in mind* for various subcomponents of the visual system. Without the tactic I have been calling artifact hermeneutics, Marr would be bereft of any principle for assigning content. Burge himself enunciates the upshot of the tactic:

> The methods of individuation and explanation are governed by the assumption that the subject has adapted to his or her environment sufficiently to obtain veridical information from it under certain normal conditions. If the properties and relations that *normally* caused visual impressions were regularly different from what they are, the individual would obtain different information and have visual experiences with different intentional content. (p. 35)

When we attribute content to some state or structure in Marr's model of vision, we must defend our attribution by claiming (in a paraphrase of Dretske on assigned functional meaning) that that is the function Mother Nature assigned this structure, the reason why it was built, and the explanation for why it was built the way it was. Had her purposes been otherwise, it might have meant$_f$ something else.

The method Burge endorses, then, must make the *methodological* assumption that the subject has adapted to his or her environment sufficiently so that when we come to assigning contents to the subject's states—when we adopt the intentional stance—the dictated attributions are those that come out veridical, *and useful.* Without the latter condition, Burge will be stuck with Fodor's and Dretske's problem of disjunctive dissipation of content, because you can always get veridicality at the expense of utility by adding disjuncts. Utility, however, is not an objective, determinate property, as the example of the two-bitser made clear. So contrary to what Burge assumes, he must relinquish the very feature that makes his conclusion so initially intriguing: his Realism about "intentional content," or in other words his belief that there is a variety of intrinsic or original intentionality that is not captured by our strategies for dealing with merely derived intentionality like that of the two-bitser.

The Realism about intentional content that Burge assumes, along with Fodor and the others, is also presupposed by Putnam, whose Twin Earth thought experiments (Putnam 1975a) set the agenda for much recent work on these issues. We can see this clearly, now, by contrasting our two-bitser with a Putnamian example. In the case of the two-bitser, the laws of nature do not suffice to single out what its internal state *really means*—except on pain of making misrepresentation impossible. Relative to one rival interpretation or another, various of its moves count as errors, various of its states count as misrepresentations, but beyond the resources of artifact hermeneutics there are no deeper facts to settle disagreements.

Consider then the members of a Putnamian tribe who have a word, "glug," let us say, for the invisible, explosive gas they encounter in their marshes now and then. When we confront them with some acetylene, and they call it glug, are they making a mistake or not? All the gaseous hydrocarbon they have ever heretofore encountered, we can suppose, was methane, but they are unsophisticated about chemistry, so there is no ground to be discovered in their past behavior or current dispositions that would license a description of their glug-state as methane-detection *rather than* the more inclusive gaseous-hydrocarbon-detection. Presumably, gaseous hydrocarbon is a "natural kind" and so are its subspecies, acetylene, methane, propane, and their cousins. So the laws of nature will not suffice to favor one reading over the other. Is there a deeper fact of the matter, however, about what they *really mean* by "glug"? Of course once we educate them, they will have to *come* to mean one thing or the other by "glug," but in advance of these rather sweeping changes in their cognitive states, will there already be a fact about whether they believe the proposition that *there is methane present* or the proposition that *there is gaseous hydrocarbon present* when they express themselves by saying "Glug!"?

If, as seems likely, no answer can be wrung from exploitation of the intentional stance in their case, I would claim (along with Quine and the others on my side) that the meaning of their belief is simply indeterminate in this regard. It is not just that I can't tell, and they can't tell; there is nothing to tell. But Putnam, where he is being a Realist about intentional content (see chapter 10), would hold that there is a further fact, however inaccessible to us interpreters, that settles the questions about which cases of glug identification don't merely *count as* but *really are* errors, given what "glug" really means. Is this deeper fact any more accessible to the natives than to us outsiders? Realists divide on that question.

Burge and Dretske argue against the traditional doctrine of privileged access, and Searle and Fodor are at least extremely reluctant to acknowledge that their thinking ever rests on any appeal to such an outmoded idea. Kripke, however, is still willing to bring this skeleton out of the closet. In Kripke's (1982) resurrection of Wittgenstein's puzzle about rule following, we find all our themes returning once more: a resistance to the machine analogy on grounds that meaning in machines is relative to "the intentions of the designer" (p. 34), and the immediately attendant problem of error:

> How is it determined when a malfunction occurs? . . . Depending on the intent of the designer, any particular phenomenon may or may not count as a machine malfunction. . . . Whether a machine ever malfunctions and, if so, when, is not a property of the machine itself as a physical object but is well defined only in terms of its program, as stipulated by its designer. (pp. 34–35)

This familiar declaration about the relativity and derivativeness of machine meaning is coupled with a frank unwillingness on Kripke's part to offer the same analysis in the case of human "malfunction." Why? Because it suggests that our own meaning would be as derivative, as inaccessible to us directly, as to any artifact:

> The idea that we lack "direct" access to the facts whether we mean plus or quus [Q or QB, in the two-bitser's case] is bizarre in any case. Do I not know, directly, and with a fair degree of certainty, that I mean plus? . . . There may be some facts about me to which my access is indirect, and about which I must form tentative hypotheses: but surely the fact as to what I mean by "plus" is not one of them! (p. 40)

This declaration is not necessarily Kripke speaking *in propria persona*, for it occurs in the midst of a dialectical response Kripke thinks Wittgenstein would make to a particular skeptical challenge, but he neglects to put any rebuttal in the mouth of the skeptic and is willing to acknowledge his sympathy for the position expressed.

And why not? Here, I think, we find as powerful and direct an expression as could be of the intuition that lies behind the belief in original intentionality. This is the doctrine Ruth Millikan calls *meaning rationalism*, and it is one of the central burdens of her important book, *Language, Thought, and Other Biological Categories*, to topple it from its traditional pedestal (Millikan 1984; see also Millikan, unpublished). Something has to give. Either you must abandon meaning rationalism—the idea that you are unlike the fledging cuckoo not only in having access, but also in having privileged access to your meanings—or you must abandon the naturalism that insists that you are, after all, just a product of natural selection, whose intentionality is thus derivative and hence potentially indeterminate.

Is Function in the Eye of the Beholder?

Attributions of intentional states to us cannot be sustained, I have claimed, without appeal to assumptions about "what Mother Nature had in mind," and now that we can see just how much weight that appeal must bear, it is high time to cash out the metaphor carefully.

Some have seen contradiction or at least an irresolvable tension, a symptom of deep theoretical incoherence, in my apparently willful use of anthropomorphic—more specifically, intentional—idioms to describe a process which I insist in the same breath to be mechanical, goalless, and lacking in foresight. Intentionality, according to Brentano, is supposed to be the "mark of the mental" and yet the chief beauty of the Darwinian theory is its elimination of Mind from the account of biological origins. What serious purpose could be served, then, by such a flagrantly deceptive metaphor? The same challenge could be put to Dawkins: How can it be wise to encourage people to think of natural selection as a watchmaker, while adding that this watchmaker is not only blind, but not even *trying* to make watches?

We can see more clearly the utility—in fact the inescapable utility— of the intentional stance in biology by looking at some other instances of its application. Genes are not the only micro-agents granted apparently mindful powers by sober biologists. Consider the following passages from L. Stryer's *Biochemistry* (1981) quoted by Alexander Rosenberg in "Intention and Action Among the Macromolecules" (1986b):

A much more demanding *task* for these enzymes is to *discriminate* between similar amino acids. . . . However, the observed *error* frequency in vivo is only 1 in 3000, indicating that there must be subsequent *editing* steps to enhance fidelity. In fact the synthetase *corrects* its own *errors*. . . . How does the synthetase *avoid* hydrolyzing isoleucine-AMP, the *desired* intermediate? (pp. 664–65; Rosenberg's emphases)

It seems obvious that this is mere *as if* intentionality, a theorist's fiction, useful no doubt, but not to be taken seriously and literally. Macromolecules do not literally avoid anything or desire anything or discriminate anything. We, the interpreters or theorists, *make sense* of these processes by endowing them with mentalistic interpretations, but (one wants to say) the intentionality we attribute in these instances is neither real intrinsic intentionality, nor real derived intentionality, but mere *as if* intentionality.

The "cash value" of these metaphors, like the cash value of the metaphors about selfishness in genes that Dawkins scrupulously provides, is relatively close at hand. According to Rosenberg, "every state of a macromolecule which can be described in cognitive terms has both a unique, manageably long, purely physical characterization, and a unique, manageably describable disjunction of consequences" (p. 72), but this may be more an expression of an ideal that microbiologists firmly believe to be within their reach than an uncontroversial *fait accompli*. In similar fashion we could assure each other that for every vending machine known to exist, there is a unique, manageably long, manageably describable account of how it works, what would trick it, and why. That is, there are no mysteriously powerful coin detectors. Still, we can identify coin detectors as such—we can figure out that this is the competence that explains their existence—long before we know how to explain, mechanically, how that competence is achieved (or better: approximated).

Pending completion of our mechanical knowledge, we need the intentional characterizations of biology to keep track of what we are trying to explain, and even after we have all our mechanical explanations in place, we will continue to need the intentional level against which to measure the bargains Mother Nature has struck (see Dennett, forthcoming b).

This might be held sufficient methodological justification for the strategy of attributing intentional states to simple biological systems, but there is a further challenge to be considered. Rosenberg endorses the view—developed by many, but especially argued for in Dennett (1969 and 1983a)—that a defining mark of intentionality is failure of substitution ("intensionality") in the idioms that must be used to characterize the phenomena. He then notes that the biologists' attributions to macromolecules, selfish genes, and the like do not meet this condition; one can substitute ad lib without worry about a change in truth value, so long as the "subject" (the believer or desirer) is a gene or a macromolecule or some such simple mechanism. For instance, the proofreading enzyme does not recognize the error it corrects *qua* error. And it is not that the synthetase itself *desires* that isoleucine-AMP be the intermediate amino acid; it has no conception of isoleucine *qua* intermediate.

The disappearance of intensionality at the macromolecular level at first seems a telling objection to the persistent use of intentional idioms to characterize that level, but if we leave it at that we miss a still deeper level at which the missing intensionality reappears. The synthetase may not desire that isoleucine-AMP be the intermediate amino acid, but it is only *qua* intermediate that the isoleucine is "desired" at all—as an unsubstitutable part in a design whose rationale is "appreciated" by the process of natural selection itself. And while the proofreading enzyme has no inkling that it is correcting errors *qua* errors, Mother Nature does! That is, it is only *qua* error that the items thus eliminated provoked the creation of the "proofreading" competence of the enzymes in the first place. The enzyme itself is just one of Nature's lowly soldiers, "theirs not to reason why, theirs but to do or die," but *there is* a reason why they do what they do, a reason "recognized" by natural selection itself.

Is there a reason, really, why these enzymes do what they do? Some biologists, peering into the abyss that has just opened, are tempted to renounce *all* talk of function and purpose, and they are right about one thing: there is no stable intermediate position.[5] If you are prepared to make any claims about the function of biological entities—for instance, if you want to maintain that it is perfectly respectable to say that eyes are for seeing and the eagle's wings for flying—then you take on a commitment to the principle that natural *selection* is well named. In Sober's (1984) terms, there is not just selection *of* features but selection *for* features. If you proceed to assert such claims, you find that they resist substitution in the classical manner of intentional contexts. Just as George IV wondered whether Scott was the author of *Waverley* without wondering whether Scott was Scott, so natural selection "desired" that isoleucine be the intermediate without desiring that isoleucine be isoleucine. And without this "discriminating" prowess of natural selection, we would not be able to sustain functional interpretations at all.

Certainly we can describe all processes of natural selection without appeal to such intentional language, but at enormous cost of cumbersomeness, lack of generality, and unwanted detail. We would miss the pattern that was there, the pattern that permits prediction and

---

5. Rosenberg (1986b):

Among evolutionary biologists, there are those who condemn the identification of anatomical structures as having specific adaptational significance, on the ground that such structures do not face selection individually, but only in the company of the rest of the organism. This makes ascriptions of adaptational "content" to a part of the organism indeterminate, since a different ascription together with other adjustments in our adaptational identifications can result in the same level of fitness for the whole organism. In the philosophy of psychology, the dual of this thesis is reflected in the indeterminacy of interpretation.

supports counterfactuals. The "why" questions we can ask about the engineering of our robot, which have answers that allude to the conscious, deliberate, explicit reasonings of the engineers (in most cases) have their parallels when the topic is organisms and their "engineering." If we work out the rationales of these bits of organic genius, we will be left having to attribute—but not in any mysterious way—an emergent appreciation or recognition of those rationales to natural selection itself.

How can natural selection do this without intelligence? It does not consciously seek out these rationales, but when it stumbles on them, the brute requirements of replication ensure that it "recognizes" their value. The illusion of intelligence is created because of our limited perspective on the process; evolution may well have tried all the "stupid moves" in addition to the "smart moves," but the stupid moves, being failures, disappeared from view. All we see is the unbroken string of triumphs.[6] When we set ourselves the task of explaining why *those* were the triumphs, we uncover the reasons for things—the reasons already "acknowledged" by the relative success of organisms endowed with those things.

The original reasons, and the original responses that "tracked" them, were not ours, or our mammalian ancestors', but Nature's. Nature appreciated these reasons without representing them.[7] And the design process itself is the source of our own intentionality. We, the reason-representers, the self-representers, are a late and specialized product. What this representation of our reasons gives us is foresight: the real-time anticipatory power that Mother Nature wholly

6. This illusion has the same explanation as the illusion exploited by con artists in "the touting pyramid" (Dennett 1984d, pp. 92ff). Schull (forthcoming) argues that the process of natural selection need not always be *perfectly* stupid, brute force trial and error of all possibilities. Thanks to the Baldwin effect, for instance, species themselves can be said to pretest some of the possibilities in phenotypic space, permitting a more efficient exploration by the genome of the full space of the adaptive landscape. Just as creatures who can "try out options in their heads" before committing themselves to action are smarter than those merely Skinnerian creatures that can only learn by real-world trial and error (Dennett 1974a), so species that "try out options in their phenotypic plasticity" can—without any Lamarckian magic—give Mother Nature a helping hand in their own redesign.

7. Pursuing Schull's (forthcoming) extension of the application of the intentional stance to species, we can see that in one sense there is representation in the process of natural selection after all, in the history of variable proliferation of phenotypic "expressions" of genotypic ideas. For instance, we could say of a particular species that various of its subpopulations had "evaluated" particular design options and returned to the species' gene pool with their verdicts, some of which were accepted by the species.

lacks. As a late and specialized product, a triumph of Mother Nature's high tech, our intentionality is highly derived, and in just the same way that the intentionality of our robots (and even our books and maps) is derived. A shopping list in the head has no more intrinsic intentionality than a shopping list on a piece of paper. What the items on the list mean (if anything) is fixed by the role they play in the larger scheme of purposes. We may call our own intentionality real, but we must recognize that it is derived from the intentionality of natural selection, which is just as real—but just less easily discerned because of the vast difference in time scale and size.

So if there is to be any original intentionality—original just in the sense of being derived from no other, ulterior source—the intentionality of natural selection deserves the honor. What is particularly satisfying about this is that we end the threatened regress of derivation with something of the right metaphysical sort: a *blind* and *unrepresenting* source of our own sightful and insightful powers of representation. As Millikan (unpublished, ms. p. 8) says, "The *root* purposing here must be unexpressed purposing."

This solves the regress problem only by raising what will still seem to be a problem to anyone who still believes in intrinsic, determinate intentionality. Since in the beginning was *not* the Word, there is no text which one might consult to resolve unsettled questions about function, and hence about meaning. But remember: the idea that a word—even a Word—*could* so wear its meaning on its sleeve that it could settle such a question is itself a dead end.

There is one more powerful illusion to scout. We think we have a good model of *determinate*, incontrovertible function because we have cases of conscious, deliberate design of which we know, in as much detail as you like, the history. We *know* the *raison d'être* of a pocket watch, or of a laying hen, because the people who designed (or redesigned) them have told us, in words we understand, exactly what they had in mind. It is important to recognize, however, that however incontrovertible these historical facts may be, their projections into the future have no guaranteed significance. Someone might set out with the most fervent, articulate and clear-sighted goal of making a pocket watch and succeed in making something that was either a terrible, useless pocket watch or a serendipitously superb paperweight. Which is it? One can always insist that a thing is, essentially, what its creator set out for it to be, and then when the historical facts leave scant doubt about that psychological fact, the identity of the thing is beyond question. In literary criticism, such insistence is known, tendentiously but traditionally, as the Intentional Fallacy. It has long been argued in such circles that one does not *settle* any questions of the meaning of a text (or other artistic creation) by "asking the author." If one sets aside the author, the original creator, as a definitive and privileged guide to meaning, one can suppose that subsequent readers (users, selecters) are just as important signposts to "the" meaning of something, but of course they are just as fallible—if their endorsements are taken as predictors of *future* significance—and otherwise their endorsements are just more inert historical facts. So even the role of the Pepsi-Cola franchise holder in selecting the two-bitser *as* a q-balber is only one more event in the life history of the device in as much need of interpretation as any other— for this entrepreneur may be a fool. Curiously, then, we get *better* grounds for making reliable functional attributions (functional attributions that are likely to continue to be valuable aids to interpretation in the future) when we ignore "what people say" and read what function we can off the discernible prowesses of the objects in question, rather than off the history of design development.

We cannot begin to make sense of functional attributions until we abandon the idea that there has to be one, determinate, *right* answer to the question: What is it for? And if there is no deeper fact that could settle that question, there can be no deeper fact to settle its twin: What does it mean?[8]

Philosophers are not alone in their uneasiness with appeals to optimality of design and to what Mother Nature must have had in mind. The debate in biology between the adaptationists and their critics is a different front in the same edgy war (see chapter 7). The kinship of the issues comes out most clearly, perhaps, in Stephen Jay Gould's reflections on the panda's thumb. A central theme in evolutionary theory, from Darwin to the present (especially in the writings of François Jacob (1977) on the *bricolage* or "tinkering" of evolutionary design processes, and in those of Gould himself) is that Mother Nature is a satisficer, an opportunistic maker-do, not "an ideal engineer" (Gould 1980, p. 20). The panda's celebrated thumb "is not,

---

8. Quine's thesis of the indeterminacy of radical translation is thus of a piece with his attack on essentialism; if things had real, intrinsic essences, they could have real, intrinsic meanings. Philosophers have tended to find Quine's skepticism about ultimate meanings much less credible than his animadversions against ultimate essences, but that just shows the insidious grip of meaning rationalism on philosophers.

anatomically, a finger at all" (p. 22), but a sesamoid bone of the wrist, wrest from its earlier role and pressed into service (via some redesigning) *as* a thumb. "The sesamoid thumb wins no prize in an engineer's derby . . . But it does its job." (p. 24) That is to say, it does its job *excellently*—and that is how we can be so sure what its job is; it is obvious what this appendage is *for*. So is it just like the q-balber that began life as a two-bitser? Gould quotes Darwin himself:

> Although an organ may not have been originally formed for some special purpose, if it now serves for this end we are justified in saying that it is specially contrived for it. On the same principle, if a man were to make a machine for some special purpose, but were to use old wheels, springs, and pulleys, only slightly altered, the whole machine, with all its parts, might be said to be specially contrived for that purpose. Thus throughout nature almost every part of each living being has probably served, in a slightly modified condition, for diverse purposes, and has acted in the living machinery of many ancient and distinct specific forms.

"We may not be flattered," Gould goes on to say, "by the metaphor of refurbished wheels and pulleys, but consider how well we work." (p. 26) From this passage it would seem that Gould was an unproblematic supporter of the methodology of reading function off prowess—which is certainly what Darwin is endorsing. But in fact, Gould is a well-known critic of adaptationist thinking, who finds a "paradox" (p. 20) in this mixture of tinkering and teleology. There is no paradox; there is only the "functional indeterminacy" that Dretske and Fodor see and shun. Mother Nature doesn't commit herself explicitly and objectively to *any* functional attributions; all such attributions depend on the mind-set of the intentional stance, in which we assume optimality in order to interpret what we find. The panda's thumb was no more *really* a wrist bone than it is a thumb. We will not likely be discomfited, in our interpretation, if we consider it *as* a thumb, but that is the best we can say, here or anywhere.[9]

---

9. We can complete our tour of two-bitser examples in the literature by considering Sober's discussion (1984) of the vexing problem of whether to call the *very first* dorsal fins to appear on a Stegosaurus an adaptation *for cooling*:

> Suppose the animal had the trait because of a mutation, rather than by selection. Can we say that the trait was an adaptation *in the case of that single organism*? Here are some options: (1) apply the concept of adaptation to historically persisting populations, not single organisms; (2) allow that dorsal fins were an adaptation for the original organism because of what happened later; (3) deny that dorsal fins are adaptations for the initial

After all these years we are still just coming to terms with this unsettling implication of Darwin's destruction of the Argument from Design: there is no ultimate User's Manual in which the *real* functions, and *real* meanings, of biological artifacts are officially represented. There is no more bedrock for what we might call original functionality than there is for its cognitivistic scion, original intentionality. You can't have realism about meanings without realism about functions. As Gould notes, "we may not be flattered"—especially when we apply the moral to our sense of our own authority about meanings—but we have no other reason to disbelieve it.

---

organism but are adaptations when they occur in subsequent organisms. My inclination is to prefer choice 3. (p. 197)

See also his discussion of the functional significance of the skin-thickness of *Drosophila* moved to different environments (pp. 209–10), and his discussion (p. 306) of how one might figure out which properties are being selected *for* by Mother Nature (now in the guise of Dawkins's crew coach): "Was the coach selecting for combinations of rowers? Was he selecting for particular rowers? We need not psychoanalyze the coach to find out." Not psychoanalysis, but at least the adoption of the intentional stance will help us do the reverse engineering we need to do to get any answers to this question.

9   Fast Thinking

One last time let us reconsider John Searle's Chinese Room Argument (Searle 1980 and forthcoming). This argument purports to show the futility of "strong AI," the view that "the appropriately programmed digital computer with the right inputs and outputs would thereby have a mind in exactly the sense that human beings have minds." (Searle, forthcoming) His argument, he keeps insisting, is "very simple"; one gathers that only a fool or a fanatic could fail to be persuaded by it.[1]

I think it might be fruitful to approach these oft-debated claims from a substantially different point of view. There is no point in reviewing, yet another time, the story of the Chinese Room and the competing diagnoses of what is going on in it. (The uninitiated can find Searle's original article, reprinted correctly in its entirety, followed by what is still the definitive diagnosis of its workings, in Hofstadter and Dennett 1981, pp. 353–82.) The Chinese Room is not itself the argument, in any case, but rather just an intuition pump, as Searle acknowledges: "The point of the parable of the Chinese room is simply to remind us of the truth of this rather obvious point: the man in the room has all the syntax we can give him, but he does not thereby acquire the relevant semantics." (Searle, forthcoming)

Here is Searle's very simple argument, verbatim:

Earlier versions of ideas in this chapter appeared in "The Role of the Computer Metaphor in Understanding the Mind" (1984e) and portions are drawn from "The Myth of Original Intentionality," in W. Newton Smith and R. Viale, eds., *Modelling the Mind* (Oxford: Oxford University Press, forthcoming) and reprinted with permission.

1. "It can no longer be doubted that the classical conception of AI, the view that I have called strong AI, is pretty much obviously false and rests on very simple mistakes." (Searle, forthcoming, ms. p. 5)

Proposition 1. Programs are purely formal (i.e., syntactical).

Proposition 2. Syntax is neither equivalent to nor sufficient by itself for semantics.

Proposition 3. Minds have mental contents (i.e., semantic contents).

Conclusion 1. Having a program—any program by itself—is neither sufficient for nor equivalent to having a mind.

Searle challenges his opponents to show explicitly what they think is wrong with the argument, and I will do just that, concentrating first on the conclusion, which, for all its apparent simplicity and straightforwardness, is subtly ambiguous. I start with the conclusion because I have learned that many of Searle's supporters are much surer of his conclusion than they are of the path by which he arrives at it, so they tend to view criticisms of the steps as mere academic caviling. Once we have seen what is wrong with the conclusion, we can go back to diagnose the missteps that led Searle there.

Why are some people so sure of the conclusion? Perhaps partly, I gather, because they so intensely want it to be true. (One of the few aspects of the prolonged debate about Searle's thought experiment that has fascinated me is the intensity of feeling with which many— lay people, scientists, philosophers—embrace Searle's conclusion.) But also, perhaps, because they are mistaking it for a much more defensible near neighbor, with which it is easily confused. One might well suppose the following two propositions came to much the same thing.

(S) No computer program by itself could ever be sufficient to produce what an organic human brain, with its particular causal powers, demonstrably can produce: mental phenomena with intentional content.

(D) There is no way an electronic digital computer could be programmed so that it could produce what an organic human brain, with its particular causal powers, demonstrably can produce: control of the swift, intelligent, intentional activity exhibited by normal human beings.

As the initials suggest, Searle has endorsed proposition (S), as a version of his conclusion, and I am about to present an argument for proposition (D), which will be sharply distinguishable from Searle's version only after we see how the argument runs. I think that proposition (S), given what Searle means by it, is incoherent—for reasons I will explain in due course. I am not convinced that proposition (D) is true, but I take it to be a coherent empirical claim for which there is something interesting to be said. I am certain, moreover, that (D) is not at all what Searle is claiming in (S)—and this Searle has confirmed to me in personal correspondence—and that my defense of (D) is consistent with my defense of strong AI.

So anyone who thinks that no believer in strong AI could accept (D), or who thinks (S) and (D) are equivalent, or who thinks that (D) follows from (S) (or vice versa), should be interested to see how one can argue for one without the other. The crucial difference is that while both Searle and I are impressed by the causal powers of the human brain, we disagree completely about which causal powers matter and why. So my task is ultimately to isolate Searle's supposed causal powers of the brain and to show how strange—how ultimately incoherent—they are.

First we must clear up a minor confusion about what Searle means by a "computer program by itself." There is a sense in which it is perfectly obvious that no program *by itself* can produce either of the effects mentioned in (S) and (D): no computer program lying unimplemented on the shelf, a mere abstract sequence of symbols, can cause anything. By itself (in this sense) no computer program can even add 2 and 2 and get 4; in this sense, no computer program by itself can cause word processing to occur, let alone produce mental phenomena with intentional content.

Perhaps some of the conviction that Searle has generated to the effect that it is *just obvious* that no computer program "by itself" could "produce intentionality" actually derives from confusing this obvious (and irrelevant) claim with something more substantive—and dubious: that no concretely implemented, running computer program could "produce intentionality." But only the latter claim is a challenge to AI, so let us assume that Searle, at least, is utterly unconfused about this and thinks that he has shown that no running, material embodiment of a "formal" computer program could "produce intentionality" or be capable of "causing mental phenomena" (Searle 1982) purely in virtue of its being an embodiment of such a formal program.

Searle's view, then, comes to this: take a material object (any material object) that does *not* have the power of causing mental phenomena; you cannot turn it into an object that *does* have the power of producing mental phenomena simply by programming it— reorganizing the conditional dependencies of the transitions between its states. The *crucial* causal powers of brains have nothing to do with the programs they might be said to be running, so "giving something the right program" could not be a way of giving it a mind.

My view, to the contrary, is that such programming, such redesign of an object's state transition regularities, is precisely what could give something a mind (in the only sense that makes sense)—but that, in fact, it is empirically unlikely that the right sorts of programs can be run on anything but organic, human brains! To see why this might be so, let us consider a series of inconclusive arguments, each of which gives ground (while extracting a price).

Edwin A. Abbott's amusing fantasy *Flatland: A Romance in Many Dimensions* (1884) tells the story of intelligent beings living in a two-dimensional world. Some spoilsport whose name I have fortunately forgotten once objected that the Flatland story could not be true (who ever thought otherwise?) because there could not be an intelligent being in only two dimensions. In order to be intelligent, this skeptic argued, one needs a richly interconnected brain (or nervous system or *some* kind of complex, highly interconnected control system) and in only two dimensions you cannot wire together even so few as five things each to each other—at least one wire must cross another wire, which will require a third dimension.

This is plausible, but false. John von Neumann proved years ago that a universal Turing machine could be realized in two dimensions, and Conway has actually constructed a universal Turing machine in his two-dimensional Life world. Crossovers are indeed desirable, but there are several ways of doing without them in a computer or in a brain (Dewdney 1984). For instance, there is the way crossovers are often eliminated in highway systems: by "stoplight" intersections, where isolated parcels of information (or whatever) can take turns crossing each other's path. The price one pays, here as on the highway, is speed of transaction. But *in principle* (that is, if time were no object) an entity with a nervous system as interconnected as you please can be realized in two dimensions.

Speed, however, is "of the essence" for intelligence. If you can't figure out the relevant portions of the changing environment fast enough to fend for yourself, you are not *practically* intelligent, however complex you are. Of course all this shows is that *relative* speed is important. In a universe in which the environmental events that mattered unfolded a hundred times slower, an intelligence could slow down by the same factor without any loss; but transported back to our universe it would be worse than moronic. (Are victims of Parkinson's disease with "orthostatic hypotension" demented, or are their brains—as some have suggested—just terribly slowed down but otherwise normal? The condition is none the less crippling if it is "merely" a change of pace.)

It is thus no accident that our brains make use of all three spatial dimensions. This gives us a modest but well-supported empirical conclusion: nothing that wasn't three-dimensional could produce control of the swift, intelligent, intentional activity exhibited by normal human beings.

Digital computers are three-dimensional, but they are—almost all of them—fundamentally *linear* in a certain way. They are von Neumann machines: serial, not parallel, in their architecture and thus capable of doing just one thing at a time. It has become a commonplace these days that although a von Neumann machine, like the universal Turing machine it is descended from, can *in principle* compute anything any computer can compute, many interesting computations—especially in such important cognitive areas as pattern recognition and memory searching—cannot be done in reasonably short lengths of time by them, even if the hardware runs at the absolute speed limit: the speed of light, with microscopic distances between elements. The only way of accomplishing these computations in realistic amounts of real time is to use massively parallel processing hardware. That indeed is why such hardware is now being designed and built in many AI laboratories.

It is no news that the brain gives every evidence of having a massively parallel architecture—millions if not billions of channels wide, all capable of simultaneous activity. This too is no accident, presumably. So the causal powers required to control the swift, intelligent, intentional activity exhibited by normal human beings can be achieved only in a massive parallel processor—such as a human brain. (Note that I have not attempted an *a priori* proof of this; I am content to settle for scientific likelihood.) Still, it may well seem, there is no reason why one's massive parallel processor must be made of organic materials. In fact, transmission speeds in electronic systems are orders of magnitude greater than transmission speeds in nerve fibres, so an electronic parallel system could be thousands of times faster (and more reliable) than any organic system. Perhaps, but then again perhaps not. An illuminating discussion of the relative speed of human brains and existing and projected hardware computers is

given by Sejnowski (forthcoming), who calculates the average processing rate of the brain at 10^{15} operations per second, which is *five
orders of magnitude* faster than even the current crop of electronic
massive parallel processors. Since the ratio of computation speed to
cost has decreased by an order of magnitude five times in the last
thirty-five years, one might extrapolate that in a few decades we will
have affordable, buildable, hardware that can match the brain in
speed, but, Sejnowski surmises, this goal cannot be achieved with
existing electronic technology. Perhaps, he thinks, a shift to optical
computing will provide the breakthrough.

Even if optical computing can provide 10^{15} operations per second
for a reasonable cost, that may not be nearly enough speed. Sejnowski's calculations could prove to underestimate the requirements by
orders of magnitude if the brain makes maximal use of its materials.
We *might* need to switch to *organic* computing to get the necessary
speed. (Here is where the argument for proposition (D) turns highly
speculative and controversial.) Suppose—and this is not very likely,
but hardly disproved—that the information-processing prowess of
any single neuron (its relevant input-output function) depends on
features or activities in subcellular organic molecules. Suppose, that
is, that information processed at the enzyme level (say) played a
critical role in modulating the switching or information processing of
individual neurons—each neuron a tiny computer using its macromolecular innards to compute its very elaborate or "compute-
intensive" input-output function. Then it might in fact *not* be possible
to make a model or simulation of a neuron's behavior that could
duplicate the neuron's information-processing feats *in real time*.

This would be because your computer model would indeed be tiny
and swift, but not so tiny (and hence not so swift) as the individual
molecules being modeled. Even with the speed advantage of elec-
tronics (or optics) over electrochemical transmission in axonal
branches, it might thus turn out that microchips were unable to keep
pace with neuronal intracellular operations on the task of determining just how to modulate those ponderously slow output spikings.

A version of this idea is presented by Jacques Monod, who speaks
of the "'cybernetic' (i.e., teleonomic) power at the disposal of a cell
equipped with hundreds or thousands of these microscopic entities,
all far more clever than the Maxwell-Szilard-Brillouin demon."
(Monod 1971, p. 69) It is an intriguing idea, but on the other hand the
complexity of molecular activity in neuron cell bodies may very well

have only local significance, unconnected to the information-processing tasks of the neurons, in which case the point lapses.

Some think there are more decisive grounds for dismissing Monod's possibility. Rodolfo Llinas has claimed to me in conversation that there is no way for a neuron to harness the lightning speed and "cybernetic power" of its molecules. Although the *individual* molecules can perform swift information processing, they cannot be made to propagate and amplify these effects swiftly. The spiking events in neural axons that they would have to modulate are orders of magnitude larger and more powerful than their own "output" state-changes, and the slow process of diffusion and amplification of their "signal" would squander all the time gained through miniaturization. Other neuroscientists with whom I have talked have been less confident that relatively slow diffusion is the only mechanism available for intracellular communication, but they have offered no positive models of alternatives. This Monod-inspired line of argument for the inescapable biologicality of mental powers, then, is inconclusive at best, and very likely forlorn.

Still, it is mildly instructive. It is far from established that the nodes in one's massively parallel system *must* be neurons with the right stuff inside them, but nevertheless this might be the case. There are other ways in which it might prove to be the case that the inorganic reproduction of the *cognitively essential* information-processing functions of the human brain would have to run slower than their real-time inspirations. After all, we have discovered many complex processes—such as the weather—that cannot be accurately simulated in real time (in time for useful weather prediction, for instance) by even the fastest, largest supercomputers currently in existence. (It is not that the equations governing the transitions are not understood. Even using what we know now is impossible.) Brainstorms may well prove just as hard to simulate and hence predict. If they are, then since speed of operation really is critical to intelligence, merely having the right program is not enough, unless by "right program" we understand a program which can run at the right speed to deal with the inputs and outputs as they present themselves. (Imagine some-one who defended the feasibility of Reagan's SDI project by insisting that the requisite control software—the "right program"—could definitely be written but would run a thousand times too slow to be of any use in intercepting missiles!)

So *if* the information processing in the brain does in fact fully avail itself of the speed of molecular-level computational activity, then the price (in speed) paid by *any* substitutions of material or architecture will prove too costly. Consider again, in this light, proposition (D):

(D) There is no way an electronic digital computer could be programmed so that it could produce what an organic human brain, with its particular causal powers, demonstrably can produce: control of the swift, intelligent, intentional activity exhibited by normal human beings.

(D) might be true for the entirely nonmysterious reason that no such electronic digital computer could run the "right program" fast enough to reproduce the brain's real-time virtuosity. Hardly a knockdown argument, but the important point is that it would be foolish to bet against it, since it might turn out to be true.

But isn't this just the wager that AI has made? Not quite, although some AI enthusiasts have no doubt committed themselves to it. First of all, insofar as we consider AI to be science, concerned to develop and confirm theories about the nature of intelligence or the mind, the prospect that actual digital computers might not run fast enough to be usable in our world as genuine intelligences would be of minor and indirect importance, a serious limitation on investigators' ability to conduct realistic experiments testing their theories, but nothing that would undercut their claim that they had uncovered the essence of mentality. Insofar as we consider AI to be practical engineering, on the other hand, this prospect would be crushing to those who have their hearts set on actually creating a digital-computer-controlled humanoid intelligence, but that feat is as theoretically irrelevant as the stunt of constructing a gall bladder out of atoms. Our inability to achieve these technological goals is scientifically and philosophically uninteresting.

But this quite legitimate way for AI to shrug off the prospect that (D) might be true glosses over a more interesting reason people in AI might reasonably hope that my biochemical speculations are resoundingly falsified. Like any effort at scientific modeling, AI modeling has been attempted in a spirit of opportunistic oversimplification. Things that are horribly complicated may be usefully and revealingly approximated by partitionings, averagings, idealizations, and other deliberate oversimplifications, in the hope that some molar behavior of the complex phenomenon will prove to be relatively independent of all the myriad micro-details, and hence will be reproduced in a model that glosses over those micro-details. For instance, suppose an AI model of, say, action planning requires at some point that a vision subsystem be consulted for information about the layout of the environment. Rather than attempt to model the entire visual system, whose operation is no doubt massively parallel and whose outputs are no doubt voluminously informative, the system designers insert a sort of cheap stand-in: a vision "oracle" that can provide the supersystem with, say, any one of only 256 different "reports" on the relevant layout of the environment. The designers are betting that they can design an action-planning system that will approximate the target competence (perhaps the competence of a five-year-old or a dog, not a mature adult) while availing itself of only eight bits of visual information on environmental layout. Is this a good bet? Perhaps and perhaps not. There is plenty of evidence that human beings simplify their information-handling tasks and avail themselves of only a tiny fraction of the information obtainable by their senses; if this *particular* oversimplification turns out to be a bad bet, it will only mean that we should search for some other oversimplification.

It is by no means obvious that any united combination of the sorts of simplified models and subsystems developed so far in AI can approximate the perspicuous behavior of a normal human being—in real time or even orders of magnitude slower—but that still does not impeach the research methodology of AI, any more than their incapacity to predict real-world weather accurately impeaches all meteorological oversimplifications as scientific models. If AI models have to model "all the way down" to the neuronal or subneuronal level to achieve good results, this will be a serious blow to some of the traditional AI aspirations to steal a march in the campaign to understand how the mind works; but other schools in AI, such as the New Connectionists or Parallel Distributed Processing groups, themselves suggest that such low-level detail will be required in order to produce significant practical intelligence in artificial minds. This division of opinion *within* AI is radical and important. The New Connectionists, for instance, fall so clearly outside the boundaries of the traditional school that Haugeland, in *Artificial Intelligence: The Very Idea* (1985), is obliged to invent an acronym, GOFAI (Good Old Fashioned Artificial Intelligence), for the traditional view, with which his book is largely concerned.

Have I now quietly switched in effect to a defense of "weak AI"— the mere modeling or simulation of psychological or mental phenomena by computer, as opposed to the creation of genuine (but artificial) mental phenomena by computer? Searle has no brief against what he calls weak AI: "Perhaps this is a good place to express my enthusiasm for the prospects of weak AI, the use of the computer as a tool in the study of the mind."(Searle 1982, p. 57) What he is opposed to is the "strong AI belief that the appropriately programmed computer literally has a mind, and its antibiological claim that the specific neurophysiology of the brain is irrelevant to the study of the mind." (p. 57) There are several ways to interpret this characterization of strong AI. I think the following version would meet the approval of most of the partisans.

The only relevance of "the specific neurophysiology of the brain" is in providing the right sort of hardware engineering for real-time intelligence. *If* it turns out that we can get enough speed out of parallel silicon microchip architectures, then neurophysiology will be truly inessential, though certainly valuable for the hints it can provide about architecture.

   Consider two different implementations of the same program—that is, consider two different physical systems, the transitions of each of which are accurately and appropriately describable in the terms of a single "formal" program, but one of which runs six orders of magnitude (about a million times) slower than the other. (Borrowing Searle's favorite example, we can imagine the slow one is made of beer cans tied together with string.) In one sense both implementations have the same capabilities—they both "compute the same function"—but in virtue of nothing but its greater speed, one of them will have "causal powers" the other lacks: namely the causal *control* powers to guide a locomoting body through the real world. We may for this very reason claim that the fast one was "literally a mind" while withholding that honorific from its slow twin. It is not that sheer speed ("intrinsic" speed?) above some critical level creates some mysterious emergent effect, but that relative speed is crucial in enabling the right sorts of environment-organism sequences of interaction to occur. The same effect could be produced by "slowing down the outside world" sufficiently—if that made sense. An appropriately programmed computer—provided only that it is fast enough to interface with the sensory transducers and motor effectors of a "body" (robot or organic)—literally has a mind, whatever its material instantiation, organic or inorganic.

   This, I claim, is all that strong AI is committed to, and Searle has offered no reason to doubt it. We can see how it might still turn out to be true, as proposition (D) proclaims, that there is only one way to skin the mental cat after all, and that is with real, organic neural tissue. It might seem, then, that the issue separating Searle from strong AI and its defenders is a rather trifling difference of opinion about the precise role to be played by details of neurophysiology, but this is not so.

A dramatic difference in implication between propositions (S) and (D) is revealed in a pair of concessions Searle has often made. First, he grants that "just about any system has a level of description where you can describe it as a digital computer. You can describe it as instantiating a formal program. So in that sense, I suppose, all of our brains are digital computers." (Searle 1984, p. 153) Second, he has often conceded that one could, for all he knows, create a brain-like device out of silicon chips (or other AI-approved hardware) that perfectly mimics the real-time input-output behavior of a human brain. (We have just given reasons for doubting what Searle concedes here.)

But even if such a device had exactly the same description at the program level or digital-computer level as the brain whose input-output behavior it mimicked (in real time), this would give us *no reason*—according to Searle—to suppose that it, like the organic brain, could actually "produce intentionality." If that perfect mimicry of the brain's control functions didn't establish that the hardware device was (or "caused" or "produced") a mind, what could shed light on the issue, in Searle's view? He says it is an empirical question, but he doesn't say how, even in principle, he would go about investigating it.

This is a puzzling claim. Although many (both critics and supporters) have misinterpreted him, Searle insists that he has never claimed to show that an organic brain is essential for intentionality. *You* know (by some sort of immediate acquaintance, apparently) that your brain "produces intentionality," whatever it is made of. Nothing in your direct experience of intentionality could tell you your brain is *not* made of silicon chips, for "simply imagine right now that your head is opened up and inside is found not neurons but something else, say, silicon chips. There are no purely logical constraints that exclude any particular type of substance in advance." (forthcoming, ms. p. 1) It is an empirical question, Searle insists, whether silicon chips produce your intentionality, and such a surgical discovery would settle *for you* that silicon chips could indeed produce intentionality, but it wouldn't settle it for anyone else. What if we opened up some third party's head and found silicon chips in it? The fact that they perfectly mimicked the real-time control powers of a human brain would give us no reason at all, on Searle's view, to suppose that the third party had a mind, since "control powers by themselves are irrelevant." (personal communication)

It is just a very obvious empirical fact, Searle insists, that organic brains can produce intentionality. But one wonders how he can have established this empirical fact. Perhaps only some organic brains produce intentionality! Perhaps left-handers brains, for instance, only mimic the control powers of brains that produce genuine intentionality! (Cf. Hofstadter and Dennett, p. 377.) Asking the lefthanders if they have minds is no help, of course, since their brains may just be Chinese rooms.

Surely it is a strange kind of empirical question that is systematically bereft of all intersubjective empirical evidence. So Searle's position on the importance of neurophysiology is that although it is important, indeed all-important, its crucial contribution might be entirely undetectable from the outside. A human body without a real mind, without genuine intentionality, could fend for itself in the real world just as well as a human body with a real mind.

My position, on the other hand, as a supporter of proposition (D), is that neurophysiology is (probably) so important that if ever I see any entity gadding about in the world with the real-time cleverness of, say, C3PO in *Star Wars,* I will be prepared to wager a considerable sum that it is controlled—locally or remotely—by an organic brain. Nothing else (I bet) can control such clever behavior in real time.

That makes me a "behaviorist" in Searle's eyes, and this sort of behaviorism lies at the heart of the disagreement between AI and Searle. But this is the bland "behaviorism" of the physical sciences in general, not any narrow Skinnerian or Watsonian (or Rylean) dogma. Behavior, in this bland sense, includes all intersubjectively observable internal processes and events (such as the behavior of your gut or your RNA). No one complains that models in science only account for the "behavior" of hurricanes or gall bladders or solar systems. What else is there about these phenomena for science to account for? This is what makes the causal powers Searle imagines so mysterious: they have, by his own admission, no telltale effect on behavior (internal or external)—unlike the causal powers I take so seriously: the powers required to guide a body through life, seeing, hearing, acting, talking, deciding, investigating, and so on. It is at least misleading to call such a thoroughly cognitivist and (for example) anti-Skinnerian doctrine as mine behaviorism, but Searle insists on using the term in this way.

Let us review the situation. Searle criticizes AI for not taking neurophysiology and biochemistry seriously. I have suggested a way in which the biochemistry of the brain might indeed play a critical role: by providing the operating speed for fast thinking. But this is not the kind of biochemical causal power Searle has in mind. He supposes there is a "clear distinction between the causal powers of the brain to produce mental states and the causal powers of the brain (together with the rest of the nervous system) to produce input-output relations." (forthcoming, ms. p. 4) The former he calls "bottom-up causal powers of brains," and it takes "but a moment's reflection" to see the falsehood in the idea that the latter are what matters to mentality: "The presence of input-output causation that would enable a robot to function in the world *implies nothing whatever* about bottom-up causation that would produce mental states." The successful robot "might be a total zombie." (forthcoming, ms. p. 5)

So that is the crux for Searle: consciousness, not "semantics." His view rests not, as he says, on "the modern conception of computation and indeed our modern scientific world view" but on the idea, which he thinks is confirmable by anyone with a spare moment in which to reflect, that strong AI would fail to distinguish between a "total zombie" and a being with real, intrinsic intentionality. Introspective consciousness, *what it is like* to be you (and to understand Chinese), is Searle's real topic. In spite of his insistence that his very simple argument is the centerpiece of his view, and that the Chinese Room "parable" is just a vivid reminder of the truth of his second premise, his case actually depends on the "first-person point of view" of the fellow in the Chinese room.

Searle has apparently confused a claim about the underivability of *semantics* from syntax with a claim about the underivability of *the consciousness of semantics* from syntax. For Searle, the idea of genuine understanding, genuine "semanticity" as he often calls it, is inextricable from the idea of consciousness. He does not so much as consider the possibility of unconscious semanticity.

The problems of consciousness are serious and perplexing, for AI and for everyone else. The question of whether a machine *could be conscious* is one I have addressed at length before (*Brainstorms*, chapters 8–11; Hofstadter and Dennett 1981; Dennett 1982b, 1985a, forthcoming e) and will address in more detail in the future. This is not the time or place for a full-scale discussion. For the moment, let us just note that Searle's case, such as it is, does not hinge at all on the very simple argument about the formality of programs and the underivability of semantics from syntax but on deep-seated intuitions most people have about consciousness and its apparent unrealizability in machines.

Searle's treatment of that case, moreover, invites us to regress to a Cartesian vantage point. (Searle's fury is never fiercer than when a critic calls him a dualist, for he insists that he is a thoroughly modern materialist; but among his chief supporters, who take themselves to be agreeing with him, are modern-day Cartesians such as Eccles and Puccetti.) Searle proclaims that somehow—and he has nothing to say about the details—the biochemistry of the human brain ensures that no human beings are zombies. This is reassuring, but mystifying. How does the biochemistry create such a happy effect? By a wondrous causal power indeed; it is the very same causal power Descartes imputed to immaterial souls, and Searle has made it no less wondrous or mysterious—or incoherent in the end—by assuring us that it is all somehow just a matter of biochemistry.

Finally, to respond for the record to Searle's challenge: What do I think is wrong with Searle's very simple argument, aside from its being a red herring? Consider once more his

Proposition 2. Syntax is neither equivalent to nor sufficient by itself for semantics.

This may still be held true, if we make the simple mistake of talking about syntax on the shelf, an unimplemented program. But *embodied, running* syntax—the "right program" on a suitably fast machine—*is* sufficient for *derived* intentionality, and that is the only kind of semantics there is, as I argued in chapter 8 (see also the discussion of syntactic and semantic engines in chapter 3). So I reject, with arguments, Searle's proposition 2.

In fact, the same considerations show that there is also something amiss with his proposition 1: Programs are purely formal (i.e., syntactic). Whether a program is to be identified by its purely formal characteristics is a hotly contested issue in the law these days. Can you patent a program, or merely copyright it? A host of interesting lawsuits swarm around the question of whether programs that *do the same things in the world* count as the same program even though they are, at some level of description, syntactically different. If details of "embodiment" are included in the specification of a program, and are considered essential to it, then the program is not a purely formal object at all (and is arguably eligible for patent protection), and without *some* details of embodiment being fixed—by the internal semantics of the machine language in which the program is ultimately written—a program is not even a syntactic object, but just a pattern of marks as inert as wallpaper.

Finally, an implication of the arguments in chapter 8 is that Searle's proposition 3 is false, given what he means by "minds have mental contents." There is no such thing as intrinsic intentionality— especially if this is viewed, as Searle can now be seen to require, as a property to which the subject has conscious, privileged access.

Q. *Compare and contrast the views of the following philosophers on the fundamental status of attributions of intentionality: Quine, Sellars, Chisholm, Putnam, Davidson, Bennett, Fodor, Stich, and Dennett.*

A.   It would be strange, and distressing, if the "major differences" between these philosophical theorists turned out to be all that major—if, in particular, it turned out that one side in each controversy was flat wrong about something important (as contrasted, say, with having put rather too much emphasis on one aspect of the truth). It would be distressing because it just shouldn't be the case that a group of such smart people might read and discuss the same books, work in the same (Anglo-American) tradition, be familiar with roughly the same evidence, endorse the same methodology, and yet some of them utterly fail to comprehend the significance of it all, in spite of their colleagues' wisest efforts at enlightening them. Everybody makes mistakes, of course, and no one is immune to confusion, but unless philosophy is just a mug's game, as some of its detractors think, other things being equal we should expect that these theorists could be seen to be making common cause, each contributing something to an emerging common enlightenment about the nature of the mind and its relation to the body and the rest of the physical world.

Happily, in this instance there is a perspective from which agreement predominates, progress can be discerned, and many of the most salient oppositions appear to be the amplified products of minor differences of judgment or taste, or of what might be called tactical overstatement. (If you think your interlocutor is missing something important, you tend to exaggerate its importance in your effort to redress the balance. Besides, the best way to get others to pay attention to you is to say something memorably "radical," with as few qualifiers and mealy-mouthed concessions as possible.) No one wants to learn that one's crusading career is just half of a tempest in a teapot, and so philosophers are typically not eager to accept such bland and ecumenical resolutions of their controversies, but it can be reassuring, and even enlightening—if not especially exciting—to remind ourselves of just how much fundamental agreement there is.

It will help us to understand the current state of play on this issue to go back a few years to the texts that set the agenda: Chisholm, in "Sentences about Believing" (1956) (see also Chisholm 1957), noted both the logical obstreperousness and apparent irreducibility of the intentional idioms and went on to pose the quandary these idioms raised for those who wanted to unify the mind and science. Some philosophers and psychologists, Chisholm noted,

> seem to have felt that it would be philosophically significant if they could show that belief sentences can be rewritten in an adequate language which is not intentional, or at least that it would be significant to show that [the irreducibility thesis of] Brentano was wrong. Let us suppose for a moment that we *cannot* rewrite belief sentences in a way which is contrary to our linguistic version of Brentano's thesis. What would be the significance of this fact? I feel that this question is itself philosophically significant, but I am not prepared to answer it. (p. 519)

Quine, working from a strikingly different starting point (his celebrated exploration of the task of "radical translation"), arrived at the same verdict: there was no way of strictly reducing or translating the idioms of meaning (or semantics or intentionality) into the language of physical science. He noted the convergence: "Brentano's thesis of the irreducibility of intentional idioms is of a piece with the thesis of indeterminacy of translation." (1960, p. 221) Not surprisingly, he also agreed with Chisholm about the philosophical importance of the question Chisholm was not prepared to answer. But unification of science has always loomed large as a goal for Quine (while it has not seemed to move Chisholm particularly), so he was indeed prepared to answer the question. In an oft-quoted passage, Quine bravely declared his allegiance to a radical brand of behaviorism (an instance of the doctrine more recently called *eliminative materialism*):

> One may accept the Brentano thesis either as showing the indispensability of intentional idioms and the importance of an autonomous science of intention, or as showing the baselessness of intentional idioms and the emptiness of a science of intention. My attitude, unlike Brentano's, is the second. (1960, p. 221)

In fact, both these passages are slightly misleading, since Chisholm, in spite of his announced reticence, has been heroic over the years in defense of Brentano's mentalistic pole (let's call it North[1]) and Quine, in spite of his ringing vow of (South) polar behaviorism, has from the outset been exploring and defending somewhat more temperate territory—along with everyone else. Anscombe (1957), Geach (1957), and Taylor (1964) made notable Northern explorations that were welcome and influential alternatives to Quine's rejection of the mental, and it soon became commonly accepted among philosophers that the phenomenon of the meaning or content of psychological states—intentionality—was neither as unapproachable by the physical sciences as Brentano and Chisholm seemed to suggest, nor as comfortably dismissable as Quine seemed to suggest. Some sort of unifying compromise must be possible, between a rigorous "reduction" of the mentalistic to the brutely physicalistic and a brusque denial of the phenomena of mind.

The Equator, to continue the geographical metaphor, had already been staked out by Sellars, in his important correspondence with Chisholm:

My solution is that "'. . .' means – – –" is the core of a unique mode of discourse which is as distinct from the *description* and *explanation* of empirical fact, as is the language of *prescription* and *justification*. (Chisholm and Sellars 1958, p. 527)

What was unique about this mode of discourse, according to Sellars's pioneering analyses (1954, 1956, 1963), was its ineliminable appeal to functional considerations. Thus was contemporary *functionalism* in the philosophy of mind born, and the varieties of functionalism we have subsequently seen are in one way or another enabled, and directly or indirectly inspired, by what was left open in Sellars's initial proposal—though this has not been widely acknowledged.[2]

---

1. Not to be confused with the East Pole, which anchors a different logical geography in Dennett 1984b and forthcoming e.

2. Sellars's influence has been ubiquitous but almost subliminal (if one judges by the paucity of citations to Sellars among functionalists). It is clear that Putnam, Harman, and Lycan (1974, 1981a, 1981b) have been quite directly influenced by Sellars, but Dennett, Fodor, Block and Lewis show the Sellars influence largely at second hand, and mainly via Putnam's very influential series of papers reprinted in Putnam 1975b. Sellars's role in the development of functionalism is made clear in Putnam's (1974) and Dennett's (1974a) commentaries on Sellars's "Meaning as Functional Classification (A Perspective on the Relation of Syntax to Semantics)," and in Sellar's reply, at the conference on Intentionality, Language, and Translation held at the University of Con-

But Quine, as just noted, was not really occupying the barren South Pole of his notorious behaviorism, in spite of what he often said. He, along side if slightly to the south of Sellars, was setting out some of the limits on any functionalist compromise. The section of *Word and Object* aptly entitled "The Double Standard" (1960, pp. 216–21) can be read today as a rich preview of the emphases and contributions of Putnam, Davidson, Bennett, Stich, and Dennett, among others.

The double standard Quine advocated depended on *how seriously* one supposed one was taking the intentional idioms.

If we are limning the true and ultimate structure of reality, the canonical scheme for us is the austere scheme that knows no quotation but direct quotation and no propositional attitudes but only the physical constitution and behavior of organisms. (p. 221)

In other words, strictly speaking, ontologically speaking, there are no such things as beliefs, desires, or other intentional phenomena. But the intentional idioms are "practically indispensable," and we should see what we can do to make sense of their employment in what Quine called an "essentially dramatic" idiom (p. 219). Not just brute facts, then, but an element of interpretation, and dramatic interpretation at that, must be recognized in any use of the intentional vocabulary.

Here we find Quine and Sellars in fundamental agreement about the not-purely-descriptive nature of intentional attribution, and just about everyone since has concurred, though with different emphases. Most, for instance, have thought Quine's claim that these idioms are merely *practically* indispensable underestimated the centrality of the role they play—but if we took out the "merely" there might be little left to debate.

What has remained an issue of strenuous debate ever since is how to play this dramatic interpretation game. What are the principles of interpretation and their presuppositions and implications? Here two chief rivals have seemed to emerge: one or another Normative Principle, according to which one should attribute to a creature the propositional attitudes it "ought to have" given its circumstances, and one or

necticut in March of 1973. The proceedings of this conference, published as a special issue of *Synthese* (1974), is also a treasury of insights on Quine's thesis of the indeterminacy of radical translation and its relation to the problem of intentionality in the philosophy of the mind. See also Harman 1968, 1986 and Lycan 1981b for further clarification of the history.

another Projective Principle, according to which one should attribute to a creature the propositional attitudes one supposed one would have oneself in those circumstances.

Under the Normative Principle we have had the various sub-varieties of the Principle of Charity (Davidson 1967, 1973, 1974, collected with others in 1985; and Lewis 1974) and the Assumption of Rationality (Dennett 1969, 1971, 1975; Cherniak 1981, 1986). Much of what Davidson and Dennett made of this theme was prefigured in Bennett's *Rationality* (1964)—though it takes some hindsight to appreciate the extent of this—but in any event, it all grows out of Quine's discussions of the need for such a principle in any exercise of radical translation:

> Wanton translation imposes our logic upon them, and would beg the question of prelogicality if there were a question to beg. . . . The maxim of translation underlying all this is that assertions startlingly false on the face of them are likely to turn on hidden differences of language. . . . The common sense behind the maxim is that one's interlocutor's silliness, beyond a certain point, is less likely than bad translation—or, in the domestic case, linguistic divergence. (1960, p. 59)

(In a footnote, Quine credits Wilson 1959 with the idea of a principle of charity, under that name.) So Quine is the father of the Normative Principle—except that one can find contemporaneous appreciation of the role of such normative considerations in individuating functional roles in Sellars.

What of the Projective Principle? Grandy (1973) developed an early version, contrasting what he called the principle of humanity to the principle of charity, and Stich (1980, 1981, 1983, 1984) has offered the most detailed and vigorous defense of this idea, but Quine is the father of this principle as well (as Stich 1983, notes, p. 84):

> When we quote a man's utterance directly we report it almost as we might a bird call. However significant the utterance, direct quotation merely reports the physical incident and leaves any implication to us. On the other hand in indirect quotation we project ourselves into what, from his remarks and other indications, we imagine the speaker's state of mind to have been, and then we say what, in our language, is natural and relevant for us in the state thus feigned. (Quine 1960, p. 219)

To complicate matters for taxonomists even further, Quine credits the ideas in his insightful discussion of the prospects for a projective principle to conversations with Davidson (Quine 1960, p. 217n). Besides, surely Sellars's elaborate analysis (1954) of functional classification of terms relative to the functions of terms in *our* language must count as the *locus classicus* of projectivist interpretation!

Levin (forthcoming) divides the contestants in this quest for interpretation principles into Rationalizers and Projectors (see also Stich 1984). She notes the tendency of mild versions of each to merge into a single view, but does not push this ecumenicism as far as Dennett (chapter 4 of this book), who argues that the opposition between Projection and Rationalization is at most a matter of emphasis. As Quine noticed from the outset, the problem with the strategy of projection is that "Casting our real selves thus in unreal roles, we do not generally know how much reality to hold constant. Quandaries arise." (1960, p. 219) Just the quandaries Stich (1983) examines in detail; quandaries that are resolvable—to the extent that they are—only by resort to normative considerations: we should project only what is *best* of ourselves, but what counts as best under the circumstances is itself a matter of interpretation.

Now if one took the attribution of propositional attitudes via intentional idioms seriously—dead seriously—there would be a real problem here: just exactly which principle or principles of interpretation give the real or *actual* propositional attitudes? But for Quine, as we have seen, this problem does not arise, since the "dramatic idiom" is just a practical necessity in daily life, subject to purely pragmatic considerations, not a way of limning ultimate reality.

Commonly the degree of allowable deviation depends on why we are quoting. It is a question of what traits of the quoted speaker's remarks we want to make something of; those are the traits that must be kept straight if our indirect quotation is to count as true. Similar remarks apply to sentences of belief and other propositional attitudes. . . . It will often happen also that there is just no saying whether to count an affirmation of propositional attitude as true or false, even given full knowledge of its circumstances and purposes. (1960, p. 218)

As Quine explained in 1970:

The metaphor of the black box, often so useful, can be misleading here. The problem is not one of hidden facts, such as might be uncovered by learning more about the brain physiology of thought processes. To expect a distinctive physical mechanism behind every genuinely distinct mental state is one thing; to expect a distinctive mechanism for every purported distinction that can be phrased in traditional mentalistic language is another. The question whether . . . the foreigner *really* believes A or believes rather B, is a question whose very significance I would put in doubt. This is what I am getting at in arguing the indeterminacy of translation. (pp. 180–81)

Let us review how we got this far. Just about everyone accepts the Brentano irreducibility thesis, but if one accepts it primarily for Quine's reasons—because one has seen that there is indeterminacy of radical translation—one will not be inclined to be a (strict) Realist about attributions of propositional attitude, and hence will not be inclined to be a Realist about psychological content (genuine or intrinsic intentionality). As Quine says, "To accept intentional usage at face value is, we saw, to postulate translation relations as somehow objectively valid though indeterminate in principle relative to the totality of speech dispositions." (1960, p. 221) Much of the debate over principles of interpretation has been displaced and distorted by a failure of the participants to come to terms with this implication of Quine's view. (The only explicit discussion of these implications I have encountered is Lycan 1981b.) Thus, for Davidson and Dennett, who are the most wholehearted Quinians on this score, there simply is no issue right where a major lacuna looms for Realists such as Fodor (and Burge and Dretske and Kripke and others—see chapter 8). The oscillations to be observed in Putnam's views over the years (1974, 1975b, 1978 (see especially his John Locke Lecture IV, pp. 54–60), 1981, 1983, 1986) trace out his explorations (North and South) of the costs and benefits of going along with Quine on indeterminacy. In his most recent works, he ends up more or less with Quine and the Quinians:

Belief-desire explanation belongs to the level of what I've been calling *interpretation theory*. It is as holistic and interest-relative as all interpretation. Psychologists often speak as though there were *concepts* in the *brain*. The point of my argument (and, I think, of Davidson's) is that there may be *sentence-analogues* and *predicate-analogues* in the brain, but not concepts. "Mental representations" require interpretation just as much as any other signs do. (1983, p. 154)

Putnam's student Fodor, meanwhile, has been pursuing a strikingly independent Northern course, defending both the irreducibility and Reality of intentional states, but—unlike Chisholm, Anscombe, Geach, and Taylor, for instance—attempting to make these irreducible realities acceptable to the physical sciences by grounding them (somehow) in the "syntax" of a system of physically realized mental representations. In *Psychological Explanation* (1968a), one of the defining texts of functionalism, Fodor resolutely turned his back on Quine (in his behaviorist trappings) and Ryle (in his quite different behaviorist trappings) and Wittgenstein (in his still different behaviorist trappings), and began sketching an account of mental events as *inner processes*, distinguished or identified by their functional properties. It looked, and was supposed to look, like quite a radical alternative. It appeared to be a way of undercutting what seemed at the time to be a stifling Behaviorist Dogma: *what goes on inside doesn't settle anything*.

While Fodor's *The Language of Thought* (1975) developed the anti-Ryle, anti-Quine theme further, the positive theory looked, for all that, not so *very* different from that of Sellars, what with its recognition of the teleological presuppositions of functional taxonomies.[3] Sellars had earlier developed his own alternative to at least one sort of behaviorism, in his Myth of our Rylean Ancestors (1956, reprinted in Sellars 1963). He imagined ancestors with a Rylean (behavioristic) language coming to postulate, as theoretical entities, certain inner episodes of Mentalese, states that were identified by their functional roles, or—what came in the end to the same thing—their meaning or intentionality (see also Sellars 1954).

Perhaps the crucial difference between Sellars's and Fodor's Mentalese functionalisms is that Sellars, in his discussions of "language entry rules" and "language exit rules" for Mentalese, recognized the need for a *sort* of "behavioristic" analysis of the semantic properties of those inner representations—what would later be called a *procedural semantics*. But in spite of Fodor's early declaration of the dependence (somehow) of semantics on function, he has resisted this step—taken most explicitly by Dennett (1969, chapter 4)—because it threatened the role he hoped to be filled by the postulated Mentalese.[4]

Chisholm and Sellars (1958, pp. 524ff), who in other regards talked past each other, were both very clear about the impossibility of *grounding* meaning in the somehow "primitive" semantic properties of an "inner" language. For Fodor, on the other hand, an inner language of thought has continued to seem like an alternative and more powerful way of *settling* questions of psychological interpretation,

---

3. It is instructive to compare Fodor's 1975 book to Harman's *Thought* (1973), a version of the language of thought with marked consonances with Quine and Sellars—though Harman never cites Sellars.

4. See Fodor 1981c for a diatribe against latter-day procedural semantics. Fodor (1975) does not cite Sellars, and in 1981a there is one reference to Sellars: "I discover, very belatedly, that an account in some respects quite like this one was once proposed by Sellars (1956). Sellars' work seems remarkably prescient in light of (what I take to be) the methodological presuppositions of contemporary cognitive psychology." (pp. 325–26)

rather than, as Quine, Sellars, Davidson, and Dennett (1973) have always insisted (and Putnam now agrees), a mere re-posing of the problem of radical translation. In order to maintain his position, however, Fodor has had to swing perilously close to the North pole of real, intrinsic intentionality—even as he makes fun of it:

My point, then, is *of course* not that solipsism is true; it's just that truth, reference and the rest of the semantic notions aren't psychological categories. What they are is: they're modes of *Dasein*. I don't know what *Dasein* is, but I'm sure that there's lots of it around, and I'm sure that you and I and Cincinnati have all got it. What more do you want? (1980, p. 71; reprinted in 1981a)

"Fodor's Guide to Mental Representation: The Intelligent Auntie's Vade-Mecum" (1985) is Fodor's own answer to our examination question, and it presents an amusing and often insightful taxonomy, if a somewhat procrustean one, as Fodor himself admits. Fodor frankly defends Realism, and presents, as his "First Anti-Realist option," Dennett's instrumentalism (p. 79). He does not take himself to refute this instrumentalism, but having dealt it some glancing blows, he sets it aside: "what with one thing and another, it does seem possible to doubt that a coherent instrumentalism about the attitudes is going to be forthcoming." He then proceeds to present his taxonomy of the other paths, but what strikes this reader is that all the positions downstream of the fork leading away from Dennett's position—the positions to which Fodor devotes the rest of his review—are by his own account so beset with quandaries that one might almost suppose him to be cataloguing an unintended *reductio ad absurdum*. In particular, Fodor cites what he calls the "idealization problem"—the principle of charity in disguise—as an unsolved problem and admits he sees "no reason to assume that the problem can be solved" within his Realistic boundaries (p. 97). He ends with the following observation: "But of the semanticity of mental representations, we have, as things now stand, no adequate account." (p. 99)

Bennett and Stich have explored two other Northern regions, resisting in their different ways the seductive climate at the Equator. Bennett (1976) explicitly rejected Quine's indeterminacy thesis (pp. 257–64), and, drawing on Taylor's (1964) analysis of teleological explanation, attempted a detailed Realistic theory of the content of what he called *registrations*, the inner representational states of animals, of which *beliefs* are the special, human subvariety. Like Dennett, and unlike Fodor and Davidson, he thus chose the strategy of trying first to get clear about the representational needs and resources of nonlanguage-using animals before attempting to build an account of human belief (or, as Dennett would say, opinion) on that foundation. In fact, the parallel tracks of Dennett's and Bennett's investigations are separated by little more than their disagreement on the indeterminacy thesis and its implications for the prospects of a "firm underlying theory" of "conceptual structures" (see Bennett's (1983) comment and Dennett's response (pp. 382–83) in *BBS*).

Stich (1983), we can now see, traced out a curving route back to the Equator: an exhaustive *reductio ad absurdum* of the hypothesis that some form of strict projectivist interpretation principle can permit one to be a Realist about content after all, despite Quine's qualms. Stich ends up joining Quine in his double standard: strictly speaking, there are no such things as beliefs, even if *speaking as if there were* is a practical necessity.

Offering somewhat different reasons, Churchland (1981) arrived at the same destination while seeming in the process to be disagreeing wholeheartedly with Dennett and Putnam. This is another case of difference in emphasis looming as a major disagreement: Churchland, unlike Dennett and Putnam, does not find the Quinian idea of a double standard attractive. That is, he does not take seriously the idea of not taking propositional attitude talk seriously—while still taking it. He acknowledges, like every other sane eliminative materialist, that for practical purposes we are going to go on talking as if there were beliefs and desires, engaging in "the dramatic idiom" as Quine says. But for Churchland, this is a dismissive acknowledgment, not the prelude to interpretation theory it is for Davidson, Dennett, and Putnam.

What further differences remain among the interpretation theorists? Dennett and Davidson have also pursued strikingly parallel but independent courses over the years, united by their acceptance of Quinian indeterminacy and their allegiance to principles of charity of interpretation. What still separates them? Haugeland observes:

Dennett . . . differs from Davidson in his ontological outlook—that is, in his attitude toward the entities addressed in the respective frameworks. Davidson restricts his discussion to events only, whereas Dennett happily includes also states, processes, structures, and the like. But this superficial discrepancy reflects a much deeper and more important divergence. It is Davidson's purpose to show that each mental event is the very same event as some physical event, and his argument depends on a doctrine about causal relations that he applies only to events. Dennett, on the other hand, not only doesn't share that aim, but apparently also wouldn't accept the conclusion. [For Dennett,] beliefs are specifiable. . . at best, by a sort of rational "equilibrium" in the intentional framework; and hence their status as entities, if distinctive, should reflect this difference in framework. In other words, perhaps Dennett should agree with Ryle:

It is perfectly proper to say, in one logical tone of voice, that there exist minds and to say, in another logical tone of voice, that there exist bodies. But these expressions do not indicate two different species of existence, for "existence" is not a generic word like "colored" or "sexed". (1949, p. 23)

Davidson, of course, would find this suggestion utterly unacceptable.

Heidegger, on the other hand, would find it entirely congenial; for his point about presence-at-hand, readiness-at-hand, and existence is precisely that they are different "ways to be." (Haugeland, unpublished, pp. 5–6)[5]

Haugeland is right: Dennett should—and did—agree with Ryle on just this point (Dennett 1969, pp. 6–18), while attempting to reconcile that with his agreement with Quine on the implications of radical translation. Davidson, on the other hand, reveals by his steadfast *ontological* realism about beliefs (as items one should hope to include in the ontology of unified science) that he has always wanted to take Quine's double standard with a grain of salt. He still hankers to take propositional attitudes more seriously than Quine would recommend, in spite of agreeing with Quine about the indeterminacy of radical translation. The "deep divergence" over ontological outlook that Haugeland correctly discerns between Davidson and Dennett can also thus be seen as merely the amplified effects of a minor difference of opinion about *just* how seriously to take the double standard.

All this convergence, among philosophers with quite different attitudes, aspirations, and methods, strengthens conviction—even more so in the light of the curious patterns of *non*-citation in the literature under review. As already noted, Dennett and Davidson, and Dennett and Bennett, virtually never cite or discuss each other despite traveling highly parallel paths through neighboring territory. Almost no one cites Sellars, while reinventing his wheels with gratifying regularity. Many other instances of unacknowledged reinvention could be cited. What explains this? The comprehension time lag, I

---

5. For heroic ecumenical hermeneutics, this drawing of Heidegger into the Quinian fold is rivaled only by Wheeler's (1986) discussion of Derrida, Quine, Dennett, and Davidson.

suspect. Philosophers are never quite sure what they are talking about—about what the issues *really* are—and so it often takes them rather a long time to recognize that someone with a *somewhat* different approach (or destination, or starting point) is making a contribution. We recognize—and cite and discuss—head-on collision courses much more readily than nearly parallel trajectories, which tend to strike us, if we notice them at all, as too obvious to comment on. Besides, it is not as if philosophers uncovered their favorite truths by pursuing elaborately chained series of laboratory experiments or on long treks into the wilderness. We are all standing around in each other's data, looking in roughly the same directions for roughly the same things. Priority squabbles may make sense in some disciplines, but in philosophy they tend to take on the air of disputes among sailors about who gets credit for first noticing that the breeze has come up.

In the case under discussion one could say that it all goes back to Quine, or that Sellars deserves the credit, or, to play a traditional melody, that it's all just a series of footnotes on Plato. From one vantage point it seems as if there is a gradual migration of theorists toward the Equator—taking what Quine calls the "dramatic idiom" of intentional attribution seriously, but not *too* seriously, treating it always as a "heuristic overlay" (Dennett 1969) or a "stance" (Dennett 1971). From this vantage point it can even appear as if there is an obvious intentional explanation of this migration: philosophers, being roughly rational intentional systems, are gradually being persuaded that Dennett is right. But that is no doubt an illusion of perspective.

Bibliography

Abbott, E. A. (1962). *Flatland: A Romance in Many Dimensions*. Oxford: Blackwell. (Originally published in 1884).

Ackermann, R. (1972). "Opacity in Belief Structures," *Journal of Philosophy*, LXIX, pp. 55–67.

Akins, K. A. (1986). "On Piranhas, Narcissism, and Mental Representation," CCM-86-2, Center for Cognitive Studies, Tufts University.

Akins, K. A. (unpublished). "Information and Organisms: or Why Nature Doesn't Build Epistemic Engines," doctoral dissertation, University of Michigan, Ann Arbor, 1987.

Amundson, R. (unpublished). "Doctor Dennett and Doctor Pangloss."

Anderson, A. R. and Belnap, N. (1974). *Entailment: The Logic of Relevance and Necessity*. Princeton: Princeton University Press.

Anscombe, E. (1957). *Intention*. Oxford: Blackwell.

Aquila, R. E. (1977). *Intentionality: A Study of Mental Acts*. University Park: Pennsylvania State University Press.

Barash, D. P. (1976). "Male Response to Apparent Female Adultery in the Mountain Bluebird: An Evolutionary Interpretation," *American Naturalist*, 110, pp. 1097–1101.

Beatty, J. (1980). "Optimal-design Models and the Strategy of Model Building in Evolutionary Biology," *Philosophy of Science*, 47, pp. 532–61.

Bechtel, W. (1985). "Realism, Reason, and the Intentional Stance," *Cognitive Science*, 9, pp. 473–97.

Bennett, J. (1964). *Rationality*. London: Routledge and Kegan Paul.

Bennett, J. (1976). *Linguistic Behavior*. Cambridge: Cambridge University Press.

Bennett, J. (1983). "Cognitive Ethology: Theory or Poetry?" (commentary on Dennett 1983a), *Behavioral and Brain Sciences*, 6, pp. 356–58.

Berliner, H. and Ebling, C. (1986). "The SUPREM Architecture: a new Intelligent Paradigm," *Artificial Intelligence*, 28, pp. 3–8.

Blackburn, S. (1979). "Thought and Things," *Aristotelian Society Supplementary Volume*, LIII, pp. 23–42.

Block, N. (1978). "Troubles with Functionalism," in C. W. Savage, ed., *Perception and Cognition: Issues in the Foundations of Psychology*. Minneapolis: University of Minnesota Press. (Reprinted in Block 1980, vol. 1.)

Block, N., ed. (1980). *Readings in the Philosophy of Psychology*, 2 vols. Cambridge, MA: Harvard University Press.

Boden, M. (1981). "The Case for a Cognitive Biology," in *Minds and Mechanisms: Philosophical Psychology and Computational Models*. Ithaca: Cornell University Press.

Boër, S. and Lycan, W. (1975). "Knowing Who," *Philosophical Studies*, 28, pp. 299–347.

Borges, J. L. (1962). "The Garden of Forking Paths," in D. A. Yates and J. E. Irby, eds., *Labyrinths: Selected Stories and Other Writings*. New York: New Directions.

Braitenberg, V. (1984). *Vehicles: Experiments in Synthetic Psychology*. Cambridge, MA: The MIT Press/A Bradford Book.

Burge, T. (1977). "Belief De Re," *The Journal of Philosophy*, 74, no. 6, pp. 338–62.

Burge, T. (1978). "Belief and Synonymy," *Journal of Philosophy*, 75, 119–38.

Burge, T. (1979). "Individualism and the Mental," *Midwest Studies in Philosophy*, IV, pp. 73–121.

Burge, T. (1986). "Individualism and Psychology," *The Philosophical Review*, XCV, no. 1, pp. 3–46.

Byrne, R. and Whiten, A., eds. (forthcoming). *Social Expertise and the Evolution of Intellect: Evidence from Monkeys, Apes, and Humans*. Oxford: Oxford University Press.

Cain, A. J. (1964). "The Perfection of Animals," *Viewpoints in Biology*, 3, pp. 37–63.

Campbell, D. T. (1973). "Evolutionary Epistemology," in Paul Schilpp, ed., *The Philosophy of Karl Popper*. La Salle, IL: Open Court Press.

Campbell, D. T. (1977). "Descriptive Epistemology: Psychological, Sociological, and Evolutionary," William James Lectures, Harvard University.

Cargile, J.(1970). "A Note on 'Iterated Knowings'," *Analysis*, 30, pp. 151–55.

Castaneda, H.-N. (1966). " 'He': A Study in the Logic of Self-Consciousness," *Ratio*, 8, pp. 130–57.

Castaneda, H.-N. (1967). "Indicators and Quasi-Indicators," *American Philosophical Quarterly*, 4, pp. 85–100.

Castaneda, H.-N. (1968). "On the Logic of Attributions of Self-Knowledge to Others," *Journal of Philosophy*, LXV, pp. 439–56.

Charniak, E. (1974). "Toward a Model of Children's Story Comprehension," unpublished doctoral dissertation, MIT, and MIT AI Lab Report 266.

Cheney, D. and Seyfarth, R. (1982). "Recognition of Individuals Within and Between Groups of Free-Ranging Vervet Monkeys," *American Zoology*, 22, pp. 519–29.

Cheney, D. and Seyfarth, R. (1985). "Social and Non-social Knowledge in Vervet Monkeys," *Philosophical Transactions of the Royal Society of London*, B 308, pp. 187–201.

Cherniak, C. (1981). "Minimal Rationality," *Mind*, 90, pp. 161–83.

Cherniak, C. (1983). "Rationality and the Structure of Memory," *Synthese*, 57, pp. 163–86.

Cherniak, C. (1986). *Minimal Rationality*. Cambridge, MA: The MIT Press/A Bradford Book.

Chisholm, R. (1956). "Sentences About Believing," *Aristotelian Society Proceedings*, 56, pp. 125–48.

Chisholm, R. (1957). *Perceiving: A Philosophical Study*. Ithaca: Cornell University Press.

Chisholm, R. (1966). "On Some Psychological Concepts and the 'Logic' of Intentionality," in H. N. Castaneda, ed., *Intentionality, Minds, and Perception*. Detroit: Wayne State University Press.

Chisholm, R. and Sellars, W. (1958). "Intentionality and the Mental," in H. Feigl, M. Scriven, and G. Maxwell, eds., *Concepts, Theories and the Mind-Body Problem*. Minnesota Studies in Philosophy of Science, II. Minneapolis: University of Minnesota Press.

Chomsky, N. (1959). "Review of B. F. Skinner's *Verbal Behavior*," *Language*, 35, pp. 26–58. (Reprinted in Block 1980, vol. 1)

Chomsky, N. (1980a). *Rules and Representations*. New York: Columbia University Press.

Chomsky, N. (1980b). "Rules and Representations," *Behavioral and Brain Sciences*, 3, pp. 1–61.

Churchland, P. M. (1979). *Scientific Realism and the Plasticity of Mind*. Cambridge: Cambridge University Press.

Churchland, P. M. (1981). "Eliminative Materialism and the Propositional Attitudes," *Journal of Philosophy*, 78, pp. 67–90.

Churchland, P. M. (1984). *Matter and Consciousness: A Contemporary Introduction to the Philosophy of Mind*. Cambridge, MA: The MIT Press/A Bradford Book.

Churchland, P. S. (1980). "Language, Thought, and Information Processing," *Nous*, 14, pp. 147–70.

Churchland, P. S. (1986). *Neurophilosophy: Toward a Unified Theory of Mind/Brain.* Cambridge, MA: The MIT Press/A Bradford Book.

Churchland, P. S. and Churchland, P. M. (1981). "Stalking the Wild Epistemic Engine," *Nous*, pp. 5–18.

Cohen, L. B.; DeLoache, J. S.; Strauss, M. S. (1979). "Infant Visual Perception," in J. D. Osofsky, ed., *Handbook of Infant Development.* New York: Wiley, pp. 416–19.

Cohen, L. J. (1981). "Can Human Rationality be Experimentally Demonstrated?" *Behavioral and Brain Sciences*, 4, pp. 317–70.

Dahlbom, B. (1985). "Dennett on Cognitive Ethology: a Broader View" (commentary on Dennett 1983a), *Behavioral and Brain Sciences*, 8, pp. 760–61.

Darmstadter, H. (1971). "Consistency of Belief," *Journal of Philosophy*, 68, pp. 301–10.

Davidson, D. (1967). "Truth and Meaning," *Synthese*, XVII, pp. 304–23.

Davidson, D. (1969). "How is Weakness of the Will Possible?" in J. Feinberg, ed., *Moral Concepts.* Oxford: Oxford University Press.

Davidson, D. (1970). "Mental Events," in L. Foster and J. Swanson, eds., *Experience and Theory.* Amherst: University of Massachusetts Press.

Davidson, D. (1973). "Radical Interpretation," *Dialectica*, 27, pp. 313–28. (Reprinted in D. Davidson, *Inquiries into Truth and Interpretation.* Oxford: Oxford University Press, 1985).

Davidson, D. (1974a). "Belief and the Basis of Meaning," *Synthese*, 27, pp. 309–23.

Davidson, D. (1974b). "On the Very Idea of a Conceptual Scheme," *Proceedings and Addresses of the American Philosophical Association*, 47, pp. 5–20.

Davidson, D. (1975). "Thought and Talk," in *Mind and Language: Wolfson College Lectures, 1974.* Oxford: Clarendon Press, pp. 7–23.

Davidson, D. (1985). *Inquiries into Truth and Interpretation.* Oxford: Clarendon Press.

Dawkins, R. (1976). *The Selfish Gene.* Oxford: Oxford University Press.

Dawkins, R. (1980). "Good Strategy or Evolutionarily Stable Strategy?" in G. W. Barlow and J. Silverberg, eds. *Sociobiology: Beyond Nature/Nurture?* A.A.A.S. Selected Symposium. Boulder, CO: Westview Press.

Dawkins, R. (1982). *The Extended Phenotype.* San Francisco: Freeman.

Dawkins, R. (1986). *The Blind Watchmaker.* Essex: Longman Scientific and Technical.

Dennett, D. C. (1969). *Content and Consciousness*. London: Routledge and Kegan Paul.

Dennett, D. C. (1971). "Intentional Systems," *Journal of Philosophy*, 8, pp. 87–106. (Reprinted in Dennett 1978a.)

Dennett, D. C. (1973). "Mechanism and Responsibility," in T. Honderich, ed., *Essays on Freedom of Action*. London: Routledge and Kegan Paul. (Reprinted in Dennett 1978a.)

Dennett, D. C. (1974a). "Why the Law of Effect Will Not Go Away," *Journal of the Theory of Social Behavior*, 5, pp. 169–87. (Reprinted in Dennett 1978a.)

Dennett, D. C. (1974b). "Comment on Wilfrid Sellars," *Synthese*, 27, pp. 439–44.

Dennett, D. C. (1975). "Brain Writing and Mind Reading," in K. Gunderson, ed., *Language, Mind, and Meaning*. Minnesota Studies in Philosophy of Science, VII. Minneapolis: University of Minnesota Press.

Dennett, D. C. (1976). "Conditions of Personhood," in A. Rorty, ed., *The Identities of Persons*. Berkeley: University of California Press. (Reprinted in Dennett 1978a.)

Dennett, D. C. (1978a). *Brainstorms: Philosophical Essays on Mind and Psychology*. Montgomery, VT: Bradford Books.

Dennett, D. C. (1978b). "Beliefs About Beliefs" (commentary on Premack and Woodruff 1978), *Behavioral and Brain Sciences*, 1, pp. 568–70.

Dennett, D. C. (1978c). "Current Issues in the Philosophy of Mind," *American Philosophical Quarterly*, 15, pp. 249–61.

Dennett, D. C. (1978d). "Why Not the Whole Iguana?" (commentary on Pylyshyn 1978), *Behavioral and Brain Sciences*, 1, pp. 103–4.

Dennett, D. C. (1980a). "Passing the Buck to Biology" (commentary on Chomsky 1980b), *Behavioral and Brain Sciences*, 3, p. 19.

Dennett, D. C. (1980b). "The Milk of Human Intentionality" (commentary on Searle 1980b), *Behavioral and Brain Sciences*, 3, pp. 428–30.

Dennett, D. C. (1980c). "Reply to Stich," *Philosophical Books*, 21, pp. 65–76.

Dennett, D. C. (1982a). "Comment on Rorty," *Synthese*, 53, pp. 349–56.

Dennett, D. C. (1982b). "How to Study Human Consciousness Empirically: or, Nothing Comes to Mind," *Synthese*, 53, pp. 159–80.

Dennett, D. C. (1982c). "The Myth of the Computer: An Exchange," *The New York Review of Books*, June 24, pp. 56–57.

Dennett, D. C. (1982d). "Why Do We Think What We Do About Why We Think What We Do?" *Cognition*, 12, pp. 219–27.

Dennett, D. C. (1983a). "Intentional Systems in Cognitive Ethology: The 'Panglossian Paradigm' Defended," *Behavioral and Brain Sciences*, 6, pp. 343–90. (Reprinted as chapter seven, this volume.)

Dennett, D. C. (1983b). "Artificial Intelligence and the Strategies of Psychological Investigation" (interview) in J. Miller, ed., *States of Mind*. London: BBC Publications.

Dennett, D. C. (1984a). "Carving the Mind at Its Joints" (review of Fodor 1983), *Contemporary Psychology*, 29, pp. 285–86.

Dennett, D. C. (1984b). "Computer Models and the Mind—a View from the East Pole," *Times Literary Supplement*, December 14, 1984, pp. 1453–54. (This is an earlier and truncated draft of Dennett 1986e).

Dennett, D. C. (1984c). "Cognitive Wheels: the Frame Problem of AI," in C. Hookway, ed., *Minds, Machines and Evolution*. Cambridge: Cambridge University Press.

Dennett, D. C. (1984d). *Elbow Room: The Varieties of Free Will Worth Wanting.* Cambridge, MA: The MIT Press/A Bradford Book.

Dennett, D. C. (1984e). "The Role of the Computer Metaphor in Understanding the Mind," in H. Pagels, ed., *Computer Culture: the Scientific, Intellectual, and Social Impact of the Computer.* Annals of the New York Academy of Sciences, vol. 426, pp. 266–75.

Dennett, D. C. (1985a). "Can Machines Think?" in M. Shafto, ed., *How We Know.* San Francisco: Harper and Row.

Dennett, D. C. (1985b). "When does the Intentional Stance Work?" (continuing commentary), *Behavioral and Brain Sciences*, 8, pp. 758–66.

Dennett, D. C. (1985c). "Why Believe in Belief?" (review of Stich 1983), *Contemporary Psychology*, vol. 30, p. 949.

Dennett, D. C. (1986a). "Engineering's Baby" (commentary on Sayre 1986), *Behavioral and Brain Sciences*, 9, pp. 141–42.

Dennett, D. C. (1986b). "Information, Technology and the Virtues of Ignorance," *Daedalus*, 115, pp. 135–53.

Dennett, D. C. (1986c). "Is There an Autonomous 'Knowledge Level'?" (commentary on Newell, same volume), in Z. Pylyshyn and W. Demopoulos, eds., *Meaning and Cognitive Structure: Issues in the Computational Theory of Mind*, Norwood, NJ: Ablex.

Dennett, D. C. (1986d). "Julian Jaynes' Software Archeology," *Canadian Psychology*, 27, pp. 149–54.

Dennett, D. C. (1986e). "The Logical Geography of Computational Approaches: a View from the East Pole," in R. Harnish and M. Brand, eds., *The Representation of Knowledge and Belief.* Tucson: University of Arizona Press.

Dennett, D. C. (forthcoming a). "A Route to Intelligence: Oversimplify and Self-monitor," in J. Khalfa, ed., *Can Intelligence be Explained?* Oxford: Oxford University Press.

Dennett, D. C. (forthcoming b). "Cognitive Ethology: Hunting for Bargains or a Wild Goose Chase?" in D. McFarland, ed., *The Explanation of Goal-seeking Behaviour*. Oxford: Oxford University Press.

Dennett, D. C. (forthcoming c). "Out of the Armchair and Into the Field," *Poetics Today*, Israel.

Dennett, D. C. (forthcoming d). "Quining Qualia," in A. Marcel and E. Bisiach, eds., *Consciousness in Contemporary Science*. Oxford: Oxford University Press.

Dennett, D. C. (forthcoming e). "The Moral First Aid Manual," 1986 Tanner Lecture, University of Michigan.

Dennett, D. C. (forthcoming f). "The Myth of Original Intentionality," in W. Newton Smith and R. Viale, eds., *Modelling the Mind*. Oxford: Oxford University Press.

Dennett, D. C. (forthcoming g). "The Self as the Center of Narrative Gravity," in P. Cole, D. Johnson and F. Kessel, eds., *Consciousness and Self*. New York: Praeger.

Dennett, D. C. and Haugeland, J. (1987). "Intentionality," in R. Gregory, ed., *The Oxford Companion to Mind*. Oxford: Oxford University Press.

de Sousa, R. (1971). "How to Give a Piece of Your Mind: Or, the Logic of Belief and Assent," *Review of Metaphysics* 25, pp. 52–79.

de Sousa, R. (1979). "The Rationality of Emotion," *Dialogue*, 18, pp. 41–63.

Dewdney, A. K. (1984). *The Planiverse*. New York: Poseidon.

Dobzhansky, T. (1956). "What is an Adaptive Trait?" *American Naturalist*, 90, pp. 337–47.

Donnellan, K. (1966). "Reference and Definite Descriptions," *Philosophical Review*, 75, pp. 281–304.

Donnellan, K. (1968). "Putting Humpty-Dumpty Together Again," *Philosophical Review*, 77, pp. 203–15.

Donnellan, K. (1970). "Proper Names and Identifying Descriptions," *Synthese*, 21, pp. 335–58.

Donnellan, K. (1974). "Speaking of Nothing," *Philosophical Review*, 83, pp. 3–31.

Dover Wilson, J. (1951). *What Happens in Hamlet*. 3rd ed. Cambridge: Cambridge University Press.

Dretske, F. (1981). *Knowledge and the Flow of Information*. Cambridge, MA: The MIT Press/A Bradford Book.

Dretske, F. (1985). "Machines and the Mental," Western Division APA Presidential Address, April 26, 1985 (printed in *Proceedings and Addresses of the APA* (1985) vol. 59, pp. 23–33.)

Dretske, F. (1986). "Misrepresentation," in R. Bogdan, ed., *Belief*. Oxford: Oxford University Press.

Dummett, M. (1973). *Frege: Philosophy of Language*. London: Duckworth.

Dummett, M. (1975). "What is a Theory of Meaning?" in S. Guttenplan, ed., *Mind and Language*. Oxford: Oxford University Press.

Enc, B. (1982). "Intentional States and Mechanical Devices," *Mind*, XCI, pp. 161–82.

Evans, G. (1973). "The Causal Theory of Names," *Aristotelian Society Supplementary Volume*, XLVII, pp. 187–208.

Evans, G. (1980). "Understanding Demonstratives," in H. Parret and J. Bouveresse, eds., *Meaning and Understanding*. New York, Berlin: Walter de Gruyter.

Ewert, J.-P. (forthcoming). "Neuroethology of Releasing Mechanisms: Prey-catching in Toads," *Behavioral and Brain Sciences*.

Fauconnier, G. (1985). *Mental Spaces*. Cambridge, MA: The MIT Press/A Bradford Book.

Feyerabend, P. (1978). *Science in a Free Society*. London: New Left Bank Publ.

Field, H. (1972). "Tarski's Theory of Truth," *Journal of Philosophy*, 69, pp. 347–74.

Field, H. (1977). "Logic, Meaning and Conceptual Role," *Journal of Philosophy*, 74, pp. 379–409.

Field, H. (1978). "Mental Representation," *Erkenntnis*, 13, pp. 9–61.

Fodor, J. (1968a). *Psychological Explanation: An Introduction to the Philosophy of Psychology*. New York: Random House.

Fodor, J. (1968b). "The Appeal to Tacit Knowledge in Psychological Explanation," *Journal of Philosophy*, 65, pp. 627–40.

Fodor, J. (1975). *The Language of Thought*. Hassocks, Sussex: Harvester Press; Scranton, PA: Crowell.

Fodor, J. (1980). "Methodological Solipsism Considered as a Research Strategy in Cognitive Psychology," *Behavioral and Brain Sciences*, 3, pp. 63–110. (Reprinted in Fodor 1981a).

Fodor, J. (1981a). *Representations*. Cambridge, MA: The MIT Press/A Bradford Book.

Fodor, J. (1981b). "Three Cheers for Propositional Attitudes," in Fodor 1981a.

Fodor, J. (1981c). "Tom Swift and his Procedural Grandmother," in Fodor 1981a.

Fodor, J. (1983). *The Modularity of Mind*. Cambridge, MA: The MIT Press/A Bradford Book.

Fodor, J. (1985). "Fodor's Guide to Mental Representation," *Mind*, XCIV, pp. 76–100.

Fodor, J. (1986). "Why Paramecia Don't Have Mental Representations," in *Midwest Studies in Philosophy*, X, pp. 3–23.

Fodor, J. (1987). *Psychosemantics*. Cambridge, MA: The MIT Press/A Bradford Book.

Frege, G. (1956). "The Thought: A Logical Inquiry," trans. by A. M. and M. Quinton, *Mind*, LXV, pp. 289–311. (Reprinted in P. F. Strawson, ed., *Philosophical Logic*. Oxford: Oxford University Press, 1967.)

Friedman, M. (1981). "Theoretical Explanation," in R. Healy, ed., *Reduction, Time and Reality*. Cambridge: Cambridge University Press, pp. 2–31.

Gardner, H. (1975). *The Shattered Mind: The Person After Brain Damage*. New York: Knopf.

Gardner, M. (1970). "Mathematical Games," *Scientific American*, 223, no. 4, pp. 120–23.

Gazzaniga, M. (1985). *The Social Brain: Discovering the Networks of the Mind*. New York: Basic Books.

Gazzaniga, M. and Ledoux, J. E. (1978). *The Integrated Mind*. New York: Plenum Press.

Geach, P. (1957). *Mental Acts*. London: Routledge and Kegan Paul.

Ghiselin, M. T. (1983). "Lloyd Morgan's Canon in Evolutionary Context" (commentary on Dennett 1983a), *Behavioral and Brain Sciences*, 6, pp. 362–63.

Gibson, E. (1969). *Principles of Perceptual Learning and Development* (Century Psychology Series). New York: Appleton-Century-Crofts.

Goldman, A. (1986). *Epistemology and Cognition*. Cambridge, MA: Harvard University Press.

Goodman, N. (1961). "About," *Mind*, 71, pp. 1–24.

Goodman, N. (1978). *Ways of Worldmaking*. Indianapolis: Hackett.

Goren, C. G.; Sorty, M.; and Wu, P. Y. K. (1975). "Visual Following and Pattern Discrimination of Face-like Stimuli by Newborn Infants," *Pediatrics*, 56, pp. 544–49.

Gould, J. L. and Gould C. G. (1982). "The Insect Mind: Physics or Metaphysics?" in D. R. Griffin, ed., *Animal Mind—Human Mind*. Berlin: Springer-Verlag.

Gould, S. J. (1977). *Ever Since Darwin*. New York: W. W. Norton and Co.

Gould, S. J. (1980). *The Panda's Thumb*. New York: W. W. Norton and Co.

Gould, S. J. and Lewontin, R. (1979). "The Spandrels of San Marco and the Panglossian Paradigm: A Critique of the Adaptationist Programme," *Proceedings of the Royal Society*, B205, pp. 581–98.

Grandy, R. (1973). "Reference, Meaning and Belief," *Journal of Philosophy*, 70, pp. 439–52.

Gregory, R. (1977). *Eye and Brain*. 3rd ed. London: Weidenfeld and Nicolson.

Grice, H. P. (1957). "Meaning," *Philosophical Review*, 66, pp. 377–88.

Grice, H. P. (1969). "Utterer's Meaning and Intentions," *Philosophical Review*, 78, pp. 147–77.

Griffin, D. R., ed. (1982). *Animal Mind—Human Mind*. Berlin: Springer-Verlag.

Hampshire, S. (1975). *Freedom of the Individual*. Expanded edition. Princeton: Princeton University Press.

Harman, G. (1968). "Three Levels of Meaning," *Journal of Philosophy*, LXV, pp. 590–602.

Harman, G. (1973). *Thought*. Princeton: Princeton University Press.

Harman, G. (1977). "How to Use Propositions," *American Philosophical Quarterly*, 14, pp. 173–76.

Harman, G. (1983). "Conceptual Role Semantics," *Notre Dame Journal of Formal Logic*, 28, pp. 242–56.

Harman, G. (1986). "Wide Functionalism," in R. Harnish and M. Brand, eds., *The Representation of Knowledge and Belief*. Tucson: University of Arizona Press.

Harman, G. (forthcoming). "(Nonsolipsistic) Conceptual Role Semantics," in E. Lepore, ed., *Semantics of Natural Language*. New York: Academic Press.

Haugeland, J. (1981). *Mind Design*. Cambridge, MA: The MIT Press/A Bradford Book.

Haugeland, J. (1985). *Artificial Intelligence: The Very Idea*. Cambridge, MA: The MIT Press/A Bradford Book.

Haugeland, J. (unpublished). "The Same Only Different."

Hayes, P. (1978). "Naive Physics I: The Ontology of Liquids," Working Paper 35, Institut pour les Etudes Semantiques et Cognitives, Univ. de Geneve.

Hayes, P. (1979). "The Naive Physics Manifesto," in D. Michie, ed., *Expert Systems in the Microelectronic Age*. Edinburgh: Edinburgh University Press.

Heyes, C. M. (forthcoming). "Cognisance of Consciousness in the Study of Animal Knowledge," in W. Callebaut and R. Pinxten, eds., *Evolutionary Epistemology: a Multiparadigm Approach*. Dordrecht: Reidel.

Hintikka, J. (1962). *Knowledge and Belief*. Ithaca: Cornell University Press.

Hofstadter, D. (1979). *Gödel, Escher, Bach: An Eternal Golden Braid*. New York: Basic Books.

Hofstadter, D. and Dennett, D. C. (1981). *The Mind's I: Fantasies and Reflections on Mind and Soul*. New York: Basic Books.

Hornsby, J. (1977). "Singular Terms in Context of Propositional Attitude," *Mind*, LXXXVI, pp. 31–48.

House, W. (unpublished). "Charity and the World According to the Speaker," doctoral dissertation, University of Pittsburgh, 1980.

Humphrey, N. K. (1976). "The Social Function of Intellect," in P. P. G. Bateson and R. A. Hinde, eds., *Growing Points in Ethology*. Cambridge: Cambridge University Press.

Hunter, I. M. L. (1962). "An Exceptional Talent for Calculative Thinking," *British Journal of Psychology*, 53–54, pp. 243–58.

Israel, D. (unpublished). "The Role of Propositional Objects of Belief in Action," CSLI Report, Center for the Study of Language and Information, Stanford University.

Ittleson, W. H. (1952). *The Ames Demonstrations in Perception*. Oxford: Oxford University Press.

Jackendoff, R. (1983). *Semantics and Cognition*. Cambridge, MA: The MIT Press/A Bradford Book.

Jackendoff, R. (1985). "Information is in the Mind of the Beholder," *Linguistics and Philosophy*, 8, pp. 23–33.

Jacob, F. (1977). "Evolution and Tinkering," *Science*, 196, pp. 1161–66.

Jeffrey, R. (1970). "Dracula Meets Wolfman: Acceptance vs. Partial Belief," in M. Swain, ed. *Induction, Acceptance and Rational Belief*. Dordrecht: Reidel.

Johnston, T. D. (1981). "Contrasting Approaches to a Theory Of Learning," *Behavioral and Brain Sciences*, 4, pp. 125–73.

Kahneman, D. (unpublished). "Some Remarks on the Computer Metaphor."

Kahneman, D. and Tversky, A. (1983). "Choices, Values, and Frames," *American Psychologist*, 39, pp. 341–50.

Kaplan, D. (1968). "Quantifying In," *Synthese*, 19, pp. 178–214. (Reprinted in *Words and Objections*, ed. D. Davidson and J. Hintikka. Dordrecht: Reidel, 1969.)

Kaplan, D. (1973). "Bob and Carol and Ted and Alice," in J. Hintikka, J. Moravcsik, and P. Suppes, eds., *Approaches to Natural Language*. Dordrecht: Reidel.

Kaplan, D. (1978). "Dthat," in P. Cole, ed., *Syntax and Semantics*. New York: Academic Press.

Kaplan, D. (1980). "Demonstratives," The John Locke Lectures, Oxford University.

Kitcher, P. (1984). "In Defense of Intentional Psychology," *Journal of Philosophy*, LXXI, pp. 89–106.

Kitcher, Ph. (1985). *Vaulting Ambition*. Cambridge, MA: The MIT Press.

Kitcher, Ph. (1987). "Why Not the Best?" in John Dupre, ed., *The Latest on the Best*. Cambridge, MA: The MIT Press/A Bradford Book.

Kiteley, M. (1968). "Of What We Think," *American Philosophical Quarterly*, 5, pp. 31–42.

Kripke, S. (1972). "Naming and Necessity," in D. Davidson and G. Harman, eds., *Semantics of Natural Language*. Dordrecht: Reidel.

Kripke, S. (1977). "Speaker's Reference and Semantic Reference," in P. French, et al., eds., *Midwest Studies in Philosophy*, II. Minneapolis: University of Minnesota Press. pp. 255–76.

Kripke, S. (1979). "A Puzzle About Belief," in A. Margolis, ed., *Meaning and Use*. Dordrecht: Reidel, pp. 239–83.

Kripke, S. (1982). *Wittgenstein on Rules and Private Language*. Cambridge, MA: Harvard University Press.

Lettvin, J. Y., et al. (1959). "What the Frog's Eye Tells the Frog's Brain," in *Proceedings of the Institute of Radio Engineers*, 1959, pp. 1940–51.

Levin, J. (forthcoming). "Must Reasons be Rational?" *Philosophy of Science*.

Lewin, R. (1980). "Evolutionary Theory Under Fire," *Science*, 210, pp. 881–87.

Lewis, D. (1974). "Radical Interpretation," *Synthese*, 23, pp. 331–44.

Lewis, D. (1978). "Truth in Fiction," *American Philosophical Quarterly*, 15, pp. 37–46.

Lewis, D. (1979). "Attitudes *De Dicto* and *De Se*," *Philosophical Review*, 78, pp. 513–43.

Lewontin, R. (1961). "Evolution and the Theory of Games," *Journal of Theoretical Biology*, 1, pp. 328–403.

Lewontin, R. (1978a). "Adaptation," *Scientific American*, 293, no. 3 (September), pp. 213–30.

Lewontin, R. (1978b). "Fitness, Survival, and Optimality," in D. H. Horn, R. Mitchell, and G. R. Stairs, eds., *Analysis of Ecological Systems*. Cincinnati: Ohio State University Press.

Lewontin, R. (1979). "Sociobiology as an Adaptionist Paradigm," *Behavioral Science*, 24, pp. 5–14.

Lewontin, R. (1981). "The Inferiority Complex," *The New York Review of Books*, October 22, pp. 12–16.

Livingston, R. (1978). *Sensory Processing, Perception and Behavior*. New York: Raven Press.

Lloyd, M. and Dybas, H. S. (1966). "The Periodical Cicada Problem," *Evolution*, 20, pp. 132–49.

Loar, B. (1972). "Reference and Propositional Attitudes," *Philosophical Review*, 80, pp. 43–62.

Loar, B. (1981). *Mind and Meaning*. Cambridge: Cambridge University Press.

Loar, B. (forthcoming). "Social Content and Psychological Content," in D. Merrill and R. Grimm, eds., *Content of Thought*. Tucson: University of Arizona Press.

Lycan, W. (1974). "Mental States and Putnam's Functionalist Hypothesis," *Australasian Journal of Philosophy*, 52, pp. 48–62.

Lycan, W. (1981a). "Form, Function and Feel," *Journal of Philosophy*, LXXVIII, pp. 24–49.

Lycan, W. (1981b). "Psychological Laws," *Philosophical Topics*, 12, pp. 9–38. (Reprinted in J. I. Biro and R. W. Shahan, eds., *Mind, Brain, and Function: Essays in Philosophy of Mind*. Norman: University of Oklahoma Press, 1982.)

MacKenzie, A. W. (unpublished). "Intentionality-One: Intentionality-Two," presented at the Canadian Philosophical Association Meetings, 1978.

Marcus, R. B. (1983). "Rationality and Believing the Impossible," *Journal of Philosophy*, LXXX, pp. 321–37.

Marks, C. (1980). *Commissurotomy, Consciousness and the Unity of Mind*. Montgomery, VT: Bradford Books.

Marler, P.; Dufty, A.; Pickert, R. (1986a). "Vocal Communication in the Domestic Chicken I: Does a Sender Communicate Information about the Quality of a Food Referent to a Receiver?" *Animal Behavior*, 34, pp. 188–93.

Marler, P.; Duffy, A.; Pickert, R. (1986b). "Voice Communication in the Domestic Chicken II: Is the Sender Sensitive to the Presence and Nature of the Receiver?" *Animal Behavior*, 34, pp. 194–98.

Marr, D. (1982). *Vision*. Cambridge, MA: The MIT Press.

Maurer, D. and Barrera, M. (1981). "Infant's Perception of Natural and Distorted Arrangements of a Schematic Face," *Child Development*, 52, pp. 196–202.

Maynard Smith, J. (1972). *On Evolution*. Edinburgh: Edinburgh University Press.

Maynard Smith, J. (1974). "The Theory of Games and the Evolution of Animal Conflict," *Journal of Theoretical Biology*, 49, pp. 209–21.

Maynard Smith, J. (1978). "Optimization Theory in Evolution," *Annual Review of Ecology and Systematics*, 9, pp. 31–56.

Maynard Smith, J. (1983). "Adaptationism and Satisficing" (commentary on Dennett 1983a), *Behavioral and Brain Sciences*, 6, pp. 370–71.

Mayr, E. (1983). "How to Carry out the Adaptationist Program," *American Naturalist*, 121, pp. 324–34.

McCarthy, J. (1960). "Programs with Common Sense," D. V. Blake and A. M. Uttley, eds. *Proceedings of the Symposium on Mechanization of Thought Processes.* National Physical Laboratory, Teddington, England: H. M. Stationery Office, pp. 75–91. (Reprinted in Minsky 1968.)

McCarthy, J. (1979). "Ascribing Mental Qualities to Machines," in M. Ringle, ed., *Philosophical Perspectives in Artificial Intelligence.* Atlantic Highlands, NJ: Humanities Press.

McCarthy, J. and Hayes, P. (1969). "Some Philosophical Problems from the Standpoint of Artificial Intelligence," in B. Meltzer and D. Michie, eds., *Machine Intelligence.* Edinburgh: Edinburgh University Press.

McClelland, J. and Rumelhart, D., eds. (1986). *Parallel Distributed Processing: Explorations in the Microstructures of Cognition,* 2 vols. Cambridge, MA: The MIT Press/A Bradford Book.

McDowell, J. (1977). "On The Sense and Reference of a Proper Name," *Mind,* LXXXVI, pp. 159–85.

McFarland, D. (1984). *Animal Behavior.* Menlo Park, CA: Benjamin-Cummings Publ.

Miller, J., ed. (1983). *States of Mind.* London: BBC Publications.

Millikan, R. (1984). *Language, Thought and Other Biological Categories.* Cambridge, MA: The MIT Press/A Bradford Book.

Millikan, R. (1986). "Thoughts Without Laws: Cognitive Science Without Content," *Philosophical Review,* XCV, pp. 47–80.

Millikan, R. (unpublished). "Truth Rules, Hoverflies, and the Kripke-Wittgenstein Paradox."

Minsky, M., ed. (1968). *Semantic Information Processing.* Cambridge, MA: The MIT Press.

Monod, J. (1971). *Chance and Necessity.* New York: Knopf Press. (Originally published in France as *Le Hasard et la Necessité.* Paris: Editions du Seuil, 1970.)

Morton, A. (1975). "Because He Thought He had Insulted Him," *Journal of Philosophy,* LXXII, pp. 5–15.

Nagel, T. (1979). *Mortal Questions.* Cambridge: Cambridge University Press.

Nagel, T. (1986). *The View From Nowhere.* Oxford: Oxford University Press.

Neisser, U. (1976). *Cognition and Reality.* San Francisco: Freeman.

Nelson, R. J. (1978). "Objects of Occasion Beliefs," *Synthese,* 39, pp. 105–40.

Newell, A. (1982). "The Knowledge Level," *Artificial Intelligence,* 18, pp. 81–132.

Nisbett, R. E. and Ross, L. D. (1980). *Human Inference: Strategy and Shortcomings.* Englewood Cliffs: Prentice Hall.

Nisbett, R. E. and Wilson, T. DeC. (1977). "Telling More than We Know: Verbal Reports on Mental Processes," *Psychological Review*, 84, pp. 231–59.

Nozick, R. (1981). *Philosophical Explanations*. Cambridge, MA: Harvard University Press.

Oster, G. F. and Wilson, E. O. (1978). *Caste and Ecology in the Social Insects*. Princeton: Princeton University Press.

Parfit, D. (1984). *Reasons and Persons*. Oxford: Oxford University Press.

Perry, J. (1977). "Frege on Demonstratives," *Philosophical Review*, 86, pp. 474–97.

Perry, J. (1979). "The Problem of the Essential Indexical," *Nous*, 13, pp. 3–21.

Popper, K. and Eccles, J. (1977). *The Self and its Brain*. Berlin: Springer-International.

Powers, L. (1978). "Knowledge by Deduction," *Philosophical Review*, LXXXVII, pp. 337–71.

Premack, A. (1983). "The Codes of Man and Beasts," *Behavioral and Brain Sciences*, 6, pp. 125–68.

Premack, A. (1986). *Gavagai! Or the Future History of the Animal Language Controversy*. Cambridge, MA: The MIT Press/A Bradford Book.

Premack, A. and Woodruff, G. (1978). "Does the Chimpanzee Have a Theory of Mind?" *Behavioral and Brain Sciences*, 1, pp. 515–26.

Prior, A. N. (1976). *Papers in Logic and Ethics*, ed. by P. Geach and A. Kenny. London: Duckworth.

Putnam, H. (1960). "Minds and Machines," in S. Hook, ed., *Dimensions of Mind*. New York: New York University Press. (Reprinted in Putnam 1975b.)

Putnam, H. (1965). "Brains and Behavior," in J. Butler, ed., *Analytical Philosophy*. Second series. Oxford: Blackwell.

Putnam, H. (1974). "Comment on Wilfrid Sellars," *Synthese*, 27, pp. 445–55.

Putnam, H. (1975a). "The Meaning of 'Meaning'," in Putnam 1975b.

Putnam, H. (1975b). *Mind, Language and Reality*. Philosophical Papers, II. Cambridge: Cambridge University Press.

Putnam, H. (1978). *Meaning and the Moral Sciences*. London: Routledge and Kegan Paul.

Putnam, H. (1981). *Reason, Truth and History*. Cambridge: Cambridge University Press.

Putnam, H. (1983). "Computational Psychology and Interpretation Theory," in *Realism and Reason*. Philosophical Papers, III. Cambridge: Cambridge University Press.

Putnam, H. (1986). "Information and the Mental," in E. Lepore, ed., *Truth and Interpretation: Perspectives on the Philosophy of Donald Davidson*. Oxford: Blackwell.

Pylyshyn, Z. (1978). "Computational Models and Empirical Constraints," *Behavioral and Brain Sciences*, 1, pp. 98–128.

Pylyshyn, Z. (1979). "Complexity and the Study of Artificial and Human Intelligence," in M. Ringle, ed., *Philosophical Perspectives in Artificial Intelligence*. Atlantic Highlands, NJ: Humanities Press.

Pylyshyn, Z. (1980). "Computation and Cognition: Issues in the Foundation of Cognitive Science," *Behavioral and Brain Sciences*, 3, pp. 111–32.

Pylyshyn, Z. (1984). *Computation and Cognition: Toward a Foundation for Cognitive Science*. Cambridge, MA: The MIT Press/A Bradford Book.

Quine, W. V. O. (1956). "Quantifiers and Propositional Attitudes," *Journal of Philosophy*, LIII, pp. 177–86. (Reprinted in Quine, *The Ways of Paradox*. New York: Random House, 1966.)

Quine, W. V. O. (1960). *Word and Object*. Cambridge, MA: The MIT Press.

Quine. W. V. O. (1969). "Propositional Objects," in *Ontological Relativity and Other Essays*. New York: Columbia University Press, pp. 139–60.

Quine, W. V. O. (1970). "On the Reasons for Indeterminacy of Translation," *Journal of Philosophy*, LXVII, pp. 178–83.

Ramachandran, V. S. (1985a). "Apparent Motion of Subjective Surfaces," *Perception*, 14, pp. 127–34.

Ramachandran, V. S. (1985b). Guest editorial in *Perception*, 14, pp. 97–103.

Raphael, B. (1976). *The Thinking Computer: Mind Inside Matter*. San Francisco: Freeman.

Reichenbach, H. (1938). *Experience and Prediction*. Chicago: University of Chicago Press.

Ristau, C. A. (forthcoming). "Thinking, Communicating, and Deceiving: Means to Master the Social Environment," in G. Greenberg and E. Tobach, eds., *Evolution of Social Behavior and Integrative Levels*, T.C. Schneirla Conference Series. Hillsdale, NJ: Erlbaum.

Ristau, C. A. (unpublished). "Intentional Behavior by Birds?: The Case of the 'Injury Feigning' Plovers."

Roitblat, H. L. (1982). "The Meaning of Representation in Animal Memory," *Behavioral and Brain Sciences*, 5, pp. 352–406.

Rorty, R. (1979). *Philosophy and the Mirror of Nature*. Princeton: Princeton University Press.

Rorty, R. (1982). "Contemporary Philosophy of Mind," *Synthese*, 53, pp. 323–48.

Rosenberg, A. (1980). *Sociobiology and the Preemption of Social Science*. Baltimore: Johns Hopkins University Press.

Rosenberg, A. (1985). "Adaptationalist Imperatives and Panglossian Paradigms," in J. Fetzer, ed., *Sociobiology and Epistemology*. Dordrecht: Reidel.

Rosenberg, A. (1986a). "Intention and Action Among the Macromolecules," in N. Rescher, ed., *Current Issues in Teleology*. Lanham, NY: University Presses of America.

Rosenberg, A. (1986b). "Intentional Psychology and Evolutionary Biology (Part I: The Uneasy Analogy)," *Behaviorism*, 14, pp. 15–27.

Russell, B. (1905). "On Denoting," *Mind*, 5, pp. 479–93. (Reprinted in Russell, *Logic and Knowledge*. London: Allen and Unwin, 1958.)

Russell, B. (1959). *Mysticism and Logic*. London: Allen and Unwin.

Ryle, G. (1949). *The Concept of Mind*. London: Hutchinson.

Ryle, G. (1958). "A Puzzling Element in the Notion of Thinking," a British Academy Lecture. (Reprinted in P. F. Strawson, ed., *Studies in the Philosophy of Thought and Action*. Oxford: Oxford University Press, 1968.)

Ryle, G. (1979). *On Thinking*, ed. by K. Kolenda. Totowa, NJ: Rowman and Littlefield.

Sacks, O. (1984). *A Leg to Stand On*. New York: Summit Books.

Sacks, O. (1986). *The Man who Mistook His Wife for a Hat, and Other Clinical Tales*. New York: Summit Books.

Savage-Rumbaugh, S.; Rumbaugh, D. M.; and Boysen, S. (1978). "Linguistically Mediated Tool Use and Exchange by Chimpanzees (*Pan troglodytes*)," *Behavioral and Brain Sciences*, 1, pp. 539–54.

Savage, C. W., ed. (1978). *Perception and Cognition: Issues in the Foundations of Psychology*. Minneapolis: University of Minnesota Press.

Sayre, K. (1986). "Intentionality and Information Processing: An Alternative Model for Cognitive Science," *Behavioral and Brain Sciences*, 9, pp. 121–60.

Schank, R. C. (1976). Research Report No. 84, Yale University Department of Computer Science.

Schank, R. and Abelson, R. (1977). *Scripts, Plans, Goals and Understanding*. Hillside, NJ: Erlbaum.

Scheffler, I. (1963). *The Anatomy of Inquiry*. New York: Knopf.

Schiffer, S. (1978). "The Basis of Reference," *Erkenntnis*, 13, pp. 171–206.

Schull, J. (forthcoming). "Evolution and Learning: Analogies and Interactions," in E. Laszlo, ed., *The Evolutionary Paradigm: Transdisciplinary Studies*. Durham: Duke University Press.

Searle, J. (1979). "Referential and Attributive," *The Monist*, 62, pp. 190–308. (Reprinted in Searle 1980a.)

Searle, J. (1980a). *Expression and Meaning*. Cambridge: Cambridge University Press.

Searle, J. (1980b). "Minds, Brains, and Programs," *Behavioral and Brain Sciences*, 3, pp. 417–58.

Searle, J. (1982). "The Myth of the Computer: An Exchange," *The New York Review of Books*, June 24, pp. 56–57.

Searle, J. (1983). *Intentionality: An Essay in the Philosophy of Mind*. Cambridge: Cambridge University Press.

Searle, J. (1984). "Panel Discussion: Has Artificial Intelligence Research Illuminated Human Thinking?" in H. Pagels, ed., *Computer Culture: The Scientific, Intellectual, and Social Impact of the Computer*. Annals of the New York Academy of Sciences, vol. 426.

Searle, J. (1985). *Minds, Brains and Science*. Cambridge, MA: Harvard University Press.

Searle, J. (forthcoming). "Turing the Chinese Room," in *Artificial Intelligence*.

Sejnowski, T. (forthcoming). "Computing With Connections" (review of W. D. Hillis, *The Connection Machine*, Cambridge, MA: The MIT Press, 1985), *Journal of Mathematical Psychology*.

Sejnowski, T. and Rosenberg, C. R. (1986). "NETtalk: A Parallel Network that Learns to Read Aloud," The Johns Hopkins University Electrical Engineering and Computer Science Technical Report JHU/EEC–86/01.

Sellars, W. (1954). "Some Reflections on Language Games," *Philosophy of Science*, 21, pp. 204–28. (Reprinted with revisions in Sellars 1963.)

Sellars, W. (1956). "Empiricism and the Philosophy of Mind," in H. Feigl and M. Scriven, eds., *The Foundations of Science and the Concepts of Psychology and Psychoanalysis*. Minnesota Studies in the Philosophy of Science, I. Minneapolis: University of Minnesota Press. (Reprinted in Sellars, 1963).

Sellars, W. (1963). *Science, Perception and Reality*. London: Routledge and Kegan Paul.

Sellars, W. (1974). "Meaning as Functional Classification: a Perspective on the Relation of Syntax to Semantics," *Synthese*, 27, pp. 417–38.

Seyfarth, R.; Cheney, D. L.; and Marler, P. (1980). "Monkey Responses to Three Different Alarm Calls: Evidence of Predator Classification and Semantic Communication," *Science*, 210, pp. 801–3.

Shaftz, M.; Wellman, H.; and Silver, S. (1983). "The Acquisition of Mental Verbs: A Systematic Investigation of the First Reference to Mental States," *Cognition*, 14, pp. 301–21.

Shannon, C. (1949). *The Mathematical Theory of Communication*. Champaign-Urbana: University of Illinois Press.

Simmons, K. E. L. (1952). "The Nature of Predator Reactions of Breeding Birds," *Behaviour*, 4, pp. 101–76.

Simon, H. (1957). *Models of Man.* New York: Wiley.

Simon, H. (1969). *The Sciences of the Artificial.* Cambridge, MA: The MIT Press.

Skinner, B. F. (1964). "Behaviorism at Fifty," in T. W. Wann, ed., *Behaviorism and Phenomenology: Contrasting Bases for Modern Psychology.* Chicago: University of Chicago Press.

Skinner, B. F. (1971). *Beyond Freedom and Dignity.* New York: Knopf.

Skutch, A. F. (1976). *Parent Birds and Their Young.* Austin: University of Texas Press.

Smith, S. B. (1983). *The Mental Calculators.* New York: Columbia University Press.

Smolensky, P. (forthcoming). "Connectionist AI, Symbolic AI, and the Brain," *AI Review*.

Sober, E. (1981). "The Evolution of Rationality," *Synthese*, 46, pp. 95–120.

Sober, E. (1984). *The Nature of Selection.* Cambridge, MA: The MIT Press/A Bradford Book.

Sober, E. (1985). "Methodological Behaviorism, Evolution, and Game Theory," in James Fetzer, ed., *Sociobiology and Epistemology.* Dordrecht: Reidel.

Sordahl, T. A. (1981). "Sleight of Wing," *Natural History*, 90, pp. 43–49.

Sosa, E. (1970). "Propositional Attitudes *De Dicto* and *De Re*," *Journal of Philosophy*, 67, pp. 883–96.

Stabler, E. (1983). "How are Grammars Represented?" *Brain and Behavioral Sciences*, 6, pp. 391–422.

Stalnaker, R. (1976). "Propositions," in A. McKay and D. Merrill, eds., *Issues in the Philosophy of Language.* New Haven: Yale University Press.

Stalnaker, R. (1984). *Inquiry.* Cambridge, MA: The MIT Press/A Bradford Book.

Stalnaker, R. (unpublished). "On What's in the Head."

Stich, S. (1978a). "Autonomous Psychology and the Belief-Desire Thesis," *The Monist*, 61, pp. 571–91.

Stich, S. (1978b). "Beliefs and Sub-Doxastic States," *Philosophy of Science*, 45, pp. 499–518.

Stich, S. (1980). "Headaches" (review of *Brainstorms*), *Philosophical Books*, XXI, pp. 65–76.

Stich, S. (1981). "Dennett on Intentional Systems," *Philosophical Topics*, 12, pp. 38–62.

Stich, S. (1982). "On the Ascription of Content," in A. Woodfield, ed., *Thought and Content*. Oxford: Oxford University Press.

Stich, S. (1983). *From Folk Psychology to Cognitive Science: The Case Against Belief*. Cambridge, MA: The MIT Press/A Bradford Book.

Stich, S. (1984). "Relativism, Rationality, and the Limits of Intentional Description," *Pacific Philosophical Quarterly*, 65, pp. 211–35.

Stich, S. and Nisbett, R. (1980). "Justification and the Psychology of Human Reasoning," *Philosophy of Science*, 47, pp. 188–202.

Stryer, L. (1981). *Biochemistry*. San Francisco: Freeman.

Taylor, C. (1964). *The Explanation of Behaviour*. London: Routledge and Kegan Paul.

Thomason, R. (1986). "The Multiplicity of Belief and Desire," in E. Lepore, ed., *Truth and Interpretation: Perspectives on the Philosophy of Donald Davidson*. Oxford: Basil Blackwell.

Touretzky, D. S. and Hinton, G. E. (1985). "Symbols among the Neurons: Details of a Connectionist Inference Architecture," *Proceedings of the Ninth International Joint Conference on Artificial Intelligence*. Los Altos: Morgan Kaufman, pp. 238–43.

Trivers, R. L. (1971). "The Evolution of Reciprocal Altruism," *Quarterly Review of Biology*, 46, pp. 35–57.

Tversky, A. and Kahneman, D. (1974). "Judgement Under Uncertainty: Heuristics and Biases," *Science*, 185, pp. 499–518.

Ullian, J. and Goodman, N. (1977). "Truth About Jones," *Journal of Philosophy*, LXXIV, pp. 317–38.

Vendler, Z. (1976). "Thinking of Individuals," *Nous*, 10, pp. 35–46.

Vendler, Z. (1981). "Reference and Introduction," *Philosophia*. (Reprinted with revisions as chapter 4 of Vendler 1984.)

Vendler, Z. (1984). *The Matter of Minds*. Oxford: Clarendon Press.

Wallace, J. (1972). "Belief and Satisfaction," *Nous*, 6, pp. 87–103.

Walton, K. (1978). "Fearing Fiction," *Journal of Philosophy*, 75, pp. 5–27.

Wason, P. and Johnson-Laird, P. (1972). *Psychology of Reasoning: Structure and Content*. London: B. T. Batsford.

Weiskrantz, J. (1983). "Evidence and Scotomata," *Behavioral and Brain Sciences*, 6, pp. 464–67.

Weizenfeld, J. (1977). "Surprise and Intentional Content," presented at the Third Annual meeting of the Society for Philosophy and Psychology, Pittsburgh, March 1977.

Wertheimer, R. (1974). "Philosophy on Humanity," in R. L. Perkins, ed., *Abortion: Pro and Con*. Cambridge, MA: Schenkman.

Wheeler, S. C. (1986). "Indeterminacy of French Interpretation: Derrida and Davidson," in E. Lepore, ed., *Truth and Interpretation: Perspectives on the Philosophy of Donald Davidson*. Oxford: Basil Blackwell.

Wilson, E. O.; Durlach, N. I.; and Roth, L. M. (1958). "Chemical Releasers of Necrophoric Behavior in Ants," *Psyche*, 65, pp. 108–14.

Wilson, E. O. (1975). *Sociobiology: The New Synthesis*. Cambridge, MA: Harvard University Press.

Wilson, N. L. (1959). "Substances Without Substrata," *Review of Metaphysics*, 12, pp. 521–39.

Wimmer, H. and Perner, J. (1983). "Beliefs About Beliefs: Representation and Constraining Function of Wrong Beliefs in Young Children's Understanding of Deception," *Cognition*, 13, pp. 103–28.

Wimsatt, W. (1974). "Complexity and Organization," in K. Schaffner and R. S. Cohen, eds., PSA and 1972 (Philosophy of Science Association). Dordrecht: Reidel, pp. 67–86.

Winograd, T. (1972). *Understanding Natural Language*. New York: Academic Press.

Wittgenstein, L. (1958). *Philosophical Investigations*, ed. by G. E. M. Anscombe. Oxford: Blackwell.

Woodruff, G. and Premack, D. (1979). "Intentional Communication in the Chimpanzee: The Development of Deception," *Cognition*, 7, pp. 333–62.

Woods, W. A. (1975). "What's in a Link?" in B. Bobrow and A. Collins, eds., *Representation and Understanding*. New York: Academic Press.

Woods, W. A. (1981). "Procedural Semantics as a Theory of Meaning," in A. K. Joshi, B. L. Webber and I. A. Sag, eds., *Elements of Discourse Understanding*. Cambridge: Cambridge University Press.

Woods, W. A. and Makhoul, J. (1974). "Mechanical Inference Problems in Continuous Speech Understanding," *Artificial Intelligence*, 5, pp. 73–91.

Zeman, J. (1963). "Information and the Brain," in N. Wiener and J. P. Schade, eds., *Nerve, Brain and Memory Models: Progress in Brain Research*, II. New York: Elsevier Publishing Co.

Index